WHITE *as* SIN

A New Paradigm
for Racial Healing

Scott Garber

To my wonderful wife, Cindi, whose personal, spiritual, and material support made this book possible.

Praise for *White as Sin*:

"In *White As Sin*, Scott Garber has written a compelling explanation and history of whiteness as a social construct, particularly how it is rooted in a sinful haughtiness that is deeply ingrained both at the personal and corporate level. Perhaps most importantly, he makes clear that white Christianity—that is, Christianity as practiced and perverted by people of European descent in the Americas going back almost 500 years—is inextricably tied to the ongoing practice and ideology of white supremacy. Scott has written this exhaustively researched book as part of the deeply necessary effort to reach white Christians with the message that white supremacy must be individually and systematically dismantled, and that this can *only* happen if white Christians everywhere join in this difficult but necessary effort. Best of all, Scott provides challenging yet eminently practical steps that white Christians can take individually and together to begin to redress America's original sin. In a time such as this, *White As Sin* is a book that white Christians need to read."

Jim Wallis, *The New York Times* bestselling author of *America's Original Sin: Racism, White Privilege, and the Bridge to a New America*, president of Sojourners, and editor-in-chief of *Sojourners* magazine

"Scott Garber gives a weighty and thoughtful progression of racialization and the sin of racism from the Garden of Eden to the fields of America, to the modern-day struggles of racial haughtiness in the 21st century. Between a historical account and an illuminating reality that racial haughtiness is an integral part of the American fabric, *White As Sin* challenges the conversation about reconciliation head on. Having served with Scott Garber for years as a reconciler I can attest to the sincerity of his heart to help us all move from being racists to gracists."

Dr. David Anderson, Senior Pastor of Bridgeway Community Church in Columbia, Maryland and author of *Gracism: The Art of Inclusion*

"Scott Garber offers a fresh perspective that will appeal to thought leaders, especially Christian leaders, who are troubled by the persistence of race-related problems in our society. *White As Sin* a serious, meaty, and quite possibly controversial book on a topic that is critically important both to Christians and to our nation."

Galen Carey, Vice President of Government Relations for the National Association of Evangelicals

Scott Garber's eloquent and powerful new work examines what he calls 'racial haughtiness," characterized "as a sinful stronghold that has never surrendered." After tracing its influence throughout history to the present day, Garber makes a compelling case for a spiritual transformation that will finally demolish the legacy of racial hierarchy.

David R. Rippey, Ed.D, Leadership Consultant

"Scott Garber is a prophetic voice uniquely positioned to do what prophets do: consider the fault-lines beneath the surface, carefully expose them, and call people to radical transformation. *White As Sin* should become required reading in every school and church across America, as the future of our society depends on recognizing the truth of Scott Garber's diagnosis and responding to the remedy he proposes. It's strong medicine. But it has remarkable potential to heal our land."

Dr. D. Brent Sandy, author of *Plowshares & Pruning Hooks* and co-author (with John Walton) of *The Lost World of Scripture.*

Acknowledgements

I would like to thank the following people for kindly lending their talents to this project:

Cover art sketch: Emily Herbst

Cover design consultation: Curtis Williams, Jr.

Author photograph: Tammy Hui

Editing: Emily Saunders

To contact the author for speaking or consultation:

scottgarber@scottgarber.com

Scripture quotations:

Table of Contents

Note: This volume contains footnotes, endnotes, and off-site notes. Endnotes are found at the end of the book, organized by chapter. They reference works that have been cited or alluded to in the text, and sometimes include additional explanations. Footnotes are found at the bottom of the page and elucidate the text to which they are linked by a lower-case letter notation. When there is additional research/background material related to the information on the page that I deemed either too detailed or too peripheral to be included in the text, endnotes, or footnotes, I have made it available in a PDF document on my website at www.scottgarber.com/was_notes.pdf. These notes are organized by chapter and numbered as indicated in the footnote. For additional information you may also contact me at scottgarber@scottgarber.com.

Chapter 1

Genesis

Like many small Northern towns, Cedarville, Ohio is not exactly a racial melting pot. More than ninety percent of its four thousand citizens are white. Fewer than one hundred African Americans call Cedarville home.

This village is also home to Cedarville University, a Baptist institution with conservative leanings. With an enrollment of over 3,000 students, the school dramatically increases the number of people in Cedarville. It does not, however, dramatically alter the local demographics, as minority representation in the student body is about the same as that of the town itself.

It seems like the kind of academic environment in which students might easily avoid multicultural issues. And perhaps they do, at least until they sign up for a class with the innocuous title *Romans & Galatians*. The professor for that course is my good friend, Chris Miller, and he has a few surprises up his sleeve.

Of course, Dr. Miller does direct his students to a deeper appreciation of the foundations of their faith, as found in these two epistles. But he doesn't let them wiggle away from passages that wrestle with the knotty ethnic/religious tensions that troubled the Early Church—or their meaning for today.

Most of the way through the semester, after weeks of exposure to the Apostle Paul's teaching about the unity of Jews and Gentiles, things come to a head in Galatians chapter two. There, in verses 11-14, Paul recalls his confrontation with the Apostle Peter over Peter's attempt to impose what Chris characterizes as "separate but equal facilities." Once his group of white, middle-class students have quite rightly recoiled at the blatant hypocrisy of Peter's position, Dr. Miller poses this unnerving question: "So, then, why do we have two Baptist churches in Cedarville?"

Now, given the fact that Cedarville contains a far higher number of Baptists than most towns its size, two churches might not seem like an excessive number. But by this time the students all know that the question has nothing to do with denominational distinctives or doctrinal disputes. There are two Baptist churches in town—one black and one white—separated by a hundred yards and hundreds of years of history.

What's most surprising about this question is the very fact that it's, well, surprising. It's not as if Dr. Miller found some Indiana Jones-style artifact in the caves of Qumran and unlocked an ancient, esoteric mystery. In fact, he would insist that Christian unity is one of the clearer and more pervasive teachings in all of the New Testament—so that "discovering" the disconnect between the biblical ideal and the experience of the American Church is rather like stumbling over the obvious. But if this incongruity is so obvious, then why is it so often overlooked?

Clearly, the problem of the segregated Church is not limited to Cedarville, Ohio. While the situation of these two Baptist churches may be hard to reconcile with Scripture, it is in perfect alignment with the racialized pattern of American church life. Cedarville's conundrum is merely a microcosm of a far more profound problem: why are there two Churches in America?

My interest in this question is not just academic; it is existential. I have been involved in multiracial/multicultural ministry since the early 1980s, long before it was trendy. Reconciling people in Christ across America's black/white divide has been my enduring passion. Unfortunately, however, this divide has proven to be enduring as well. Even as many of our major social institutions have become significantly more integrated, the color-coded Church remains an anachronistic embarrassment to its Founder and Lord.

Frustrated by the stubborn recalcitrance of this racial rift, I embarked upon a serious historical investigation, hoping that a deeper understanding of how we got into this mess would somehow show us how to get out of it. Not surprisingly, I found no shortage of explanations for our ecclesiastical apartheid. The segregated Church has been shaped by a myriad of events, personalities, politics, institutions, economics, theological perspectives, and social psychologies—all played out over the course of several centuries.

True enough, but still unsatisfying. What I really needed to know was: what *caused* these causes? I kept digging, and as my understanding increased, so too did my unease. Indeed, I was often tempted to exercise my white privilege—to turn my head and look away. But deep inside I wanted to see how our past would affect me if I allowed my spirit to steep in it. So I did.

After nearly an entire month immersed in the study of lynching, I experienced a brutal epiphany. Soul-weary from so much sadistic savagery masquerading as justice, I came across an old-time photo of a large, sturdy tree. From one of its branches hung a noose. Dangling forlornly from that noose was a charred, black body. The image itself was not unlike so many others I had seen. But on that day one more horrific image proved one too many. All of a sudden, the sepia scene began to melt into an impressionistic blur, and my chair began to quake, rhythmically convulsed by my disconsolate weeping. What seemed like a whole box of tissues later, my sobbing finally subsided—but my sorrow did not.

My grief endured, in part, because such a prolonged exposure to inhumanity had left an indelible mark on me. More importantly, however, there came a point at which lynching became more than awful; it became shameful as well. You see, the perpetrators had a certain profile. They were white, American, and Christian. And as much as I wanted to believe that I wasn't *like* them, I could not deny that I *was* them.

Lynching did not just come out of nowhere, nor was it a one-off atrocity. This extraordinary evil was part and parcel of the far more ordinary but no less sinister reality of white-on-black American life—a reality long characterized by dominance, cruelty, belittlement, marginalization, and ill will. Lynching may have been the terrible tip of the iceberg, but the tip of the iceberg has something in common with the rest of the iceberg. It's all ice.

But what was that ice? What could have led us whites to initiate, perpetuate, and then tolerate the evils of racial imposition and oppression? Given the consistency of this historical pattern, we could hardly have been acting out of character. But wait… if we were not acting *out* of character, then we must have been acting *according* to character. Which means that, in order to do these despicable things, we must have already been the kind of people who would do them.

That awful notion sent a shiver through my soul. But then came the even more unsettling corollary questions. If we were once that kind of people, how do we know that we are not still that kind of people? What if racial injustice was not just the product of white *activity* but, rather, of white *identity*?

Fast-forward several years to the present day. After carefully examining the moral pathology of our racial dysfunction in the light of these questions, I have reached two inescapable conclusions. First: things are the way they are, because we are the way we are. And, second: if we want those things to be different than they are, we must be different than we are.

The change I'm talking about is fundamentally spiritual in nature. Now, that may sound like good news for Christians, since we specialize in spiritual solutions; but if we want to be part of that spiritual solution, we must first stop being part of the spiritual problem. And if we want to be part of that spiritual solution, we must stop thinking about spiritual change as a strictly private matter. Our response to social sin must affect both the world within in us *and* the world around us.

As followers of Christ, we have the potential be on the vanguard of this great moral challenge of our time. But if we want to lead, we have to go first. We have to take the medicine ourselves. *White as Sin* offers a prescription— a prescription for change, a new paradigm for racial healing.

This new paradigm arrives at a critical moment in our history, because the national conversation about race has changed significantly in recent years. When I first began working on this book, many pundits were wondering aloud if we might be entering a post-racial era. Less than a third of all whites thought that racism was a major problem.[1] The majority believed that the country had already done everything necessary to ensure equal rights for blacks.[2]

But then came the deaths of Trayvon Martin, Eric Garner, and, most notably, Michael Brown. That police shooting of a young black man in Ferguson, Missouri, the roiling protests that followed, and the ongoing attention given to the plight of African Americans in the justice system began to erode the white fantasy of a post-racial society. Freddie Gray's death while in police custody and the urban chaos that engulfed portions of Baltimore further undermined that wishful narrative. Weeks later a disturbed white supremacist named Dylann Roof opened fire during a midweek Bible study at Emanuel African Methodist Episcopal Church in Charleston, SC, killing nine. Then, Chicago police took a whole year to release the video of an officer shooting Laquan McDonald sixteen times. Perhaps we were not one big, happy, colorblind family after all.

The occasional injustice might be dismissed as a mere exception to the rule of racial equality. But as every spectator became a potential cameraman, these "exceptions" started to feel far less exceptional. A constant rollout of new injustices on the one hand and emboldened black responses on the other kept the media fixated, bringing long-forgotten and disquieting images of racial unrest back into white living rooms. Forced to face a too-big-to-be-ignored phenomenon, whites began to re-assess the state of race relations.

In a single year, from 2014-2015, white sensitivities underwent an astonishing adjustment. Polls showed that in 2014 whites saw race relations as "generally good" vs. "generally bad" by a margin of 60% to 37%, respectively. By mid-2015 that number had more than reversed itself, with only 33% saying that race relations were "generally good," versus 62% who disagreed.[3] During that same year (2014-2015) the percentage of whites affirming that further changes were needed in order to achieve equal rights rose from 39% to 53%.[4]

By mid-2016 we were in the throes of a presidential campaign, and the emergence of then-candidate Donald Trump added fuel to the fire. His brand of nationalism hearkened back to a lost greatness, appealed to white self-interest, and offered implicit protection for the existing racial hierarchy. Trump's actions after becoming President—particularly his response to the white supremacists who rallied in Charlottesville, Virginia—further exacerbated racial tensions. In December 2017, Pew Research found that 60% of Americans believed that Trump had had a negative effect on race relations, while only 8% thought he had improved them.[5]

As current events keep the race question front and center, concern about the state of race relations remains elevated for a majority of Americans, whites included. The share of Americans who classify racism as a "big problem" has more than doubled since 2011.[6] A half century after the Civil Rights Movement, we are coming to grips with the fact that progress is not inevitable.

Given the remarkable recalcitrance of this problem, it's hard not to wonder, *what* is going on with race in America? If you work or reside in a multiracial environment, this question matters; if you want to live in a nation or worship in a church that lives up to its creed, this question matters.

As I investigated this *what* question, however, it pointed me to another question that, I have come to believe, matters even more. I'm talking about the *why* question. If we know only *what* is happening but not *why*, then we can describe our misfortune, perhaps even complain about it more precisely, but we remain powerless to change it. In order to find a cure, we must first understand the cause of our affliction.

Therefore, this book is intentionally and unapologetically obsessed with the *why* question—and even more obsessed with its answer. *White as Sin* identifies the moral malware in the root directory of our racial identity, demonstrates how it energizes both our past and present racial reality, and proposes a new paradigm for racial healing.

Perhaps you're tired of talking about race but seeing no progress. If so, I hope you'll be encouraged that the journey we're about to embark on in this book can, indeed, lead us to a better place. Perhaps you're tired of talking about race, period. I get that. But our racial dysfunction isn't going to just go away—or solve itself. The only way to get beyond talking about race is to actually do something about it. In order to discover that something, let's begin at the beginning, with America's original sin.

Chapter 2

Original Sin

In March of 2008, Senator and presidential candidate Barack Obama found himself besieged by controversy on account of racially-charged remarks made by his pastor, Rev. Jeremiah Wright. With his candidacy in serious jeopardy, the future president seized the moment with a bold national address about race, in which he referred to slavery as "America's original sin."[1] The extensive media coverage that accompanied the speech cemented Mr. Obama's association with this catchphrase; but he is certainly not the first or the last to make use of such theological terminology to stress the foundational role that slavery played in defining our racial reality.

Given the seminal nature of this historic transgression, the designation of slavery as our "original sin" has an undeniable resonance. Note, however, that American slavery was not a random development. That "original" sin also had an origin—and not just in the Garden of Eden but in the formative cultural, religious, and moral dynamics that defined the white American psyche.

We are about to embark upon a forensic examination of that inner reality, an investigation that will cast "America's original sin" in a somewhat different light, one that is more akin to the traditional theological use of the term.[a] In theological parlance, *original sin* refers not so much to an original sinful *act* but to the *condition* of sinfulness that resulted from that act, a condition that has affected the entire human race ever since. In a similar vein, I am using this original sin metaphor to denote a sinful condition, the driving moral force behind not just slavery but behind all sorts of racial injustices.

What is this original sin, this driving moral force? I am convinced that the ultimate explanation for (and solution to) our racial divide is not merely historical or institutional or sociological or even psychological; it is spiritual. Slavery was certainly the incubator from which a long litany of social ills emerged. But all of these symptoms, from slavery to 20th-century segregation to 21st-century racial dysfunction, are products of a common moral pathogen.

---

[a] The fact that I employ the term "original sin" somewhat differently than others is not intended as a critique or correction of their usage. When used as a metaphor, the term can have several legitimate applications.

Not surprisingly, socio-historical treatments of racial domination do not typically frame this issue in such openly moralistic terms. Nevertheless, they do recognize a *pattern* of white domination moving episodically through time. In order to explain this pattern, they must postulate the existence of a psycho-social constant—a phenomenon capable of producing generation after generation of racial imposition. They typically locate this ongoing dynamic in both our institutions as well as in our collective psyche. They call it racism.

Racism is very, very real, but *talking* about racism is often surreal. Why is that? First, because its connotations overpower its denotations, and, second, because those denotations themselves are problematic. As a result, the *language* of racism poses some significant problems for our investigation of "America's original sin."

Let's begin by thinking about its denotations. For some, racism equals anti-black animus; for others it can also be anti-white or anti-any-color animus. Some hold that only whites can be racists; others insist that it is an equal-opportunity misdeed. Some believe that slavery caused racism; others think it's the other way around. Some view racism as primarily an institutional reality; others see it as primarily an individual matter. Some think that you must actually discriminate against others to be a racist; others think that you're a racist if you're inclined to discriminate, even if you don't actually do so.

The term *racism* ends up being applied to virtually every aspect of our racial dysfunction. It might refer to either the cause or the effect of that dysfunction—or both. Depending on the person or the community with whom you are speaking; *racism* might refer to an ideology, an attitude, a social custom, a practice, a perspective, a tool of power, a structure of power, or any combination thereof.

Nevertheless, a lot of people still think they know what *racism* means. And maybe they do know what it means—to them. But it's a lot harder to know what *racism* means to anybody else, let alone to everybody else.

As if this lexical morass were not sufficiently problematic, consider the connotations of this terminology. Racism has acquired a nearly singular status in the pantheon of social transgressions. People will often admit to other personal weaknesses—even to being sinners. But to be a racist is to be a pariah, making it basically an inadmissible flaw. There's a reason why even the members of the KKK wear hoods.

Ridding oneself of racism is not the kind of thing that you can be "working on." People might talk about how failure has made them more patient or even share their battles with addiction. But nobody's going to crow about being somewhat less racist this year than last.

Though we can't agree about the meaning of *racism*, we do agree about what it means to be a racist. We tell ourselves: "To be a racist is to be a terrible person, and since I am not a terrible person, I am not a racist."

The erudite can and do debate the "proper" definition of *racism*, a discussion that can be helpful for exploring the nature of the phenomenon itself. But if anyone thinks they can, by force of logic or linguistics, control how others perceive and react to this terminology, I fear they are mistaken. Facilitating a collective conversation on race is already challenging enough without the additional complication of self-defeating semantics.

For the purposes of this book, "racism-speak" is particularly unhelpful. I'm trying to talk about racial dysfunction in a therapeutic way—that is, in a way that promotes healing. And in order to have that curative conversation we must first agree on the nature of the problem. If, however, that agreement requires us to: 1) share a common cognitive and affective response to this language, and 2) admit that I/we are in some sense racist, then that effort is likely to be about as successful as it has been thus far.

Wary of the pitfalls of this terminology and hoping to cast our discussion in a fresh light, I will avoid using *racism* as an explanatory principle.[b] Since mine is a spiritual thesis, it seems more appropriate to present it in the language of biblical morality. Admittedly, this approach introduces its own set of challenges. My hope, however, is that a less-encumbered nomenclature will help open our hearts and minds to a significant paradigm shift.

So, if we eschew *racism* as the most apt descriptor for "America's original sin," and if we refuse to reduce that sin to the practice of slavery—how can we describe this problem? What immoral constant has dogged us throughout our history? What spiritual phenomenon defined America's racial beginnings, fuels our racial present, and helps explain all that happened in between?

I have to admit that when it first came to me, I was a bit underwhelmed. A proper theory, it seems, benefits from a name with a certain scientific cachet. As explanations for human behavior go, however, this one sounded more like something from a Charles Spurgeon sermon than from the

---

[b] Various Christian writers have addressed the "sin of racism," and I applaud their moral acumen. Nevertheless, it seems to me that the language of racism complicates rather than facilitates that discussion. Therefore, I do not employ this terminology in my own exposition, even though the language of racism will appear in citations and in my interaction with the thoughts of others.

Diagnostic and Statistical Manual of Mental Disorders. It didn't end in *ism* or *osis*. It wasn't so much a syndrome as a sin, and not even one of those that get a lot of airtime. It was just haughtiness—or so I thought.

Yes, it was haughtiness. But it wasn't *just* haughtiness, because there's nothing trivial or trifling about haughtiness when it's *racial* haughtiness. Mixing haughtiness with racial identity is like mixing *Mentos* with *Diet Coke*; it's going to erupt—overflowing into supremacy, domination, and oppression.

Haughtiness is, of course, a form of pride. But the term carries with it some very specific nuances that are useful for our purposes. According to The American Heritage Dictionary, to be *haughty* is to be "scornfully and condescendingly proud." Haughtiness is not just how one thinks about oneself; it bolsters that self-assessment by debasing others, displaying an "arrogant superiority to and disdain of those one views as unworthy" (Vocabulary.com). In certain contexts pride might seem justifiable or even admirable, but not haughtiness. Its inherently superior pretensions render it invariably contemptible.

For some readers, such an unapologetic emphasis on morality might be unwelcome or at least unfamiliar. After all, race relations is a phenomenon that social scientists typically address in the language of sociology, psychology, politics, and economics. My purpose, however, is not to substitute a spiritual treatment of the subject for a scientific one. Rather, I'm offering a dedicated lens through which we can appreciate the phenomenon of evil as it exists in racial identity. Sin is real, and it matters; but sin does not exist in a vacuum. I have depended heavily on the social sciences to help me think about how that evil was shaped by its environment and how it has shaped that environment in return.

Other readers might welcome such a moral critique but worry that my emphasis on *personal* morality is just another attempt to privatize and spiritualize a problem with important institutional and societal implications. As the argument of this book unfolds, I trust that my overall strategy will become more evident. But let me say a word up front about the nexus between the individual and corporate aspects of this problem.

I do, indeed, stress the need for personal moral engagement and response. In part, this is because I'm convinced of its relevance. But it's also because my particular white target audience is generally quite attuned to matters of individual morality but hesitant to contemplate whiteness writ large. Therefore, trying to engage them on this issue primarily at the corporate level is like trying to pick up a plastic spoon with a magnet.

We must also keep in mind that the individual and the collective aspects of this issue, while certainly distinguishable, are not easily divisible. The collective psyche is the product of the individual psyches of which it is comprised. On the other hand, those individual psyches are shaped by the collective psyche in which they are nurtured. Racial haughtiness, in particular, is inherently corporate in nature, and the social ills that emanate from it create self-perpetuating institutional dynamics that cannot be resolved simply by personal penitence.

So, I do intend to address the institutional aspects of this problem. In fact, I want to fundamentally alter that conversation, because that conversation is currently stuck in a rut. It is a rut created by well-worn narratives—*all of which* are operating under the influence of racial haughtiness.

The first such narrative sees white advantage as *slipping*. According to this mindset, whites are losing their hegemony, and that is reason for white alarm. Efforts to address racial injustice have resulted in an overreach, leading to reverse discrimination. Restoring the "proper" equilibrium would require us to do less rather than more.

A second narrative conceives of white advantage as *static*. That is, now that we have created the proper legal framework for racial justice, the most important reform is over and done. What remains is to manage the status quo.

The problem is that the social equilibrium we are managing is not equal. As a result, whites must occasionally cede small portions of their advantage (whether cynically or compassionately), in order to ameliorate the most egregious effects of that inequality. These minor calibrations, combined with a commitment to "better race relations," serve to mitigate the frustration of the disenfranchised and to keep the societal boat from rocking.

A third narrative aspires to white advantage as *shared*. Recognizing that whites enjoy a disproportionate slice of social wellbeing, this approach embraces sharing as an ethical ambition rather than a necessary evil required to sustain the status quo. Because the redistribution of social goods on this scale requires a mechanism more robust than mere philanthropy, subscribers to this narrative are generally more open to governmental intervention.

The often-acrimonious tension between these three narratives serves to obscure just how much they have in common. For these competing strategies are actually united by a shared presupposition—*the appropriate permanence of white advantage*. Those who actively try to shore up its slippage are certainly the most straightforward advocates of this dogma. But even those who are willing to share their advantage are rarely thinking in terms of social parity. They, too, assume that whites will continue to control the nature and extent of such sharing from their perpetual position atop the racial hierarchy.

As a result of this unintentional ideological collusion, every one of these three narratives ends up being the opposite of equality. No matter which approach dominates, white hegemony remains a categorical imperative and an uninterrupted social reality.

The key element in the phrase "the appropriate permanence of white advantage," is the word "appropriate." What would make an unequal racial hierarchy seem "appropriate?" Well, the material benefits we whites derive from social dominance would certainly make it attractive. But there is a considerable difference between "attractive" and "appropriate." I am convinced that what ultimately makes white dominance seem *appropriate* is the sin of racial haughtiness. Haughtiness breeds a subtle sense of deservedness that arises, not from a rational *calculation* of worthiness (supremacist arguments notwithstanding) but from an immoral *presumption* of greater worthiness.

As long as this institutionalized inequality seems appropriate at some level, we can never really get rid of it. It will morph; it will evolve; it will shapeshift; but it will never disappear—because it is ultimately a manifestation of a racial identity steeped in the sin of haughtiness. For this reason, our new paradigm for racial healing must begin with a moral accounting.

But there's a problem—this moral accounting requires an understanding of contemporary whiteness and the extent to which it is defined by racial haughtiness. And white people trying to comprehend whiteness is a bit like fish trying to comprehend water.

Nevertheless, there may be a way for us to create the necessary distance between ourselves and the object of our contemplation, even when we are that object. I say that, because what we are today is the product of what we've been becoming. So, if we look backward and trace the development of original sin over time—if we observe what our racial identity has been becoming—we can kind of sneak up on ourselves from behind.

That sweeping survey begins in the next chapter, as we examine the rise of haughtiness in the European mindset from which our Founding Fathers drew their cultural heritage.

Chapter 3

The Lie

The Genesis account of the Garden of Eden finds Adam and Eve walking and talking with God himself in an unspoiled, idyllic, innocence. But, then, only a few verses later that bliss is suddenly replaced by disobedience, shame, and estrangement. What happened? Well, it's not easy to wrap our minds around the twisted logic of sin, but this much is clear—they had help. That catalyst was none other than a lie introduced by the Evil One.

Likewise, white America's "original sin"[a] of racial haughtiness is animated by a lie—a convenient untruth called superiority. All sinful pride is powered by superiority, which causes us to think of ourselves as more worthy than we really are. Haughtiness, however, goes a step further, prompting us to think of ourselves as more worthy than someone else.

Racial haughtiness requires a human foil, someone to play the inferior "other" to our supposedly superior selves. Once we have identified this less-deserving counterpart, we quite naturally go about giving them exactly what they deserve—which is, of course, less. And, so, the lie of superiority becomes the demonstrable fact of dominance, completing the sinful circularity.

But just how did this superiority dynamic develop in actual historical events? Let's pick up the story in the 4th century A.D. After the conversion of Constantine in the early part of that century, Christianity began its transformation from an increasingly influential movement to a religious institution identified with a particular geopolitical reality. In 380 A.D., the Emperor Theodosius issued the Edict of Thessalonica, making Christianity the "official" religion of the Roman Empire[b] which, at the time extended well beyond Europe into Asia Minor, the Middle East, and North Africa.

About a century later, however, the Roman Empire dissolved, and though Christianity remained the dominant faith in the corresponding territories, it no

---

[a] From here forward, unless specifically noted, the term *original sin* will refer to racial haughtiness rather than to the traditional theological concept.
[b] "Official" can be defined in more than one way. This edict identified Nicene Christianity as the true apostolic religion vis-à-vis its Arian counterpart. It wasn't until later that the public practice of other religions was forbidden.

longer enjoyed the all-powerful protection of the imperial military and political apparatus. After its founding in 622 A.D., Islam began flexing its muscle in the vacuum left by Rome's demise. A series of caliphates conquered considerable territory along the southern tier of Christendom, circumscribing official Christianity to an essentially European geography.

Soon after the Great Schism between the Eastern and Western Churches took place in 1054, the Western Church became the primary protagonist in the Crusades, which began in 1095 and lasted for about two centuries. These loosely organized military campaigns retook relatively small portions of the territory lost to Muslim conquests, only to lose it again after the crusades came to an end. Along the way, however, the crusades militarized the mission of the Church, consolidating power around the popes and fusing Christianity with Western European political aims, cultural norms, and ethnic identity. As the Renaissance dawned, and with it the science and technology necessary to project global influence, Western Europe and the religion associated with it were poised to take center stage in the looming confrontation between organized Christianity and non-Christian cultures.

At the dawn of the colonial era in the 15th century, a rivalry erupted between Portugal and Castile (the precursor to modern-day Spain) over the rights to newly "discovered" lands.[c] The Portuguese gained the upper hand in this competition in 1455, when Pope Nicholas V issued a papal bull entitled *Romanus Pontifex*. This papal pronouncement gave King Alfonso and Prince Henry of Portugal the right: [my emphasis below]

> to invade, search out, capture, vanquish, and subdue all Saracens [Muslims] and pagans whatsoever, and other enemies of Christ wheresoever placed... and *to reduce their persons to perpetual slavery*, and to apply and appropriate to himself and his successors the... dominions, possessions, and goods, and to convert them to his and their use and profit...[1]

Note that this Pontiff deemed it appropriate to assign not only newly discovered *lands* to the political entities that comprised Christendom—but also the *people* who lived there, along with all of their rights and possessions.

---

[c] I am indebted to Prof. Willie James Jennings for his excellent and extensive treatment of the incident that follows and of Acosta and Valignano, who appear later in this chapter (*The Christian Imagination: Theology and the Origins of Race*. New Haven: Yale University Press, 2010). I have summarized his material, along with other sources. Unless specifically noted, the interpretation is my own, and quotes are drawn from the original sources.

This astounding claim sparked a centuries-long debate within the Church. Subsequent papal pronouncements significantly altered the terms of *Romanus Pontifex*, including those regarding slavery, but the principle of laying claim to the "heathen" world nevertheless prevailed throughout the colonial period.

Portugal's Prince Henry (the Navigator) wasted no time in carrying out his Christian duty in nearby Africa. From his point of view, the responsibility to conquer, enslave, and Christianize heathen peoples constituted a single mandate, a seamless strategy. His chronicler, an intellectual by the name of Zurara, recorded the scene on August 8, 1444, as a Portuguese ship entered the port of Lagos with a cargo of 235 slaves from a previously unexplored area of Africa along the coast of modern Angola. This early and dramatic account juxtaposed European (racial) identity with that of their African captives, as they disembarked from the slave vessels:

> ...Amongst them were some white enough, fair to look upon, and well-proportioned; others were less white like mulattoes; others again were as black as Ethiops and so ugly, both in features and in body, as almost to appear (to those who saw them) the images of a lower hemisphere.[2]

Lançarote, the leader of the expedition, presented the slaves to Henry as his plunder from the land to which they had been sent in the service of God and the Crown.[3] In turn, the prince gave an offering comprised of the best of the slave lot to remain in the service of the Church.[4] Zurara notes that Henry was particularly pleased by "the salvation of those souls that before were lost"[5]—as if these Africans had voluntarily walked down the aisle to the tune of "Just as I Am" rather than being forcefully loaded onto a slave ship.

In spite of the pious trappings of this event, Zurara could not escape the blatant inhumanity of the scene unfolding before him.

> But what heart could be so hard as not to be pierced with piteous feeling to see that company? For some kept their heads low and their faces bathed in tears, looking one upon another, others stood groaning and dolorously, looking up to the height of heaven, fixing their eyes upon it, crying out loudly, as if asking help of the Father of Nature...

> But to increase their sufferings still more... then was it needful to part fathers from sons, husbands from wives, brothers from brothers. No respect was shown either to friends or relations, but each fell where his lot took him.... And who could finish that partition without very great toil? For as often as they had placed them in one part the sons, seeing their fathers in

another, rose with great energy and rushed over to them; the mothers clasped their other children in their arms, and threw themselves flat on the ground with them; receiving blows with little pity for their own flesh, if only they might not be torn from them.[6]

Zurara then seemed to apologize for his own sense of compassion in this heartfelt, if condescending, prayer:

I pray Thee that my tears may not wrong my conscience; for it is not their religion but their humanity that maketh mine to weep in pity for their sufferings. And if the brute animals, with their bestial feelings, by a natural instinct understand the suffering of their own kind, what wouldst Thou have my human nature to do on seeing before my eyes that miserable company, and remembering that they too are the generation of the sons of Adam?[7]

Despite his humanitarian misgivings, the royal chronicler nevertheless remained committed to the ends that justified the means. As he detailed the advantages the slaves would come to enjoy in Portugal, he foreshadowed a rationalization that would be repeated all too often in the coming centuries:

And so their lot was now quite the contrary of what it had been; since before they had lived in perdition of soul and body; of their souls, in that they were yet pagans, without the clearness and the light of the holy faith; and of their bodies, in that they lived like beasts, without any custom of reasonable beings— for they had no knowledge of bread or wine, and they were without the covering of clothes, or the lodgment of houses; and worse than all, they had no understanding of good, but only knew how to live in a bestial sloth.[8]

As Europeans continued to colonize, their missionary endeavors generated certain ecclesiastical concerns. What were the best methods for drawing unbelievers into the Christian fold? How could they gauge the depth/authenticity of the converts' Christian experience? And which peoples were best suited for Church leadership?

During the latter part of the sixteenth century two Jesuit missionary theologians, José de Acosta and Alessandro Valignano—one located in the West and the other in the East—responded to these questions, elaborating hierarchies of the spiritual and intellectual capacities of different groups. While these were ostensibly religious issues, European explorers and missionaries tended to view them through a collective (ethnic) rather than an individualistic lens. Quite naturally, then, outward indications of ethnicity became associated with broad stereotypes.

Acosta taught at the Jesuit college of Salamanca, Spain, after serving fifteen years as a scholar and church leader in Peru . The Italian Valignano—trained in law, philosophy, and theology—was appointed head of all missions in the Far East. These two highly qualified individuals, who were probably familiar with each other's work,[9] came to strikingly similar conclusions about the pedagogical possibilities of the world's peoples.

Acosta divided non-Europeans, whom he called "barbarians," into three groups. The first and most advanced had both complex social structures as well as a literary tradition capable of advancing their respective civilizations from one generation to the next. These included the Chinese, the Japanese, and the inhabitants of eastern India. Acosta concluded that these societies could be converted by reason rather than by conquest.

The next class consisted of those civilizations with little or no literacy or philosophy but who nevertheless had a well-defined social order and government. These societies, including the Peruvians and Mexicans, needed cultivation in order to be better prepared to live as Christians. Acosta believed that the rule of the European colonizers would provide this needed boost.

The lowest group were deemed savages—illiterate hunters and gatherers with no developed system of governance. These docile creatures, who didn't even possess normal human emotions, could be won over either through flattery or, if that failed, by force.[10]

Valignano, for his part, was favorably impressed by the Japanese and contrasts them with the (Asian) Indians: [my emphasis below]

> There is a difference between the Indian and Japanese Christians… for each one of the former was converted from some individual ulterior motive, and since they are *blacks*, and of small sense, they are subsequently very difficult to improve and turn into good Christians; whereas the Japanese usually become converted, not on some whimsical individual ulterior motive… but only in obedience to their lord's command; and since they are *white* and of good understanding and behavior… when they are instructed they become very good Christians.[11]

Valignano concocted a detailed breakdown of those who might qualify for service in the Church, starting with the most adequate—purebred Europeans—and working down through a series of racial mixtures until he got to those who were "clearly beyond the veil of possibility for service… those [he] termed the 'dusky races, [as they are] stupid and vicious…'"[12]

So, haughtiness emerged when Europeans began to project their power onto other people groups. Their sense of superiority inevitably included a strong religious sentiment, because Christianity was almost completely identified with the European geography in which it exercised its hegemony. As the colonial enterprise unfolded, a more self-conscious, European Christian identity would evolve. Believing their faith to be absolutely superior to every other, it was not hard for them to imagine that the culture baptized by that faith was at least relatively superior to every other.

With religion and culture so intertwined, the European way became the standard, representing God's plan for how people should think and be and interact. It was a standard that European Christians applied, not only when judging the cultural merits of others but also when evaluating their religious aptitudes—and sometimes their very personhood.

This supposed European superiority was initially rooted in a religio-cultural calculation, not an overtly racial one. But since the existing cultures and religions were distributed geographically and ethnically, they naturally aligned with certain physical differences. Confusing correlation with causation, it did not take long for European Christians to infer that perceived differences in human capacity and behavior were racial/ethnic in nature.

Given the Europeans' ethnocentric assumptions, it's not surprising that the racial hierarchy they created was heavily prejudiced in favor of whiteness. *White* became the standard and *black* its deficient counterweight. So much so that whiteness was not only a color marker; it could also be applied to peoples whose cultural organization paralleled that of the Europeans.

For instance, though Valignano referred to the Japanese as *white*, others, who did not share his high regard for that culture, sometimes called the same people *black*. Francisco Cabral, Portuguese superior of the mission to Japan, did not favor the use of indigenous clergy, because, as he said, the Japanese "are Niggers and their customs barbarous.'"[13] Historian C. R. Boxer says that the Portuguese tended to regard even the children of European parents born in the East as good for nothing and sometimes referred to them as "niggers."[14/d]

So, *white* came to represent that which was good and normative; *black* became a derogatory designation, one that might or might not correlate with

---

[d] Because this terminology is offensive to me and to others, I do not employ it as a designation for black people, either in America or elsewhere. I do, however, include it in quoted material, sometimes to retain the virulence of the original quote and sometimes (as in the case of transcriptions of interviews with former slaves) to maintain the integrity of historical speech patterns.

skin color. The blackest of the "black" were black Africans, typically regarded as uncivilized and brutish.[15] As Willie James Jennings observes, from the 15th century onward "both Iberian empires remained essentially a 'pigmentocracy' …based on the conviction of white racial, moral and intellectual superiority— just as did their Dutch, English, and French successors."[16]

Thus began the lie—racial haughtiness in its primordial state. It is not so much a lie that liars tell to others (though they do), as a lie that liars tell to themselves. This lie of superiority says: "We are good; we are right; we are normative. Compared to us, others are, in one degree or another, defective."

As God's chosen representatives, these Europeans believed that God had conferred upon them both the theological mandate as well as the practical wherewithal to subjugate inferior peoples. They saw their dominance as not only just but actually beneficent. It seemed just, because it allowed everyone to occupy the place they deserved. And it seemed kind, because, by putting the best people (themselves) in power, they could help others become better.

Lies are, of course, easier to believe when they provide us with greater social and material benefits. Lies are also easier to believe when they contain a kernel of truth. In this case that kernel of truth was *chosenness*, a recurring, but twisted theme in the history of haughtiness.

Scripture, indeed, teaches that Christians are chosen by God. But, in this case, the "elect" ignored the consistent Scriptural teaching in Deuteronomy 7 and 9, as well as Romans 11 and other passages, that God's choice is not based on the superior merit of the chosen, but on the ultimately mysterious rationale of grace. That is, God's exceptional goodness to some is *not* bestowed in response to their exceptionalism, either individually or collectively.

For that reason, chosenness should never lead to haughtiness. As the Apostle Paul reminds us in Romans 3:27, boasting (or any high-mindedness) "is excluded." The only proper response to grace is a spirit of humility.

Grace should make us humble, not only in spirit but also in service. Though Christ's followers are called to share in his glory, that future reality is promised to those who also "share in his sufferings" (Romans 8:17)—not to those who inflict suffering in his name. Christ's own example in Philippians 2:5-8 shows that, rather than dominating others we deem *less than us*, we are to make ourselves *less than others*. European Christians clearly stumbled out of the gate regarding this rather central responsibility.

Chapter 4
Haughtiness Crosses the Atlantic

European colonialism remained the dominant force in world politics for several centuries, as Protestant countries joined their Catholic counterparts in re-drawing the world map. At the heart of their expansionist vision was the conviction that they had both the right as well as the responsibility to dominate. This ethnocentric European hubris was still in vogue even toward the end of the 19th century, when slavery had been abandoned and secularism was supplanting religious sentiment.

Jules Ferry, twice Prime Minister of France and himself a secularizing reformer, addressed the Chamber of Deputies on July 28, 1883:

> Gentlemen, ...we must say openly that indeed the higher races have a right over the lower races... I repeat, that the superior races have a right because they have a duty. They have the duty to civilize the inferior races... In the history of earlier centuries these duties... have often been misunderstood... But, in our time, I maintain that European nations acquit themselves with generosity, with grandeur, and with sincerity of this superior civilizing duty.[1]

This same haughty spirit crossed the Atlantic to the American colonies, where it became the foundation for a racialized society. But what were the factors that determined how this mentality filtered into the American experience? In this chapter, I examine three foundational influences that shaped American haughtiness: a chosen-nation mentality imported from England, an avaricious approach to economics, and the socio-political peculiarities of colonialism.

A chosen-nation mentality

After defeating the Spanish Armada in 1588, the English leveraged their naval advantage to become the dominant colonial power. Other European nations saw their colonizing mission as a way to also fulfill the Christianizing mission of the Roman Catholic Church. But England, which had its own Church, tended to fuse these secular and spiritual duties together under the umbrella of its own nationalistic identity.[a] As a result, the mission of the kingdom of God and the mission of the British state became inseparable when projected upon the world stage.

That a "chosen people" identity took shape in England during the 16th and 17th centuries is hardly a matter of historical dispute. In early 2010, the BBC ran a TV documentary series entitled "The Seven Ages of Britain." The third of those ages, covering the century from 1509-1609, was advertised as "the creation of an enduring myth: England as God's chosen nation."[2]

The publication of *Foxe's Book of Martyrs* in 1563, helped to solidify England's sense of itself as both an alternative to a decadent Catholicism as well as a representative of God's kingdom on earth. John Spencer Hill, professor of English at the University of Ottawa, regards this book as "the most important assertion of national vocation in Elizabethan England... According to Foxe, scripture and history alike declared that the divine purpose was about to be fulfilled in the chosen people of England..."[3]

Pastor and hymn writer Isaac Watts[b] (1674-1748) further cemented this image in the popular imagination. Watts, who penned such classic hymns as "Joy to the World," and "When I Survey the Wondrous Cross," thought that the Psalms needed to be recast in a more vernacular verse form to which people could relate. In so doing, however, he actually re-envisioned the Psalter, wresting it from its original Hebrew context and resetting it so that Britain became the protagonist of the biblical narrative. Take, for instance, these excerpts from his version of Psalm 67. The bold text represents the King James Version, followed by Watts' rendition of the verses indicated:

(1) God be merciful unto us and bless us; and cause his face to shine upon us.

"Shine, mighty God, on Britain shine, with beams of heavn'ly grace;
Reveal thy power through all our coasts, and show thy smiling face."

(6) Then shall the earth yield her increase; and God, even our own God, shall bless us.

"Earth shall obey her Maker's will, and yield a full increase;
Our God will crown his chosen isle, with fruitfulness and peace."

---

[a] The French, too, had a sense of national calling rooted in their own exceptionalism and their civilizing duty. Their outlook, however, relied more heavily on Enlightenment values than on a "chosen nation" identity.
[b] Willie James Jennings offers a valuable and more extensive treatment on Watts' contributions in *The Christian Imagination,* pp. 210-220.

(7) God shall bless us; and all the ends of the earth shall fear him.

"God the Redeemer scatters round, His choicest favors here,
While the creation's utmost bound, shall see, adore, and fear."[4]

In this striking example of nationalistic supersessionism,[c] Britain is transformed into God's "chosen isle" to which the peoples of the world must turn to see God's saving work. [d] And this worldview, fueled by a religiously-charged exceptionalism, traveled quite comfortably from England to New England and beyond during the formative years of America's national consciousness. Even now, in the 21st century, it is not too much to say, along with journalist John B. Judis, that the way America views its role in the world is "based on Protestant millennial themes that go back to seventeenth-century England."[5] This religio-cultural hubris, born in Western Christendom and filtered through the spirit of imperial Britain, became the stage onto which "our fathers brought forth on this continent a new nation."

Avaricious economics

Even as England was beginning its New World colonization, it was also experiencing a tremendous economic expansion at home. Between 1530 and 1680, its population doubled, increasing the internal market, even as the nation was exponentially increasing its role in the global economy. This boom was due, in part, to an entrepreneurial spirit that was lacking across most of the continent. Changes in the way that wealth was created, however, also led to economic polarization. Those who had significant land holdings prospered, supplying food and clothing to the growing markets, while those who owned little or no land found themselves marginalized by the scale of the new economic reality. [6]

The result of this domestic situation in Britain was that nearly everyone became a potential player on the new American scene—a wealthy investor class; groups of religious dissenters, who were often members of the middle class; and the down-and-outers who had been victimized by demographic and

---

[c] Supersessionism is the doctrine that the Church has replaced Israel in the plan of God. Its nuances cover a wide range of interpretations, but here this replacement is applied to a specific Christian nation.

[d] Watts was atypical in a formal sense, a dissenter who pastored an independent congregation outside the Anglican Church. This fact, however, may make his commitment to the country's religious calling more rather than less remarkable, demonstrating the breadth of this nationalistic appeal.

economic changes. To facilitate this move to the New World, joint stock-trading companies (the precursors to modern corporations) pooled the funds of various investors to establish colonies in the New World—including both the Virginia Company of London and the Massachusetts Bay Company. Unlike other European colonies, America's economic vitality did not depend on the royal treasury or on a missionary force financed by the Church. Rather, the colonists and their sponsors relied on a broad-based private protagonism.

The American colonists, then, were not in America because it was their ancestral home or because they knew no other reality. Rather, they chose to come in search of *prosperity*. Thomas K. McCraw of Harvard Business School characterizes this uniqueness: "No nation has been more market-oriented in its origins and subsequent history than the United States of America. The very settling of the country... was one long entrepreneurial adventure... Capitalism did come in the first ships... and that proved to be momentous for the nation's future..."[7]

While such material aspirations may seem innocent enough, the inevitable intersection between economics and ethics resulted in a good deal of give and take. And ethics did its share of the giving. McCraw observes: "The line between virtuous profit and damnable avarice was blurry then, as it remains today."[8]

Popular patriotic sentiment loves to extol our national commitment to this virtuous profit obtained through ingenuity and hard work. And there was undoubtedly much of that. But we're not so quick to recognize its powerful alter ego, which McGraw characterizes as "damnable avarice." It was, however, precisely this greedy tendency, catalyzed by haughtiness, that led to the creation of a slave society.

Avarice can be distinguished from the legitimate pursuit of wealth by a myopic self-interest that leads us to ignore our own ethical principles and to exploit other people. When avarice takes hold, wealth ceases to be the result of industry and instead becomes its focus. Economic activity is no longer a matter of glorifying God or contributing to the common good or even fulfilling our personal responsibility. When wealth becomes its own justification, the temptation to extract it from others through oppressive means can overpower moral restraints.

Avarice was certainly present in Europe as well, leading as it did to colonial exploitation and slave trading. Europeans, however, stopped short of embracing slavery in their own social midst, a compunction that was, sadly, lacking in America. As we trace the history of racial exploitation, we shall see that Americans, even devoutly Christian Americans, ran a whole series of moral stop signs, exploiting and even enslaving others in their personalized "pursuit of happiness."

In a competition among valued equals one may gain a relative advantage over another, but moral sensibilities limit just how much loss people will inflict upon their fellows in pursuit of personal gain. Haughtiness, however, erodes the bonds of *fraternité*, dividing people into classes of relative worthiness. Doing unto others as you would have them do unto you doesn't seem quite so binding if the others are not really like you in the first place.

When it comes to avarice, the American Church has never posed a serious challenge to the cultural status quo. Why? Because both institutionally and individually we, its constituents, are implicated. If we are to ever deal with the consequences of avarice on our racial history, we must first recognize what it means to be under its influence.

The socio-political peculiarities of colonialism

Politics and economics have always been intertwined, and that symbiotic relationship was never more visible than during the colonial period, when imperial political aspirations and global commerce fed off one another. In the age of competing nation-states, beginning in the 16th century, the prize became money; enough money to build a military capable of expanding one's own empire while protecting that empire against encroachment from others. The politics of the day revolved around exploiting one's own colonies, while squelching the competition through protectionist measures—all in an effort to maintain a cash-producing trade surplus.

For example, the Navigation Acts of the mid-17th century called for all trade between England and its colonies to be transported by English or colonial ships. Certain colonial products could be sold only in Britain. And all trade between continental Europe and the colonies had to pass through England first, where taxes were collected.

England did not allow slavery in the mother country. Nevertheless, they (along with other European powers) established quite a different policy in the colonies. American settlers, though English, were also colonists and took advantage of this bifurcated ethic. The use of slave labor was an economic advantage that, once established, eventually became impossible to do without. As a result, even when the Americans gained their independence from England, they could not shake their dependence on slavery.

Though America was a colony, it was, importantly, a colony populated primarily by (English) Europeans. In most other colonies the European powers controlled and exploited the indigenous people and/or replaced them with slaves. They themselves, however, emigrated to those colonies in relatively small numbers and were often absentee landowners.

America was a very different story. Climate, as it turns out, was the key to allowing blacks and whites share this geographical space. Europeans considered themselves ill-suited for the tropics, where most of the rest of colonial slavery took place, but the temperate North American weather allowed them to live here in large numbers. Conditions in the southern states proved ideal for crops that lent themselves to plantation agriculture. Africans thrived in America as well, avoiding many of the diseases that decimated their numbers in the Caribbean. So much so that the black population continued to multiply naturally,[e] even after the legal importation of slaves ended in 1808.

As a result, for many European Americans blacks were not some far off exotic novelty but part of the fabric of their everyday lives. Whites had an ethnic "other" close at hand, sometimes even in the same household. For that reason Europeans living in America developed attitudes toward black people and modes of interaction with them that Europeans living in Europe did not. As America's original sin filtered through this peculiar arrangement, the result was a uniquely racialized society.

Haughtiness, then, was already part and parcel of European self-identity in the colonial era. This attitude, originally manifested as a religio-cultural hubris, was already acquiring racial overtones by the time the first English settlers made their way to these shores. But it took the perfect storm of opportunities and influences described above for haughtiness to evolve into a white-over-black American society, a legacy that still haunts us today.

It's true that only a relatively small percentage of whites ever actually owned slaves. Nevertheless, the original sin of racial haughtiness still poisoned an entire pool of people. Nearly everyone believed that whether or not the African was your slave, he or she was certainly not your equal. And the haughty complicity of that social compact allowed a slave society to flourish for a quarter of a millennium.

---

[e] By "naturally" I mean through procreation. As later chapters make clear, the conditions under which this procreation occurred were not always natural.

Chapter 5

From Indians to Africans

More than one hundred years before British settlements began to multiply in North America, the slave trade made its first mark on our history through none other than Christopher Columbus. Returning from his first voyage to the New World, he wrote to King Ferdinand and Queen Isabella, "that he could, with their help, 'give them slaves, as many as they shall order.'"[1] On his second voyage, Columbus loaded up five hundred Indian slaves, two hundred of whom died en route, their bodies tossed into the sea.[2] And so began the notorious commerce known as the trans-Atlantic slave trade—not from east to west, bringing Africans to the New World, but from west to east, transporting members of the indigenous population to Europe.

Why did they do it? The motivational mix that first launched colonial slavery didn't differ much from the mentality that sustained it more than three centuries later—haughtiness excited by avarice. Tzvetan Todorov writes in *The Conquest of America*: "The desire for wealth and the impulse to master— certainly these two forms of aspiration to power motivate the Spaniards' conduct; but this conduct is also conditioned by their notion of the Indians as inferior beings, halfway between men and beasts."[3]

While the Iberians continued their colonial enterprise in the southern part of the Americas, by the early 17th century the English were landing on North American shores. These new colonists interfaced with the Indians, not simply as conquistadors but as settlers, as co-inhabitants. Some of these initial encounters were relatively friendly, such as the oft-recounted relationship between Massasoit, leader of the Wampanoag Confederacy, and the Pilgrims of the Plymouth Colony.[4] In general, however, the English attitudes toward the Indians did not differ greatly from those of the Spanish—that is, that the Indians were an inferior race that could rightly be used in whatever way most benefited the colonists. As a result, the relationship between colonists and natives evolved into dynamic mix of treaties, trading, wars, and slavery.

In his magnum opus, *Magnalia Christi Americana*, the famous New England clergyman, Cotton Mather set forth his jaundiced view of the Indians:

> These doleful creatures are the veriest ruines of mankind, which are to be found any where upon the face of the earth.... Their way of living is infinitely barbarous... No arts are understood among them, except just so far as to maintain their brutish conversation, which is little more than is to be found among the bevers upon our streams.[5/a]

To complicate matters further, even as the colonists were busy taking advantage of the Indians, they were also trying to convert them to Christianity. Indeed, when "King James... granted special charters establishing the Virginia [colony], he specifically called for 'propagating the Christian Religion to such people, as yet live in darkness and miserable ignorance of the true knowledge and worship of God.'"[6] The very charter of the Massachusetts Bay Colony stated that "the principall Ende of this Plantacion"[7] was to "wynn and incite the Natives of Country, to the Knowledg and Obedience of the onlie true God."[8] The charters of several other colonies as well as the Articles of Confederation for New England echoed similar intentions.

Apart from the incongruities inherent in the colonists' less-than-loving attitudes and behaviors, their evangelistic efforts were hampered by the fact that even friendly contact with Europeans often proved deadly for Native Americans, who had no defenses against imported diseases. Though it appears that these first settlers did not intentionally use pathogens as weapons, they nevertheless viewed the decimation of the Native American population as providential. John Winthrop, governor of the Massachusetts Bay Colony and author of the "shining city on a hill" imagery, wrote: "Gods hand hath so pursued them, as for 300 miles space, the greatest parte of them are swept awaye by the small poxe,"[9] concluding that "God hathe hereby cleered our title to this place."[10] Not surprisingly, Winthrop did not interpret the settlers' own rampant mortality rates through the same theological prism.

The scale of this catastrophe is staggering. The pre-Columbian population of Native Americans in what is now the United States[b] is uncertain, with estimates ranging from less than a million to 10 million.[11] Though the starting point may be hard to fix, the final result is nevertheless crystal clear. "By 1900, the Native American population in the United States had dwindled to approximately 250,000."[12] Though many Indians were killed in warfare or

---

[a] Throughout the book I retain the original spellings found in historic texts.

[b] The historical context limits this consideration to the contiguous 48 states.

perished as they lost their habitat, it is estimated that imported diseases were responsible for 75 to 90 percent of the population decrease.[13]

During the early colonial period, Native Americans were enslaved throughout the colonies, but nowhere more so than in the Carolinas. Historian Seymour Drescher recounts that,

> in the 1670s and 1680s, Carolina's labor force consisted primarily of European indentured servants. When the supply of indentured servants declined and planters could not successfully compete for African slaves, the colonists turned towards Native Americans. By 1710, Indian slaves made up a quarter of the colony's bound laborers.[14]

The British eventually found a more beneficial use for Indian slaves throughout the Southeast—exporting Native American labor and using the profits to purchase Africans.

> Once slaves became something to be bought and sold... a powerful new dynamic began shaping the [Indians'] lives... Indian slave raiders captured slaves, mostly women and children, by the thousands and sold them to English, French, and Dutch slavers, who shipped them to the sugar plantations in the Caribbean.[15]

Even as European settlers hastened to exploit the ubiquitous supply of Indian labor, black Africans were already being introduced into America. The first African slaves in what is now the U.S. were brought by Spanish explorers to the Carolinas in 1526. The first African slaves in the British colonies arrived in Jamestown in 1619, just ten years after its founding. They, not the Indians, would eventually become the dominant racial foil for white Americans.

There were, of course, significant differences between Native Americans and Africans, differences that would define the nature of the oppression that each would suffer. Indians had a sense of belonging in their land and could escape into familiar territory, whereas newly imported Africans were completely out of their element. The Africans had already lost everything, whereas Indians still had something to lose. And African slaves were a valuable asset rather than a bellicose enemy, meaning that their masters neither sought nor celebrated their demise.

In spite of these differences, we can observe a common thread in the white treatment of both Indians and African Americans. Whites consigned both to the status of racial *other*. Whites subjected both to despotic treatment. Whites denigrated the very personhood of both groups. And whites justified the subordination of both groups with a missionary mandate.

Regardless of the identity of the victims, the haughty outlook of the oppressors was eerily similar. In the end, however, Africans proved to be more vulnerable. In the racial hierarchy inherited by America's settlers, Africans commanded even less respect than Native Americans, and that inferior image was reinforced by their wholly servile role. If the decimation of Indian populations demonstrated that God was on the side of white dominance, what would their absolute control over the destinies of imported Africans prove about the rightness of that racial order?

What made the American experience unique was certainly not the *fact* of slavery, since slavery is as old as human history. Or even the importation of foreigners. Nevertheless, what became known as "our peculiar institution" was just that, in part because of the sheer scale of the American slave enterprise. While a *society with slaves* is the historical rule, *slave societies* are the rare exception.

A *society with slaves* is one in which "slavery is only one of several other systems of labor,"[16] whereas a *slave society* is one in which "slavery is the foundation of the economic and social order."[17] The list of genuine slave societies is a short one: Athens, Roman Italy, parts of the Americas between 1500-1900, certain areas in Africa, and (briefly) Nazi Germany.[18/c] If the requirement is that slavery be "the foundation of the economic and social order," then the enduring institution that took root in the southern American colonies and the subsequent slave states clearly qualifies.

Not only was American slavery similar to that of classic slave societies like Rome in terms of its social and economic importance, but consider the historic scale of Southern slavery. A careful estimate of slavery in ancient Rome yields "a figure of around two million slaves out of a population of about six million at the time of Augustus..."[19] meaning that "approximately one in every three persons in Rome and Italy was a slave."[20] Compare that to the slave population of the Deep South in the nineteenth century. According to the 1860 census, slaves accounted for one-third or more of the population in seven southern states, including two, Mississippi and South Carolina, in

---

[c] Historian Seymour Drescher refers here to areas of Africa where the slave population numbered between 25% and 50% and where slave labor was the key to agricultural production. Other historians expand this overall list somewhat, but the relative paucity of slave societies remains clear. For more on Nazi Germany, see: www.scottgarber.com/was_notes.pdf, Note 5.1.

which slaves constituted a clear majority.[21] Slavery on this scale is rare in the annals of human history.

By contrast, in 1860, the North was comprised of states that had already outlawed slavery[d] and border states with relatively modest slave populations. Neverthless, slavery benefited the economy of even the free states. Historians dispute the importance of *slave labor* to the New England economy, but there can be no doubt that the *slave trade* was vital to that region.

> The Massachusetts slave trade gave work to coopers, tanners, sailmakers, and rope makers. Countless agents, insurers, lawyers, clerks, and scriveners handled the paperwork for slave merchants. Upper New England loggers, Grand Banks fishermen, and livestock farmers provided the raw materials shipped to the West Indies on that leg of the slave trade. Colonial newspapers drew much of their income from advertisements of slaves for sale or hire. New England-made rum, trinkets, and bar iron were exchanged for slaves.[22]

Even after the North had outlawed slavery, "its ships continued to carry slaves to Southern ports, and slave-grown cotton to Europe. The North reaped the profits of the Southern plantations, and the federal government collected the tariffs."[23] Perhaps only the South could be classified as a *slave society*, but because of the symbiotic economic relationship between the North and South, the entire country owed much of its economic vitality to slavery.

It's impossible to say just how America would have developed without slavery, but until Emancipation the slave economy was vital to our national wealth. Historian Herbert S. Klein concludes that "export agriculture and effective colonization would not have occurred on the scale it did if enslaved Africans had not been brought to the New World. Except for precious metals, almost all major American exports to Europe were produced by Africans."[24]

African slaves and their Native American counterparts were not the only "unfree" contributors to the American economy. During the colonial period more than half of all European immigrants came here as indentured servants.[e]

---

[d] For more background information on the prolonged process of Northern emancipation, see: www.scottgarber.com/was_notes.pdf, Note 5.2.

[e] This may be a conservative estimate. Professor James Horton (George Washington Univ.) claims that "upwards of 80 percent of Europeans... who came to British North America came in a state of indentured servitude." "Race – The Power of an Illusion: Background Readings: Interview with James O. Horton," www.pbs.org/race/000_About/002_04-background-02-04.htm.

In fact, the very first Africans to arrive in the British American colonies often worked right alongside white laborers.

This picture of mixed servitude is, however, somewhat deceiving. Since slavery was practically unheard of in England, initially there was simply no legal category for perpetual bondage, so Africans could not be classified as "slaves," even if that was their destiny. The overwhelming majority of white indentured servants (aside from prisoners) came to the colonies voluntarily, while Africans were taken forcibly into servitude. Whites usually worked four to seven years to pay for their passage to the new world; their servitude functioning as the first rung on the ladder of upward mobility. The few black people who did work their way to freedom were far more likely to end up in northern ghettoes.

In any case, it did not take long for racial distinctions to arise in the status of white and black "servants," creating an official class called "slave" that was particular to black people.

> The first official legal recognition of chattel slavery as a legal institution in British North America was in Massachusetts, in 1641, with the "Body of Liberties." Slavery was legalized in New Plymouth and Connecticut when it was incorporated into the Articles of the New England Confederation (1643). Rhode Island enacted a similar law in 1652. That means New England had formal, legal slavery a full generation before it was established in the South. Not until 1664 did Maryland declare that all blacks held in the colony, and all those imported in the future, would serve for life, as would their offspring. Virginia followed suit by the end of the decade. New York and New Jersey acquired legal slavery when they passed to English control in the 1660s. Pennsylvania, founded only in 1682, followed in 1700, with a law for regulation of servants and slaves.[25]

And, so, permanent chattel slavery was established in America, in the North as well as the South. While the institution evolved differently in different sectors of the country, we shall see that this was more a function of economic viability than of virtuous principle. Whatever moral responsibility we, as a society, bear for embracing this institution cannot be mitigated by recasting slavery as an aberration localized by time or place. Slavery was not just a Southern problem; it was a national phenomenon—and a national sin.

Chapter 6

The Master-Slave Relationship

Apart from the Bible, the best-selling book of the nineteenth century, was *Uncle Tom's Cabin* by Harriet Beecher Stowe. Published in 1852, its depiction of the relationship between masters and slaves created an indelible and stereotypical image of slave life, one that continues to influence the public imagination even today. Since that time, historical research has provided a more thorough understanding of the master-slave dynamic than is possible in a propagandistic literary snapshot. Nothing in that expanded historical record, however, in any way mitigates the moral affront depicted in Stowe's novel.

In the following pages, I explore the master-slave relationship, not simply to establish the historical record (a task already undertaken by many capable historians), but to better appreciate the interpersonal denigration and exploitation that has left an indelible psycho-spiritual imprint on race relations today. The historical viewpoint of an oppressed people is necessarily quite distinct from that of their oppressors. So, not surprisingly, whites and blacks have very different affective appreciations of the master-slave experience. I trust that this chapter will help to bridge that gap, by generating a common outrage toward that disgraceful history.

There were two different dynamics at work in the master-slave relationship. The first was the constant, everyday fact of white-over-black dominance that was established during the several centuries of American slavery. The second involved the less universal but all-too-common patterns of abuse in the context of an already illicit slave system. Let's begin with the more mundane, yet still powerful influence of the institution itself.

The very fact that certain people within our society owned other people (not just their labor but their very selves) established predictably disastrous precedents for interracial relationships. The value of slaves could be expressed in dollars and was dependent only to their ability to produce. Hence, the masters who bought and sold them ultimately established their worth.

Prof. Willie James Jennings comments:

> The lens through which the masters looked at the slaves and
> taught slaveholding society to look at black flesh was one of

use-value. How useful is black flesh? Was the black body docile, friendly, loving, industrious, and positive? or was it malicious, rebellious, deceitful, lazy, and haughty? I am careful to say "body" and not "person," because black flesh was first a commodity.[1]

In order to justify this utilitarian treatment, some of slavery's proponents went so far as to deny black personhood altogether.[a] Rev. John Dixon Long, an abolitionist and minister in the Methodist Episcopal Church in the mid-nineteenth century, recalls his conversation "at the table of a rich, haughty slaveholder,"[2] who asked him:

"Mr. Long, do you believe that the negroes are a part of the human race?"

"Yes, sir," I replied.

"Well, I do not,' said he. "I believe that they are a species of monkey."

...His treatment of his slaves [Long explained] was in accordance with his theory. Yet he was more consistent than those who hold that they are of the same blood as ourselves, and yet treat them like brutes—who hold to their common origin with ourselves from Adam, and their common redemption by Christ, and yet sell them like oxen.[3]

This outright denial of black humanity seems, however, to have been something of a minority position. The bigger issue was one of *truly equal* personhood, a status admitted by few whites on either side of the slavery issue. James Warley Miles, an Episcopal priest who in 1850 became the Chair of History and Intellectual Philosophy and Greek Literature at the College of Charleston, "ridiculed the abolitionist assertion that the negro is 'a man and a brother'.... 'No one,' Miles wrote, 'denies that the negro is a man; but the abolitionists never consider what *kind* of man he is.'"[4]

Even the Great Emancipator, Abraham Lincoln, did not believe in anything resembling real equality. In an 1858 debate, Lincoln's opponent, Stephen Douglas, stated unequivocally, "I do not regard the negro as my equal, and positively deny that he is my brother or any kin to me whatever."[5] With Douglas doing his best to tag Lincoln with the abolitionist label, the future President felt compelled to clarify his view of racial equality:

---

[a] For more background on the three-fifths Constitutional compromise, see: www.scottgarber.com/was_notes.pdf, Note 6.1.

> I agree with judge Douglas he [the black man] is not my equal in many respects—certainly not in color, perhaps not in moral or intellectual endowment. But in the right to eat the bread, without leave of anybody else, which his own hand earns, he is my equal and the equal of Judge Douglas, and the equal of every living man... I have no purpose to introduce political and social equality between the white and the black races. There is a physical difference between the two, which, in my judgment, will probably forever forbid their living together upon the footing of perfect equality; and inasmuch as it becomes a necessity that there must be a difference, I, as well as Judge Douglas, am in favor of the race to which I belong having the superior position..."[6]

The establishment of a white-dominated society was a logical extension of the Euro-American belief in a divinely-ordained social hierarchy in which the superior race dominated the inferior for the benefit of all concerned. But not only did the slave society reflect that belief; it inevitably served to validate that belief as well. Centuries of experience with black subservience seemed to confirm that such a state was not only natural but normal. Joseph Dodderidge, a Southern critic of slavery, summed up this symbiotic circularity between prejudice and experience when he wrote in 1824: "We debase them to the condition of brutes, and then we use that debasement as an argument of perpetuating their slavery."[7]

Given the prevailing views of relative black worth and white assumptions about their own dominance, about the best one could hope for in the context of the master-slave relationship was a (relatively) benign paternalism. And this familial metaphor was, indeed, common among masters who considered themselves kindly disposed toward their slaves. Historian Eugene Genovese comments: "The aristocratic ethos, however offensive to many in its extreme formulations, rested squarely on a world view in which some (slaves, women) were naturally subordinate to others whose domination they accepted in return for a protection without which they could not hope to survive."[8] This ideal was captured in the common expression, "my family, white and black."[9] In fact, it was not uncommon for Southern slave owners to record "the births and deaths of slaves in their family Bibles."[10/b]

---

[b] This paternal interest on the part of 19th century Southern owners "was absent in the North, for the most part, and the colonies there had to resort to laws to prevent masters from simply turning their slaves out in the streets when the slaves grew old or infirm." (www.slavenorth.com, "Introduction")

George Washington, who often referred to his slaves as part of his family, typified this sort of scrupulous paternalism. He came to view his responsibility as that of making "the Adults among them as easy & comfortable in their circumstances as their actual state of ignorance and improvidence would admit..."[11] But he also understood the paternalistic relationship to be mutual, writing, "It has always been my aim to feed & cloath them well, & be careful of them in sickness—in return, I expect such labour as they ought to render."[12]

The barbarous downside of paternalism was that it perpetuated the institution of slavery by masking its true nefarious nature. Rather than an arrangement in which a white elite forcibly subjugated people based on racial identity, paternalistic sentiments made slavery feel more like a mutually beneficial social contract—or even one in which whites were doing a favor for those in bondage. Some believed that "the negro... found happiness only when under the tutelage of a white master."[13]

As offensive as such paternalistic pretensions might seem, even that condescending ideal was rarely achieved. And this less-than-equal vision of black humanity often resulted in abuse and deprivation. The catalog of cruelty that was part of the slave experience is a long one—the lack of a personal history or even a birth date; the impossibility of legal marriage; the separation of family members; the overwork; the exposure to the elements; the denial of religious and secular education; the scarce provision of food and clothing; the whippings; and the sometimes even more grievous physical abuse, including branding with a hot iron.[14]

Slaveholders who considered their slaves to be less than fully human didn't stop to consider how their own treatment of the slaves served to drain the humanity out of them. Frederick Douglass held that dehumanization was a necessary concomitant of the slave enterprise:

> I have found that, to make a contented slave, it is necessary to make a thoughtless one. It is necessary to darken his moral and mental vision, and, as far as possible, to annihilate the power of reason. He must be able to detect no inconsistencies in slavery; he must be made to feel that slavery is right; and he can be brought to that only when he ceases to be a man.[15]

As atrocious as such systemic mistreatment might seem, it was the quotidian reality of slave life. In order to maintain this system of chattel slavery such accouterments were deemed necessary. And because this master-slave dynamic was "necessary," it also seemed morally justifiable to slavery's practitioners and proponents.

The power differential inherent in slavery, however, gave rise not only to these "mundane" forms of racial oppression, but to even more grievous violations of black personhood, extraordinary abuses for which no coherent moral justification could be offered. Among these was the sexual abuse of slaves. W.E.B. DuBois once wrote:

> I shall forgive the white South much in its final judgment day: I shall forgive its slavery, for slavery is a world-old habit; I shall forgive its fighting for a well-lost cause, and for remembering that struggle with tender tears: I shall forgive its so-called "pride of race." ...But one thing I shall never forgive, neither in this world nor the world to come: its wanton and continued and persistent insulting of black womanhood which it sought and seeks to prostitute to its lust.[16]

As DuBois indicated, conflict and even oppression are part and parcel of human history, but certain offenses simply overwhelm our sensibilities, creating seemingly impassable relational barriers. With God's help reconciliation is, of course, possible—but only when and if we face the truth of what actually occurred and share a common affective response to that truth. That is why we cannot whitewash the master-slave relationship by failing to view it at its worst.

If absolute power corrupts absolutely, when that control involves members of the opposite sex, licentious behavior is a predictable, albeit horrific, result. Even so, given the professed religiosity of many masters, it is shocking to discover the degree to which the sexual abuse of slaves was not only commonplace but also broadly tolerated. The prima facie evidence that such large-scale immorality has, in fact, occurred is the fact that "fully 58 percent of African-American people, according to geneticist Mark Shriver at Morehouse College, possess at least 12.5 percent European ancestry (... the equivalent of one great-grandparent)."[17]

There is also considerable testimony from former slaves that such abuse was a regular feature of slave life. The sexual abuse of slaves took at least two forms—the sexual imposition of the master (or sometimes the mistress, household members, or acquaintances) and slave breeding. I shall explore them in that order.

Real anecdotes from former slaves, compiled in the 1930s before the last of the slave generation passed away, illustrate the despotic lust of the slaveowners toward their powerless victims.

My master often went to the house, got drunk, and then came out to the field to whip, cut, slash, curse, swear, beat and knock down several, for the smallest offense, or nothing at all. He divested a poor female slave of all wearing apparel, tied her down to stakes, and whipped her with a handsaw until he broke it over her naked body. In process of time he ravished her person and became the father of a child by her.

Besides, he always kept a colored Miss in the house with him. This is another curse of Slavery—concubinage and illegitimate connections—which is carried on to an alarming extent in the far South.... A white man thinks nothing of putting a colored man out to carry the fore row [front row in field work] and carry on the same sport with the colored man's wife at the same time.[18]

Former slave Sylvia Watkins of Tennessee reminisced somewhat matter-of-factly about master/slave "relationships":

In them times white men went with colored gals and women bold[ly]. Any time they saw one and wanted her, she had to go with him, and his wife didn't say nothin' 'bout it. Not only the men, but the women went with colored men too. That's why so many women slave owners wouldn't marry, 'cause they was goin' with one of their slaves.[19]

Harriet Jacobs, a young slave girl who eventually escaped and became an abolitionist, shared her experience:

...I now entered on my fifteenth year—a sad epoch in the life of a slave girl. My master began to whisper foul words in my ear.... He peopled my young mind with unclean images, such as only a vile monster could think of.... He told me I was his property, that I must be subject to his will in all things...[20]
My master was, to my knowledge, the father of eleven slaves. But did the mothers dare to tell who was the father of their children? Did the other slaves dare to allude to it, except in whispers among themselves? No, indeed! They knew too well the terrible consequences.[21]

Though these practices were seldom mentioned in public, they seem to have been a well-known "secret." In the mid-19th century, responding to abolitionist pressure, Southern clergymen like the Rev. Robert L. Dabney began to push for reform of the slave practice. When he insisted that the black woman must be "the mistress of her own chastity,"[22] there was no need to explain how that differed from the norm.

Terrible as it was, the predatory sexual imposition of masters with respect to their slaves was only part of the sexual abuse that occurred under slavery. One of the most debasing aspects of the entire enterprise was the practice of slave breeding. Some have tried to minimize the extent of slave breeding or deny its existence altogether,[c] but former slaves tell a consistent story. In addition, there are also historical records, such as a 1796 advertisement from Charleston, South Carolina, offering fifty slaves who had been "purchased for stock and breeding Negroes."[23]

After visiting a Georgia plantation, Englishwoman Francis Ann Kemble observed:

> ...Many indirect inducements [are] held out to reckless propagation, which has a sort of premium offered to it in the consideration of less work and more food counterbalanced by none of the sacred responsibilities which hallow and ennoble the relation of parent and child; in short, as their lives are for the most those of mere animals, their increase is literally mere animal breeding, to which every encouragement is given, for it adds to the master's live-stock and the value of his estate.[24]

Thomas Jefferson Randolph, grandson of Thomas Jefferson, wrote of the annual average of 8,500 slaves who had been sent to other southern states over the previous twenty years: "It is a practice, and an increasing practice in parts of Virginia, to rear slaves for market. How can an honorable mind... bear to see this ancient dominion converted into one grand *menageries* where men are to be reared for market like oxen for the shambles?"[25]

Thomas Jefferson himself not only made an unacknowledged concubine out of one of his teenage slaves (Sally Hemmings, who ultimately bore him six children,)[d] but also managed to see the hand of God at work in the slave-breeding enterprise. "'I consider the labor of a breeding woman as no object, and that a child raised every two years is of more profit than the best laboring man,' Jefferson advised his overseer. 'In this case, as in all other cases,

---

[c] Perhaps the most well-known example is historian Robert William Fogel, whose book, *Time on the Cross: The Economics of American Negro Slavery*, contains a chapter entitled "The Myth of Slave Breeding." Using economic and demographic data, he argues that slave breeding was not a viable enough financial investment to have worked. However, he largely ignores the direct evidence of the practice cited here and noted in many other histories.

[d] Not acknowledged by Jefferson at the time but now recognized by The Thomas Jefferson Foundation. See: www.monticello.org/site/plantation-and-slavery/sally-hemings.

Providence has made our duties and our interests coincide perfectly.'"[26] How convenient.

It seems that few slaveholders dedicated their entire operation to slave breeding, but once the profitability of slave-dependent agriculture began to decline in the northernmost slave states, a strong economic incentive arose to supply slaves for areas in which they were still in high demand. This led to a variety of slave-breeding, or at least slave-raising/rearing, enterprises. Not content to allow procreation to simply occur as the natural result of family life, these owners pro-actively and selectively facilitated the reproductive process, in order to produce more numerous and desirable offspring.

For the masters this was simply a "business model," but the testimony of a former slave speaks to the trauma experienced by the young women who were reduced to baby factories.

> Dere am one thing Massa Hawkins does to me what I can't shunt from my mind... After I been at he place 'bout a year [at age sixteen], de massa come to me and say, "You gwine live with Rufus in dat cabin over yonder. ...I's thought dat him mean for me to tend de cabin for Rufus and some other niggers...

> We'uns has supper, den I goes here and dere talkin', till I's ready for sleep and den I gits in de bunk. After I's in, dat nigger come and crawl in de bunk with me 'fore I knows it. I says, "What you means, you fool nigger! You's teched in de head... I puts de feet 'gainst him and give him a shove and out he go on de floor 'fore he know what I's doin'.

> Dat nigger jump up and he mad... He starts for de bunk and I jumps quick for de poker. It am 'bout three foot long and when he comes at me I lets him have it over de head. Did dat nigger stop in he tracks!...

> De nex' day de massa call me and tell me, "Woman, I's pay big money for you and I's done dat for de cause I wants yous to raise me chillens. I's put yous to live with Rufus for dat purpose. Now, if you doesn't want whippin' at de stake, yous do what I wants."

> I thinks 'bout massa buyin' me offen de [auction] block and savin' me from bein' sep'rated from my folks and 'bout bein' whipped at de stake. Dere it am. What am I's to do? So I 'cides to do as de massa wish and so I yields....

> I never marries, 'cause one 'sperience am 'nough for dis nigger. After what I does for de massa, I's never wants no truck with any man. De Lawd forgive dis cullud woman, but he have to 'scuse me and look for some others for to 'plenish de earth.[27]

Behind this colorful storytelling lies a deeply disturbing reality. In their pursuit of profit a despotic white ruling class cavalierly ignored not only the normal human sensibilities of the young slave women in their care—they ignored their own professed moral standards as well. Take the case of Mr. Covey, the former owner of Frederick Douglass.

> In the beginning he was only able—as he said—"to buy one slave;" and scandalous and shocking as is the fact, he boasted that he bought her simply "as a breeder." This young woman (Caroline was her name) was virtually compelled by Covey [who locked her up every night with the same man] to abandon herself to the object for which he had purchased her; and the result was the birth of twins at the end of the year.

> ...No better illustration of the unchaste, demoralizing, and debasing character of slavery can be found, than is furnished in the fact that this professedly Christian slaveholder... was shamelessly and boastfully encouraging and actually compelling, in his own house, undisguised and unmitigated fornication, as a means of increasing his stock.[28]

The master-slave relationship, an indispensable part of slavery itself, damaged not only the slaves but the owners as well. Their absolute control over other human beings brought out the very worst in them. This was nothing less than gentrified villainy—the powerful using the powerless to satisfy their own wanton desires, whether economic or carnal. And, make no mistake, the master-slave relationship is still being felt, because it was more than just an offense; it was an affront, an atrocity, an abomination—the kind of wound, that even when it heals, still leaves an ugly scar.

Chapter 7

Justifications for Slavery

American slavery, as just described, was so appalling that it might seem indefensible. Nevertheless, slavery had its defenders, and their justifications helped sustain the institution for centuries. Some of those arguments have since been abandoned. Some are now used to rehabilitate the moral standing of earlier generations. Some still resonate with a certain audience today.

What relevance do these justifications have for the historical survey in which we are presently engaged? I'm trying to demonstrate that racial haughtiness has been an immoral constant in white identity, one that has changed its manifestations but not its essence. If, however, the justifications offered for slavery have some actual validity, or if they were, in fact, the true and legitimate motivation for American whites' involvement in slavery, then a very different set of conclusions might logically follow.

For instance, if slavery is defensible, then past generations of white Americans were, perhaps, not the perpetrators of immoral haughtiness but simply righteous people living in a less enlightened era. And if slavery is shown to be defensible, our forebears have not so much bequeathed to us a legacy of haughtiness but, rather, a legacy of social evolution in which racial issues should work themselves out without the need for a moral accounting.

These historic justifications matter a great deal to racial reconciliation, because truth matters to reconciliation. Was slavery an immoral atrocity indicative of the worst of whiteness, or was it more like a pothole along the road to justice for all? Until and unless black people and white people share a common vision of this practice that defined race relations in America, there aren't enough verses of Kumbaya to ever bring the two races together.

Biblical justifications for slavery

For those of us who take biblical authority seriously, the justifications for slavery that are grounded in Scripture itself are potentially the weightiest. Let's be honest. Looking at this issue from a 21st century vantage point, it would be handy if the Bible simply offered a blanket denunciation of the principle of slavery and a blanket prohibition of its practice. That is not the case, however. Slavery is more or less accepted as a fact of life throughout the biblical text, and its practice is regulated rather than forbidden.

Dr. Richard Fuller famously stated in 1845, "What God sanctioned in the Old Testament, and permitted in the New, cannot be sin."[1] For many Bible believers, such a pronouncement had (and perhaps still has) an incontrovertible ring of authenticity. It sounds simple, straightforward. The reality, however, is considerably more complex.

Even in Israel, law and morality were not synonymous. That is, there were moral ideals for which the corresponding legal statutes accommodated themselves to the reality on the ground. Ideally, divorce would not have existed among God's people, but marriages nevertheless did break up, and so there were provisions for divorce, regulating the practice and protecting those involved. God's ideal was that there should be no poverty in Israel (Dt. 15:4), but there were provisions in the law to care for the poor. Scripture's attitude toward slavery represents yet another case in which God chose to regulate the existing reality rather than to impose the moral ideal.

But what was that moral ideal? Throughout both testaments we find a God who aspires to freedom. That conception of freedom differed from its modern-day, humanistic counterpart, however. The basis for freedom in the covenant community was soteriological. Yahweh redeemed his people out of slavery in Egypt, not to secure their personal or political autonomy but in order that they might become *his* servants. It was, therefore, inappropriate for God's people to be enslaved to anyone else, as Lev. 25:39 makes clear: "Because the Israelites are my servants, whom I brought out of Egypt, they must not be sold as slaves."

There were, nevertheless, certain social circumstances under which one could temporarily lose the exercise of that essential freedom. The slavery that existed among the Israelites was actually more like indentured servitude and functioned as a sort of social safety net—a less than ideal arrangement designed to deal with less than ideal circumstances. Debtors could sell themselves or their family members into slavery due to economic hardship (Dt. 15:12, Ex. 21:7-10, 2 Ki. 4:1). Likewise, destitute thieves might become slaves, in order to make restitution for their crimes (Ex. 22:2-3).

The Torah did, however, set some significant parameters for this institution. Hebrew bondsmen were not to be treated like slaves but rather like hired workers (Lev. 25:39-40). Masters had the right to use corporal punishment to enforce their servants' compliance, but anyone who killed a slave would be punished, and maiming a slave (even knocking out a tooth) resulted in the slave's freedom (Ex. 21:20-21, 26-27). In no case could an Israelite be forced to serve more than six years (Ex. 21:2-4).[a] Sabbath rest applied to all slaves (Ex. 23:12). And, at the end of their period of service, slaves were to be sent away with significant startup capital, so that they could re-enter society as a functioning member of the community (Dt. 15:12-15).

This same ideal of soteriological freedom is present in the New Testament as well. "But now having been set free from sin, and having become slaves of God..." (Rom. 6:22) The Apostle Paul expanded on the implications of that status in 1Cor. 7:21-23, advising those who were freepersons in civil society: "You were bought at a price; do not become slaves of human beings." To those in bondage he said, "If you can gain your freedom, do so." It seems clear, then, that freedom, not bondage, is the status that best conforms to Christian spiritual reality.

The Apostle Paul did not directly challenge the social institution of slavery, but he did expand on the humanitarian ethos already present in the intra-Israelite context. Masters were to treat their slaves with Christian consideration (Eph. 6:8). This involved not threatening them (and presumably not brutalizing them, either) or even exerting their authority as if it were absolute, since all were servants/slaves of Christ (Eph. 6:9). In addition, masters were to treat their slaves justly (Col. 4:1), providing for them adequately and being devoted to their welfare (1 Tim. 6:2). In fact, Paul instructed them to treat their slaves as they themselves would want to be treated (Eph. 6:9).

It might be true that "what God sanctioned in the Old Testament, and permitted in the New, cannot be sin." But the implication behind this appeal to the biblical model is that what God sanctioned/permitted in Scripture was the *same thing* that existed in America. Indeed, that premise is essential to the entire justification—but that premise is entirely false. Even if we were to grant the legitimacy of some form of slavery under *certain* conditions, those were definitely not the conditions under which American slavery operated.

Speaking of conditions, there is a very important point to be made here about historical conditions and the progressive illumination of God's will. In biblical times we see God permitting and regulating a less-than-ideal social practice in a historical context in which it was already ubiquitous. Such was

---

[a] Two circumstances could reduce this term to less than six years: (1) if the debt were paid off or (2) if the jubilee year fell during the six years of servitude.

the case regarding slavery in both the Ancient Near East as well as in the Roman Empire. By the dawn of the colonial period, however, the progressive influence of the Christian ethos had practically eliminated slavery altogether in Christianized societies. So, once the ideal had been approached, what possible motivation would Christians have to revert to an inferior model?

There are two readily identifiable motivations for this reversion, neither of which is biblically justifiable. One is greed, and the other is haughtiness. Europeans generally believed that it was improper to enslave their own countrymen or (European) Christian believers in general. But once they had access to a source of bound labor that they also considered to be inferior, they breached this moral barrier with the greatest of ease. Any social system designed to satisfy such sinful motivations can hardly claim moral justification.

Even if there had been some legitimate rationale for reverting to an inferior social model, the slave society our forefathers created was morally inferior to that earlier model in almost every way. It provided no positive social benefit to the enslaved. It lacked similar humanitarian protections. It placed no limitations on the length of servitude. It held no promise of freedom. It showed little regard/respect for the enslaved persons. And it did not recognize the equality of those who were fellow believers.

Slavery, therefore, cannot be defended by appealing to the biblical ideal. Nor can it be justified by any realistic comparison to the relatively benign versions of slavery that existed among members of the Early Church or in Israel's covenant community. Anyone looking for a "biblical" precedent for American slavery must look to its practice between Israel and foreign nations.

On the surface, this approach might seem promising. According to Jewish law, Israelites were allowed to purchase foreign slaves or capture them in war, holding them in perpetual bondage without all of the safeguards afforded to fellow Israelites.[b] The pertinent text in this regard is Lev. 25:44: "Your male and female slaves are to come from the nations around you; from them you may buy slaves."

Note, however, that though there were special provisions for foreign slavery, Israelites did not have *carte blanche* to go around reducing any and all foreigners to slavery. As Roland DeVeaux observes: "Besides the free citizens of Israel who formed 'the people of the land,' and traveling foreigners

---

[b] Hebrew masters held broad rights over such slaves, but unlike their American counterparts, those slaves were guaranteed Sabbath rest and protected against extreme cruelty.

who could count on the customs of hospitality but were not protected by law (Dt. 15:3, 23:20), part of the population consisted of resident foreigners, the *gerim*."[2] The legal status of resident foreigners was roughly equal to that of Hebrew Israelites, as established in Leviticus 19:34: "The foreigner residing among you must be treated as your native-born. Love them as yourself..." Ex. 12:49 is even more specific: "The same law applies both to the native-born and to the foreigner residing among you."[c]

It appears, then, that foreigners who were *permanent* residents could be enslaved only under the same conditions as other Israelites. And even though temporary residents could sell themselves into permanent slavery (Lev. 25:44b), they could not be taken forcibly. Unless and until they sold themselves (most likely because of indigence) they remained free, protected by the laws against kidnapping (Ex. 21:16) and Ancient Near Eastern customs concerning sojourners.

So, then, just who were these "foreigners" who could be enslaved under relatively less humane conditions? The vast majority of such slaves were acquired as the spoils of war. Victorious soldiers might take slaves home with them—mostly women and children, as the men were often killed to prevent future uprisings (Numbers 31:15-18, Dt. 21:10 ff., Judges 5:30). If the town they went to fight against surrendered rather than resisting, however, its people (men and women) were to become slaves of Israel (Dt. 20). These slaves were far more likely to end up serving the king of Israel than individual Israelites. He might subject them to forced labor in large public works projects (2 Sam. 12:31, 1 Kings 9:15 ff.) or simply convert that country to a tribute-paying vassal (2 Sam. 8:2) without actually enslaving individuals.

In theory, there were other nations in the surrounding area with whom the Hebrews were not at war and from whom they could purchase slaves. But Israelite families rarely had more than a few slaves, and these were usually assigned domestic duties. For such purposes the supply of slaves from war may have been largely sufficient and more economical than purchasing them.

This narrow slice of Israel's slave enterprise is the only class of slavery that even resembles the American variety. But even this narrowly-defined precedent is problematic, because America is not the chosen nation. Today's "people of God" are not co-terminus with any political or ethnic identity.

---

[c] Though this verse refers specifically to the Passover, to which circumcised foreigners were invited, it seems to rest on a broader principle (Lev. 19:34).

It is, therefore, impossible to divide the world into Christian nations (who have the supposed right, either individually or collectively, to play the part of ancient Israel) and heathen nations (cast in the role of foreigners). Politically speaking, anyone who is not a citizen of your country is a foreigner, whether they are Christian or not. And, spiritually speaking, a "foreigner" would be any and everyone who is not a true Christian believer, whether they live in your country or not. Of course, pro-slavery interpreters did not use this Old Testament precedent to justify the enslavement of *white* "foreigners," either because they were citizens of other countries or because they were unconverted members of their own society.

The means by which African slaves were acquired creates yet another contradiction with the biblical model. Though the Israelites had the right to slave plunder from nations that posed a military threat to them, they did not have the right to wage war solely for the purpose of acquiring slaves.[d] But this is exactly what the early enslavers did, targeting black Africans, who posed absolutely no threat to them and were, therefore, not legitimate targets of war.

It's true that once their Africans victims started to resist, white slavers changed their tactics and began buying slaves from other Africans. It would be disingenuous to suggest, however, that this new strategy somehow ceased to be a warlike acquisition. Though intra-African slavery did exist, it was the demand created by the trans-Atlantic slave trade itself that incentivized Africans slave raiders (armed with European weaponry) to exponentially expand the scope of their enterprise. White slavers got others to act as their armed proxies—but they could not delegate their moral responsibility.[e]

Biblical rationalizations notwithstanding, not only the practice but the very institution of American slavery was simply sinful. It reversed the progress of the European Christian tradition. It was uniquely barbarous. In contrast to its biblical counterpart, the American institution was thoroughly racialized; it relied on kidnapping and brutal oppression; it ran roughshod over the basic humanity and morality of its victims. It twisted Scripture in its own

---

[d] Not all foreigners were legitimate enemies. God told the Israelites that they were not to conquer certain nations in the region (Dt. 2). In addition, David and Solomon made numerous treaties with other nations (1 Ki. 5, 9, 10).
[e] Such methods left slave owners/traders open to charges of being "man-stealers," those who reduce free persons to bondage against their will. The term appears in 1 Tim. 1:10 (KJV), a concept taken from Exodus 21:16, which talks about "stealing" a man (KJV)—a capital offense whether or not the kidnapped person was subsequently sold.

defense. And, as if that were not enough, American slavery was motivated by greed and fueled by haughtiness, for which there can be no justification.

The Curse of Ham

There is yet another biblical defense of slavery that both predates slavery in America and has also managed to outlive it. This justification does not rely on specious precedents. It does not aspire to the merely permissible. It attempts to vindicate American slavery based on God's revealed design for the black race. I'm talking about the Curse of Ham.[f]

Its source is Genesis 9:20-27, which recounts how Noah's son, Ham, finds his drunken father lying naked in his tent. Ham proceeds to tell his brothers, who walk backward into the tent and cover up their father without observing his nakedness. When Noah awakens and discovers what has happened, he delivers a curse to Ham and pronounces a blessing on the other two brothers.

The outlines of the Curse of Ham interpretation of this passage, are as follows: 1) Ham sinned and received a curse of slavery from his father, Noah. 2) Ham was the progenitor of black African peoples. 3) Therefore, blacks were doomed to bondage by virtue of this curse, so that their enslavement was nothing more than the fulfillment of their divinely appointed destiny.

The Curse of Ham was by no means a novel interpretation cooked up by American Christian slaveholders. Though they certainly co-opted it, the origins of the curse theory go much further back and much further afield. Historian David Goldenberg characterizes this interpretation as "the single greatest justification for Black slavery for more than a thousand years."[3]

Moreover, its influence was not limited to the American South. John H. Hopkins, the first Episcopal Bishop of the Diocese of Vermont, wrote in 1864:

> The Almighty, foreseeing this total degradation of the [black] race, ordained them to servitude or slavery under the descendants of Shem or Japheth, doubtless because *he judged it to be their fittest condition* [italics his]. And all history proves how accurately the prediction has been accomplished, even to the present day.[4]

Pope Pius IX also indicated his adherence to this interpretation as late as 1873 in the following prayer: "Let us pray for the most wretched Ethiopians

---

[f] For a more in-depth consideration of this topic, see "The Curse of Ham" at https://www.scottgarber.com/was_notes.html.

in Central Africa, that Almighty God may at length move the curse of Cham [Ham] from their hearts…"[5]

Even the demise of American slavery did not put an end to this interpretation, which continued to be used as a rationale for white dominance writ large. C. I. Scofield's study Bible,[g] which eventually sold more than two million copies, played an important role in keeping the Hamitic myth afloat. In Scofield's first edition notes on Genesis 9:24 -25, he affirmed: "a prophetic declaration is made that from Ham will descend an inferior and servile posterity."[6] He went on to say in his comments on v. 27: "A prophetic declaration is made that from Japheth will descend the 'enlarged' races. Government, science, and art, speaking broadly, are and have been Japhetic [Caucasian], so that history is the indisputable record of the exact fulfillment of these declarations."[7/h]

Anecdotal evidence suggests that this interpretation continues to exercise some influence, even to this day. While writing this book, I came across two well-educated and sincere Christians, one white and one black, who had been taught and still believed (at least until they were exposed to this critique) that the Curse of Ham interpretation was the proper understanding of Genesis 9.

The great irony of this enduring myth is that it is patently and demonstrably false. As per the Curse of Ham interpretation, Genesis 9 does identify Ham as the guilty party and Noah as the one who spoke the curse to him. But the text also makes it clear that the target of that malediction was not Ham but his son, Canaan. Genesis 9:25 clearly says: "Cursed be Canaan! The lowest of slaves will he be to his brothers." Canaan's descendants, the Canaanites, settled along the Mediterranean in the area of Palestine and *were not black*. They were eventually conquered by the incoming nation of Israel, and many of the survivors did, in fact, become slaves (Joshua 9:23, Judges 1:27-35)—a fact that seems to explain the prophetic relevance of the passage.

How, then, has this interpretation managed to last so long and to be so influential? Goldenberg notes four factors that have helped perpetuate the myth: "[1] *explanation*—an attempt to make sense of the Bible; [2] *error*—a

---

[g] In the church of my youth this Bible was so popular that when congregants were directed to a passage of Scripture, the reference was often accompanied by the page number in the Scofield Reference Bible.

[h] The note on Gen. 9:24-25 and its Hamitic identification remained unchanged until the release of the *New Scofield Reference Bible* in 1967. It rightly asserts that the "descendants of Canaan, one of Ham's sons, will be servants to their brothers (Gn. 9:25-26)." Even so, the ethnocentric 9:27 note remains.

mistaken recollection of the biblical text; [3] *environment*—a social structure in which the Black had become identified as a slave; and [4] *etymology*—a mistaken assumption that Ham meant "black, dark.'"[8]

This curious story does, indeed, beg for an *explanation*, though the biblical text does not offer one. Why was the curse pronounced on Canaan, who (as far as we know) had nothing to do with the incident, when Ham was the guilty party? Once this curse was associated in the popular imagination with Ham, however, the *error* of referring to it as the "Curse of Ham" was more easily committed, cementing the erroneous identification. *Environment* certainly had a lot to do with the popularity of the Hamitic myth. There is a long history of black enslavement, and the mind naturally looks for a rationale to explain why things are as they are. *Etymology*, however, also played an important role in popularizing this explanation. Convinced that the name "Ham" referred to blackness, white interpreters found it plausible that he, rather than his son, was actually the intended recipient of this curse.

The identification of *Ham* with ancient root words signifying *black, dark*, and/or *hot* gained currency in England as early as 1660.[9] This notion was further popularized by Augustin Calmet, a French Benedictine, in his 1722 Bible Dictionary, which was later translated into English.[10] Bishop Thomas Newton, a British scholar who relied heavily on Calmet's work, became quite influential in America and popularized this theory in the latter half of the eighteenth century.[i] "Eventually, 'almost every Southern writer on the Ham myth' used the philological argument that *Ham* meant 'black,' 'dark,' and 'hot.'"[11]

The true etymology of *Ham* remains a mystery,[12] but modern linguistic research clearly demonstrates that these theories were based on faulty assumptions about which root words could conceivably have a phonetic association with the name. So, while we can't say exactly where the name came from, there is no evidence relating *Ham* to blackness.

---

[i] Newton's story is a fascinating one. He (incorrectly and possibly deceitfully) used Calmet as the justification for a textual emendation, changing Gen. 9:25 to refer not to "Canaan" but to "Ham the father of Canaan." Episcopal Bishop John Hopkins (quoted above) then cited Newton extensively in his defense of the morality of slavery. See: David M. Whitford, *The Curse of Ham in the Early Modern Era: The Bible and the Justifications for Slavery*, (Farnham, England; Burlington, VT; Ashgate Publishing Ltd., 2009), 142 ff. Also, Stephen R. Haynes, *Noah's Curse: The Biblical Justification of American Slavery* (Oxford, New York; Oxford University Press, 2002), 39.

The bottom line is that this Curse of Ham interpretation has no real support in either exegesis, linguistics, or history. It is, in fact, a baseless myth used to legitimize black slavery. How, then, can we explain its enduring influence? Certainly, the need for an exegetical explanation, the repetition of an erroneous identification, the existence of a slave environment, and the acceptance of a mistaken etymology all helped to facilitate and perpetuate this myth. But it seems that nothing short of haughtiness could have ever made it truly convincing to the pious devotees of Scripture who swallowed it hook, line, and sinker.

The Missiological Justification for Slavery

The Curse of Ham was not the only rationale used by advocates of slavery. For five hundred years, from the 15th century Portuguese to the 19th century Americans, pro-slavery Christians touted the evangelistic potential of slavery as a justification for the practice. As a Rhode Island church elder exclaimed upon seeing a slave ship coming into port, "An overruling Providence has been pleased to bring to this land of freedom another cargo of benighted heathens to enjoy the blessings of a Gospel dispensation."[13][j]

While slavery's proponents touted the evangelistic virtues of the slave system, they nevertheless feared its consequences. The specter of insurrection generated a very real conflict of interest between the need for religious education and the danger posed by a literate slave population. Insurrection, however, was not the only threat. Slave owners sensed that Christianity's egalitarian ethos could eventually undermine their entire institution. As a result, even when the owners did expose their bondsmen to the Christian message, the slaves' role in the community of faith remained entirely subservient. Most masters, however, found it more expedient to avoid the issue entirely by simply refusing to evangelize their slaves.

---

[j] In addition to the strictly missiological argument, some have insisted that purchasing African slaves was actually a humanitarian gesture, since victorious African tribes kept only women and children as slaves, killing off the men. There does seem to be some historical evidence of this practice, but the justification remains problematic. It applies only to men, and only to those who would have been enslaved anyway, not to those hunted down to fulfill white demand. That latter group was never in danger of being killed off, as they were far too valuable in trade with the Europeans. This "humanitarian rescue" might seem more authentic and less self-serving if those purchased had been transported under humane conditions to eventual freedom.

In its 1730 report, England's Society for the Propagation of the Gospel referenced this situation, calling it "a great Reproach to the Christian Name, that so many Thousands of Persons should continue in the same State of Pagan Darkness, under a Christian Government, and living in Christian Families, as they lay before..."[14] The Society blamed the "Masters themselves... some [of whom] have been so weak as to argue, the Negroes had no Souls; others that they grew worse by being taught, and made Christians."[15]

It's not surprising, then, that the number of African converts was quite low. As late as the 1790 census only 4% of the slaves in Virginia were church members.[16] Though meaningful statistics are difficult to come by,[k] Albert J. Raboteau's conclusion that "the majority of slaves... remained only minimally touched by Christianity by the second decade of the nineteenth century"[17] seems reasonable.

Many of the slave conversions that did occur came as the result of the evangelistic preaching of the First and Second Great Awakenings rather than the efforts of established church bodies. These revivalist meetings not only reached people that the institutional church was never going to reach; they also fueled the growth of denominations like the Baptists and the Methodists, whose informal worship style was more amenable to the slaves' sensibilities.

It is, of course, true that the vast majority of African Americans eventually came to identify with the Christian faith. And all believers certainly welcome this ultimate outcome. But that end does not justify the means. Sinful behavior motivated by selfish attitudes cannot be rehabilitated by a happy ending.

The truth of the matter is that the entire religious justification for slavery was a canard. The motivation behind American slavery was not a missionary concern for the peoples of Africa. This appeal to Scripture and evangelism, however sincerely espoused in its time, was simply an a posteriori attempt to legitimize a sinful status quo.

Eschewing the ideals of both the Old and New Testaments, pro-slavery Christians appropriated the biblical examples that best advanced their selfish and supremacist agenda. They augmented their theological misidentifications with an ill-founded curse and then triumphantly cast themselves as the

---

[k] There is no statistical basis for the popular notion that the slave population was overwhelmingly Christian. Wood traces various sources that range from 4% church membership in 1790, to 6.5% in 1830, to 8% in 1840, to 12% in 1860. (Forrest G. Wood, *The Arrogance of Faith*, 139-141.) There were, of course, many slaves who attended church who were not members, and in some cases significant religious life took place on the plantations.

missionary heroes of the entire malevolent enterprise. But, alas, they were neither missionaries nor heroes.

Children of Their Time?

If slavery's proponents and its beneficiaries were neither missionaries nor heroes, then what were they exactly? I have insisted that neither their attitudes toward black people nor the institutional bondage they perpetuated were morally justifiable, and I imagine that many readers concur in this assessment. Nevertheless, there seems to be a sense that, even if the moral choices of yesteryear cannot be justified, the people who made those choices were, in some curious way, still justified in making them. Because, it is supposed, they were just children of their time.

Of course, we are all unavoidably children of our time. Every generation is subject to its own historical limitations. Nevertheless, every generation, including our own, makes moral choices for which they are genuinely responsible. I believe that once we consider the gamut of influences under which slave-era Christians operated, it will become clear that they should have known better and could have done otherwise.

To be fair, many of the social influences felt by early slave owners tended to justify slavery rather than question it. Like other colonies located in this hemisphere, America was expected to produce goods and profits for the European metropolis, using slave labor. And popular opinion considered servitude to be entirely appropriate, or at least perfectly normal.

In addition to the social mores of the time, American settlers were also influenced by an ambivalent Western legacy of moral reasoning concerning slavery. A Spanish legal code from the thirteenth century, known as *Las Siete Partidas (The Seven-Part Code)*, laid the groundwork, calling slavery "contrary to human reason"[18] and "the vilest thing in this world except sin,"[19] but nevertheless recognizing "birth, self-alienation, and especially war as valid grounds for enslavement."[20] Catholic theologians agreed that only a "just" war could justify the enslavement of the vanquished. But since "the Church did not, usually, confront governments head-on over the issue,"[21] what could have been an important qualification turned into a giant moral loophole.

There was, of course, plenty of opposition to slavery from Northern abolitionists, particularly toward the end of the slave period. But a couple of factors mitigated their influence in the areas where slavery was practiced. Southern religious leaders denounced the abolitionists as infidels or liberals who were unfaithful to Scripture. In addition, the abolitionists' message was often lost or overshadowed by the politicized context in which it was communicated, so that it came across as self-righteous and self-serving.

In spite of cultural influences that reinforced or ineffectually challenged the morality of slavery, there were other voices that Christian proponents and practitioners of slavery might have heeded. There were minority religious groups—mostly Quakers, Anabaptists, and early Methodists—who opposed slavery (or at least slaveholding) for sound theological reasons.

Then there was the Bible itself. Though Scripture offered no outright prohibition of slavery, America's version clearly operated in gross violation of biblical norms. Moreover, the individual conscience, when enlightened by the Holy Spirit, should not be discounted. Certain aspects of slavery so assaulted basic Christian sensibilities, that red flags should have been flying.

There were also social influences that could have opened American eyes, like those of England and France, America's cultural mentors. English sensibilities rejected the idea of slavery at home, considering itself "too pure an Air for Slaves to breathe in." (Cartwright Decision, 1569).[1] The implicit biblical aversion to enslaving God's people was the basis of the "English common-law principle, which dated at least from the Protestant Reformation, that one cannot enslave a Christian."[22] Throughout the centuries of American slavery, the French proudly proclaimed that "there are no slaves in France."[23/m]

While both of these countries engaged in the convenient inconsistency of permitting and even promoting slavery in their colonies, by the nineteenth century, the tide was turning in English and French public opinion about the propriety of slavery even in the colonies. The British abolished slavery in most of their Empire in 1833, and France followed suit in 1848.[n] America did not, however, follow their lead, as slavery reform got bogged down in factionalism and the realities of domestic economics and politics.

---

[1] Spain and Portugal did import a relatively small number of slaves, but England, France, and the Netherlands shared a common commitment to the "Freedom Principle," the notion that any slave setting foot on their sovereign soil would thereby be free.

[m] Due to some inconsistencies in the laws this was not absolutely true, but the French commitment to the "Freedom Principle," insured that "Every slave who sued for freedom within the Admiralty Court of France ... won the case." Sue Peabody, *There Are No Slaves in France: The Political Culture of Race and Slavery in the Ancien Régime* (New York: Oxford Univ. Press, 2002), 3.

[n] Technically, France was the first to abolish slavery (1794). But two years later Napoleon reinstated it, so that the final abolition did not occur until 1848.

So, yes, Americans of the slave era were children of their time. But not all the children of that time created slave societies on their own shores. Though America was a colony and therefore fell within the colonial exclusion permitting slavery, the colonists themselves certainly had some input on the kind of society they wanted. America was unlike some of the other European holdings in this hemisphere, which were largely populated by uneducated natives and occupied by a small European contingent. This was a colony comprised of European immigrants and boasted of one of the highest literacy rates in the world, arguably higher than that of either England or France.°

Ignorance is, therefore, no excuse; and that goes double for religious ignorance. James Fisch, Pastor of the French Evangelical Church in Paris, visited the United States in 1863. Observing the disconnect between our religious zeal and our sense of racial justice, Rev. Fisch wondered: "How it is possible that a country so imbued with Christianity could have maintained slavery; and how it is that a third of its population defends it all hazards?"[24]

Our forebears can hardly be excused for being children of their time, when they were decidedly *behind* their time. In any case, quite apart from whatever our times are telling us, we Christians can never allow ourselves to be reduced to the mere sum of our environmental influences. For though we are necessarily children of our time, we are also quite especially children of God. As such, we are both called and empowered to pursue an incrementally illuminated vision of God's righteous ideal—not to bend the revealed will of God in order to justify a haughty and self-serving agenda.

° Measuring literacy is a bit tricky (usually those able to sign their wills), and the exclusion of Indian and slave populations constitutes an important asterisk. Even including those populations, however, the American literacy rate was quite high compared to others of the colonial period. For more information see Harvey J. Graff, *Literacy and Social Development in the West: A Reader,* Cambridge, Cambridge University Press, 1981, pp. 183-200.

Chapter 8

The Ecclesiastical Response to Slavery

In previous chapters we observed how haughtiness, pimped by greed, gave rise to centuries of racial dominance and oppression. It's particularly sad to note that many of the people who perpetrated and/or defended this evil enterprise were professing Christians. One would hope, however, that where individuals went astray, their church bodies and church leaders might have the prophetic perspicacity to see through this fog of self-interest and superiority.

Unfortunately, that was not the case. In the South, the Church offered little ecclesiastical opposition to the institution of slavery, allowing the unacceptable to become accepted. Northern religious sentiments more often ran contrary to slavery, but their response was often inconsistent and mostly ineffectual. Moreover, even those denominations that did denounce the evils of slavery were blind to the evil of racial haughtiness in their own hearts.

The Denominational Response to Slavery

In general, the historic denominations' responses to slavery represented a giant capitulation to interests other than those of love and justice. There were a couple of notable exceptions, namely the Mennonites and the Quakers. Their opposition to slavery had a common beginning in the 1688 Germantown Protest. This denunciation of other local Quakers who had become slaveholders was the first recorded stand against slavery in the Americas.[1]

Mennonite opposition to slavery was by far the staunchest of any denomination. All the way "through the 1860s Virginia Mennonites barred slaveholders from membership."[2] But in spite of their positive example, the Mennonites did little to alter broader societal mores, due to their miniscule numbers[a] and separatist mindset.

The far more numerous Quakers (the 5th largest church body in 1776)[3] had a more inconsistent record on slavery but a much greater impact on the cause of abolition. Ironically, "the Quakers were among the most prominent

---

[a] Of the 3,228 congregations in the American colonies in 1776, only 16 were Mennonite. (See the following endnote for citation.).

slave traders during the early days of the country,"[4] and the abolitionist cause took quite some time to develop in their midst. George Fox, one of the fathers of the Quaker movement, sought to reform slavery, advocating for eventual freedom for slaves who had served well but not condemning the practice of slavery per se.[5]

The Germantown Protest, though historic as a first, turned out to be something of a nonstarter. A few months after its signing, the Quaker meeting deemed the slavery issue "so weighty that we think it not expedient for us to meddle with it here."[6] Even the 1688 document itself was subsequently lost, until it was rediscovered and published in 1844.

In the mid-18th century, Quakers began to shift seriously toward the (mostly gradualist) abolitionist position. This change coincided with the passing of influential Quakers who had been part of the colonial establishment, but it was also spurred by a new generation of reformers, the most notable of whom was Anthony Benezet. He founded the first school for black children in Philadelphia, wrote prolifically on the subject, and had a profound personal impact on John Wesley, the father of Methodism. He also founded the first abolition society in America and was influential in the 1780 passage of Pennsylvania's Emancipation Act, the first in North America.

The broader Quaker movement continued to lean toward abolitionism, prohibiting slave trading in their midst in 1758 and slaveholding as well by 1776. They helped turn Pennsylvania into a haven for runaway slaves. In 1790 the Quakers even petitioned Congress to abolish slavery, but, despite widespread sentiment in favor of the measure, the House refused to act.

With the fortunes of slave agriculture withering in the northernmost slave states and those of the Deep South not yet fully developed, this would have been the moment to act. Three years later the cotton gin appeared on the scene, causing production to explode from 3,000 bales in 1790 to 178,000 bales in 1810 to 3.8 million in 1860.[7] This development made cotton king, slaves highly valuable, and morality far too expensive.

For all the relative enlightenment of the Quakers, their contribution should be kept in perspective. Though they represented 10% of all church members in 1776, at that time only 12% of the American public claimed church membership, so the Quakers' social and political influence was still quite limited.[8] Note, too, that their unified opposition to slavery came rather late in the game, and they made little effort to convert slaves to the Christian faith. All in all, they seemed far more concerned with their own standing before God vis-à-vis the issue of slavery than with the impact of slavery on the oppressed. And this was the legacy of America's *most progressive* major religious body on the matter of slavery.

Congregationalists were more numerous, but their influence was largely restricted to the Northeast. Regardless, they embraced a wide variety of opinions concerning slavery, which Frederick Douglass once characterized (and perhaps oversimplified) as follows: "The most ardent friends of the slaveholders are in the highest grade of church office, while those in an inferior station, are invariably on the side of humanity and Christianity..." [9] Puritans, the forerunners of the Congregationalists, had certainly supported slavery when it was economically viable for them, and they continued to reap huge profits from the slave trade long after they had ceased to own slaves.

Historically, the Anglican Church was the most dominant tradition in the South, particularly among the slave-owning elite, and they had neither the will nor the means to impose discipline with regard to participation in slavery. The Church's official non-emancipation policy and general attitude of following Caesar's lead on socio-political matters made it a haven for planters (and, conversely, an unattractive destination for slaves). When Northern abolition rhetoric heated up in the nineteenth century, many of those who propounded a biblical defense of slavery were Anglican clergymen.

Perhaps the most interesting case is that of the Methodist Episcopal Church, which took a strong initial stand against slavery, a position that withered rather swiftly in the face of a populist pro-slavery backlash. John Wesley, the founder of Methodism, was vehemently opposed to slavery. Following his lead, American Methodist leaders affirmed at their 1780 meeting: "Does this conference acknowledge that slavery is contrary to the laws of God, man, and nature, and hurtful to society; contrary to the dictates of conscience and pure religion, and doing that which we would not that others should do to us or ours? ...Yes." [10] Four years later, in the conference that marked the official beginning of the Methodist Church, they reiterated that it was contrary to their most precious principles "to hold in deepest abasement... so many souls that are all capable of the image of God." [11] And they committed themselves to find "some effectual method to extirpate this abomination from among us," [12] requiring all slaveholding Methodists to free their slaves within a year and prohibiting slaveholders from becoming members after that time.

Despite the tough and oft-repeated anti-slavery rhetoric of the Methodists in those early years, it seems that the prescribed sanctions were never consistently applied. In fact, only six months after the 1784 statement a large portion of the practical prescriptions were suspended "till the deliberations of a future conference."[13] Their bold stance had run headlong into the recalcitrance of slaveholding members, ambivalence from many others in both the North and South, and even legal difficulties concerning emancipation laws in various states.

This conflict between ideological purity and practical inconsistency doesn't seem to have dampened Methodism's appeal. Between its founding and its schism over slavery, Methodism grew from a few thousand people to become the largest denomination in the United States. Slaveholding among Methodists, however, grew at an equally august rate. Just before the North/South split of 1844-45, "25,000 communicants owned 208,000 slaves—over 9 percent of the total slave population—and 1,200 Methodist clergymen were themselves slaveholders."[14] After the split "every minister elevated to the rank of bishop in the Methodist Episcopal Church, South, between 1846 and the Civil War was a slaveholder."[15] In sixty-four years this denomination went from active opposition to slavery, to ignorance of the issue, to attempts to maintain unity, to regional schism over slavery.[b]

Similar patterns emerged in the Baptist and Presbyterian churches. Early pronouncements depicted slavery (or at least slave trading/holding) as sinful. But since these denominations exercised little control over individual congregations, such stances were sometimes opposed and widely ignored with little consequence. So, anti-slavery rhetoric gradually gave way to a general truce on the matter. Slavery was framed as a social rather than a spiritual issue, and denominational disapprobation increasingly fell upon the abolitionists as schismatic rabble-rousers.

As a result, Baptists finally split (North/South) over slavery in 1845. Presbyterians suffered a compound fracture. After dividing over doctrinal issues into the New School and the Old School in 1837, the New School divided once again over slavery in 1857. In 1861 the Old School followed suit, splitting over a range of sectional disagreements, including slavery.[16]

Congregational Life during Slavery

While Christian denominations were alternatively dividing over, running from, or caving in on the issue of slavery; blacks and whites were still interfacing at the local church level. Throughout the slave era those slaves

---

[b] For more background on the Methodists' attempts to maintain unity and their ultimate division, see: www.scottgarber.com/was_notes.pdf, Note 8.1.

who attended church did so with their masters, so, in a broad sense their churches were integrated. But even when masters and slaves were together, the way they shared that space was quite segregated, as the racialized social distinctions present in slave society did not stop at the door of the church.

One of the great inequities of this "integrated" Church was the instruction offered to the slaves, a propagandist curriculum that put more emphasis on making them better slaves than on making them better Christians. In 1709 the famous Puritan divine, Cotton Mather, produced a catechism for slaves called "The Negro Christianized," in which he interpreted the fifth commandment, to honor father and mother, not as having to do with natural family relationships but with subjection to one's master.[17] The tenth commandment against covetousness was defined as, "I must be Patient and Content with such a Condition as God has ordered for me."[18]

More than a hundred years later Charles Colcock Jones published the widely used "A Catechism for Colored Persons," urging slaves "…not to give saucy answers; and even when they are whipt for doing well, to take it patiently…"[19] It also insisted that their simple station was happier than that of their masters, who were forced to shoulder the burdens of social dominance.[20]

At least this catechism held out the hope of eschatological equality, affirming that "there will be no difference there [in heaven], but what more holiness or more sin makes."[21] Such equity in the presentation of the afterlife was not a given. Some slaves were not even informed about heaven or, alternatively, were told that there was no heaven for them or that they would continue to serve whites in glory or even go to a separate, segregated eternal reward.[22] One former slave heard from his minister that there would be "a wall between [the black and white sections of heaven], but there will be holes that will permit you to look out and see your mistress as she passes by."[23] Another was taught that "if they be good niggers and not steal their master's eggs and things, they might go to the kitchen of heaven when they died."[24]

Though some slaves bought into this theological folklore, they far more commonly conceived of heaven as a place where scores would be settled and they would enjoy a reversal of fortunes.[25] The notion of a happy coexistence in an egalitarian afterlife seemed to stretch the imagination of both masters and slaves. Slavery imposed such a perverse deformation of human identity that even heaven was viewed through the prism of segregation.

From the very beginning the presence of slaves in church made their masters uneasy, fearing that church membership might somehow lead to emancipation. Apart from the logic inherent in such a notion, the colonial slaveholding class, overwhelmingly English in its ancestry, had a nagging cultural sensitivity related to the inelegance, if not immorality, of enslaving a fellow Christian. Whites insisted that baptism shouldn't lead to freedom, because that prospect would tempt slaves into insincere conversions. The real threat, however, was the implosion of the institution of slavery itself.

Because of the important practical implications of church membership for slaves, colonial legislatures weighed in on the matter early and often. A 1667 Virginia law declared:

> "Whereas some doubts have arisen whether children that are slaves by birth, and by the charity and piety of their owners made partakers of the blessed sacrament of baptism, should by virtue of their baptism be made free; It is enacted and declared by this grand assembly, and the authority thereof, that the conferring of baptism doth not alter the condition of the person as to his bondage or freedom; that diverse masters, freed from this doubt, may more carefully endeavor the propagation of Christianity..."[26]

Such was the planters' paranoia on this issue, however, that, as historian Eugene Genovese observed: "Although... the law clearly stated that baptism would not imply emancipation, slaveholders throughout the British and even French colonies continued to fear that Christian slaves would be declared free."[27] As a result, Virginia, Maryland, and Carolina reinforced their seventeenth-century statutes at least three times over the next half century.

This colonial preoccupation was felt in Britain as well. When "Bishop of London Edmund Gibson proclaimed in 1727 that 'Christianity does not make the least alteration in civil property,' the Anglican Church became the first Protestant denomination to adopt a formal no-emancipation policy."[28/c] Two years later, the King's Attorney and the Solicitor General of England rendered an opinion on the status of slaves who might enter Great Britain or Ireland with their masters, concluding that "baptism doth not bestow freedom on him, nor make any alteration in his temporal condition in these kingdoms."[29]

Even with this carefully stacked legal deck in hand, slaveholders were still nervous about the implications of Christian liberty. So, slaves were quite often required to renounce any aspirations to freedom as a condition of their baptism. Dr. Francis LeJau, a missionary of the Anglican Society for the Propagation of the Gospel, insisted that slaves affirm the following: "You

---

[c] Forrest G. Wood's *The Arrogance of Faith* offers an excellent treatment of this issue on pages 117-119, which I have summarized above.

declare in the presence of God and before this congregation that you do not ask for the Holy Baptism out of any desire to free yourself from the duty and obedience you owe to your master while you live?"[30]

This segregated integration within the walls of the church, however contradictory, more or less "worked" during the first two centuries of slavery. Since most masters were not trying very hard to convert their slaves, there were not that many black people in the churches, anyway. But as the 19th century unfolded, a curious confluence of social and spiritual factors, from populist revivals to slave rebellions, led to a modest but significant increase in the number of black converts and church members.

The Second Great Awakening not only resulted in the conversion of many slaves; it also had a profound spiritual impact on the slaveholders, who then felt a burden for the spiritual welfare of their slaves. That Awakening also fired up the Christian abolitionist movement and, with it, criticism of the abuses of slavery. In response, some Southern divines—trying to show that a Christianized slave society was not an oxymoron but a legitimate social alternative—began to push for reforms, including religious training.[d]

There was, however, another important catalyst for change among the slaveholding class—the fear of rebellions. In particular, the 1831 Nat Turner uprising, in which sixty whites lost their lives, created a ripple effect across the South.[e] Though such events were rare (this was the most serious uprising in American history), the white ruling elite became permanently paranoid about just how outnumbered they were compared to the slave population.

This fear led to a variety of knee-jerk responses. Some states, noting that Turner had been educated and that he had gained his following in a religious community, restricted the teaching of blacks. Virginia passed a law that "banned all negroes, slave or free, from preaching or holding religious meetings unattended by a licensed white minister."[31] A North Carolina statute went even further, forbidding any black person from preaching whatsoever.[32]

Ironically, however, as Genovese observes, "a great burst of proselytizing among the slaves [also] followed the Nat Turner revolt. Whereas many slaveowners had previously feared slaves with religion… they now feared slaves without religion even more. They came to see Christianity as primarily a means of social control."[33] In order to avoid the risks inherent in literacy, however, religious instruction was generally limited to oral training.

---

[d] For more background, see: www.scottgarber.com/was_notes.pdf, Note 8.2.
[e] For more on Turner, see: www.scottgarber.com/was_notes.pdf, Note 8.3a.

The net result of all these influences was that in the decades before the Civil War there was a significant spike in church attendance among blacks. In some rare cases, black people even constituted a majority of the congregants. How did white churches and their leaders respond?

In general, the most fraternal biracial atmosphere existed in the Baptist churches. Though their association with their masters was typically noted on the membership role, slaves were received into membership in the same way as their white counterparts, held to similar standards, cared for as members, often addressed as "brother" or "sister," and formally transferred by letter to new congregations when they "moved." Of course, social distinctions were in no way erased, so there could be little interracial "fellowship," in the form of socializing between whites and blacks. But slaves were at least regarded as persons with genuine religious needs.

The Baptists were also more prone to recognize the spiritual giftedness of their black members. Men who showed talent and a sense of calling were sometimes licensed as exhorters or preachers and occasionally even ordained. A few even preached to mixed or white-only audiences. Black deacons were not uncommon and helped to care for the needs of their own congregants. Slaves sometimes had limited voting power to affirm these black deacons, but only after they had been vetted by whites. Janet Duitsman Cornelius observes: "Black preachers and deacons were useful to the white church...; they monitored the behavior of their fellow slaves and diverted their search for freedom to expectations of judgment day."[34]

Not only among Baptists but across denominational lines, the very physical layout of their meetings negated the possibility of true Christian unity. Black Christians, whether slave or free, had their own pews or, in larger churches, a separate gallery. Abolitionist James Birney observed that "the 'negro pew' is almost as rigidly kept up in the free States as in the slave."[35/f] Some churches had separate services, with black congregants often meeting on Sunday afternoons. The exception was communion Sunday, when they would often meet together. However, this symbol of Christian equality was pretty much ruined by the fact that blacks had to wait until whites had finished taking communion before they could be served.

Black worshipers were generally welcome in the white-controlled churches, and some congregations even made special efforts to reach out to them out of genuine concern for their spiritual welfare. But as liberating as

[f] For an illustration of segregation as practiced in Northern churches, see: www.scottgarber.com/was_notes.pdf, Note 8.3b.

the church environment may have felt compared to plantation work, exposure to the Christian message naturally raised expectations—expectations which could never be satisfied in a relationship with haughty fellow congregants who were convinced of their own innate superiority. The very premise of slave society was inimical to the gospel the Church proclaimed.

Not only slaves but even free black Christians were trapped in an inherently and deliberately unequal relationship with white Christians. Whether the mechanism for maintaining white dominance was slavery or some other form of social hierarchy, whites, who were convinced of their inherent superiority, could not contemplate living as social equals with blacks. They were more afraid of the "mongrelization" of the white race through racial amalgamation than they were of the most dreaded diseases of the time.

The most popular "final solution" to this problem during the early part of the nineteenth century, one that came to be endorsed by some denominations, was that of African colonization—sending free blacks and newly manumitted slaves to Africa. In 1816 the American Colonization Society (ACS) was formed and began to raise money to compensate slaveholders who would free their slaves to populate the settlement of Liberia in West Africa, which the society officially founded in 1822. Carefully avoiding any stand on the issue of slavery per se, they managed to appeal to both gradual abolitionists and slaveholders—though not always for the same reasons.

The *Historical Encyclopedia of World Slavery* comments: "Ironically, many Southern colonizationists saw the ACS as a means for making slavery more secure, and they believed the colonization of free blacks would remove people who allegedly corrupted the morals of slaves and encouraged them to escape.... [Others] felt that removing free blacks would promote national progress and safety."[36] On the abolitionist side, some "argued that removing free blacks to Africa would remove them from the ill effects of white prejudice,"[37] allowing them to flourish. Still others "hoped that blacks from the United States would plant Christianity in Africa."[38]

A lot of (white) people, it seems, could find something to like about colonization, but the idea never generated much enthusiasm among black people. Many considered the United States to be their native soil and had no desire to return to Africa. Others distrusted any idea that was so appealing to the white ruling class. Many even rejected the offer of freedom in exchange for emigration. AME leader Richard Allen opposed the plan as a scheme designed to deport black abolitionists and weaken the movement.[39]

African colonization turned out to be a colossal failure.[g] During the first 25 years of emigration, from the ACS founding to Liberian independence in 1847, "a mere 12,000 emigrants had moved under the auspices of the society."[40] (Out of 320,000 *free* blacks in the U.S., per the 1830 census). As late as 1860 only 4,000 freed slaves had been relocated, approximately one-tenth of one percent of the slave population.

This debacle went far beyond the recruiting effort. Prior to 1842, more than 40% of the U.S. emigrants to Liberia died in their first six years there. The new colony struggled constantly with poverty. The Americo-Liberians, as they came to be known, established themselves as a ruling elite that dominated the indigenous peoples, emulating a familiar example. And Liberia did not become a beacon of Christianity on the African continent.

When the ACS eventually lost its influence, a new champion of colonization arose—none other than Abraham Lincoln, who was determined to establish a black settlement in Panama. He secured significant funding from Congress for this project (in the middle of a war) and appointed James Mitchell as Commissioner of Emigration. But the idea was widely rejected by black leaders, as well as by authorities in Central America. Political and military developments soon moved Lincoln toward emancipation, but recent evidence suggests that he may have continued to secretly pursue colonization options even after that time.[41] Though Lincoln's dream was never realized, other colonization efforts continued into the twentieth century.

The sentiments that fueled the colonization movement are not insignificant to the dynamic of church life during the antebellum period and beyond. What were black Christians to do, when many of their white fellow church members wanted to either exploit them as slaves or to be rid of them entirely? When the President of the United States—who is remembered as a friend of the black cause—calls in representatives of your race to tell you that you are essentially *personae non gratae* and therefore should go somewhere far, far away, what are you to conclude about the possibilities of Christian brotherhood in these United States?[42/h]

---

[g] This was not because of a lack of funding; rather, because so few slaves were manumitted and so few owners had to be compensated, the ACS typically had more money than it could disburse.

[h] On August 14, 1862, President Lincoln summoned five free black ministers to the White House to enlist their help in recruiting other free blacks for colonization, saying: "You and we are different races... Whether it is right or wrong I need not discuss, but this physical difference is a great disadvantage to us both, as I think your race suffer very greatly... while ours suffer from

The Rise of the Black Church Tradition

Throughout the slave era, black Christians experienced racial separation, even in the "integrated" churches. Indeed, black congregants were often relegated to their own services—though, given the demeaning treatment they received in a mixed assembly, such segregation could be a welcome relief. If the black contingent was large enough, these segregated meetings sometimes became quasi-independent congregations led by blacks under white tutelage.

Though such services allowed slaves a modicum of freedom, they often supplemented traditional worship in "hush harbors," amidst the rhythms of the Ring Shout. Janet Duitsman Cornelius explains: "Hush harbors were meeting places, usually secret, which slaves created outside the plantations quarters… typically in forests, in dugouts and hollows, or by river banks."[43] Former slave Susan Rhodes commented, "We used to steal off to de woods and have church like de spirit moved us—sing and pray to our own liking and soul satisfaction…"[44] For its part, "Ring Shout was a dance-like form of Christian worship done by African-American slaves, mostly before the Civil War. It involves moving in a counterclockwise circle, singing, clapping, stomping and beating on the floor rhythmically with a stick or broom."[45]

In addition to the typical biracial churches and their clandestine alternatives, a few independent black churches existed during the final century of the slave era. "The first known black churches in America [are] generally acknowledged to have been the African Baptist or 'Bluestone' Church on the William Byrd plantation in… Virginia in 1758, and the Silver Bluff Baptist Church, located… not far from Augusta, Georgia."[46] A slave preacher named George Liele established this latter congregation in the mid-1770s, and two of his protégés started new churches in the Savannah area in the late 1780s.

As time went on, however, increasingly restrictive laws made such religious independence more difficult. For example, Mississippi's Poindexter Code (1822-23) and subsequent legislation stipulated that religious services had to "be conducted by a regularly ordained or licensed white minister, or

---

your presence. …Even when you cease to be slaves, you are yet far removed from being placed on an equality with the white race. …On this broad continent, not a single man of your race is made the equal of a single man of ours…. There is an unwillingness on the part of our people, harsh as it may be, for you free colored people to remain with us…"
(https://quod.lib.umich.edu/l/lincoln/lincoln5?page=viewtextnote;rgn=full+text, 371-373.) More detail at: www.scottgarber.com/was_notes.pdf, Note 8.4.

attended by at least two discreet and respectable white persons, appointed for that purpose by some regular Church or religious society."[47]

Despite these restrictions, other black Baptist churches began to arise in major metropolitan areas, where a higher proportion of free blacks could be found. For instance, in 1841 the First Baptist Church of Richmond, Virginia created the First African Baptist Church. Though it had white leadership—in order to conform to both legal requirements and social pressure—the church did have its own separate identity and building. The model proved to be a popular one. "The 1,000 black members in 1841 grew to 2,591 by 1849. The First African Baptist Church generated three additional African Baptist churches in Richmond by 1860."[48]

The most significant development in racially separate worship came out of Philadelphia. In 1787, church officials at St. George's Methodist Episcopal Church pulled a group of black congregants off their knees while they were praying in order to relocate them to a new blacks-only gallery.[49] Among them was a black preacher named Richard Allen, who desired to remain Methodist but saw the need for a church in which black people would not be treated as an inferior caste. So, "in 1794 Bethel AME (African Methodist Espiscopal) was dedicated with Allen as pastor. To establish Bethel's independence from interfering white Methodists, Allen... successfully sued in the Pennsylvania courts in 1807 and 1815 for the right of his congregation to exist as an independent institution."[50] The following year, 1816, Allen met with other black Methodists and established the African Methodist Episcopal Church.

This was the first black denomination capable of operating totally apart from white control. The AME Zion Church, born out of similar circumstances in New York, followed close behind. Though these denominations established a few congregations in the South, most of their growth took place in the Midwest and Northeast until after the Civil War. Black religious independence, which began as an exception, quickly became the rule after Emancipation.

It's hard to blame black Christians for voting with their feet, as an oxymoronic apartheid unity is hardly worth preserving. Nevertheless, the resulting separation and its color-coded ecclesiastical traditions now make it all the more complicated to unite the divided house that haughtiness built.

Chapter 9

Emancipation, Reconstruction, and Redemption

As a youngster, I learned that on New Year's Day, 1863 Abraham Lincoln's Emancipation Proclamation freed the slaves from centuries of bondage. I imagined the Great Emancipator, tall and gaunt in his long black coat, his eyes misty with compassion. As he put his pen to the blessed document, slaying the savage dragon of slavery, delighted black children frolicked in the background, celebrating the news that they were henceforth and forever free. And, having done this historic deed, Abe managed a tired but satisfied smile, a gentle tear of joy trickling across his craggy cheek.

As I later discovered, the real story was not quite so cinematically heroic. This proclamation, while certainly momentous, was far more about politics than about justice. And while Emancipation marked a turning point in black history, it did not mark a turning point in the history of white haughtiness.

In August of 1862 Lincoln made his racial and political priorities clear in a letter to New York Tribune editor, Horace Greeley:

> My paramount object... is to save the Union, and is not either to save or to destroy slavery. If I could save the Union without freeing any slave I would do it, and if I could save it by freeing all the slaves I would do it; and if I could save it by freeing some and leaving others alone I would also do that. What I do about slavery, and the colored race, I do because I believe it helps to save the Union; and what I forbear, I forbear because I do not believe it would help to save the Union.[1]

Lincoln's "emancipation" strategy was designed to win the war and, thereby, preserve the Union. The President, however, found himself in a delicate situation with the border states, which, while still part of the Union, nevertheless practiced slavery. In order to avoid alienating these important allies, the Emancipation Proclamation specified that "all persons held as slaves within any State or designated part of a State, the people whereof *shall then be in rebellion* [emphasis mine] against the United States, shall be then, thenceforward, and forever free."[2]

In this manner, the President "liberated" the slaves in the Confederacy without immediately affecting slavery within what remained of the Union or

Union-controlled territories. Secretary of State Seward, co-signer of the document, could not avoid this bit of sarcasm: "We show our sympathy with slavery by emancipating slaves where we cannot reach them and holding them in bondage where we can set them free."[3]

Lincoln's edict had little immediate impact on the institution of slavery, but it did have important strategic implications. It bolstered the moral rationale for the war in the North; it allowed the Union to recruit runaway slaves for the war effort; and, last but certainly not least, just when England and France were considering recognizing the sovereignty of the Confederacy, this proclamation re-cast the war as a struggle for human freedom, winning popular and political support for the Union cause abroad.

So, this proclamation was neither a philosophical declaration of human rights nor a magic wand of instant liberty—but its long-term consequences were nevertheless significant. In one fell swoop this executive order cut through the political logjam that had stymied other efforts to abolish slavery. It eventually led to the demolition of that abominable institution. And, even though Emancipation was not primarily (or even secondarily) concerned with the future fortunes of the enslaved, it nevertheless ushered in one of the most remarkable eras in American history—Reconstruction.

Given the fact that the government had no plan for assimilating four million former slaves into free society, just how did blacks manage a dozen years of significant social progress after the Civil War? The most important factor was the gritty initiative of the new African Americans themselves, but bold congressional action and Northern philanthropy also played a role. Conspicuously absent from that list is Presidential action, which, particularly in the early years, nearly aborted Reconstruction's launch altogether.

Lincoln's priority was to re-integrate the Southern states into the Union as quickly and as seamlessly as possible, and he began that effort even before the war's end with his "Ten Percent Plan," launched in December of 1863. According to this plan, if as few as ten percent of a state's citizens state swore allegiance to the United States, it could be restored to the Union. A new state constitution had to denounce secession and affirm emancipation. In exchange, all confederates other than high-ranking officers and government officials would be pardoned, and the planters' property (other than their slaves) would be protected. There would be no federal occupation or assistance for the freedmen, and the details of reconstruction would be largely left to the states.

As subsequent history demonstrates, this plan would have spelled disaster for black people. But Lincoln never fully implemented it. By the end of 1864

Arkansas, Louisiana, and Tennessee met the plan's requirements and formed alternatives to their Confederate state governments. These initiatives, however, did not enjoy popular support within their respective states, and the Radical Republican Congress refused to seat their elected representatives.

When Lincoln was assassinated early in his second term, Vice-President Andrew Johnson became President. This Tennessean was a strong supporter of the Union—but also an outspoken supporter of states' rights and white supremacy. During his tenure the confrontation between the executive and legislative branches would become exponentially more entrenched.

Congress recessed from the summer of 1865 until December of that year, giving Johnson time to implement his own incredibly lenient plan to re-admit Confederate states to the Union. He required only that they invalidate their acts of secession and form a new government, electing delegates from among *whatever portion* of the voting population was loyal to the Union.

Johnson's haste to hit the reset button not only led to overly permissive policies regarding the former Confederacy, it also undermined African-American fortunes. Take, for instance, the infamous "promise" of "forty acres and a mule." That story began with Gen. William Tecumseh Sherman, who was concerned about how to handle the thousands of slave refugees who had followed his army across Georgia. In response he issued Special Field Orders, No. 15 on January 16, 1865, offering each former slave family "not more than forty acres of tillable land"[4] in the Sea Islands and along the Atlantic coast from Charleston south into very northern Florida. And the mule? Sherman also instructed Gen. Rufus Saxton to lend farm animals to black settlers from the military stock that were too decrepit for further service.[5]

In the beginning it was not clear just what the terms of the land deal would be. Sherman's order spoke of somehow providing a "possessory title in writing,"[6] but that was still "subject to the approval of the President of the United States."[7] Barely six weeks later, however, in March of 1865, Congress clarified that issue. It created the Freedman's Bureau, authorizing the *leasing* of "not more than forty acres"[8] of abandoned or confiscated lands to the freedmen, with an option to "*purchase* the land, and receive such titles thereto as the United States can convey" [emphasis mine].[9]

Though this program was never really the straightforward land giveaway that it might seem in the popular retelling, it nevertheless could have been an attractive opportunity for the former slaves. Indeed, in the six months after Sherman's order 40,000 African Americans flooded into these 400,000 acres. Later that same year, however, President Johnson began pardoning the

Confederates from whom the land had been confiscated and returning it to them, effectively undermining the program.

Taking advantage of Johnson's liberality, by the end of 1865 every former Confederate state except Texas had a new constitution. Not surprisingly, they also passed a whole spate of Black Codes, denying African Americans the right to vote, serve on juries, hold office, own property, and travel freely.[10] When Congress finally came back into session, elected representatives from some of the Southern states actually showed up in their Confederate uniforms! The new Senator from the state of Georgia was none other than Alexander Stephens, fresh from his recent gig as the Vice President of the Confederacy.

The existing Republican Congress was not pleased. In fact, they refused to seat these Southern officials and sent them home. Then, in the mid-term elections of 1866 the Republicans won an overwhelming victory, and Congress took charge of Reconstruction. To be sure, Johnson vetoed almost every piece of Reconstruction legislation, but Republicans had the super-majority necessary to override his vetoes and press ahead with their policies.

That ambitious agenda provided important legal protections for black Americans. Though the Thirteenth Amendment (1865) abolished slavery throughout the United States, it created no positive rights for the freed slaves. The Fourteenth Amendment (1868) did, however, include such provisions, making blacks full citizens and guaranteeing (at least in principle) due process for all. Finally, the Fifteenth Amendment (1870) enshrined the right to vote, noting specifically that this right cannot be denied on account of "race, color, or previous condition of servitude."[11] Notably, it did not include women.

In addition to the Fourteenth and Fifteenth Amendments, Congress passed a series of Reconstruction Acts that grouped the Southern states into five districts and established military rule in them, overseeing the process of voter registration and elections while protecting civil rights. Congress required the former Confederate states to ratify the Fourteenth Amendment and write new constitutions that included voting rights for black males. By 1870 eleven southern states had complied with these terms and had been re-admitted to the Union.

President Johnson did his best to oppose this process with vetoes and bigoted diatribes. His 1867 State of the Union address was a case study in haughty fear-mongering, predicting a degrading future in which blacks would not only "govern themselves" but "rule the white race."[12] The confrontation between Johnson and Congress culminated in the spring of 1868, when the House of Representatives voted to impeach him. The Senate, however, ended up acquitting him by a single vote, a verdict that was almost certainly influenced by the fact that Johnson was not running for re-election that fall.

Between 1866 and 1875 Congress passed four additional Civil Rights Acts to protect the voting rights of African Americans, to guard against racial terrorism, and to specifically guarantee "the full and equal enjoyment of the accommodations, advantages, facilities, and privileges of inns, public conveyances on land or water, theaters, and other places of public amusement."[13] Though these legal protections were certainly groundbreaking, they did little to erase the serious economic disenfranchisement that was common among former slaves. To respond to those needs, in 1865, the federal government established the Bureau of Refugees, Freedmen, and Abandoned Lands—popularly referred to as the Freedman's Bureau.

> It issued food and clothing, operated hospitals and temporary camps, helped locate family members, promoted education, helped freedmen legalize marriages, provided employment, supervised labor contracts, provided legal representation, investigated racial confrontations, settled freedmen on abandoned or confiscated lands, and worked with African American soldiers and sailors and their heirs to secure back pay, bounty payments, and pensions.[14]

The Bureau did manage a measure of social triage, but it faced overwhelming challenges in trying to establish a social and economic beachhead from which former slaves could enter mainstream American life. Black people had neither capital nor land. The infrastructure of the South had been devastated by war. And, to make matters worse, impoverished Southern whites resented and resisted black progress.

In the new economic matrix of the South, the planters still had something the freedmen did not—land. But blacks now had something the white man needed—labor. This balance of supply and demand led to the practice of sharecropping, a system in which black people farmed white-owned land. Sharecropping gave the former slaves at least some hope of eking out a living, but it also helped the landowners, who paid workers with a portion of the crop and avoided hiring laborers in a cash-starved economy.

Though black farmers were free to negotiate the terms of their labor, most sharecropping arrangements ended up being highly favorable to the white landowners. In addition, blacks often had no money to buy food and supplies until the crops came in, so they were forced to buy on credit from plantation stores. This arrangement proved to be fertile ground for white chicanery, so that sharecroppers often found themselves still indebted to the store at the end of the season—a vicious cycle that reduced them to virtual serfdom.[15]

Some African Americans did make incremental gains in wealth over time through hard work and good fortune, but most were mired in dire poverty and de facto second-class citizenship. Ironically, the black economic woes of Reconstruction stood in sharp contrast to their progress in other areas like education, politics, and religion.

Several new realities fueled the historic expansion of African-American education during Reconstruction. First and foremost was the initiative of the African-American community itself. Self-sustaining, indigenous schools began to pop up even before the war's end under the tutelage of educated blacks. Hungry for that which had been so long denied, African Americans made education a priority, making incredible sacrifices to attain it.

The Freedman's Bureau also played an important role in expanding educational opportunities. They rented "buildings for schoolrooms, provided books and transportation for teachers, superintended the schools, and offered military protection for students and teachers against the opponents of black literacy."[16] The bureau did not run the institutions, but it built 630 schools in its first five years and established institutions of higher learning, including Howard University and the Hampton Institute. Eventually the Bureau helped established some 4,000 schools that educated up to 250,000 students at once.[17]

Another vital resource for educational growth was Northern philanthropy, which worked hand-in-hand with the Freedman's Bureau in funding and operating schools. "Within "thirty years of the war's end, Northern philanthropists had sent an estimated $15.7 million [$384 million, 2019] to Southern states."[18] Most of this money came from church mission societies, and it was vital to the infrastructure of black education during Reconstruction and beyond, until public education became more widely available.

Some of the new state constitutions even established public education systems, though most states had little money for them. South Carolina, for example, passed the first such measure in 1870. By 1871 they were educating thirty-two percent of school-age children, and by 1875 that number had increased to fifty percent. (Other states lagged far behind this pace.) In theory, educational opportunity was open to all, but in these (mostly) segregated school systems, the actual allocation of scant resources was typically unfavorable to African Americans.

White supremacist groups did not manage to derail this burgeoning educational enterprise, but it was not for lack of trying. They regularly terrorized students, teachers, Northern missionaries, and government officials involved in education. They also burned many schoolhouses to the ground; it is estimated that "Between 1868 and 1871... Klansmen in Alabama [alone] committed more than 100 murders and thousands of acts of violence and intimidation."[19]

In response to these terrorist tactics the federal government passed a series of Enforcement Acts, culminating in the Ku Klux Klan Act of 1871. Under these acts many thousands of people were arrested. Some 3,000 were eventually indicted. Many of those pled guilty but received only suspended sentences. Only 600 were convicted, resulting in fines and/or very limited jail time. Only 65 were ever sentenced for five or more years in a federal penitentiary, and all of them were released early.[20] The problem was that law enforcement, prosecution, and the rendering of verdicts depended largely on the officials and citizenry of the state in which the offenses occurred.

If black advances in education were encouraging, African-American political activity was genuinely impressive—even by modern standards. In the former Confederacy:

> 703,000 adult black men but only 627,000 whites were eventually registered to vote during military Reconstruction. To be sure, in some states white disenfranchisement was self-imposed by alienated whites. But military application of loyalty oaths and loyalty challenges helped assure that five states ended up with black electoral majorities.[21]

This black advantage at the ballot box helped cement Republican control of the South, insuring policies that were at least sympathetic to black concerns.

Not only did black people turn out to vote, they often found themselves voting for black candidates, as Yale Prof. David Blight explains:

> ...Approximately 200 African-Americans in the Southern states served in state legislatures, in state government and executive positions, and ultimately in the U.S. Congress. Sixteen African-Americans from ex-Confederate states were elected to the U.S. Congress, two to the U.S. Senate ... Of the 1,000 delegates to Constitutional writing conventions, in 1868, '69, ...268 of them were black. About 680 African-Americans served in the lower houses of state governments during Reconstruction. Four presided as speakers of those houses. There were 112 African-Americans who served in State Senates during Reconstruction. There were at least 41 black sheriffs... five black mayors of Southern cities... 145 blacks who served on city councils...[22]

The white population, scandalized by the prospect of being either ruled or represented by blacks, levied numerous objections against this trend—and some of their complaints were legitimate. There were, indeed, numerous carpetbaggers[a] in the political mix. And some of the new black office holders turned out to be unscrupulous—though it would be hard to argue that there was any more corruption in their ranks than among their white counterparts.

Black candidates were also presumed to be uneducated, since few had the opportunity for formal schooling. But their level of formal education must be kept in historical perspective. Most "of the major Negro leaders during Reconstruction had more formal education than Abraham Lincoln. 10 of the 22 Negroes who served in Congress had attended college; five of them were lawyers. Both of the Negro Senators had attended college."[23]

Not surprisingly, such a threat to the establishment did not go unchallenged, and the angry white sentiment that filled the South became fertile ground for the Ku Klux Klan and similar organizations. Founded in Tennessee in December of 1865, by 1867 the KKK had begun to spread to other states. A year later it had infected the entire South and was primed to influence the election of 1868. According to David Blight, that year blacks:

> ...went to the polls in extraordinary numbers... and many of them died doing it.... There were more than 200 political murders in the State of Arkansas alone... In twenty-two Georgia counties, with a total of 9,300 black men listed on the voting rolls, [Ulysses] Grant tallied only eighty-seven votes.[24]

Why didn't somebody do something? Well, eventually (1870) Congress passed the 15th Amendment, guaranteeing the right to vote. But that law proved to be only as effective as its enforcement, which was spotty at best. In reality, there was limited sympathy, even in the North, for black voting rights. Northern politicians forced Southern states to grant the vote to blacks in their new state constitutions, even though most Northern whites opposed black voting rights in their own states. As late as the 1868 Presidential election, most of the Northern and border states still did not allow black Americans to vote.

The black Church, which had maintained a low profile under slavery, came into its own during Reconstruction. Whereas only a few years earlier many slaves had not been permitted to attend worship services under any

---

[a] "Carpetbagger" was a pejorative term used by Southerners to describe Northern politicians who moved into the former Confederate states after the war to seek political office, in spite of having no local connections.

circumstances, now that they were free not only to worship but free to do so apart from white domination, they quickly took advantage of this freedom.

During Reconstruction, the black church was not only a center of spiritual sustenance but, as the single social institution that black people truly controlled, it also became an operational center for addressing economic, social, and political concerns. Black pastors were not just spiritual leaders; by the nature of the case they became community leaders as well. They eventually wielded enormous political influence, and many even ran for office. During Reconstruction more than 200 of the 1,500 blacks elected to office were ordained ministers, including AME minister Hiram Revels from Mississippi, the first African American elected to the U.S. Senate.

Several factors contributed to the spectacular black church growth in the postbellum South. The same white Northern philanthropy that helped establish schools also assisted in the building of churches, as most of that money came from church mission societies. More importantly, Northern black missionaries combined forces with former slaves, who, buoyed by their newfound independence, were motivated to build their congregations.

The most successful outreach was that of the AME Church, whose ministers and missionaries began arriving immediately after Emancipation. They organized the North Carolina, Georgia, and South Carolina conference in 1865 with just 4,000 members. By 1876, only eleven years later, it had grown to some 300,000 members.[25]

These aggressive missionary efforts, combined with white enthusiasm for dispatching black Christians to a "more suitable" congregational home, led to a mass exodus of black people from white-controlled congregations. For instance, in 1860 the Methodist Episcopal Church South had 207,766 black members, but six years later only 78,742 remained.[26] Some of the remaining black leaders asked the denomination to establish an independent black Methodist church. In 1870, their white counterparts approved the idea, helped ordain black ministers, and established the CME Church (then *Colored,* now *Christian* Methodist Episcopal). In 1875, white Methodists transferred church property valued at about $1 million (1875 dollars) to CME trustees.[27]

This highly beneficial, though paternalistic, arrangement, which CME Bishop L. H. Holsey termed "fatherly directorship,"[28] came at a price. The CME church had to agree to refrain from political activity, which was a hallmark of their AME cousins. In this manner white Christians managed to rid themselves of the pesky problem of relating to free black people in the same congregation, muzzle the church as a social agitator, and look benevolent all at the same time.

Baptist churches also experienced phenomenal growth during this time. Rather than being controlled by a hierarchy, these congregations were independently governed. As a result, they did not feel quite the same urgency to form black denominational structures. Many black congregations continued to be associated with the white church through the African Baptist Missionary Society, though some also joined black Baptist associations. The two black Baptist conventions that had existed in the North before Emancipation merged in 1867 and welcomed a host of new congregations from the South. There was friction, however, between the better educated and more staid Northern black contingent and its Southern counterpart, which was comprised of ex-slaves. That tension resulted in a convention split along geographical lines in 1879.[29]

Like other institutional advances during Reconstruction, the burgeoning black Church met resistance from white supremacists, including the KKK. Their targeting of churches had nothing to do with theological differences, as black Christians shared the same general beliefs as the whites who oppressed them. Rather, it was the church as a center of power that made it a threat to white hegemony, prompting church burnings and vandalism, along with intimidation and violence directed against church leaders and missionaries.

On the opposite end of the spectrum, white Christians in the North—motivated by a combination of evangelistic zeal, compassion, paternalism, and the sense that God had helped secure a Union victory in order to end slavery—funneled significant development aid to the former slave population. Their invaluable assistance was, however, accompanied by a certain degree of hypocrisy, given the fact that they did little to better the lives of the African Americans in their own back yard. Northerners, who generally had little contact with black people and faced no threat from their numbers, found it pretty easy to support civil rights in the abstract, or better yet, in the South.

Despite the many challenges faced by black Americans, they made enormous advances during Reconstruction. The dynamo of African-American initiative created a host of fraternal, benevolent, and mutual aid societies, including "burial societies, debating clubs, Masonic lodges, fire companies, drama societies, trade associations, temperance clubs, and equal rights leagues... [They] raised money to establish orphanages, soup kitchens, employment agencies, and poor relief funds."[30]

Nevertheless, by the middle of 1875, Frederick Douglass was worried; he could already see the pendulum of history heading into a threatening, descending arc. In his Independence Day remarks Douglass wondered aloud, "If war among the whites brought peace and liberty to blacks, what will peace among the whites bring?"[31]

The impressive institutional gains of Reconstruction were possible only because federal troops occupied the South. Federal protective protagonism reached its apex with the 1871 passage of the Ku Klux Klan Act, cementing the demise of the original Klan.[b] But soon afterwards, a series of circumstances conspired to turn the momentum back toward states' rights and against black interests. This counter-revolution, which saw whites reassert their dominance over Southern institutions, became known as "Redemption."

What forces sent black fortunes swinging in the opposite direction? Four seminal influences allowed Redemption to triumph.

The first influence was *psychic*. Weary of war, the nation was also tiring of the adversarial nature of Reconstruction. With the passage of the Fifteenth Amendment in 1870, Northerners believed they had created a legal framework that would allow African Americans to manage on their own. It seems not to have mattered a great deal whether such an expectation was realistic; what mattered was that whites had fulfilled their own sense of due diligence in the matter. They were anxious for reconciliation between North and South and wanted to move on with the great national project of America.

The second influence was *economic*. What became known as the Panic of 1873 began in Europe and quickly spread to the United States. In a matter of year and a half wheat lost three-quarters of its value, while manufacturing workers saw their wages cut in half, leading to major labor unrest.[32] The effects of this economic emergency would last for years, and under such financial pressure even Northern sympathizers became distracted from the issue of African-American rights and development. Justice had once again priced its way out of the marketplace.

Simultaneously, a third factor was making its mark on the national landscape in the form of a *legal* challenge. In 1873, the Supreme Court ruled in the Slaughterhouse Cases that the Fourteenth Amendment protected civil rights only at the *federal* level but not in *state* matters. This interpretation undermined the Amendment by rendering it inapplicable in most cases.

And then came Colfax, Louisiana. Following the 1872 gubernatorial election in Louisiana, both Republicans and Democrats claimed victory and set up parallel governments. That led to violent exchanges, including one that

---

[b] The KKK remained moribund until it was reconstituted in 1915. More details of that episode can be found in the following chapter.

became known as the Colfax Massacre. A white paramilitary force attacked a contingent of black people (many of whom were members of the state militia) who were holed up in the county courthouse. Fire was set to the building, and a number of blacks were killed trying to escape. The rest of their force surrendered, at which point forty men were summarily executed, their corpses left to rot. State officials reported that some of the bodies were mutilated or eaten by dogs and vultures. Death toll estimates range from 62 to 150.[33]

Only nine men were ever tried for this heinous crime, and only three convicted. In 1876 the case reached the Supreme Court (*United States v. Cruikshank*). Building on the Slaughterhouse verdict, they ruled that only the states, not the federal government, had the right to prosecute under the "due process" and "equal protections" provisions of the Fourteenth Amendment. This decision turned the responsibility for policing the henhouse back to the foxes, leading to an exponential increase in white-on-black terrorism.

The fourth and final contributing factor to the demise of Reconstruction was *political*. In the early 1870s, the KKK and other white supremacist groups succeeded in forcing white unionists, carpetbaggers, and scalawags out of the South, leaving African Americans to defend their own rights. Aided by the economic crisis, White Democrats began winning back their seats, and by 1874 Democrats had taken control of the U.S. House of Representatives.

Then, in 1876, a disputed Presidential election turned into a political event that definitively marked the end of Reconstruction. In that contest between Rutherford B. Hayes and Samuel Tilden, Tilden clearly won the popular vote, but the returns in four states were unclear. The final result would depend on those disputed electoral votes.

Congress appointed a special commission to resolve the issue. After some backroom negotiations, Democrats accepted Hayes's election in exchange for certain considerations, among them the withdrawal of federal troops from the former Confederacy. With no one to protect black voting rights, Democrats soon re-took those state legislatures, and Redemption was all but complete.

Looking at this entire period through the prism of America's original sin, we can see that the seeds of Redemption were present in Emancipation itself. It is one thing to abolish slavery, but quite another to address racial haughtiness. Whites disagreed about slavery, but they firmly agreed about this—they did not want to live and work and worship next to black people. Even the radical social change of Reconstruction did not significantly alter whites' belief in their own racial superiority.

U.S. Senator from Mississippi (Dem.) L.C.Q. Lamar, whom historian Mark Noll notes, "was regarded as a moderate,"[34] wrote a letter in the mid-1870s in which "he articulated harshly the message that drove 'redemption' in the South and won it a measure of respect in the North:"[35]

> Draw a line on the side of which you see property, intelligence, virtue, religion, self-respect, enlightened public opinion, and exclusion from political control; and on the other the absolute unchecked political supremacy of brute numbers, and there you will behold not one attribute of free government, but the saddest & blackest tyranny that ever cursed the earth.[36/c]

At the outset of Reconstruction, Northern sensibilities differed from those in the South. Some felt a sense of responsibility for the enormous refugee crisis created by the war. Many believed that God had secured their victory, and they feared that they might forfeit that divine favor if they left blacks with no guarantee of rights. By granting power to black people, Northeners also punished the South and established political control for the Republican party.

Whatever its initial motivation, this short-lived Northern concern was soon trumped by white social solidarity, economics, and diminishing political gains. After teasing African Americans with the prospect of equality, whites succumbed to the mammoth gravitational pull of haughtiness.

At first glance, postbellum Church history might seem to be an exception to this rule. Rather than whites marginalizing black Christians by excluding them from white congregations, it looks more like a flood of African Americans joyously fleeing their ecclesiastical captivity and establishing their own institutions. And since this exodus appears to be voluntary, it might also appear to be something other than a consequence of haughtiness. *Segregation* calls to mind a discriminatory social separation imposed by a racially-defined oppressor. *Voluntary separation*, however, seems more benign—more like a convenient and mutually beneficial parting of the ways. In the context of the Church, however, even voluntary separation is a morally deficient condition.

In his "Letter from a Birmingham Jail," Dr. King quoted theologian Paul Tillich as saying that "sin is separation."[37] That pithy statement may run the risk of conflating the two elements, but it also contains an important truth—

---

c For nearly 100 years, Reconstruction was viewed as a period of inept, corrupt government. But once the premise of black inferiority disappeared, a different vision of Reconstruction, as an unsuccessful yet noble experiment in progressive democracy, became dominant. See: Eric Foner, "The New View of Reconstruction," *American Heritage*, October/November, (1983): 10-15.

sin does *involve* separation, or as King later and more helpfully restated it, "estrangement."[38] Any act of sin involves a certain estrangement from God and then exacerbates that condition. And sin often involves estrangement from others as well, once again contributing to further estrangement.

The good news of the gospel is not merely its power to overcome the influence and the penalty of sin, as an impersonal moral and juridical force, but ultimately to restore those estranged relationships, whether on the vertical or the horizontal plane. To the extent that sin involves separation, salvation, in its fullness, must involve reconciliation and reconnection.

Despite this correlation between sin and separation, it's important to note that not all separation is an *act* of sin. Sometimes the physical distance of separation is merely a recognition of an estrangement that already exists and the inability of an oppressed party to effectively pursue reconciliation in the resulting context. For example, a woman who flees from her husband's abuse is not causing an estrangement but merely protecting herself from the consequences of relational alienation that already exists. Such was the lot of African Americans escaping from an ecclesiastical institution that had denied them the most basic respect for centuries. Even after Emancipation, black people remained second-class citizens, faced with a Hobbesian choice between "separate but sort of equal" or "together but thoroughly unequal."

But while the black separation from the white-controlled Church may not have been a sinful *act*, the condition of estrangement itself was, nevertheless, a morally deficient *condition*, because it flew in the face of God's revealed will for his people. As exhilarating as it might have felt for black Christians to get out of Egypt, they were not really entering an autonomous Promised Land but merely escaping into the relational no-man's-land of the wilderness. The real Promised Land is not racial autonomy but rather racial harmony.

Ideally, this separation would have caused white Christians to take note of what haughtiness had wrought and change their ways. But they did neither; rather, they chose to bid good riddance to the racial "problem" as it walked out the door. Over time that separation hardened into divorce, putting asunder that which God intended to be joined. And now, a century and a half later, that estrangement continues.

Chapter 10

The Legal Structure of Jim Crow Society

> Come listen all you galls and boys,
> I'm going to sing a little song,
> My name is Jim Crow.
> Weel about and turn about and do jis so,
> Eb'ry time I weel about I jump Jim Crow.

In 1828, a white entertainer in blackface named T. D. "Daddy" Rice began touring the country with this original ditty, popularizing the onstage persona of Jim Crow, a happy-go-lucky, dancing buffoon. In just a few years, Jim Crow became a stock character in minstrel shows around the country, and by 1840, "Jim Crow" was already being used as a racial slur. After Reconstruction, the term became associated with restrictive race laws, and by 1900 it was being used to denote the era defined by such laws.[1]

While the South became infamous for its Jim Crow legislation, Jim Crow's social impact was certainly not circumscribed by geography. Most of the Northern states had abolished slavery long before it disappeared in the South. Therefore, Northern whites had already adapted their own supremacist attitudes towards free blacks, employing a combination of de facto and de jure segregation[a] to consign black people to second-class citizenship. Most Northern states denied voting rights to blacks, and schools and other public facilities were often segregated. During and after the Civil War some of these restrictions were ameliorated, but an overt racial hierarchy remained.

By contrast, the Jim Crow system in the South was a far more dramatic and far-reaching phenomenon. It was also more revolutionary (or counter-revolutionary), as it came on the heels of the historic gains of Reconstruction and the pushback of Redemption. It was also more ubiquitous and enduring.

Consider the demographics of the time: "In 1870 over 90% of African Americans lived in the South, over 80% in the rural South."[2] So, for all intents and purposes, the Southern Jim Crow experience became America's defining interracial dynamic until the second half of the twentieth century.

---

[a] De jure segregation was codified in the law, whereas de facto segregation depended on social custom without a formal legal basis.

The country underwent enormous change during this lengthy period, transforming itself into an industrial juggernaut, adopting a grand national mission, experiencing a tidal wave of European immigration, and rising to become a major power on the world stage. Given the tremendous social transformation that was occurring, it is remarkable that, after the onset of Jim Crow, race relations evolved so little. Haughtiness not only managed to maintain its grip on the American soul; it found systemic and institutional expression in the asymmetrical reality of segregation.

In order to be "successful," the apartheid system of Jim Crow needed to control the behavior of an ostensibly free black population that actually outnumbered its white counterpart in many localities. That control depended on three factors working in conjunction: 1) an implicit sense of one's place in the racial/social hierarchy that was reinforced at every level of society, 2) extra-legal mechanisms designed to produce fear, and 3) a legal framework that lent official sanction to the entire arrangement.

The legal framework of Jim Crow was anchored in a judicial mentality that emerged during Redemption, one that interpreted the Constitutional Amendments and civil rights legislation of Reconstruction so narrowly as to thwart their original intent. That left black civil protections in a vacuum, a vacuum eventually filled by Jim Crow laws that codified white dominance.

The first major step in post-Reconstruction white dominance occurred in October of 1883, when the Supreme Court, by a margin of 8-1, declared the 1875 Civil Rights Act unconstitutional. This Act forbade racial discrimination by private businesses in hotels, conveyances, and other public spaces. But the Court argued that the civil protections of the 14th Amendment regulated only racial discrimination as perpetrated by the state, not by private persons or entities. This ruling opened the door to broad social segregation, as whites still controlled nearly all privately held but publicly accessed facilities.

The seriousness of this judicial stab in the back was not lost on AME Bishop Henry McNeal Turner, a leading black churchman and social activist. In a letter to the ministers and members of the Eighth Episcopal District dated Jan. 4, 1884, he reacted to the decision: "A terrible crisis is upon us; heaven is insulted, our civilization is disgraced! …To the negro in this country… this decision is known to be a fearful blow, a civil shame, an inhuman outlaw, upon more than seven millions of American citizens…"[3]

His initial outrage was not misplaced. A decade later Turner reflected on the fallout from this infamous ruling:

...That decision alone authorized and now sustains all the unjust discriminations, proscriptions and robberies perpetrated by public carriers... It fathers all the "Jim-Crow cars" into which colored people are huddled and compelled to pay as much as the whites, who are given the finest accommodations. It has made the ballot of the black man a parody, his citizenship a nullity and his freedom a burlesque. It has ingendered [sic] the bitterest feeling between the whites and blacks, and resulted in the deaths of thousands, who would have been living and enjoying life today.[4]

Some of the earliest Jim Crow legislation sought to segregate railroad cars. Tennessee passed the first such law in 1881, and other Southern states followed shortly thereafter. When Louisiana passed its own Separate Car Act in 1890, a small Citizens' Committee comprised of black professionals resolved to test the constitutionality of the law. It was an incident that would lead to one of the most far-reaching civil rights decisions in American history.

The Committee first challenged segregated railroad cars engaged in *inter*state travel and won that case in a Louisiana district court. Next, they decided to target the law on the *intra*state level. They chose Homer Plessy, a light-skinned "Creole of Color" who could pass for white. The Committee had already alerted the conductor as to Plessy's racial identity, and when he boarded the train on June 7, 1892, he was detained.

The district court ruled, however, that the Louisiana law was not unconstitutional when applied to intrastate travel. The Louisiana Supreme Court upheld this verdict the following year, and the case eventually reached the U.S. Supreme Court, which ruled in 1896. Their verdict in the *Plessy v. Ferguson* case dealt a crushing blow to black aspirations. This famous verdict established the legitimacy of "separate but equal" treatment for whites and blacks, a principle that was used to justify the maintenance of a separate but thoroughly *un*equal society for many decades to come.[b]

Though local ordinances and customs varied from place to place, during the early 20th century access to public facilities became generally segregated across the Southern states. Whites and blacks could not participate in the same public amusements such as parks, pools, and sporting activities. They were not typically allowed to attend the same theater, but when they did there were separate seating sections. Ticketing and waiting facilities were segregated.

---

[b] For more background on the legal rationale behind the majority opinion and the prescient dissent, see: www.scottgarber.com/was_notes.pdf, Note 10.1.

Blacks and whites were not permitted to use the same water fountains or toilets. They could not occupy the same sections of trains or buses or ride in the same taxis. They had separate schools and, often, separate hospitals; hospitals that served both races might have separate, color-coded entrances.

When the two races did interact socially, black people had to show public deference to whites. Richard Wormser, who wrote and directed the PBS documentary series, *The Rise and Fall of Jim Crow*, describes the rules:

> Blacks had to address white people as Mr., Mrs., or "Mizz," "Boss," or "Captain" while they, in turn, were called by their first name, or by terms used to indicate social inferiority— "boy," "aunty," or "uncle." Black people, if allowed in a store patronized by whites, had to wait until all white customers were served first... They had to give way to whites on a sidewalk, remove their hats as a sign of respect when encountering whites, and enter a white person's house by the back door.[5]

Jim Crow laws were ubiquitous, arcane, and seemingly arbitrary. Georgia had a law against "colored" barbers cutting the hair of white females. In Alabama, white female nurses were not allowed to care for black men. There, even interracial billiard games were illegal. Florida required white and black juvenile delinquent facilities to be separated by at least a quarter mile. In Georgia, neither race could play baseball on any lot located less than two blocks from a playground dedicated to the other race. Louisiana mandated that racially distinct ticket offices for the circus be at least twenty-five feet apart.

Mississippi imposed heavy fines and/or jail time on anyone found guilty of publishing material promoting either racial equality or intermarriage. North Carolina insisted that schoolbooks be used only by whichever race had used them first. Texas insisted on separate library branches for blacks, administered by a black person. White and black members of the North Carolina militia were not allowed to serve together, and black troops could be commanded only by whites. In Oklahoma fishing, boating, and swimming were racially segregated by law; the telephone company had to provide separate phone booths for each race if anyone complained about sharing.[6]

To be sure, segregation took place in the North as well, but in most localities there simply were not enough black people to make the creation of redundant facilities (like separate restrooms) practical. Instead, arrangements ranged from uneasy mixing to the outright exclusion of blacks. But whether the segregation was de facto or de jure, the message was eerily similar.

Though Jim Crow laws were clearly designed to enforce a system of white dominance, one might nevertheless wonder why such a draconian system of social separation was necessary. There were two primary motivations behind these regulations. First, most whites believed that black people were morally and physically unclean, as evidenced by the frequency with which racial epithets were modified by the words *dirty* or *filthy*. Second, by limiting social mixing, they hoped to avoid the über-taboo of interracial sex and/or marriage, a powerful prejudice that continues to haunt race relations to this day.

Georgia physician L. C. Allen presented a paper to the American Public Health Association in Jacksonville, Florida in November of 1914 that illustrates white attitudes toward black hygiene:

> It is undoubtedly true that the negro race has deteriorated physically and morally since slavery times... The present generation of negroes have grown up amid very unfavorable surroundings, and without home training, or discipline. Many of them have not had a bath since infancy. They live very irregular lives. They often roam about at night, some of them indulging in licentious debaucheries of the most disgusting character. Their homes are filthy, and their home language unchaste. Their girls early learn evil ways.[7]

While it's true that many black people of that time lived in deplorable conditions and therefore did not enjoy the refinements that affluence could provide, this white prejudice concerning black hygiene has endured through changing times. In their 1950 study on prejudice in which whites were asked to describe blacks' personal qualities, sociologists Bettelheim and Janowitz recorded the most common category of responses as "sloppy, dirty, filthy."[8] The result of this belief was a legal separation that kept the two races from coming into personal contact or even touching the same objects.

There was, however, an even more profound and visceral repugnance that manifested itself through anti-miscegenation[c] laws.[9] Such legislation first appeared in the Maryland colony in 1664. A Massachusetts anti-miscegenation law dating from 1705 declared itself "An Act for the Better Preventing of a Spurious and Mixed Issue."[10] In a paper read to the New York Historical Society in 1843, Charles Hoffman commented on the situation in

---

[c] The term *miscegenation* is derived from the Latin words *miscere* (to mix) and *genus* (race). It appeared for the first time in an 1863 pamphlet as a method for resolving racial tensions. These statutes are sometimes referred to as *miscegenation* laws, though the meaning is the same as *anti-miscegenation*.

his state during colonial times. He said that New Yorkers were "early taught that nature had placed between them [and their slaves] a barrier, which it was in a high degree criminal and disgraceful to pass; they considered a mixture of such distinct races with abhorrence, as a violation of her laws."[11]

Forty-one states eventually passed anti-miscegenation statutes. By 1887, eleven had repealed those laws. None of the other states, however, followed suit until 1948, beginning a twenty-year period in which fourteen more states lifted their prohibitions. The remaining sixteen were nullified by the 1967 Supreme Court decision in *Loving v. Virginia*.[12]

Those sixteen states eventually moved to formally repeal their already outlawed laws. Alabama was the last to do so in the year 2000, though even at that late date *forty percent of the voters still voted against annulment*.[13] The law might still be on the books if not for the bold moral stance of Governor Don Siegelman, who argued that failure to repeal "would send the wrong message to the corporate world."[14]

Anti-miscegenation laws reflected a social sensibility that went far deeper than just the legal level. Even when the legal prohibition of interracial marriage disappeared, there was no massive backlog of interracial couples waiting to tie the knot. Gallup polling from 1968, the year *after* anti-miscegenation laws were declared unconstitutional, showed that only 20% of Americans approved of interracial marriage, while 73% disapproved.[15] The rate of interracial marriages between blacks and whites (about 1 in 800) remained virtually unchanged from the 1960 census to that of 1970.[16]

In order to understand the enduring power of this taboo, we must consider the myth of racial purity. The purpose of this myth was much like that of classic myths (traditional beliefs or narratives used to support or explicate some portion of a worldview). During Jim Crow, racial purity served as an organizing principle for white supremacy.[d] If this fundamental *we/they* dichotomy were allowed to disappear, haughtiness would find itself frustrated for lack of an inferior *other*.

This dichotomy, in which *we* are better than *they*, allowed whites to justify their own dominance and the racial hierarchy of Jim Crow. Working from the

---

[d] Commenting on his own experience in the former Yugoslavia, theologian Miroslav Volf observes: "The 'will to purity' contains a whole program for arranging our social worlds—from the inner worlds of our selves to the outer worlds of our families, neighborhoods, and nations…" Miroslav Volf, *Exclusion and Embrace: A Theological Exploration of Identity, Otherness, and Reconciliation* (Nashville: Abingdon Press, 1996), 74.

haughty presumption of their own superiority, whites attributed "undesirable" black qualities to an innate inferiority, fearing that any amalgamation would result in what Jeremiah Jeter, editor of Virginia's *Religious Herald*, called "the *mongrelization* of our noble Anglo-Saxon race."[17]

Black men were believed to possess voracious sexual appetites and a penchant for chaste white women. Protecting the purity of the race, therefore, required a prophylactic social distance between the two. Not only was the thought of such sexual comingling inherently abhorrent, but the mulatto fruit of such liaisons, who represented the loss of racial purity, were considered a threat to the future of the white race.

That threat flowed from two fears that might seem mutually exclusive. On the one hand, the term *mulatto* derives from the Spanish and Portuguese *mulato*, a form of *mula* or *mule*.[e] Like mules, mulattos were widely thought to be either infertile or to have difficulty reproducing—at least among themselves. So, this racially impure stock might not have much of a future.

On the other hand, mulattos were considered a threat, because they might pass as whites, resulting in inadvertent racial amalgamation. Whites were so paranoid about this possibility that in some places they instituted the "one drop" rule—anyone who had any black genetic makeup whatsoever must therefore be considered black. In *Plessy v. Ferguson* the U.S. Supreme Court had adopted a sufficiently draconian 7/8 standard to distinguish between the two "separate but equal" races at the federal level. But during the early 20th century one-drop standards (or their de facto equivalents) became the rule across the Southern U.S. and sometimes in the North. It wasn't until the 1967 *Loving v. Virginia* decision that all such laws were declared unconstitutional.

There was, of course, more than a little bit of hypocrisy and willful ignorance involved in this pursuit of racial purity, because consensual sex between whites and blacks was not exactly rare, nor were mulattos. Albert Bushnell Hart,[f] an esteemed Harvard historian writing on the South in 1910, claimed that there were "two million deplorable reasons in the South for believing that there is no Divinely implanted race instinct against

---

[e] There is some debate about this etymology. The Arabic *muwallad* (person of mixed ancestry) has also been suggested. The *Real Academia Española* claims, however, that the Spanish usage is documented centuries earlier. See: www.websters-online-dictionary.org/definitions/mulatto.

[f] Hart himself is a curious case study in racial haughtiness. While he trained and promoted W.E.B. Dubois, served as a trustee of Howard University, and promoted black rights; he nevertheless believed that blacks were inferior.

miscegenation."[18] The 1910 U.S. Census confirms this elevated number, dividing "negroes" into two groups—black (7,777,077) and mulatto (2,050,686).[19] A popular folk saying in Louisiana's black community during the 1930s insisted that "you could feed all the pure whites in Louisiana with a nickel's worth of red beans and a dime's worth of rice."[20]

Racial purity should be regarded as a myth, not only because of its power as an organizing principle; its mythological character is also evident in its dependence on folk beliefs. In this case those folk beliefs have to do with the nature of race itself. Throughout this period, it was generally believed that the races were fixed biological families marked by a set of immutable traits that defined the members of each race. This physical identity, in turn, correlated with certain predictable personal, social, and psychological qualities.

Since the mapping of the human genome, we know far more about the relationship between "race" and genetics. We know that, while genetic variety exists and can even be mapped into general geographical pools, significant overlapping of traits occurs between these groups, so that "racial" distinctions are not accurate predictors of human capacity or behavior. We also know that such distinctions are not fixed or immutable; they are merely descriptive groupings of what *is*, rather than hard and fast categories of what *ought to be*.

The myth of racial purity, however, needed an *ought*. Anti-miscegenation sentiments sought that *ought* on two fronts—racial science (aka scientific racism) and conservative Christianity. Though the two eventually diverged, early attempts at racial theory were often considered a complement to the biblical account of creation. This pseudo-scientific, observational approach to natural history—largely a projection of white supremacist prejudices—produced extra-biblical taxonomies, typically based on continental divisions, that described the various races and their accompanying qualities.

The *ought* inherent in every iteration of scientific racism was that biological superiority justified domination by the superior group. According to Janet Brown, British historian of science, in the 19th century "...evolutionary views, and then the new science of genetics, gave powerful biological backing to partition society according to ethnic difference or promote white supremacy."[21] It was supposed that in the course of human development one group (inevitably Caucasian and most often Northern European) emerged as the most advanced,[g] and this advancement was

---

[g] The specific mechanisms for this superiority varied from the Lamarckian (linear) to the Darwinian (branched) models of evolution. For more

threatened by racial amalgamation. Racial science enjoyed strong popular and academic support in the U.S., until the horrors of Nazi Germany illustrated what such theories can lead to when taken to their extreme—not just the marginalization of "inferior" peoples, but their very destruction.

Secular supremacists and many theologically liberal Christians relied on racial science rather than Scripture to support their view of a segregated, racially pure society. Even some Bible-believing Christians were enchanted by one scientific approach or another, as these cloaked their prejudice in the garb of objectivity. Ultimately, however, what these whites really longed for was a Scriptural justification for their die-hard commitment to racial purity and the racial hierarchy. It seems, however, that they ran short of theological enthusiasm and exegetical ammunition. Eugene Genovese comments: "No postbellum defense of racial dictatorship and segregation compared in biblical scholarship and intellectual power to the defense of slavery."[22]

Rather than elaborating a thoroughgoing racial theology, they instead opted for a hunker-down conservatism. With Redemption complete and the societal cards once again stacked in their favor, white Christians sought refuge in the support of law and order and the social status quo. They just wanted to pursue a pietistic, personal faith, devoid of any prophetic boat-rocking.

To the extent that they did make any special appeal to the Bible, it centered on two principles—separation and Divinely-ordained station. It's true, of course, that both the Old and New Testaments emphasize the principle of separation. But Jim Crow Christians made some (theo)logical leaps in the way they applied the principle to racial segregation.

In the New Testament separation is unambiguously *moral* rather than ethnic or racial. In fact, the story of the Church, from the Great Commission onward, is a story of global inclusivity. The initial rift between Jews and Gentiles was a problem to be fixed rather than a good to be pursued.

The picture painted in the Old Testament, however, takes some sorting out, largely because the community of faith and the nation of Israel were so closely identified. Therefore, when God told his people to remain separate from the nations around them and, in particular, not to intermarry with them, at first reading it may not be clear what the basis for that separation really was. Supporters of white dominance and racial purity seized upon this superficial correlation to find support for segregation.

---

background, see: Edward Larson, *Evolution: The Remarkable History of a Scientific Theory* (New York: Modern Library, 2006).

To suppose that the ban on marriage between Israelites and non-Israelites was a matter of racial purity, however, represents a compound blunder. First, it superimposes a modern view of race onto a context where it doesn't fit at all, and, second, it ignores the stated purpose of the restriction. The prohibition against Jews marrying foreigners had nothing whatsoever to do with genetics or physical appearance. In fact, many of their forbidden neighbors were fellow Semites. The prohibition was all about the foreigners' devotion to other gods and the impact that idolatry would have on the nation of Israel.

Deuteronomy 7:3-4, speaking of the inhabitants of Canaan, says: "Do not intermarry with them. Do not give your daughters to their sons or take their daughters for your sons, *for they will turn your children away from following me to serve other gods*, and the LORD's anger will burn against you and will quickly destroy you." Separation was about avoiding idolatry, not about protecting racial purity. Foreigners (Ruth, Rahab, et. al.) who became part of the faith community of Israel, were not a threat, as demonstrated by the elite biblical genealogies in which they appear.

Supporters of racial purity appealed not only to separation texts but also to passages that affirmed God's sovereign dividing of peoples into nations according to his design. Deuteronomy 32:8 says: "When the Most High gave the nations their inheritance, when he divided all mankind, he set up boundaries for the peoples according to the number of the sons of Israel." In Paul's discourse on Mars Hill he referred to this same phenomenon, when he said, "From one man [KJV, *one blood*] he made all the nations, that they should inhabit the whole earth; and he marked out their appointed times in history and the boundaries of their lands." (Acts 17:26)[h]

Scripture clearly says that God established the location of the nations and determined the peoples who would populate them, but that simply shows his sovereignty over human affairs. It requires quite a leap of logic to then surmise that those boundaries were meant to be impermeable and eternal, much less that they somehow represent God's desire to ghettoize humanity according to color, which was clearly not the basis for the national distinctions.

---

[h] Both quotations involve textual issues. The Masoretic Text of Dt. 32:8 ends with "sons of God" instead of "sons of Israel," as per the Septuagint and the Dead Sea Scrolls. The exact interpretation is not without difficulties in either case, but it matters little for this discussion, because both options refer to a model of God's choosing that he followed in the establishment of nations. In the case of Acts 17:26 the Byzantine texts read "blood" instead of the older manuscripts' "men," but both refer to a single ancestral, genetic line.

Acts 17:26 was a singularly ironic proof text for Christian segregationists, because in it Paul was *refuting* Athenian pretensions of racial superiority. They claimed to be the only Greeks descended from truly indigenous stock, free from barbarian blood. New Testament scholar, F. F. Bruce, comments: "…But this pride was ill-founded. All mankind was one in origin—all created by God and all descended from a common ancestor. This removed all imagined justification for the belief that the Greeks were innately superior to the barbarians, as it removes all justification for comparable beliefs today."[23]

Segregationists needed God-ordained, immutable racial categories, but Scripture neither makes any such inference, nor is their existence historically/scientifically demonstrable. In fact, God himself was sovereignly re-arranging the international map on a constant basis. Throughout biblical times, people traveled and mixed and intermarried, and that circumstance has in no way disrupted God's design, except when it led to religious syncretism.

In spite of this dearth of Scriptural support, many white conservative Christians continued to believe that God himself had segregated the races—a view that was still popular when the *Dake Annotated Reference Bible* was first published in 1961. That first edition contained an extended note on Acts 17:26 entitled "30 Reasons for Segregation of Races."[i] Jim Crow Christians may not have been any more guilty of racial haughtiness than their secular counterparts, but the fact that they co-opted their own Sacred Text to justify their prejudice certainly aggravates that moral responsibility.

---

[i] Finis Dake died in 1987, but the family continues to market his study Bible. In response to complaints about the racist nature of this note and other references to divinely-ordained segregation, the family changed the wording from "segregation" to "separation." That did not fix the problem, however, and in 1997 they removed the offensive notes. The older versions are still in use, however, and the list of "30 Reasons" is still available on the web, posted by both supporters and detractors. For the family's explanation of their response to this issue, see: www.dake.com/dake/position.html.

Chapter 11

Vigilante Violence and the Reign of Terror

In 1939 Billie Holliday recorded a controversial, bluesy ballad entitled "Strange Fruit."[1][a] Though *Time* magazine proclaimed it "the song of the century" in 1999,[2] many white people are nevertheless unfamiliar with this classic protest song. Those who have heard its graphically poetic description of putrefying "fruit" (inspired by the 1930 lynching of two young African-American men in Marion, Indiana[3]) would have a hard time forgetting it—but perhaps an even harder time talking about it.

The past that we find most difficult to discuss in racially-mixed company is likely to contain the very pain that divides us. And among those taboo topics, no subject is more assiduously avoided than lynching. It's tempting to think that if we just leave the toxic waste of our racial history buried as deep as possible, we might thereby escape its effects. The reality is, however, that until it is unearthed and properly disposed of, this legacy will continue to leach hurt and shame and distrust, poisoning the groundwater of race relations.

If the sexual abuse of slaves was slavery at its worst, then lynching was surely Jim Crow at its worst. Lynching reveals the real harm in haughtiness, by taking it to its logical and moral extreme—sadism masquerading as justice. Lynching was not, however, the only form of violence that buttressed segregation. Let's consider this atrocity in the broader historical context of individual and mob violence that characterized this era.

Individual Vigilante Violence

Having lost the Civil War and with it their slave economy, Southern whites were determined not to lose their racial dominance as well. Two of their principle weapons in the struggle to hold on to supremacy were the legal system and the economy. Having re-taken all three branches of government during Redemption, they passed and enforced black codes designed to control

---

[a] For more background, see James Cone's thought-provoking lecture, "Strange Fruit: The Cross and the Lynching Tree," delivered at Harvard Divinity School on Oct. 19, 2006, www.hds.harvard.edu/multimedia/video/strange-fruit-the-cross-and-the-lynching-tree.

and marginalize the African-American population. In addition, whites continued to control the means of production, and with it black economic opportunity. Employment discrimination during Jim Crow was often quite overt, with white employers announcing that "Negroes need not apply."[4] When a black person did have a job, the threat of losing it was usually enough to enforce social subservience.

The white obsession with controlling the vast numbers of free blacks was, however, a perennially nervous one. Uneasy about the efficacy of their "legitimate" political and economic might, whites also relied on the coercive power of extralegal violence. It was nothing less than terrorism, the threat and use of vigilantism to guarantee conformity in a white-over-black society.

On the private front, this terrorism led to intimidation, attacks, and murders. In the public arena it took the form of race riots and lynching. Black people frequently disappeared or turned up dead for even minor violations of Jim Crow etiquette. According to bluesman Poppa Jazz: "They had to have a license to kill everything but a nigger. We was always in season."[5]

Of course, the vast majority of white people were never actively involved in murder, but as historian Steve Martinot explains: "Enforcement of this [Jim Crow] system was expected of the entire white population, which was granted impunity, both legally and personally."[6] Despite the widespread use of lethal vigilante violence, between Reconstruction and 1966 only one white Southerner was ever convicted of the first-degree murder of a black person, and that was mass murderer John Williams (1921).[7]

As late as 1955, vigilante violence was still a way of life in some areas. That summer a fourteen-year-old from Chicago named Emmet Till was visiting relatives in Mississippi. One day, while hanging out with some friends at a local grocery, he allegedly whistled at a white woman who worked there. Four days later his badly beaten body surfaced in the Tallahatchie River, a 75-pound cotton gin fan lashed to his neck with barbed wire.

The woman's husband, Roy Bryant, and his half-brother, J. W. Milam, were tried for the murder. In his closing remarks, defense attorney John Whitten rallied the all-white jury: "[I am sure] that every last Anglo-Saxon one of you men on this jury has the courage to set these men free."[8] After barely of an hour of deliberation they did exactly that. One juror quipped, "If we hadn't stopped to drink pop, it wouldn't have taken that long."[9]

A few months later, journalist William Bradford Huie interviewed defendant J. W. Milam for *Look* magazine. Milam admitted to the killing but insisted that they had only intended to scare the young man, blaming the eventual outcome on Till's recalcitrance and claiming, "I'm no bully...I never hurt a nigger in my life. I like niggers—in their place... But I just decided it was time some people got put on notice...."[10]

The Till case was unusual in that the killers were even brought to trial. Local law enforcement could usually be counted on to turn a blind eye to such vigilante justice, as it made their job of maintaining the social order just that much easier. And the police didn't just wink at racial wrongdoing; they were some of its primary perpetrators.

Race Riots

In addition to the unquantifiable but ever-present threat of personal vigilantism, the Jim Crow era saw a great deal of mob violence against African Americans. This took two primary forms—race riots and lynching. While lynching was an overwhelmingly Southern phenomenon, race riots tended to occur more often in Northern, urban settings.

Southern blacks, lacking upwardly mobile employment opportunities and basic civil rights, embarked on an epic migration from the rural South to the urban North. In a single decade, from 1910 to 1920, more than a half million African Americans fled the South, settling in Northern industrial centers.[11] In a two-year span between 1916 and 1918 Chicago's African American population doubled from 50,000 to 100,000.[12]

Northern whites did not exactly welcome this influx with open arms— especially the working class, for whom black labor amounted to economic competition. Indeed, black hires were often regarded as strike breakers.

That very scenario provoked the East St. Louis race riot of 1917. Aluminum Ore, the largest processor of bauxite in the world, paid attractive wages to black workers, in part to undermine the (white) union. At one point during 1916-1917 more than a thousand black people per month were moving to East St. Louis. Tensions began to rise, based on rumors that blacks were planning a race war and constituted a threat to white women.

After a packed-out, incendiary meeting between union forces and city officials, in which cries of "East St. Louis must remain a white man's town" were heard, mobs began to form. Groups of whites began indiscriminately attacking blacks in the downtown area. The police did little more than transport the wounded to the hospital and disarm the black population. Estimates indicate that 40-200 blacks died in the fracas, along with at least 8 whites. As a result, thousands of African-American families fled the city.

In more recent times the term "race riot" has been associated with black uprisings, but during Jim Crow these events were perpetrated by white mobs. Often ignited by rumors and abetted by police action, race riots wreaked tremendous havoc on African Americans and their communities. And this was no passing fad; the first of the seven largest race riots occurred in Wilmington, North Carolina in 1898, and the last took place in Detroit, Michigan in 1943.

This trend reached its apex during the "Red Summer" of 1919, when some 25 race riots took place from rural Arkansas and small-town Texas to major cities like Charleston, Knoxville, Tulsa, Washington, and Omaha. Chicago, however, suffered the worst violence of that fateful summer—38 deaths (15 whites and 23 blacks), 520 injuries (178 whites and 342 blacks), and more than 1,000 black homes destroyed.

The race riot phenomenon demonstrates that neither white haughtiness nor anti-black animus were limited to the South. The use of extra-legal actions to protect one's way of life was not the exclusive province of a few pointy-hooded radicals. In fact, the threat of vigilante violence at the hands of average citizens seemed to follow the black population wherever it went.

Lynching

As disturbing as we might find the aforementioned forms of reactionary vigilantism, they pale in comparison to the sheer barbarity of lynching. Its painful memory continues to cast a long shadow of doubt over any and all assumptions about moral progress, for there is no starting point from which lynching constitutes a step in the right direction.

Lynching takes its name from Charles Lynch, a Virginia planter and Justice of the Peace. During the Revolutionary War, Lynch presided over extralegal courts designed to punish British loyalists. What came to be known as "lynching" was, at the time, mostly non-lethal corporal punishments like whipping and tarring and feathering.[13] In the antebellum period the vast majority of those lynched were white, since slaves were considered property and could not be taken from their masters without due process. After Reconstruction, however, lynching became an extra-legal form of execution, a means of social control aimed primarily at African Americans (though many whites were also lynched, often for sympathizing with blacks).

In large lynching events a mob of bloodthirsty avengers was joined by a host of curious onlookers, sometimes numbering in the thousands. Though lynching usually involved hanging, this was not always the case. Some victims were shot or burned at the stake (sometimes in addition to being strung up), and these killings were often accompanied by beatings, torture, and mutilations. Lynchings took place in every part of the country, though the vast majority were concentrated in the Southern and border states.

In popular parlance the term itself was used with some flexibility, but the Tuskegee Institute, the principle compiler of statistics on lynching, developed a consistent working definition based on four criteria: "(1) There must be legal evidence that a person was killed; (2) The person must have met death illegally; (3) A group must have participated in the killing; (4) The group must have acted under pretext of service to justice, race, or tradition."[14/b]

Lynchings usually involved a single victim or a small number of targets. Most often the victims were hunted down by a lynching party, though it was not uncommon for them to be taken from police custody, often with official collusion and rarely with any significant resistance. Elected officials regularly turned a blind eye to lynching, and some went so far as to brazenly associate themselves with it. One Mississippi candidate for sheriff remarked that he expected to pick up votes for just being a suspect in a lynching.[15]

How many people have been lynched in the United States? Available figures represent only a fraction of the actual number, because statistics had to be culled from thousands of local newspapers, which were far too numerous for any research team to monitor.[c] Even those partial numbers, however, are shocking—4,473 people from 1882-1968 (1,297 whites and 3,446 blacks.)[16/d]

That amounts to nearly one (reported) lynching every week for eighty-two years. These incidents, however, were not evenly distributed throughout the Jim Crow era. Nearly 3,000 occurred in the first twenty years for which statistics have been tabulated, 1882-1901.[17] The peak year was 1892, when 230 lynchings occurred. This early frequency created a legacy of terror to which later and less frequent acts of vigilante violence served as a sufficient reminder.

---

[b] Excludes victims of individual vigilante violence. Includes lynchings that occurred during race riots, but not indiscriminate victims of mob violence.

[c] By 1880, there were 11,314 different newspapers and periodicals in America—17,616 by 1890. See: Robert Percival Porter, Carroll Davidson Wright, United States Census Office. 11th Census; *Census Reports: Eleventh Census: 1890, Volume 6, Part 3* (Washington: Govt. Printing Office, 1892-97), 649.

[d] For more background on the sources for lynching statistics, see: www.scottgarber.com/was_notes.pdf, Note 11.1.

In an 1892 report, published in Philadelphia's Christian Recorder, Rev. E. Malcolm Argyle captures the capacity of lynching to terrorize the black population of Arkansas:

> There is much uneasiness and unrest all over this State among our people, owing to the fact that the people (our race variety) all over the State are being lynched upon the slightest provocation... In the last 30 days there have been not less than eight colored persons lynched in this State.... Verily the situation is alarming in the extreme. At this writing 500 people are hovering, upon wharves in Pine Bluff, awaiting the steamers to take them up the Arkansas River to Oklahoma.

> ...It is evident that the white people of the South have no further use for the Negro.... The white press of the South seems to be subsidized by this lawless element, the white pulpits seem to condone lynching. The colored press in the South are dared to take an aggressive stand against lynch law. The Northern press seems to care little about the condition of the Negroes South. The pulpits of the North are passive. Will not some who are not in danger of their lives, speak out...? For God's sake, say or do something, for our condition is precarious in the extreme.[18]

The way in which lynchings were publicized served to exacerbate their grisly effect. These were often very public spectacles, preceded by published announcements. Newspaper accounts then carried the reports to a broader audience, and gruesome photographs of the victims were widely circulated. Richard Lacayo, writing in *Time* magazine, noted that "even the Nazis did not stoop to selling souvenirs of Auschwitz, but lynching scenes became a burgeoning subdepartment of the postcard industry."[19] The Postmaster General finally banned violent images on postcards in 1908, but postcards depicting lynchings continued to be produced and circulated by other means.

One of the more revolting "spectacle lynchings," an event that was circulated far and wide through film and print, took place in Waco, Texas in 1916.[20] Waco was at the time a growing city of more than 30,000 that touted its own progressiveness. It boasted sixty-three churches and was home to the Baptist-affiliated Baylor University, as well as two black colleges.

In May of that year a seventeen-year-old black farmhand named Jesse Washington was arrested for the rape and murder of his employer's wife. The young man, who was illiterate and deemed "feeble-minded," signed a confession that he could not have written or even read. Whether he signed it because he was actually guilty and/or because doing so was supposed to keep him from being lynched, no one knows.

The trial was over in an hour, and the jury deliberation took a mere four minutes. Immediately afterward a mob, which eventually swelled to an estimated ten thousand, put a chain around his neck and dragged him into the town square. The police not only offered no resistance—the mayor and chief of police watched from a nearby window as the crowd stripped the young man, beat him with a variety of objects, castrated him, doused him with oil, and repeatedly lowered him into a bonfire. When he tried to climb the chain to escape the flames, they cut off his fingers. Once Jesse Washington had burned to death, the crowd dragged his charred remains through the city streets. His teeth and other body parts were taken and/or sold as souvenirs.

A macabre postcard commemorates the event, depicting a partially dismembered and blackened figure hanging in the foreground, surrounded by onlookers. A young white man appears at the left of the postcard, which he sent to his parents with the inscription, "This is the barbecue we had last night. Your son, Joe."[21]

Mob executions were not unknown in other countries, but lynching, as we know it, seems to be a rather original American contribution to the history of infamy. As political economist James Cutler wrote in 1905: "The practice whereby mobs capture individuals suspected of a crime, or take them from officers of the law, and execute them without any process at law, or break open jails and hang convicted criminals, with impunity, is to be found in no other country of a high degree of civilization."[22]

Speaking of civilization, where were America's white Christians during lynching's heyday? Their rare opposition and all-too-frequent involvement prompted theologian Reinhold Niebuhr in 1923 to say, "If there were a drunken orgy somewhere, I would bet ten to one a church member was not in it…. But if there were a lynching I would bet ten to one a church member was in it."[23]

Few clergymen openly supported lynching, but they seldom interfered with it. The fact is that dissenters risked becoming the focus of mob violence themselves.[e] Some did dare to offer general denunciations of the practice or

---

[e] After the grisly lynching of Sam Hose in 1899, Baptist pastor Len Broughton of Atlanta suggested that blacks should be relocated to the tropics rather than lynched. For even that mild challenge to populism his church was vandalized, and he received one of Hose's charred finger bones in the mail. See, Kathleen

after-the-fact criticisms, but far and away the most common response was a pregnant silence. Preachers preferred to focus on matters of personal piety, social concerns like temperance, and foreign missions.[f]

Toward the end of the 19th century, whites were consumed by a passion for national unity and reconciliation. Therefore, any effort to protect black rights that might pit whites against whites was regarded as divisive. Henry Ward Beecher, a Congregationalist minister and renowned abolitionist leader before the war, typified this willingness to sacrifice black welfare on the altar of white solidarity, saying: "You must not be disappointed or startled because you see in the newspapers accounts of shocking barbarities committed upon these people [the freedmen]."[24] He urged his fellow Northerners to have "patience with Southern men as they are, and patience with Southern opinions as they have been, until the great normal, industrial, and moral laws shall work such gradual changes as shall enable them to pass from the old to the new."[25]

Other well-known Christian figures—in an apparent effort to keep their base of ministry as broad as possible—made pragmatic choices about which fights to pick. The most influential evangelist of the early Jim Crow period, Dwight L. Moody, had a policy of conducting integrated evangelistic meetings in the North. When he went to Augusta, Georgia, however, "the white leaders let Moody know in unguarded language that if he had come to Georgia to bring social revolution rather than the gospel he should go home."[26] A conflicted Moody eventually gave in to the pressure, setting a pattern that remained unchanged in Southern evangelism campaigns until Billy Graham began to integrate his meetings in the 1950s.

One of Moody's contemporaries, a Southern evangelist by the name of Sam Jones (1847-1906), outlived Moody and for a time "assumed the mantel of America's premier popular preacher."[27] Moody, who often spoke against other social ills, was practically silent on the subject of lynching.[g] Jones, on

---

Minnix, *Laughter in the Amen Corner: The Life of Evangelist Sam Jones* (Athens: University of Georgia Press, 2010), 201.

[f] For more background on the relationship between white churches and lynching, see: www.scottgarber.com/was_notes.pdf, Note 11.2.

[g] Moody was roundly criticized for his silence by Ida B. Wells. See: Ida B. Wells-Barnett, *The Red Record: Tabulated Statistics and Alleged Causes of Lynching in the United States* (Project Gutenberg Ebook, 2005, reprinted from the original pamphlet published in 1895). I was able to find only one rather bland statement made by Moody on the subject (in East Northfield, Massachusetts, 1899): "Lynching is unknown in the old country [England],

the other hand, criticized mob violence[28] but laid the ultimate responsibility at the feet of black people.[29] In Jones' opinion a lynching, when necessary, should be a "decent affair,"[30] although he conceded that certain particularly heinous crimes might warrant a more gruesome response.[31]

The lack of prophetic outcry from white America's pews and pulpits was initially seconded by the silence of the meta-ecclesiastical church bodies. As time went on, however, and gruesome spectacle lynchings became widely publicized, national leaders felt compelled to say something. By the 1920s and 1930s the Federal Council of Churches (forerunner of the National Council of Churches) and virtually every Christian denomination had taken formal stands against lynching. By 1934, even the state conferences of the *Methodist Episcopal Church, South* in Georgia, North Carolina, Virginia, Florida, and North Alabama had adopted resolutions against lynching.[32]

While these denunciations were a welcome and altogether appropriate response, they came too late in the game to be of much practical value. In 1920, when this institutional anti-lynching movement first began to gather steam, 89% of all lynchings had already taken place, and the practice was in decline. By the 1934 resolutions, 97% of this activity was over and done. There was also a significant disconnect between the denunciations offered at the denominational level, where it had little effect on local lynching activity, and the near silence of churches and church affiliations in the affected areas.[33]

Some church bodies did support a more substantive Congressional measure, the Dyer Anti-Lynching Bill of 1922. Unfortunately, however, that bill never became law. It would have "provided fines and imprisonment for persons convicted of lynching in federal courts, and fines and penalties against states, counties, and towns which failed to use reasonable efforts to protect citizens from mob violence."[34] That legislation, sponsored by the NAACP and supported by the Federal Council of Churches, passed the House, but Southern legislators killed it in the Senate by means of a filibuster.

While many opposed the Dyer bill as unconstitutional, because it overturned states' rights in favor of federal imposition, some Congressmen dared to reveal their true agenda. Their rallying cry was the protection of white women against the supposedly unfettered lust of black rapists (which in their view might be any black male with opportunity). It is a chilling example of racial haughtiness exacerbated by ignorance.

Rep. William Driver of Arkansas made his case on the House floor:

and we are having lynchings by the scores and hundreds." See: *Moody's Latest Sermons*, (Chicago: Bible Institute Colportage Association, 1900), 117.

We must remember that we are the product of a civilization of thousands of years, while the Negro is comparatively a child in moral training. He is an emotional being without our mental processes and control of passion, and therefore with but little moral restraint. He is a slave to his appetite and will respond to a mere suggestion without thought of consequences.... with his distorted and immoral conception, the probabilities are only too great that he will feel himself licensed to yield to his unbridled passion.... [But let it be clear that] when a brute, black or white, places his lecherous hand upon our women, he commits suicide.[35]

As Rep. Thomas Sisson of Mississippi explains his position, one is forced to question the sincerity of his opening statement:

No good man in the South believes in lynching as a method of enforcing law. But as long as rape continues lynching will continue. For this crime, and this crime alone, the South has not hesitated to administer swift and certain punishment... We are going to protect our girls and womenfolk from these black brutes. When these black fiends keep their hands off the throats of the women of the South then lynching will stop, and it is never going to stop until that crime stops. [Applause]

...Even if you do pass this law I say that your law will fail. You shall not successfully promote, encourage, foster, and protect the rapist by this law.... I would rather the whole black race of this world were lynched than for one of the fair daughters of the South to be ravished and torn by one of these black brutes. Now, if this be treason, make the most of it. [Applause]."[36]

The image of the black brute plays a prominent role in these pronouncements, as it did in Jim Crow mythology in general. The docile, childlike representations of blacks that were common during slavery took a sinister turn after Reconstruction, turning the black man into the boogey man. Depictions of black males as depraved and violent served as a justification for the brutality of lynching.

This monstrous image was popularized in books such as Charles Carroll's *The Negro a Beast* (1900) and *The Tempter of Eve* (1902), which argued that blacks were the descendants of a pre-Adamite line and that the serpent in the Garden of Eden was a black man. During that same decade a Baptist minister by the name of Thomas Dixon wrote a series of three novels in which the Ku Klux Klan saved noble whites from the black scourge. In the first volume, *The*

Leopard's Spots, dispirited Confederate soldiers return home to face a new enemy: "In every one of these soldiers' hearts, and over all the earth, hung the shadow of the freed Negro, transformed by the exigency of war from a Chattel, to be bought and sold, into a possible Beast to be feared and guarded. Around this dusky figure every white man's soul was keeping its grim vigil."[37]

Dixon's second installment, *The Clansman*, featured a black protagonist who rapes a white woman and is subsequently lynched by a heroic KKK. This 1905 novel sold more than *one million* copies. Ten years later, D. W. Griffith made it into a movie, *The Birth of a Nation*. The first film ever screened at the White House,[h] it went on to become the top-grossing silent film of all time,[38] etching the image of the black brute into the minds of millions of Americans and resurrecting the Klan as a protagonist on the stage of vigilante violence.[i]

Black-on-white rape was not unheard of, but most such charges were nothing more than false accusations designed to increase the likelihood of lynching. Many of the sexual liaisons that did occur were consensual, but a rape charge protected the white woman's reputation if pregnancy ensued or if the relationship came to light.

Though rape was often cited as the main reason for lynching, available statistics do not support that claim. The plurality of accusations (41%) lodged against lynching victims (1882-1951) were for murder. Only 19% were even *accused* of rape; 6% percent were lynched for attempted rape, 5% for robbery and theft, 4% for felonious assault, and 2% for insult to white persons. 23% were executed for other causes, including offenses as trivial as arguing with a white person, attempting to register to vote, defending oneself, testifying against a white man, proposing to a white woman, and peeping in a window.[39/j]

Only *first-degree* murder could be counted upon to produce a death sentence in the courts, and those constituted only a portion of the total homicide figures. Even a rape charge did not guarantee a death sentence in court. A study of 288 black men tried for rape in Virginia between 1900 and 1961, showed that 87 per cent (230) ended up being convicted of some (often lesser) crime, but only 22 per cent of those were executed. Only 21 per cent

---

[h] Dixon and Woodrow Wilson were friends from their days at Johns Hopkins. It was widely reported that Wilson approved of the film and found it realistic, but that account has been challenged by others close to the former president.
[i] For more background on the various iterations and impact of the Ku Klux Klan, see: www.scottgarber.com/was_notes.pdf, Note 11.3.
[j] For more information on black-on-white crime during Jim Crow, see www.scottgarber.com/was_notes.pdf, Note 11.4.

even received the maximum sentence for their respective offense, and some of those were later pardoned by governors.

It's clear, then, that even biased, all-white juries were more dispassionate in their consideration of black crime than impassioned lynch mobs, which were constituted for only one purpose. Those seeking certain vengeance did not trust the legal system to produce the desired result or to send a sufficiently blunt message. As a result, mobs often kidnapped their lynching victims from police custody, even after they had been convicted in a court of law.

Lynching's Legacy

It would be morally convenient to regard lynching as a historical anomaly, one somehow unrelated to the national character. But when we're talking about a public atrocity that was perpetrated with virtual impunity for the better part of a century, its significance cannot be so easily dismissed. Lynching is nothing less than the logical and moral extreme of racial haughtiness.

Whatever the phenomenon of lynching says about the national character of that time, perhaps the more pressing question has to do with its implications for today. Thankfully, we no longer live in the era of lynching, but to what extent does the era of lynching still live in us? It can't be easy to undo the damage to black male identity or to untwist a twisted white identity. Nor can we un-reveal what lynching revealed about the depth of our racial divide.

Let's think about these legacy items one at a time. Though lynch mobs certainly did not spare black women, the fact remains that 95% of the black people who were lynched during Jim Crow were men.[40] This should come as no surprise, since the myth of the black brute was the primary justification for this extra-legal practice. However, this myth had far less to do with the honor of white women than with the honor of white men. The black sexual conquest of white women, whether forced or consensual, real or imagined, constituted a threat to white male dominance, to white male identity, and to the paradigm of white racial superiority.

It is no accident, therefore, that castration was a common feature in lynchings.[k] This was not about limiting the accused's capacity for sexual violence; he was going to die anyway. Rather, the act of emasculation and the

---

[k] Amy L. Wood estimates that one third of those lynched were emasculated. See: *Lynching and Spectacle: Witnessing Racial Violence in America*, 1890-1940, (Chapel Hill: University of North Carolina Press, 2009), 98.

severed genitalia—sometimes distributed as souvenirs—became chest-thumping tokens of white male dominance.

The physical mutilations associated with lynching symbolize one of the sad legacies of Jim Crow, the psychic emasculation of the black male. That assault on black manhood was a carry-over from slavery, when black men were forced to stand by while their families were disbanded and their wives were assaulted, powerless before the "real" man of the house.

Jim Crow brought greater independence but not greater esteem for the black man. Having lost his primary source of social value as unpaid labor, he became little more than unwanted competition. The racial etiquette of that era, both explicit and implicit, still required him to treat whites with great deference. Black men were feared as predators, despised as a retrograde form of humanity, denied equal standing by an apartheid society, and dogged by the constant threat of vigilante violence for any reason or none at all. As a result, many had no choice but to tiptoe through life.

Without over-analyzing the black male psyche, it's worth noting that centuries of assault on one's value and personhood—to say nothing of the emotional exclamation point of lynching—cannot be easily erased. This internal code cannot be re-written by enacting civil rights legislation or even by electing a black president. As long as black men are viewed with suspicion, marginalized as "others," and despised as lesser—the legacy of lynching lives on.

The Jim Crow reality also teaches us something important about the nature of white identity. It shows us that haughtiness, as a feature of that identity, transcends slavery. Even with slavery dismantled and more or less discredited, whites hastened to re-create a new hierarchy that enforced their haughty notions of racial superiority/inferiority. What we are dealing with, then, is a sin that cannot be vanquished by simply changing social institutions. Haughtiness just finds a new mask behind which to manifest itself.

Certainly, there were practical benefits, like money and power, that whites continued to enjoy by virtue of their continued control of the racial hierarchy. Segregation, however, provided not only a practical but also a psychological benefit. Jim Crow was more than the product of a rational calculus designed to protect or enhance white dominance; it was the projection of an intuitive sense of racial identity. There is no other way to understand the breadth and the depth of both the implicit and explicit messaging of Jim Crow. At some fundamental level, segregation simply felt right to whites, because it corresponded to and reinforced their haughty self-image.

In this transition from slavery to Jim Crow we see the depth of America's racial divide. That divide that was not healed by abolishing slavery. Neither was that divide healed by eliminating Jim Crow nor by civil rights nor by affirmative action nor by incremental improvements in black wellbeing. That's because the social conditions that continue to remind us of this divide are not its ultimate cause, just its incidental manifestation.

I don't mean to say that these milestones were not important. They were. Moreover, each new milestone of racial justice creates a space, a window of opportunity in which the fundamental issue itself *could* be addressed. To date, however, we have not taken advantage of that opportunity on any significant scale. And to whatever degree whiteness continues to be characterized by haughtiness, our racial divide will remain.

Chapter 12

The Church and Jim Crow

The enduring reality of Jim Crow not only institutionalized the racial divide in American society; it had a similar effect on the American Church. As early as 1880, the separation of white and black churches was largely a fait accompli, and, as the two separate bodies continued to grow, they were, by the very nature of the case, growing apart. In order to understand this new, segregated dynamic and its implications, this chapter examines that racially-defined ecclesiastical landscape one color at a time.

Black Churches

During Jim Crow, the Church continued to be the only social institution in which African Americans enjoyed self-determination, and black churches experienced dramatic growth. In just sixteen years, between 1890-1906, their membership increased from 2.6 million to 3.6 million. Baptists alone accounted for 70% of that growth, with the National Baptist Convention claiming over two million adherents in the 1906 religious census.[1/a]

As black churches grew numerically, they also expanded their institutional footprint. The church became a primary community outlet and a source of social services—helping their members to find jobs and learn new skills as well as ministering to the sick, the elderly, and the destitute. At the denominational level, they also built their own institutions of higher learning and began preparing future generations of leaders.

Segregated black society mirrored its white counterpart, and, in more populous areas, that included a partially parallel economy. African Americans started their own insurance companies, savings and loan associations, barber/beauty shops, funeral parlors, etc.—and that eventually helped to create a black "middle class." Local pastors played the role of gatekeepers for connections and opportunities, and thus became influential power brokers.

---

[a] These numbers (in both 1890 and 1906) were self-reported and may be somewhat exaggerated, but the rates of growth were nevertheless significant.

In the North, black preachers often interlaced the theme of racial justice with their old-time religion, but Southern black preachers, living under the threat of vigilante violence, focused almost exclusively on the latter. There were a few exceptions, like AME Bishop Henry McNeal Turner, who was also President of Atlanta's Morris Brown College. An advocate of black separatism, Turner famously announced: "We have every right to believe that God is a Negro."[2] Such boldness was, however, rare and usually short-lived.

Initially, there was hesitance in some quarters about formal ecclesiastical separation from whites, a hesitance motivated in part by theological concerns but perhaps even more by the possible loss of economic assistance. By 1906, however, no more than five percent of all black church members found themselves in white-controlled denominations, and even many of those were ensconced in all-black congregations. Black congregational life was both a fresh breeze of spiritual autonomy as well as a welcome respite from the second-class status African Americans endured in the broader society.

This institutionalized separation between black and white churches has now lasted more than a century, complicating contemporary attempts at reunification. Over time institutions take on a life of their own, exhibiting an instinct for self-preservation. Not only that, but by the end of Jim Crow, distinct worship traditions had become an ingrained feature of racial identity itself. As a result, any future ecclesiastical rapprochement would require everyone to give up something of themselves.

White Churches

Protestants

The African-American struggle to create a parallel existence in the shadows of segregation was their defining reality, and their churches were at the forefront of that struggle. For white Protestants, however, once their black counterparts were out of sight, they were largely out of mind.

In any case, many Protestants were more worried about the "Catholic problem" than the "Negro problem." African Americans were a known and controlled element, but the Catholic population was expanding rapidly. Catholics became a prime target of the early 20th century incarnation of the Ku Klux Klan and were regarded as a threat to Americanism, the Protestant faith, and Anglo-Saxon racial purity. White Protestants were also preoccupied with scientific secularism and the theological divide between fundamentalists and modernists. Moreover, they were busy eradicating social ills at home and playing the role of God's chosen nation on the world stage.

Many conservative Christians, in the mold of D. L. Moody and Billy Sunday, believed that an increase in conversions would naturally promote a more positive public morality. Therefore, they insisted that evangelism and personal piety, not social reform, remain the focus of their faith. This slice of Protestantism did not share the progressives' confidence in government intervention or their postmillennial optimism. As the 20th century wore on, more and more conservative evangelicals turned to dispensational premillennialism, an eschatological perspective that reinforced their mentality of non-engagement.

Located on the opposite end of the theological spectrum were the proponents of the Social Gospel. They dominated the Federal Council of Churches, and their ideological leader, Walter Rauschenbusch, was the most iconic theologian of the Social Gospel movement. Rauschenbusch held to a Christianized version of the inevitability of progress, i.e., that the continued influence of the Kingdom of God would ineluctably redeem society.

Though divided by their theological opposition, most liberal and conservative Christians nevertheless agreed on a couple of key points relative to race. First, whether owing to divine fiat or the vagaries of human evolution, whites were superior to blacks. And, second, even if Jim Crow was a less than ideal social arrangement, its reform was not an urgent matter.

Throughout this period fundamentalists remained myopically focused on their own agenda and unconcerned about America's ecclesiastical apartheid. But even the Federal Council of Churches did not engage with the issue until the Second World War.[3] It wasn't until 1946 that they finally renounced "the pattern of segregation in race relations as unnecessary and undesirable and a violation of the gospel of love and human brotherhood."[4] Furthermore, they pledged to "work for a non-segregated church and a non-segregated society."[5]

This statement was indeed historic, but its aspirations should not be exaggerated. "Non-segregated" really meant "not forcibly separated" rather than "truly integrated," a condition hardly anyone was anxious to achieve. As Methodist historian Peter Murray points out, in the same FCC meeting that adopted this resolution "there was an attempt to keep African American vice president of the FCC Dr. Benjamin E. Mayes [sic] off the rostrum when President Harry Truman addressed the council."[6]

Earlier in the Jim Crow period, during the Progressive Era,[b] evangelicals had pursued a robust social agenda—fighting social ills like alcoholism, urban blight, child labor issues, and the abuses of unfettered capitalism. Eschewing a reductionist theology, their vision of the Good News combined personal transformation with a pro-active approach to social betterment.

In spite of that robust social awareness, however, neither racial justice writ large nor even segregation in the Church figured in their list of wrongs to be righted. As Historian Barry Hankins of Baylor University has observed, in the aftermath of the Civil War, "race would not be a central concern for the most influential political or religious leaders again until the Civil Rights era. Not a single, prominent white political reformer of the Progressive Era... made racial injustice a consistent theme."[7]

The progressive movement's brightest political light was William Jennings Bryan,[c] a theological fundamentalist who has nevertheless been characterized as the "most left-leaning candidate ever to receive a major party nomination for the US presidency."[8] But, in spite of his progressive posture on a wide variety of issues, Bryan had precious little to say about segregation, as he could not afford to alienate Southern Democrats.

One progressive evangelical leader who did speak out about race would have served the cause far better by saying nothing at all. Josiah Strong, one of the founders of the Social Gospel movement, and its leading evangelical proponent, served as General Secretary of the Evangelical Alliance from 1886-1898, a position he acquired after the publication of his most famous book, *Our Country: Its Possible Future and Its Present Crisis*. Had he not been so influential, he might now be easily dismissed as a crackpot.

Not content with mere *white* supremacy, *Our Country* is nothing less than a manifesto of *Anglo-Saxon* supremacy, which Strong insisted has found its most exalted manifestation in the United States of America. Strong was convinced that this slice of white America was God's chosen instrument to determine the future of humankind and was "destined to dispossess many weaker races, assimilate others, and mold the remainder, until, in a very true and important sense it has Anglo-Saxonized mankind."[9] He even went so far

---

[b] The Progressive Era, which variously dates from the mid-1890s to the 1920s, was characterized by a strong belief that moral crusading, the rise of science, and the power of government could cure societal ills, many of which were linked to rapid urbanization and industrialization.
[c] Bryan was nominated by the Democratic Party in 1896, 1900, and 1908 but lost all three elections.

as to proclaim that, like it or not, "the extinction of inferior races before the advancing Anglo-Saxon… certainly appears probable."[10]

The Progressive Era featured a heady mix of romantic nationalism, global imperialism, and missionary zeal. Senator Albert J. Beveridge invoked that very spirit, as he urged his colleagues to annex the Philippines:

> This question is deeper than any question of party politics; deeper than any question of the isolated policy of our country; deeper than any question of constitutional power. It is elemental. It is racial. God has not been preparing the English-speaking and Teutonic peoples for a thousand years for nothing but vain and idle self-contemplation and self-admiration. No! He has made us the master organizers of the world to establish order where chaos reigns. He has given us the spirit of progress to overwhelm the forces of reaction throughout the earth. He has made us adepts in government that we may administer government among savage and senile peoples…. And of all our race He has marked the American people as His chosen nation finally to lead in the regeneration of the world. This is the divine mission of America, and it holds for us all profit, glory, happiness possible to man. We are trustees of the world's progress, guardians of its righteous peace.[11]

The final third of the nineteenth century ushered in an age of American exceptionalism, a "divinely-sanctioned" haughtiness unseen since the era of Isaac Watts. Granted, this rah-rah protagonism may have been more about money and power than about global redemption, but the religious and secular motivations eventually became so enmeshed as to be indistinguishable. Such an epic sense of calling was necessary to overcome the long-standing American tendency toward isolationism and get a previously self-conscious country to assume the role of superhero on the world stage.

Amidst this focus on a grandiose mission, the situation of blacks within America was largely ignored, and conveniently so, as it called into question the vaunted capacity of white Americans to solve everyone else's problems. Those who did think that something ought to be done about segregation simply subsumed African-American progress within the scope of America's larger manifest destiny. There would be eventual progress for black people (within the scope of their capacities, of course) as WASP-ish America exported Christianized civilization to a waiting world, at which point a rising religio-cultural tide would lift all boats.

Catholics

The relationship between the Catholic Church and black Americans during Jim Crow was, let's say, complicated. On the one hand, the Vatican seems to have been genuinely interested in outreach to the black community and in maintaining some level of equality in the mass. In practice, however, our society's original sin affected white Catholics and Protestants alike, so that in spite of official pronouncements, significant segregation occurred in both Catholic church life as well as in its parochial schools.

When black people migrated north in search of jobs, they became competition for immigrant Catholics, and there was often open hostility between the two factions. The Catholic Church suffered from its immigrant association in the eyes of African Americans, who saw the Church bending over backward to provide for the needs of these incoming white Europeans, while doing little to ameliorate black suffering.

Concerned about how to minister to black Americans, in 1912 the Vatican dispatched Archbishop Giovanni Bonzano to examine the situation and propose solutions. He basically ignored the input of American priests familiar with the realities of black Catholics and resisted their calls for training black priests. It seems he was troubled by black moral proclivities and insisted that they preferred white priests, because blacks believed them to be superior.

Fearing that Bonzano's tactless approach would raise eyebrows in Rome, American Cardinal Gibbons filed a more diplomatic report. He stressed the Church's recent positive efforts on behalf of black people and pronounced himself deeply committed to black souls and in favor of a black clergy. Nevertheless, citing the delicate nature of the American situation, he went on to excuse himself from doing anything about the black situation other than to wish that he could. It seems that his report did accomplish one thing—it managed to placate Rome for some time.[12]

During Jim Crow, black Catholics often enjoyed a greater level of spiritual equality than their Protestant counterparts in white-controlled congregations. Such a comparison becomes less meaningful, however, when you consider that by 1890, most black Protestants had already fled the white Church. Historian David Southern observed that, even among Catholics, over time "Jim Crow parishes replaced Jim Crow pews in white-dominated churches."[13/d]

---

[d] Southern maintains that this strategy paralleled the creation of "racial parishes" for various European nationalities, a practice the Second Plenary

What black Catholics really lacked was their own leadership. Forrest Wood notes that "only two black Americans were ordained as Catholic priests in the nineteenth century, and as late as 1930 there were only three working in the American church."[14] For its part, the Vatican challenged the U.S. Church to develop black clergy and founded a seminary in Bay St. Louis, Mississippi[15/e] dedicated to that end. By 1945, the number of black priests in the U.S. had risen to twenty-one. While this was a significant increase, by that time there were almost three million black Catholics in the U.S.

W.E.B. Du Bois, the President of the NAACP and frequent critic of white Protestants, expressed admiration for the historic contributions of Catholicism and even collaborated in a Knights of Columbus publication. While he insisted that he was not "an enemy of Catholicism,"[16] he nevertheless minced no words in his evaluation of Catholic relations with the black community:

> The Catholic Church in America stands for color separation and discrimination to a degree equaled by no other church in America, and that is saying a very great deal... The white parochial schools, even in the North, exclude colored children, the Catholic high schools will not admit them, the Catholic university at Washington invited them elsewhere and scarcely a Catholic seminary in the country will train a Negro priest. This is not then a case of blaming the Catholic Church for not doing all it might—it is blaming it for being absolutely and fundamentally wrong today and in the United States on the basic demands of human brotherhood across the color line.... Because Catholicism has so much that is splendid in its past and fine in its present, it is the greater shame that "nigger" haters clothed in its Episcopal robes should do to black Americans in exclusion, segregation and exclusion from opportunity all that the Ku Klux Klan ever asked."[17]

Pentecostals

During Jim Crow a new religious phenomenon shook the nation, offering great initial promise for racial reconciliation. In 1906 the Azusa Street revival began in Los Angeles under the leadership of William Seymour, a Holiness preacher who was himself the son of slaves. For over three years the Azusa

---

Council of 1866 had allowed "as an expedient, but [which] became increasingly the rule after the 1890s." See endnote for citation.

[e] By comparison, the much smaller Episcopal Church raised up eighty-six black priests between 1866 and 1900. See endnote, p. 72.

Street revival conducted three services a day, seven days a week. Thousands of people reported a fresh experience with the Holy Spirit marked by glossolalia, known as speaking in tongues. This awakening was unique, not only because of the unusual religious manifestations that accompanied it, but also for the fact that many whites joined with the African-American core.

Seymour had studied under Charles Fox Parham, a controversial white supremacist preacher and pioneer of the Pentecostal movement. Parham's informal training school in Texas did not allow blacks to study with whites, but Parham nevertheless allowed Seymour to listen outside the room with the door ajar. Seymour, who considered Parham a kind of mentor, kept him abreast of the revival's progress, and in October of 1906 invited him to Los Angeles to see this phenomenon for himself.

Parham was immediately put off by what he saw as emotional excesses, and he characterized the gathering as "a darky camp meeting."[18] He was especially offended by racial mixing, complaining that worshipers were "crowded together around the altar like hogs, blacks and whites mingling; this should be enough to bring a blush of shame to devils, let alone angels, and yet this was all charged to the Holy Spirit."[19] He added that "frequently a white woman, perhaps of wealth and culture, could be seen thrown back into the arms of a 'buck nigger,' and held tightly as she shivered and shook in freak imitation of Pentecost. Horrible, awful shame!"[20] Parham criticized Seymour and tried to assume leadership of the movement, causing Seymour to eventually bar him from the Azusa Street Mission.

A few years later, in 1911, Seymour had a similar experience with a powerful white preacher named William Durham. Seymour invited Durham to preach at Azusa Street while he went on an extended trip, and Durham attracted large crowds. He also used the opportunity to promote a variation on Pentecostal doctrine that won over many followers. By the time Seymour returned, Durham was poised to take over the ministry. After Seymour finally locked him out, Durham began another mission nearby to which many of the Azusa Street congregants, particularly whites, followed him. It is difficult to determine just how much of the split was doctrinal and how much was racial.

The Pentecostal/charismatic movement was born in a whirlwind of optimism about its potential to bridge the racial divide. And why not? It had no ecclesiastical history of oppression or segregation to overcome. Its free-flowing style of worship offered a comfortable common ground for both blacks and whites. Its distinguishing element was religious *experience* rather than religious *tradition* with its racial/cultural trappings. And the movement was integrated at its very roots. Nevertheless, after the integrated idealism of Azusa Street's beginnings, black and white Pentecostal practitioners were not able to make a marriage out of that initial courtship.

Whites within the movement were simply not prepared to walk together with black people as equals. Harvard professor Harvey Cox observes that, whereas Seymour finally came to see unity across racial lines as a more telling sign of spiritual awakening than speaking in tongues, the white Pentecostal pioneers disagreed. "Uncomfortable under black leadership and embarrassed by the opprobrium heaped on them for 'worshipping with niggers,' they finally opted to reject the interracial fellowship and keep the tongues."[21]

The Encyclopedia of American Religious History calls William Durham "the most significant figure in the shaping of the Assemblies of God,"[22] a white-controlled denomination that began two years after his death in 1912. Charles Mason—who, like Durham, had his initial Pentecostal experience at Azusa Street—went on to found the Church of God in Christ, now the largest black denomination in America. Charles Parham's star quickly faded, and in his later years he spoke favorably about the KKK. William Seymour ended up as the pastor of a small black church on Azusa Street, his dreams of Spirit-filled racial reunification already long dead when he passed away in 1922.

In summary, the American Church, in nearly all of its incarnations, opted for the one solution the Apostle Paul refused to even contemplate for the Early Church—separation along ethnic/racial lines.[f] But that separation was not a solution—nor could it be—because division cannot heal a divide.

To be honest, nearly everyone was happy with the new arrangement. Whites rid themselves of a problem they didn't quite know how to deal with, and blacks managed to escape their second-class status, at least on Sundays. Their churches experienced explosive growth, contributing significantly to both the spiritual and temporal welfare of their members.

Over time, however, that separation became a de facto divorce, an institutionalized spiritual apartheid that continues to undermine the integrity of American Christianity to this day. That great divorce placed blacks beyond the reach of dysfunctional domination—but also beyond the reach of functional fellowship. The great divorce limited the damage haughtiness can do, but it did not limit haughtiness itself. And, so, the great divorce continues.

---

[f] Though the Roman Catholic Church did not split into autonomous, race-based factions, there was intra-Church segregation during Jim Crow.

Chapter 13

The Winds of Change

Throughout the centuries-long history of haughtiness there was plenty of bad news and even some worse news, but precious little good news. As America and the American Church entered the second half of the twentieth century, however, change—real change—was in the air. This was not a mad dash from apartheid to utopia, but somehow a society steeped in centuries of overt, in-your-face racial dominance at least began *talking* about racial justice. What moved that needle along "the arc of the moral universe?"[a]

It's not as if whites somehow grew weary of racial dominance; nor did haughtiness take a holiday. But, in the fullness of time, the right people, conditions, and events converged to produce what came to be known as the Civil Rights Movement. The mythical romanticism that now surrounds this period of intense social ferment tends to blur our memory about how it was received, what it accomplished, and what it left undone. Perhaps this chapter can refresh that memory.

Precursors to a movement

Five developments during the latter part of the Jim Crow period set the stage for the monumental changes of the Civil Rights era. The *first* was the growth of federal power during the first half of the 20th century. This ramping up of federal authority would prove necessary, as it had been during Reconstruction, to overcome the intransigence of state and local governments regarding segregation.

The growth of the federal government began in earnest around the time of First World War. Later, Roosevelt's New Deal, forged in response to the Great Depression, greatly "expanded the federal government's role as a guardian of social welfare,"[1] more than doubling the federal budget before WWII.[2] These two global conflicts required huge government expenditures, and even though those outlays abated in peacetime, the federal budget (in

---

[a] A phrase that originated with Theodore Parker, now associated with Martin Luther King Jr. See: http://quoteinvestigator.com/2012/11/15/arc-of-universe/

constant dollars) never declined to less than double what it had been before each war.[3]

The *second* important precursor to the Civil Rights Movement was World War II itself. In the popular mind, the U.S. was cast as democracy's champion, protecting the world from Hitler's racist fascism. But this image was clearly at odds with the country's own treatment of its black citizens, creating an uncomfortable moral dissonance and an appetite for its resolution.

In 1944 Cpl. Rupert Trimmingham and eight other black soldiers were en route from one base to another in the state of Louisiana, when they stopped at a railway lunch room to get a cup of coffee. They were not allowed in the white dining area, however, so they were forced to take their coffee in the kitchen. Meanwhile, two dozen German prisoners of war, accompanied by their American guards, sat down and enjoyed a pleasant meal alongside the lunchroom patrons.

Incensed by this obvious injustice, Trimmingham detailed the incident in a letter to *Yank* magazine, asking, "What is the Negro soldier fighting for?"[4] *Yank* received thousands of letters in response—like this one, written by Cpl. Henry S. Wootton Jr., and co-signed by two other soldiers.

> Dear Yank: I am writing to you in regard to the incident told in a letter to you by Cpl. Trimmingham (Negro)... Gentlemen, I am a Southern rebel, but... I think this incident is a disgrace to a democratic nation, such as ours is supposed to be... I wonder what the "Aryan supermen" think when they get a first-hand glimpse of our racial discrimination... A lot of us, especially in the South, should cast the beam out of our own eyes before we try to do so in others across the seas.[5]

For the first time in American history racial identity posed a serious threat to our *national* identity—and right in the middle of a life-and-death conflict. As a result, existential loyalties began trumping ancient prejudices. The times they were a-changin'.

The *third* important precondition for the Civil Rights Movement was the advent of the television. In 1950, less than one in ten households owned a TV; by 1960, nine in ten had one. The murder of Emmet Till, school integration, bus boycotts, church bombings, marches, standoffs between local and federal powers—not to mention the oratory of black civil rights crusaders—it was all piped into the living rooms of white Americans, who otherwise would never have experienced these events so dramatically, if at all.

Not only did this new medium engage the moral sentiments of whites, it also helped to unite African Americans, as news about the Civil Rights Movement and racial injustices was generally suppressed by the Southern print media. Jack Nelson, a reporter for the *Atlanta Constitution* during the late 1950s and early 1960s, later recalled that though a few brave journalists "risked lives and fortunes to report the civil rights struggle," the *Constitution*, like most Southern newspapers, paid little or no attention to the march on Selma, Alabama, even though it was the hottest story in the nation.[6]

The *fourth* factor was a watershed institutional change. President Truman, concerned about the negative PR of Jim Crow, noted in his memoirs that "we could not endorse a color line at home and still expect to influence the immense masses that make up the Asian and African peoples. It was necessary to practice what we preached..."[7] So, he signed Executive Order #9981 on July 26, 1948: "It is hereby declared to be the policy of the President that there shall be equality of treatment and opportunity for all persons in the armed services without regard to race, color, religion, or national origin."[8/b]

This Executive Order would turn out to be the most significant advance in black civil rights between Reconstruction and the Supreme Court's 1954 landmark decision. For the first time in history, African Americans had a legitimate career choice in which they participated with whites on what was, at least ostensibly, a level playing field. And even though black people had far fewer options when it came to claiming their military benefits in the still-segregated society, the GI Bill and federally backed loans nevertheless helped many African Americans pursue education and home ownership.

Fifth, there was the rise of black advocacy itself. As Martin Luther King Jr. said, "We know through painful experience that freedom is never voluntarily given by the oppressor; it must be demanded by the oppressed."[9]

In 1951, thirteen black plaintiffs, led by the NAACP, filed a class action lawsuit against the Board of Education in Topeka Kansas. Though they lost their challenge to school segregation in District Court, the case eventually made it all the way to the U.S. Supreme Court. There, four similar cases were subsumed under the Kansas appeal. Thurgood Marshall, chief counsel for the NAACP, championed the cause. In May of 1954, the Court rendered its unanimous *Brown v. Board of Education* decision that "in the field of public education, the doctrine of 'separate but equal' has no place. Separate

---

[b] There was both a moral and a political calculus involved in this decision, as Truman needed African-American votes for his 1948 presidential bid.

educational facilities are inherently unequal."[10] With this historic opinion, the entire legal foundation of the Jim Crow edifice began to crumble.

Black protagonism

With all these precursors percolating, the stage was set, but set for whom? In order for these Civil Rights rumblings to become a movement, black leadership was necessary. And not just any leader, but someone capable of mounting a three-pronged, simultaneous offensive: 1) mobilizing ordinary black people, 2) interfacing with the white power structure, and 3) exerting moral pressure on the broader white society. Enter Martin Luther King Jr.

In 1954, while working on his Ph.D. dissertation at Boston University, Dr. King became pastor of the Dexter Ave. Baptist Church in Montgomery, Alabama. The following year, Rosa Parks, Secretary of the local NAACP, refused to give up her seat on a public bus and was arrested and fined $10. Montgomery's black community responded by organizing a bus boycott, and they chose the recently arrived clergyman to lead the effort.

Three hundred eighty-one days later, the boycott ended. The courts had struck down the city's bus laws as unconstitutional. African Americans had proved that well-organized, grassroots opposition could challenge Jim Crow. And Rev. Martin Luther King Jr. had established himself as a major player in the unfolding Civil Rights Movement.

There were, of course, many important figures other than King who contributed to the success of this march to freedom, but there was no one else during his time who possessed the same combination of skills— communicator, organizer, political activist, and theologian/moral philosopher. It is, then, no accident that the Civil Rights era was roughly co-terminus with Dr. King's own career or that he became the iconic face of the Movement.

Despite his passion, gifts, and moral conviction; Martin Luther King Jr. was not a paragon of all virtue. Allegations that he was guilty of plagiarism as a graduate student and of adultery while carrying the torch of racial justice are now generally admitted as fact, even by his admirers.[11] For some whites, these shortcomings not only tarnish Dr. King's virtual halo; they somehow nullify everything he stood for. We should not lose sight, however, of our ample human capacity for moral inconsistency and compartmentalization. Theoretically incompatible light and darkness are existentially juxtaposed in every human psyche. And every good deed is done by a sinner.

In this book, I have not hesitated to point out the lapses of some our most revered national figures. We cannot fall into the trap of historical hagiography if we want to know the truth about our past and ourselves. But that doesn't mean that we should not also appreciate and honor their contributions. As *The New York Times* once editorialized, "Martin Luther King's courage was not copied; and there was no plagiarism in his power."[12] With all things duly considered, I still consider him the most influential American of the twentieth century.[c] A framed poster of a pensive Dr. King hangs on my office wall.

In 1957, King helped found the Southern Christian Leadership Council and became its first president. First called the Southern Negro Leaders Conference on Transportation and Nonviolent Integration, it sought to coordinate the many localized groups that were working for racial justice into a broad moral crusade. In their original manifesto they defined their mission, expounding principles that would resonate throughout King's career:

> We call upon all Negroes in the South and in the nation to assert their human dignity... to seek justice and reject all injustice, especially that in themselves... [and to] refuse further cooperation with the evil element which invites them to collude against themselves in return for bits of patronage.

> ...Non-violence is not a symbol of weakness or cowardice, but as Jesus demonstrated, non-violent resistance transforms weakness into strength. ...No matter how great the provocation... [we must] dedicate [ourselves] to this motto: "Not one hair of one head of one white person shall be harmed." We... believe this spirit and this spirit alone can overcome the decades of mutual fear and suspicion that have infested and poisoned our Southern culture.

> In this same spirit... we call upon white Southern Christians to realize that the treatment of Negroes is a basic *spiritual* [emphasis mine] problem. We believe that no legal approach can fully redeem or reconcile man. We urge them in Christ's name... to see that all persons, regardless of color or creed, who seek the saving grace of Christ are accepted as equals in their churches.[13]

---

[c] I am not alone in this assessment. A 1999 Gallup Poll ranked King as the most-admired American of the century (www.gallup.com/poll/20920/martin-luther-king-jr-revered-more-after-death-than-before.aspx). In his own time, however, King was among the top ten admired men only in 1964 and 1965. Only in 1964 did his positive rating (43%) top his negative rating (39%).

Historian David Chappell observes:

> It may be misleading to view the civil rights movement as a social and political event that had religious overtones. The words of many participants suggest that it was, for them, primarily a religious event, whose social and political aspects were, in their minds, secondary or incidental.[14]

After all, the movers and shakers of the Civil Rights movement were not sociologists or economists or political scientists.[d] They were mostly preachers, and they had to rely on the tools in their toolbox to repair the problem. Rev. Fred Shuttlesworth, a co-founder of the SCLC along with Dr. King, said it succinctly in 1958: "This is a religious crusade, a fight between light and darkness, right and wrong, good and evil, fair play and tyranny. We are assured of victory because we are using weapons of spiritual warfare."[15]

With King and other ministers at the forefront, black churches became the locus of inspiration and a launch pad for practical protest. This religious packaging of civil rights did not generate nearly the same enthusiasm on the other side of the racial ledger, however. Though I was just a youth, I vividly remember my own pastor calling Dr. King a communist, which was just about the worst thing you could say about anyone during those days.

Despite his inclusive appeal to white Christians and his invocation of a common moral foundation for racial justice, King was perennially disappointed with the response of white Christians. In the spring of 1963, Martin Luther King Jr. went to Birmingham, Alabama, to protest the segregation that existed there. When local officials threw him in jail, eight white clergymen wrote an open letter to a local newspaper, entitled, "A Call to Unity," in which they criticized King's methods and timing. In his response, now famously known as "Letter from a Birmingham Jail," King expressed his own sentiments.

> I have been so greatly disappointed with the white church and its leadership... When I was suddenly catapulted into the leadership of the bus protest in Montgomery, Alabama, a few years ago... I felt that the white ministers, priests and rabbis of the South would be among our strongest allies. Instead, some have been outright opponents, refusing to understand the freedom movement and misrepresenting its leaders; all too many others have been more cautious than courageous and

---

[d] For further perspective on the impact of economic/political influences vs. the moral/spiritual angle, see: www.scottgarber.com/was_notes.pdf, Note 13.1.

have remained silent behind the anesthetizing security of stained glass windows.[16]

That disappointment did not adhere only to the clergy but to whites in general, particularly to those with moral sensitivities. In *Stride Toward Freedom* King expressed his oft-repeated warning that "the greatest tragedy of this period of social transition was not the strident clamor of the bad people, but the appalling silence of the good people. Our generation will have to repent not only for the acts and words of the children of darkness but for the fears and apathy of the children of light."[17]

White response

Martin Luther King's true opposition was never the nightstick-toting, fire-hose-wielding, pointy-hat-wearing white extremists. Ironically, for all the harm they inflicted, they often end up playing the role of a media foil that won considerable sympathy for the Movement. Behind the headlines, however, lurked a far vaster and more subtle defense of white dominance.

It's not as if the Civil Rights Movement was birthed amidst a white outcry, demanding that somebody please do something about racial injustice. In 1954, only a very narrow majority (55%) of Americans approved of the Supreme Court's *Brown v. Board of Education* ruling, with a full 40% opposing it. Five years later that approval had climbed to only about 60%, with 53% telling Gallup that the historic school desegregation decision had "caused a lot more trouble than it was worth."[18]

Whatever level of positive sentiment did exist was not evenly distributed across the country. Southern whites demonstrated particularly significant opposition to desegregation. In June of 1961 Gallup asked, "Generally speaking, do you think that integration should be brought about gradually, or do you think every means should be used to bring it about in the near future?"[19] Only 23% of all Americans opted for the more immediate route, while 61% favored a gradual approach. By comparison, only 13% of Southerners wanted to see integration in the near future, while 52% preferred to go slowly. A full 22% *volunteered* the opinion that integration should *never* take place, even though that was not one of the options given in the poll.[e]

---

[e] Though there was a negative reaction to desegregation in the North as well, only 7% of national poll respondents said that integration should never happen (including the 22% of Southerners who volunteered that response).

Given the threat that the Civil Rights Movement posed to white dominance in the South, such stonewalling should come as no surprise. In fact, in early 1956 a movement arose in Virginia in response to Sen. Harry Byrd Sr.'s call for "massive resistance." The state itself conspired to block the implementation of the Supreme Court's *Brown v. Board of Education* decision. Virginia officials selectively suspended school attendance rules and provided white students with tuition grants to private, segregated schools. With the nearly universal support of the state's press, they created a Pupil Placement Board to keep black students out of white schools. If a school came under a federal desegregation order, they simply closed it. They harassed black families who sought redress in the courts and created a commission to mount a public relations campaign in favor of states' rights and segregation.

When federal judges finally ordered that black students be admitted to white schools in Front Royal and Norfolk in 1958, Virginia's governor closed all nine of them. More than a year later, in January of 1959, the courts finally ordered the state to reopen and desegregate the schools. Prince Edward County, however, closed all its public schools the following September, sending the white students to private schools and leaving black students with no local schooling options whatsoever. The schools did not reopen until forced to do so by the U.S. Supreme Court in 1964.

This massive resistance movement spread to other states across the South as well. In March of 1956, eighty-two U.S. representatives and nineteen senators (about 20% of the entire Congress) signed what was known as the Southern Manifesto. It accused the Supreme Court of judicial abuse and pledged to use all legal means to resist school desegregation.[20]

The following year, 1957, after the entire Arkansas legislature had signed the Southern Manifesto, nine properly enrolled black students attempted to enter Little Rock Central High School. Gov. Orval Faubus blocked their access, calling out the National Guard to "prevent violence." This led to a confrontation with President Eisenhower, who promptly federalized the Guard and ordered in additional troops to guarantee the students' safety.

The National Guard remained in place from September until May. The next fall Gov. Faubus closed all four Little Rock high schools, backed by a local referendum that passed by a three-to-one margin. After what became known as "the lost year," Little Rock public high schools reopened under court order in 1959 and began gradual desegregation.[21]

School desegregation was the first domino in a series that threatened to unravel an entire white-over-black way of life, and the dominant desperately tried to keep that first domino from falling. In fact, "State legislatures in Alabama, Georgia, Mississippi, South Carolina, and Virginia adopted resolutions of 'interposition and nullification' that declared the Court's decision to be 'null, void, and no effect.'"[22] In 1957, black Michigan Congressman Charles C. Diggs lamented that Southern powerbrokers had won the first round in the battle for compliance, stating: "We cannot point to one instance of submission by Mississippi, Georgia, South Carolina, or Alabama to the Supreme Court's three-year-old decision outlawing school segregation."[23] Though segregationists would not ultimately prevail, the effort they expended in a losing cause speaks volumes about their commitment to white dominance.

After the passage of the 1964 Civil Rights Act, Southern whites reacted by manipulating the electoral process in ways that marginalized black voters. Legal but nonetheless discriminatory tactics like poll taxes and literacy/constitutional tests were supplemented by extra-legal intimidation— violence, loss of employment, credit denials, and the blacklisting of African-American commercial enterprises.

Despite these barriers, across much of the South black voter registration had been gradually increasing since the Second World War. For its part, Congress tried to reduce the obstacles to black voting by enacting federal voting rights legislation in 1957, 1960, and 1964. The problem, however, was enforcement, which usually required aggrieved African Americans to seek legal redress by filing suit. As a result, by 1964 only about 23% of voting-age black people were registered nationally. [24]

The most stubborn and most organized resistance was in the Deep South. Mississippi had by far the lowest statewide index of registered black voters— just 6.7% in 1964.[25] When several major civil rights groups launched their "Freedom Summer" voter registration drive in 1964,[f] white supremacists struck back against the activists. In Neshoba County, the Sheriff arrested three civil rights workers for speeding and locked them up pending "further investigation." Upon their release they were promptly executed by the Klan.[g]

In that fall's election there were widespread efforts to keep registered black voters from participating. Propaganda about how the Civil Rights Act could be used against whites convinced many employers across the South to

---

[f] For this project the SNCC, CORE, SCLC, NAACP, and others formed Council of Federated Organizations (COFO).

[g] The FBI later uncovered a conspiracy between law enforcement and the KKK, resulting in twenty-one arrests.

force their black employees to work overtime on Election Day in order to keep them away from the polls. In Houston, Texas fliers were distributed, warning black voters that anyone who had ever had any sort of run-in with the police, even a traffic ticket, would have to check in with the Sheriff before voting. President Lyndon Johnson, in a conversation with Vice President Humphrey, described these tactics as "just the meanest, dirtiest, low-down stuff that I've ever heard"[26]—which, considering the source, is saying quite a bit.

By 1965, frustration with the suppression in Dallas County, Alabama led to protests and police violence, prompting the "Bloody Sunday" march in Selma.[h] Eight days later, in response to those events, President Johnson gave his historic "We Shall Overcome" speech, calling on Congress to pass the Voting Rights Act. That legislation authorized the U.S. Attorney General "to appoint federal registrars to oversee voter registration in political subdivisions where literacy tests were previously used and where fewer than half the voting age residents were registered to vote or actually voted in 1964."[27] This enforcement focused particularly on Alabama, Georgia, Louisiana, Mississippi, North Carolina, South Carolina, and Virginia.

The results of this pro-active approach were immediate. The 23% of African Americans registered to vote across the U.S. before the Act increased to 61% in five years; in the same period, black voter registration in Mississippi increased tenfold.[28] Increased registration helped to usher in a new generation of black civic leadership. In 1965 there were fewer than 100 black elected officials in the seven targeted Southern states; ten years later there were 963.[29]

While there was no truly equal reaction for the Civil Rights Movement, there was, not surprisingly, an opposite one. This white backlash was very real and very effective in certain localities. Ultimately, however, it could not sustain segregation, a notion gutted of its social appeal and moral merit.

The wave of egalitarian enlightenment that swept across the country during these years did not get everyone soaking wet. As a result, even after the demise of de jure segregation, the ongoing moral constant of white racial

---

[h] In 1961, the county had 15,000 voting-age blacks (57% of the population). But due to white obstruction and intimidation, only 130 blacks were registered to vote. Even after two years (1963-65) of intensive voter registration efforts by SNCC, that number climbed to only 335 blacks vs. 9,542 whites. See: "Selma: Breaking the Grip of Fear," *Veterans of the Civil Rights Movement: 1963 – January-June*, http://www.crmvet.org/tim/timhis63.htm#1963selma1.

haughtiness guaranteed that de facto segregation would prove far more resistant.

Though Dr. King had reason to be disappointed with the white response, his message was not really lost on religious leaders or their constituents. Note that King prefaced his criticism of Birmingham's white ministers by saying, "I am not unmindful of the fact that each of you has taken some significant stands on this issue." Without the provocation of the Civil Rights Movement they would never have stuck out their necks even as far as they did.

Preachers are easily influenced by what I call "prophetic envy." Desirous of being spiritual guideposts to their followers, they don't want to appear completely tone deaf to an issue with moral relevance that affects their flock. Even if they are too timid to take up the cause on their own, they may at least try to establish themselves as a "balanced" voice, recognizing the more obviously valid aspects of a controversial position, while maintaining a safe distance of deniability from its more unpopular and/or radical elements.

Even in their silence, the "good people"—whether clergy or not—were still listening. They sensed something in the morality of the message, and they were moved by the activists' courage. Their unspoken sympathies were rarely passionate enough to challenge the racial hierarchy; few went so far as to join the marches. But, eventually, many joined the cause—or at least found no reason to actively oppose it. A Harris Poll found that by November of 1963, 63% of Americans supported the Civil Rights Act, which banned racial discrimination in employment, voting, and the use of public facilities, backing that proscription with federal law enforcement. By May of 1964, that number had increased to 70%.[30]

Though the civil rights message produced legislative outcomes, it was not fundamentally a legal reform movement but a moral reform movement. David Chappell suggests that "perhaps what historians frequently call the Second Reconstruction could just as rightly be called the Third Great Awakening."[31] Indeed, it's impossible to understand or to explain the Civil Rights Movement without taking into account its spiritual character. There's no way to re-package white self-interest attractively enough to change the dynamics of racial dominance.

The impact of the Civil Rights Movement was nothing short of monumental. In a few short years it ended Jim Crow; it created previously unimaginable opportunities; it affirmed and codified black rights; and it elevated the discussion about equality to a new quantum level, altering white notions of superiority.

In order to appreciate the true impact of these historic accomplishments, however, we must understand both what the Civil Rights Movement did—and what it left undone. For if we do not recognize its limitations, we might too hastily conclude that such a spiritually-oriented juggernaut might have well have swept away racial haughtiness right along with Jim Crow segregation. Let's examine the unfinished business of the Civil Rights Movement, both socially and spiritually, and then think about how those shortcomings influenced the future of racial haughtiness.

The first thing that the Civil Rights Movement left undone also turns out to be the main thing. In his book, *The Strength to Love*, King made the ultimate objective crystal clear:

> Court orders and federal enforcement agencies are of inestimable value in achieving desegregation, but desegregation is only a partial, though necessary, step toward the final goal which we seek to realize, genuine intergroup and interpersonal living. Desegregation will break down legal barriers and bring men together physically, but something must touch the hearts and souls of men so that they will come together spiritually because it is natural and right.... True integration will be achieved by true neighbors who are willingly obedient to unenforceable obligations.[32]

This ultimate objective, which Martin Luther King Jr. dubbed "the beloved community," remains to this day an elusive dream. There simply is no such racially-inclusive community that could reasonably be described as "beloved" operating on any significant scale in American society—or even in the American Church. What we have are color-coded communities that cannot pretend to be "beloved," because they are not even proximate. Whites and blacks remain deeply divided, not only by physical distance but by cultural and relational distance as well.

That brings us to a second major piece of unfinished business from the Civil Rights Movement—something we might call "empty equality." Coming out of this era, there was both good news and bad news concerning equality. The good news was that in a few short years white people, who had never shown much enthusiasm for equality, now generally embraced the notion. The bad news was that the ways blacks and whites defined that equality were as different as—well, as different as black and white.

Martin Luther King Jr. struggled to get his mind around this black/white disconnect concerning the nature of equality, saying: "Negroes have proceeded from a premise that equality means what it says, and they have taken white Americans at their word when they talked of it as an objective. But most whites in America in 1967, including many persons of goodwill, proceed from a premise that equality is a loose expression for improvement."[33]

Dr. King complained that in spite of advances in civil rights, the black/white divide remained a stark reality, saying:

> Of the good things in life he [the black person] has approximately one-half those of whites; of the bad he has twice those of whites. Thus, half of all Negroes live in substandard housing, and Negroes have half the income of whites. When we turn to the negative experiences of life, the Negro has a double share. There are twice as many unemployed. The rate of infant mortality (widely accepted as an accurate index of general health) among Negroes is double that of whites.[34]

King went on to highlight the disparities in education, employment, and military service—all of which remained entirely unequal. Of course, in 1967 very little time had elapsed since the passage of the most sweeping civil rights legislation, making it hard to gauge the actual impact of these laws. We might, therefore, wonder if Dr. King wasn't just a little impatient. But if we fast-forward fifty years and compare the today's black reality with that of 1967, it's clear that something about equality did, indeed, get lost in translation.

Now, a half century later, the unemployment rate for blacks is still double that of whites.[35/i] The black infant mortality rate is now more than double that of whites.[36/j] Compared to whites, black people are more than twice as likely to be arrested[37/k] and more than *five* times more likely to be incarcerated.[38/l] The median income of African American households, as a percentage of its white counterpart, remains essentially unchanged since 1967.[39/m] The median net worth of white households is *ten* times that of black households.[40/n] Even education hasn't eliminated this divide, as the greatest disparity between the two races is now to be found among the college-educated.[41]

---

[i] The average ratio for 2017 (most recent reporting year, *mrry*) = 1.97 to 1

[j] The ratio for 2015 (*mrry*) = 2.44 to 1

[k] The ratio for 2014 (*mrry*) = 2.27 to 1

[l] The ratio for 2016 (*mrry*) = 5.3 to 1

[m] As Dr. King indicated, he was rounding off the numbers, and we don't know if he was referring to the mean or the median. The 1967 median income of blacks compared to whites was closer to 60% than 50%. The relative racial income disparity has remained remarkably constant. The median household income for blacks in 2016 was just over 60% of its white counterpart.

[n] Actual figures for 2016 (*mrry*), whites = $171,000 vs. blacks = $17,600

The failure to create a beloved community or to create meaningful equality surely rank as two of the major disappointments of the Civil Rights Movement. And, as Dr. King was well aware, the two issues are integrally related. You cannot get from dominance to equality without sacrifice on the part of the dominant. Unless and until the dominant are willing to sacrifice themselves for the good of others, they will continue to sacrifice others for their own good.

In order to maintain its momentum, the Movement had to accomplish these two elusive goals. What no one seemed to even realize, however, was that in order to accomplish these goals something else had to happen. Somehow someone had to tear down the stronghold of haughtiness, which is absolutely antithetical to both true equality and to the beloved community.

Dr. King certainly recognized the moral nature of the civil rights struggle. He believed that sin was at the root of racial dominance. It seems, however, that he may not have realized the extent of that root system. Especially in the beginning, it's not clear that he understood that the "good people" were infected with the same moral pathogen as the "bad people." It simply manifested itself differently. Perhaps naively, he believed that when the "good people" were confronted with the truth, they would see the light and enthusiastically create equality.

He eventually disabused himself of that that naiveté, adopting a far more cynical view of white morality. King came to realize that there was some hidden aspect of white identity that he had not managed to address. In a speech to the SCLC staff in late 1966, he lamented the superficial nature of the civil rights gains and concluded that while the Movement "represented a frontal attack on the doctrine and practice of white supremacy, it did not defeat the monster of racism."[42] King was clearly frustrated by this recalcitrant "something," which I believe we can now identify as white haughtiness.

Even if King had recognized racial haughtiness as such, it's hard to know what he would or could have done about it. Black leaders who mounted too much of a frontal challenge to the benignity of whiteness (*a la* Malcolm X)° were relegated to a minority audience and marginalized from access to power. For black activists to be heard, their appeal had to be palatable to whites, who were willing to embrace a dream but not a personal indictment. Some whites could imagine themselves being part of the solution, as long as they didn't

---

° For more background on Dr. King's relationship with Malcolm X and Black Nationalism, see: www.scottgarber.com/was_notes.pdf, Note 13.2.

have to admit to being part of the problem. They might resist evil as it existed in the less enlightened, but not as it existed in their own souls.

Though Dr. King died somewhat disillusioned, it's possible that the Civil Rights Movement accomplished just about all that the moment would allow. After all, overcoming racial injustice was not something that black people could do *without* white people; nor was it something they could do *to* white people. Any progress in the direction of justice that requires a change on the part of free moral agents, particularly those who are advantaged by a sinful system, is likely to be incremental or episodic.

Even the fact that the Movement invoked the power of God was never a guarantee that it would be more than a partial victory. Had it not been for Divine enablement, this partial victory would certainly have been even more limited. It was at least a step in the direction of what Francis Schaeffer called "substantial healing," the best we can hope for in this age.

That said, the racial healing that began in the civil rights era was not nearly substantial enough. Not enough for Martin Luther King Jr., and not nearly enough for God. Unfortunately, however, that change *was* substantial enough for many white people—too substantial for some of them. In the next chapter I drill down into this white response, as we attempt to understand its long-term impact on racial haughtiness.

Chapter 14

"Yes, but..."

In order to achieve its legislative successes, the Civil Rights Movement had to change the conversation about equality. Where would its leaders find the necessary ideological leverage? Well, they were mostly preachers, so they naturally turned to the pages of Scripture.

Even though the Bible had long been used to support the racial hierarchy, civil rights protagonists turned it into a motor for change by highlighting its egalitarian emphases. This appeal was enhanced by the growing acceptance of the principle of human rights, as enshrined in the UN's 1948 Declaration of Universal Human Rights.[a] This two-pronged argument broadened the ideological base of equality, allowing it to be couched in either religious or secular vernacular. As a result, the "self-evident" truths of the oft-invoked Declaration of Independence suddenly seemed far more evident.

But if most whites eventually affirmed equality, why then did/does de facto segregation continue? Why was/is there still such an enormous gap between white and black social wellbeing? And why did/do many whites find these inequitable situations to be acceptable, or at least not so unacceptable that they feel compelled to resolve them?

I believe the answer can be found in the nature of the equality question itself—not as one might expect it to be answered on philosophical level, nor as black people expected it to be answered, but as whites have chosen to interpret it. And, as it turns out, the way whites have chosen to answer this equality question is somewhat more nuanced than just "yes" or "no."

Of course, during slavery, the answer was a straightforward "no." Black people were considered inferior to whites and were treated as such. During the Jim Crow period, however, the answer became "no, but." Blacks were not so inferior that they deserved to be enslaved, but not equal enough to avoid a second-class citizen status—hence, the "separate but equal" rationalization.

---

[a] Article 1 of that document states: "All human beings are born free and equal in dignity and rights. They are endowed with reason and conscience and should act towards one another in a spirit of brotherhood." ("The Universal Declaration of Human Rights," www.un.org/en/documents/udhr/)

Then came the Civil Rights Movement, and with it a quantum leap in the white conceptualization of equality. Suddenly, whites began to answer the equality question in the (kinda/sorta) affirmative. But even though whites generally embraced the *language* of equality, their "yes" was really "yes, but." That is, in principle they supported racial equality, but something still whispered in their ears that black people were *other* and that in their *otherness* they were also somehow less.

Granted, an equivocal answer to equality is nonsensical. Equality is a rather absolute notion—something like perfection. There may be many gradations of imperfection, but there's only one degree of perfection. Likewise, there may be many gradations of inequality, but unless the two entities being compared enjoy a very similar status, it does not make sense to talk about them as being equal, when, in fact, they are *un*equal.

While the term itself ought to be unequivocal, what whites really had in mind when they affirmed equality came with significant qualifications. They could say "yes" to equality as a moral ideal. They could say "yes" to equality as a legal principle. They could say "yes" to equality as slogan. *But*—they were unwilling to say "yes" to an actual dismantling of the racial hierarchy.

Social Dominance Theory, proposed by Sidanius and Pratto, helps us to understand why this definitive *yes* is so hard to say.[b]

> Human societies tend to organize as group-based social hierarchies in which at least one group enjoys greater social status and power than other groups. Members of dominant social groups tend to enjoy a disproportionate share of *positive social value*, or desirable material and symbolic resources such as political power, wealth, protection by force, plentiful and desirable food, and access to good housing, health care, leisure, and education. Negative social value is disproportionately left to or forced upon members of subordinate groups in the form of substandard housing, disease, underemployment, dangerous and distasteful work, disproportionate punishment, stigmatization, and vilification.[1]

So, our answer to the equality question determines how we distribute social value. When the answer was "no," we got slavery. When it changed to "no, but," we got Jim Crow. But then the Civil Rights Movement came along, and the answer to equality changed from "no, but" to "yes, but." And "yes, but" gave us what we have now—an unequal equality. Never mind that white

---

[b] For more on SDT, see www.scottgarber.com/was_notes.pdf, Note 14.1.

people tend to think of their "yes" as an unqualified affirmative. Since our answer to the equality question determines the distribution of social value, if we simply work backwards from the actual distribution of social value in America, we'll see that what feels like "yes" is really "yes, but."

The magic of "yes, but" is that it allows its purveyors to heartily affirm equality in nearly any theoretical form while denying it in nearly every tangible form, to champion equality without changing the actual equation, to say "amen" to equality in the abstract without reapportioning social value.

But why would someone who believes in equality in principle be resistant to equality in practice? There is, of course, the matter of self-interest, and that is no small matter. Redistributing wealth and power diminishes the relative social value of those who enjoy a more than equal share of it.

But while this motivation is very real and even compelling for some people, there are people of principle who might, under the right circumstances, relinquish their disproportionate social value. That is, if they were really convinced that they were getting more than they deserved, relative to someone else who was getting less than they deserved. The problem, then, is not just whether someone selfishly wants to keep their disproportionate share—but whether they truly consider that share to be disproportionate.

"Yes, but" contains an affirmation—a cognitive commitment to the ideal of equality. However, "yes, but" also contains an adversative—a sense of deservedness that springs from an immoral attitudinal addiction to racial haughtiness. As a result, "yes, but" allows the haughty to *feel* more deserving than others, even though they *know* that everyone is equal.

Not surprisingly, "yes, but" created an enormous psychic dissonance that was new to whiteness. When the answer to equality was "no," that was simple. Even "no, but" created very little conflict for white identity. "Yes, but" is different. It pits a sinful attitude against our cognitive commitments—and cognitive commitments cannot vanquish sinful attitudes, even when they render those attitudes logically incoherent.[c] When you deny evil its rationalization, it does not surrender; it just finds a new justification.

---

[c] Some sociologists have also observed the resistance of racial prejudice to cognitive persuasion. Stephen Voss warns that we shouldn't rely too heavily on education to combat prejudice, because "racial stereotypes are not likely to fold in the face of disconfirming evidence (no matter how persuasive)." D. Stephen Voss, "The Rational Basis of Symbolic Racism," Paper prepared for the annual meeting of the Midwest Political Science Association, Chicago, IL, April 27-30, 2000. www.uky.edu/~dsvoss/docs/pspapers/mwpsa00.pdf.

Faced with the seemingly impossible task of marrying mutually exclusive values like equality and haughtiness, whites found not just one but at least three ways to make the incompatible, compatible. These new, largely unconscious, rationalizations allowed a haughty white identity to assimilate the civil rights message, adapting to a new reality without addressing its own fundamental character.

The first rationalization involved *a shift from white supremacy in principle to white meritocracy in practice.* The key to this adjustment was the compartmentalization of equality and superiority. "Equality" was relegated to ontological and legal theory— that we are all equal in our basic humanity, and from that fact certain fundamental rights can be inferred. Those rights make us equal before the law, precluding any degrees of citizenship.

It did not follow from this formal sense of equality, however, that any two individuals were actually equal in terms of their capacities, cultural refinement, or accomplishments. And those who were superior in any or all of these senses might still be deemed worthy of greater social value. Not so coincidentally, many whites still considered black intelligence, morality, civilization, and productivity to be inferior to that of whites. Sure, there were exceptions on both sides, and broad-minded whites might even concede that especially talented blacks should have access to all the prosperity they could acquire. But, in general, such an outcome was not to be expected or cultivated.

This interpretation of equality and superiority allowed whites to affirm egalitarian principles, to join their black counterparts in denouncing past injustices like slavery and segregation—to even welcome a new era of African-American freedom—all this while maintaining a recalibrated notion of superiority. Perhaps that superiority had been downgraded from a question of kind to one of degree, from a categorical absolute to a relative advantage. But, no matter, superiority is superiority, and haughtiness needs just enough of it to rationalize its desire for dominance. Sociological research indicates that dominant groups can relinquish a sizable measure of their control and still satisfy their need for superior status by preserving what is known as a "diminishing difference" between themselves and their supposed inferiors.[2] After all, superiority is by nature a relative measure, not an absolute one.

There is evidence that whites did, in fact, engage in just such a compartmentalization of equality and superiority. A November 1963 Harris poll found that nearly two-thirds of all whites supported the Civil Rights Act. The same poll, however, found that up to 70% "were willing to agree that

Blacks smell different, have looser morals, want to live off the handout, have less native intelligence, breed crime, and are inferior to Whites."[3]

Poll numbers help to quantify the extent of these beliefs, but I recognize this tension between equality and superiority for a different and more personal reason. I grew up during the sixties, the same era when Bettelheim and Janowitz used an open-ended survey to catalogue the terms that whites most frequently used to describe black people, such as:

- sloppy, dirty, filthy
- depreciate property
- taking over, forcing out the whites
- lazy, slackers at work
- low character, immoral and dishonest
- lower standards, lower class
- ignorant, low intelligence
- troublesome and cause disturbances
- smell bad, have a body odor
- carry diseases
- spend their money on a good front, don't save[4]

I remember hearing all of these in my youth, and I undoubtedly subscribed to much of this collective bias myself. I don't think I even met a black person until I was twelve or so. There were no black children in my school district. So, I had no experiential basis to question the prejudices I was absorbing from the white society around me.

It might seem surprising that whites who held such opinions would be drawn toward the civil rights message. How can we explain this seeming incongruity? First, consider that even today many white Americans believe in equality and still cling to some of these (or other) negative stereotypes.[d] Second, it is not uncommon for our formal professions of principle to bend under the weight of our personal moral inclinations and/or self-interest.

Consider the case of evangelical Christians, who are known as staunch pro-life advocates. Indeed, about three out of four disapprove of abortion as a means to resolve unplanned/unwanted pregnancies.[5] And yet, according to the National Association of Evangelicals, nearly a third of unplanned pregnancies among evangelicals end in abortion (vs. 40% in the general population).[6]

---

[d] While surveys still detect such prejudices, it is not possible to make direct comparisons between today's stereotypes and those of yesteryear, because an increase in political correctness over time has made respondents less willing to be candid. This phenomenon is known as "social desirability bias."

The shifting social and moral tectonics of the Civil Rights Era *did* manage to change the white response to the equality question from "no, but" to "yes, but." But the civil rights message *did not* vanquish haughtiness, and it *did not* eliminate white dominance. It simply replaced a more severe system of dominance with a more benign one. Old-time white supremacy was out, leaving in its place a form of meritocracy tilted in favor of whites.

Racial meritocracy was not, however, the only new and improved pathway to dominance. A second rationalization saw whites gravitating to *dominance by definition.* In this view there need not be an inherent or ontological difference between the races—not even superior performance. Even if black people should prove to be the equal of whites in every respect, in America, whites would still retain a preferential status simply by definition.

This superiority by definition is based on the "fact" that white identity and culture have long defined what it means to be American. The country was founded by white Europeans; and the history, the thought, the character, the organization, and the ethos of America were all determined by whites. Nearly all the historical cultural icons were white as well. According to a definitional view of dominance, in this country the white way is the right way, because that is categorically who *we* are. The bottom line of this dominance by definition is that some people end up being more equal than others.[e]

Many years ago, my family and I spent some happy years living in the Catalán region of Spain, an area with its own peculiar culture, language, and history. At one point, in fact, we thought that our work would keep us in Spain permanently, and we investigated the possibility of becoming citizens. When one of our friends heard about our interest in citizenship, she quipped, "Well, you can become Spanish, but you will never be Catalán."

I had no aspirations to become Catalán, but I was nevertheless a bit taken aback by the remark. The incident illustrates an important principle: social identity is defined not only by the cohesive inclusivity of the ingroup but also by its exclusionary ability to define the *other.*

---

[e] Many immigrant white ethnicities have also faced their share of difficulties assimilating into the Anglo-American context and finding acceptance. Aided, however, by a common Western heritage, an aversion to intermarriage that did not rise to the level of the white/black miscegenation hysteria, and two world wars that redefined the *us vs. them* dynamic; whites have more or less coalesced around a sense of whiteness that is, if nothing else, not black.

Civil rights could (ostensibly) ensure that black Americans had full legal status, but haughtiness continued to resist genuine inclusion. Blacks might be accepted as American citizens, but they were not thereby invited to help define what it means to be an American. For most whites, black people were not part of the *we* but part of the *they* that delimits what *we* means.

The third, and perhaps the most subtly destructive rationalization regarding the equality/superiority dialectic is *relational worthiness.* Relational worthiness requires neither competitive superiority nor cultural priority. Rather, it is the tendency for whites to value whiteness, not because it is better but just because they are associated with it and therefore prefer it. Whiteness, as such, might be defined in terms of aesthetics, values, culture, or other factors.

But, wait—isn't there such a thing as a totally natural and innocent ethnocentrism whereby people exhibit a preference for that which is associated with their ingroup? Can't people enjoy a cultural comfort zone without that preference implying something sinister? Yes, that certainly can be the case. The Apostle Paul demonstrated just such a healthy affinity with his own Jewish identity and heritage.

That worked for Paul, because, while he valued his Jewishness, he was at the same time pouring out his life as an apostle to the Gentiles and championing the cause of an integrated Church. He was not only loving others he loved as himself; he was loving his natural and former enemies *sacrificially.* In spite of his devotion to his Jewish identity, he stood up to the most powerful apostle of all, when Peter engaged in ethnically discriminatory behavior. Paul went so far as to associate with the outgroup in the cause of loving justice (Gal. 2:11-14).

So, yes, a righteous ethnocentrism is possible—but it's tricky, especially if we're not truly committed to others in the way that Paul was. Or if we nurture a sense of white exceptionalism. Or if we are so used to white privilege that it has become a birthright.

Under the influence of unredeemed ethnocentrism, our affinity with our own ingroup magnifies the importance of *our* people and *our* interests. These may not *be* better than other people and their interests, but they *become* more important to us. We empathize with our group's aspirations and are angered when our people are treated unfairly, because in some way we feel as if we are part of the same whole. And so, in the end, *we* become subjectively more worthy of our affection and solidarity than *they* are.

Ethnocentrism certainly affects minority groups as well, but it presents some particular challenges for historically dominant groups like white Americans, especially white American Christians, whose chosen ethic obligates them to a higher standard than mere tolerance or civility. How do you heed the command to "in humility consider others better than yourselves," (Philippians 2:3) when, in fact, you're far more attuned to and appreciative of your own issues? When your social advantage has been won at the expense of others, how can you achieve justice for those whose concerns seem less important? If the advantaged do not empathize with the pain of the disadvantaged more than they enjoy their own dominance, how can these disparities ever be overcome?

But can't we love everyone and still love one class of people more? The problem with such a view of relational worthiness is that, in a historical context in which the self-interests of each group have been pitted against one another, simply loving some people more becomes an especially pernicious method of insuring the continued dominance of the dominant. Outwardly, this approach may seem victimless and even benign. After all, it's not a matter of ill will; it's just not caring quite enough to change the status quo, because the concerns of those who are like us register as more worthy of our attention than the concerns of those who are not.

To illustrate this phenomenon of relational worthiness, consider what happens when a pretty, young white girl gets killed or goes missing. Their stories dominate the press, their smiling "before" photos and the images of their anguished families becoming familiar faces. Stories such as those of JonBenét Ramsey (1996 murder unsolved), Laci Peterson (her husband found guilty of murdering her and her unborn child in 2002), and Natalee Holloway (missing in Aruba since 2005, declared legally dead in 2012) occupied the national imagination for months and even years. None of them were celebrities before their demise, but there is now a *Wikipedia* page dedicated to each of the victims. A Google search yields over a half million results for Natalee, three-quarters of a million results for Laci, and well over a million for JonBenét.

Contrast this with the coverage afforded to the loss of young black women. It's hard to even think of a case that has received significant national attention, even though they are far more likely to be the victims of such tragedies. I happen to know about one of the more publicized cases (46,000 results on Google), because Myesha Lowe was gunned down in a drive-by shooting directly in front of my Washington, DC residence in July of 2004.

Myesha, a precocious fifteen-year-old honors student who had once met First Lady Hillary Clinton, received a fair amount of attention for a black victim. One of the dozens of bullets sprayed from the semi-automatic weapon that killed her entered our upstairs window, and the local media wanted to find out how I felt about it. CNN, too, wanted to interview me. I told them, "If you want to talk about the real issues, fine. But if you just want to probe a white person's distress about a hole in his window, while a black girl had a hole in her head, don't waste my time." They never came back.

Myesha was one of twenty-four juveniles murdered in Washington, DC in 2004, all of them black. Nine were female.[7] Unlike Myesha, most got little publicity beyond a possible obituary. There is no *Wikipedia* page in her name or, as far as I can tell, in the name of any other black girl who died as a murder victim. In response to Laci Peterson's murder, in 2004 Congress passed the Unborn Victims of Violence Act, otherwise known as Laci and Connor's Law. In the wake of Myesha's murder, Congress ignored a written plea from DC's Mayor, voting 250-171 to not only repeal the District's current gun laws but also to legalize the very kind of semi-automatic weapon that killed her.

The fact that the stories of these black youngsters are not told is not a function of their frequency. Even though there are about six whites for every black person in the United States, the number of murder victims from each group is almost identical.[8] It's just that the African-American stories are simply not as compelling to a white audience. It's not that they don't matter at all; they just don't matter as much. And that disparity in relational worthiness makes white dominance seem somehow more appropriate.

Even if "yes, but" suffers from all the drawbacks mentioned above, isn't "yes, but" still better than "no, but?" Well, yes, but... Maybe as an incremental rung on the ladder of progress "yes, but" represents some sort of progress. But, when a half century later "yes, but" has effectively become the top rung of the ladder, that is no longer cause for celebration.

At this point "yes, but" is no longer worth celebrating, but it is worth fixing. "Yes, but" came about, because we tried to affirm equality without disavowing haughtiness. The unfinished business of this generation is to turn "yes, but" into "yes, period." And that will require not just changing our answer but changing our very selves.

Chapter 15

Civil Rights and the Ecclesiastical Landscape

As the shock waves of the civil rights era reverberated throughout American society, they shook up not only our secular institutions but our religious ones as well. But that seismic shift did not look and feel the same on both sides the racial fault line. In this chapter we try to understand those disparate consequences for black and white churches respectively—and why, rather than bringing them closer together, it drove them even further apart.

For the better part of a century, black churches had been socially conservative institutions. While their contributions to the African-American community were enormous, they were focused on ameliorating black suffering within the existing structures and strictures of a white-dominated society. The hope they proclaimed was largely future and eternal; they had done little to challenge to the legitimacy of the racial hierarchy itself.

As the Civil Rights Movement unfolded, the response of the black Christian community was by no means monolithic. On one hand, many were enthusiastic about the march to freedom; on the other, some black leaders had created comfortable ghetto fiefdoms and believed they had more to lose than to gain by challenging the status quo. In Martin Luther King's own National Baptist Convention, the power brokers were mostly gradualists, and his more aggressive tactics in pursuit of civil rights caused considerable controversy.[a]

Internal power struggles among black elites continued throughout the Civil Rights Movement, as did a vigorous debate about strategy. As late as 1964 a Gallup Poll showed that only 55% of *non-whites* thought that the current mass demonstrations would actually help the cause of racial equality.[1] In spite of their differences over strategy, however, the vast majority of African Americans came to believe that the time for fundamental change had come, and they embraced Dr. King as the iconic leader of that movement. By 1963, his personal approval rating among blacks reached as high as 88%.[2]

---

[a] In 1961, after the denomination removed King from his position on a denominational board, he helped form the Progressive National Baptist Convention, which embraced a more activist approach toward civil rights.

Primed to challenge the paradigms of the past and influenced by events on the ground, the message of freedom and hope proclaimed from black pulpits became increasingly infused with temporal implications. Weary of simply attenuating the effects of a white hierarchy while passively perpetuating it, this sleeping giant awoke. In just a few short years, black churches crossed a double solid line and left their historic lane, mounting a conscious challenge to America's longstanding racial hierarchy.

Not only did that transformation alter the ethos of African-American churches; it forever changed the prospects for Christian racial reconciliation. White and black churches had always been associated with different interests, but the unchallenged appropriateness of white hegemony had kept them from becoming actual adversaries. The two factions might have even imagined themselves as working on behalf of the same Kingdom along parallel lines. But given the long history of the white Church as a hierarchy-enhancing institution, with the onset of the Civil Rights Movement the two traditions found themselves on opposite sides of the challenge to white dominance itself.

The prophetic message of equality held an undeniable appeal for many white Christians, but its implications for white dominance were troubling. Something about the practical agenda of civil rights sent the subliminal message, "Don't pull on that loose string!" So, most white Christians beat a tactical retreat, offering neither overt support nor opposition to the Movement and buying time to sort out their identity vis-à-vis this new reality.

The record shows that white churches, caught in the crossfire of competing commitments, felt their way forward quite cautiously on this issue. Of course, their responses varied depending on their geography and their theological commitments. Northern evangelicals, according to Emerson and Smith in *Divided by Faith*, "seemed more preoccupied with other issues— such as evangelism, and fighting communism and liberalism."[3] As a result, the message of civil rights got squelched by competing priorities.

Just how did these evangelical commitments influence their response to the Civil Rights Movement? First, evangelicals viewed any involvement with social issues as an implicit de-emphasis on evangelism, if not a dangerous dabbling in the social gospel. Second, when a 1965 Gallup Poll asked about the extent of Communist involvement in civil rights demonstrations, nearly three quarters of Americans considered it significant.[4] So, understandably, anti-communist evangelicals were wary. Third, evangelicals saw civil rights leaders as leaning toward the theological left—a view that was influenced by the fact that the few white Christians who *were* active in civil rights were liberal Protestants and Catholics.

Yes, evangelicals were otherwise occupied, and those occupations were at odds with their perceptions of the Movement. As a result, "yes, but" was about as much enthusiasm as they were going to muster. Historian George Marsden observes that, "most… did not think it their duty to oppose segregation; it was enough to treat the blacks they knew personally with courtesy and fairness."[5]

White Southern evangelicals, however, could not embrace the Northern laissez-faire attitude toward an issue so intimately intertwined with their history and their daily lives. But they, too were conflicted. David Chappell observes: "The historically significant thing about white religion in the 1950-60s is not its failure to join the civil rights movement. The significant thing, given that the church was probably as racist as the rest of the white South, is that it failed in any meaningful way to join the *anti*-civil rights movement."[6]

What kept them on the sidelines? Southern evangelicals had three principle commitments of their own—Scripture, law and order, and missions. However appropriate segregation might have seemed to Southern whites, most came to accept the fact that no positive argument could be made on behalf of it from Scripture. Given their devotion to the Bible as the standard for faith and practice, evangelicals opted to relegate matters of segregation and desegregation to the social rather than the spiritual sphere—a categorical judgment that located the issue outside of the Church's purview.

Though these evangelicals did not find biblical warrant for segregation, they did believe that Scripture supported law and order. Indeed, this commitment had long lent support to the racial hierarchy itself. But when the Supreme Court came down on the side of desegregation, Christians were caught in a bind. The only way to justify civil disobedience against the law of the land was to argue that it was inherently immoral. But they had already eliminated that line of argument by declaring the issue purely social in nature.

So, while Southern Christians had no real enthusiasm for desegregation, Southern churches made no concerted effort to oppose it. In fact, when the Gray Amendment (the beta version of the Southern Manifesto, designed to nullify the Supreme Court's decision) was being debated in Virginia, "state senator Ted Dalton reportedly stated, 'The politicians lined up almost solidly for the amendment and the preachers almost solidly against it.'"[7]

World War II gave Americans a new awareness of the broader world, resulting in a flurry of missionary activity during the 1950s and beyond. The Southern Baptist Convention, in particular, was heavily invested in international outreach. Between 1948 and 1964 their foreign missionary force grew from 600 to almost 1,900. The familiar refrain from returning missionaries, however, was that racial strife in America was affecting their ability to minister in the non-white world. And this collision between their commitment to missions and their segregationist sentiments limited the Southern evangelical defense of the existing order.

For most white evangelicals, regardless of their geographic location, civil rights remained more of a civil than a moral issue. *Christianity Today (CT),* the flagship magazine of evangelicalism, wrote an average of less than two articles per year on the subject between 1957 and 1965,[8] despite the fact that the topic dominated the national news and had an unmistakable Christian connection. Though *CT* sent coeditor Frank Gaebelein to investigate civil rights stories, the magazine later admitted that his "dispatches from Martin Luther King's marches in the South went unpublished for fear of giving the impression that civil rights should be part of the Christian agenda."[9/b]

The most influential figure in American evangelicalism during the civil rights era, and arguably in American religion itself, was the founder of *Christianity Today*, Rev. Billy Graham. After some initial waffling on segregation during his early ministry, in 1954 he decided that all his campaigns would be integrated. This seems to have reflected his own unfolding conscience on the matter, his theology of human equality at the foot of the cross, and his sense of what would best promote his evangelistic enterprise. The decision was unquestionably historic, a son of the South breaking with the uniform Jim Crow legacy of evangelists who refused to hold integrated meetings in segregated states, even when they did so elsewhere.

An interesting relationship developed between the two leading churchmen of that day, one black and one white. In 1957 Graham asked Dr. King to appear with him in his New York evangelistic campaign, hailing him as a leader of a "great social revolution." The evangelist even posted King's bail after a protest arrest on one occasion. He also encouraged whites to support desegregation, invoking the law and order argument.

---

[b] For more background on *Christianity Today* and its editorial perspective of that time, see: www.scottgarber.com/was_notes.pdf, Note 15.1.

As the Movement grew, however, Rev. Graham had trouble reconciling King's "great social revolution" with his own commitment to that very law and order principle, and never asked him to appear at another evangelistic event. He was generally critical of black protest disturbances. While Dr. King was incarcerated in Birmingham, Graham urged his "good personal friend"[10] to "put on the brakes a little bit."[11] And after King dreamed aloud in August of 1963 that "one day, down in Alabama... little black boys and black girls will be able to join hands with little white boys and white girls as sisters and brothers," [12] Graham countered that "only when Christ comes again will little white children of Alabama walk hand in hand with little black children."[13]

The relationship between these two men illustrates what can happen to racial justice and harmony when parsed along the lines of one's relationship to the social/racial hierarchy—and why even well-meaning white and black Christians in the post-civil rights era would have difficulty pursuing reconciliation and creating common life. Ostensibly "shared" commitments, like racial justice and law and order, were prioritized so differently that what looked similar in principle looked very different in practice. What Dr. King called "the fierce urgency of now,"[14] when translated into *whitespeak*, became "a non-pressing preference for someday"— hardly a reason to rock the boat.

The notable absence of white evangelical involvement in a movement championed by black Christians further estranged the two religious traditions. Had white and black Christians joined forces as a counter-cultural force for change, the future might have looked brighter for racial reconciliation. But with black Christians squarely arrayed against the traditional racial hierarchy that white evangelical Christianity supported, powerful conflicts of interest precluded anything more than a sentimental notion of unity.

While white evangelicals defined the Southern religious landscape during the civil rights era, mainline denominations still dominated the national scene.[15] Especially in the north, these church bodies tended to be influenced by theological liberalism, which placed a premium on the social gospel. As a result, the black struggle for racial justice resonated with many mainline clergymen (and to a lesser degree the with laity). And, compared to their evangelical counterparts, these denominations proved to be relatively more involved and supportive of the Civil Rights Movement, particularly through the National Council of Churches.

In June of 1963, the NCC, on behalf of its thirty-one constituent denominations, created the *Commission on Religion and Race*. This body helped sponsor the 1963 March on Washington and urged its clergy to participate with Dr. King in the 1965 voting rights march in Selma, Alabama.[c] They sent a delegation to lobby Congress on behalf of the Civil Rights Act. One of their resolutions called "on the churches to declare open membership, to engage in interracial activities with other churches, and to inquire about the policies of companies and enterprises with which churches do business."[16]

Despite the cooperation and practical support provided by mainline churches, Chappell makes a strong case that "the alliance between black Christian civil rights groups and American liberals was more an alliance of convenience than one of deep ideological affinity."[17] In part that's because both theological as well as secular liberalism, "had in common a very unprophetic faith in human autonomy and self-improvement."[18]

Though mainline Christians did occasionally participate in acts of solidarity with black protesters, their involvement was not numerically significant until late in the game. Indeed, proactive advocacy was not the liberals' principle strategy. Mainline theologians took a more benign view of human sinfulness than King and his cohorts, so they were more content to allow education and progress to bring about racial enlightenment.

The black theological orientation was a study in contrast. Like "the Hebrew prophets, these thinkers believed that they could not expect that world and those institutions to improve.... They had to try to force an unwilling world to abandon sin—in this case, 'the sin of segregation.'"[19] The nexus between their anthropology and the social gospel was in many ways more akin to that of the progressive evangelicals of the late 19th century (except that those evangelicals, as we have seen, did not connect the dots to racial justice).

Despite their differing attitudes toward civil rights as a religious issue, liberal-leaning whites suffered from the same problem as their evangelical counterparts—they were white, and racial haughtiness was part and parcel of white identity. Mainline churches may have been more sensitive to racial justice, but in the end they remained hierarchy-enhancing institutions under the influence of white self-interest. They were willing to point a finger at "the problem" but unwilling to point it at themselves. Unfortunately, no Christian

---

[c] Some 450 clergy participated in the march. I have found no official accounting of the denominational representation, but there was a delegation of 35-40 Catholic priests, some 45 Unitarians, and as many as a dozen rabbis. The rest appear to have hailed overwhelmingly from mainline denominations.

critique can be truly prophetic if judgment does not begin in the house of God, and theirs did not.

The Roman Catholic experience of civil rights was quite different from that of Protestants. African Americans had historically represented a very distinct minority among U.S. Catholics. Neither slavery nor Jim Crow had ever split the Church along racial lines. And many Catholics had themselves suffered marginalization at the hand of a WASP-ish majority in the not too distant past on account of either their ethnicity and/or their faith.

Perhaps because of these differences, the Catholic Church in America—at least in its upper echelons—demonstrated both an engagement with race relations as well as a comprehension of its spiritual nature. As early as 1943 the Conference of Catholic Bishops issued a statement calling not only for political equality but for "fair economic and educational opportunities, a just share in public welfare projects, good housing without exploitation, and a full chance for the social advancement of their race."[20] Fifteen years later, in 1958, just as the Civil Rights Movement was gathering steam, they released another document, entitled, *Discrimination and the Christian Conscience*. In it they recognized that "the heart of the race question is moral and religious,"[21] clearly distinguishing themselves from the many Protestants who wanted to relegate the problem to the social and political sphere. They stated categorically that enforced segregation was incompatible with a Christian view of humankind and the obligations of neighborly love. In addition, they called upon all Americans to root out bitterness and hatred from their hearts.

The Roman Catholic Church, however, suffered from the nexus between Catholicism and white identity. Some of those connections were as obvious as the Church's legacy of white, European leadership and its overwhelmingly white American constituency. After all, in 1960 African Americans constituted less than 2% all U.S. Catholics.

The identification of the Catholic Church with whiteness was widespread in the black community during the civil rights era and beyond. Father Rollins Lambert was the first African American ordained in the Archdiocese of Chicago (1949) and later served as an advisor on African Affairs for the United States Conference of Catholic Bishops (1975-1987). In 1963, Father Lambert flatly told the St. Louis Archdiocese Institute on Human Rights Conference: "The Roman Catholic Church in the United States is identified by Negroes as a white man's church."[22]

Nearly two decades later, in 1984, the Black Catholic Bishops would return to this theme in a pastoral letter entitled *What We Have Seen and Heard.* They argued that since the Church "is essentially universal, hence, Catholic," that it was neither "a 'White Church' nor a 'Euro-American Church.'"[23] But why, then, did they feel the need to repeat this theological mantra? As they explained, it was "to counter the *assumption* [emphasis mine] that to become Catholic is to abandon one's racial heritage and one's people."[24]

While the Catholic Church deserves credit for creating a more integrated environment than did the Protestant churches of that era, the experience of black Catholics shows that the perception of white dominance in their Church had some basis in reality. In 1963, Father Lambert complained: "White Catholics may concede that there is a place in the Church for Negroes, but traditionally that place has been there, not here—at a distance, not in our parish."[25] More than two decades later, America's ten black bishops reported that "American blacks [still] suffer discrimination in the Roman Catholic Church."[26] They recognized that through its official condemnations of racism "the church has spoken" but asked, "has the church listened to itself?"[27]

Though at one time many Catholics had themselves been on the receiving end of discrimination, by the time of their 1958 statement on race, the bishops acknowledged that the once-despised Catholic immigrant "has achieved his rightful status in the American community."[28] By 1960, there were 42 million Catholics in the United States, making it far and away the largest single religious body. And, as Catholicism became mainstream in America, the values of Catholics largely merged with those of the white Protestant majority.

Like mainline Protestant proponents of racial reform, American Catholics were limited by the fact that they were ensconced within the very hierarchy they were ostensibly trying to change. Which meant that the Church might rock the boat a little, but certainly not enough to capsize it. Even the bishops' urgent-sounding gradualism was too radical for many Catholics in the trenches, who felt threatened by racial change. These more conservative sentiments inevitably formed part of the backdrop against which American Catholicism interfaced with the Civil Rights Movement.

The disconnect between the course charted at 35,000 feet and the realities on the ground was, at times, palpable. During the difficult days of Milwaukee's 1967 racial tensions a troubled lay person wrote to activist priest, Father James Groppi:

It is not fair to shove people of another race down our throats. The Archbishops, Bishops, priests, the president, Robert Kennedy, and other people advocating open housing sit in their single homes and tell us who to live with.... When all the people I have mentioned live in the middle of row houses with people of other races I will too.[29]

With evangelicals on the sidelines (at best) and mainline Protestants saddled with the weight of history and their own white identity issues, Catholics missed an opportunity to become a far more prophetic voice with game-changing influence. Yes, they took seriously the moral dimension of the country's racial problems, and they possessed a certain moral authority as a national body that had not split along racial lines. But the Church failed to recognize its own complicity in haughtiness, trying to lead from a position of (self-)righteousness, when America really needed a model of penitence.

By the middle of the 20th century the institutional rift between black and white churches was already well-established. Theology, however, had never been a line of demarcation between the two, as the faith and polity of black churches was essentially a hand-me-down from their white forebears. But then black liberation theology arrived on the scene.

This theological perspective first surfaced on July 31, 1966, when fifty-one black churchmen—members of an *ad hoc* group called The National Committee of Negro Churchmen (NCNC)—took out a full-page ad in *The New York Times*, proclaiming their view of race relations from a "black power" viewpoint. Not endorsed or even officially acknowledged by the largest black denominations, this document articulated the divide between white and black churches along the lines of the existing racial hierarchy.

In a section of the statement directed to white churchmen, the NCNC members rejected the notion that integration was the answer to the racial schism, writing: "The Negro Church was created as a result of the refusal to submit to the indignities of a false kind of 'integration' in which all power was in the hands of white people."[30] That integrated, white-over-black hierarchy was the focus of their challenge. They insisted that "without this capacity to participate with power... integration is not meaningful."[31]

With the publication of *Black Theology & Black Power* (1969) and *A Black Theology of Liberation* (1970), James Cone, a Professor of Systematic Theology at Union Theological Seminary who died in 2018, became the leading spokesperson for black liberation theology. As he described it, his thought arose from the confluence of the messages of Malcolm X and Martin Luther King Jr., whom he called "the most important and influential Christian theologian in America's history."[32] Though many white theologians had addressed the social implications of the Gospel, it was King who connected God's salvific activity to the black struggle for freedom, and, as Cone explained, "transformed our understanding of the Christian faith by making the practice of justice an essential ingredient of its identity."[33]

Dr. Cone wrote: "[King] helped define my Christian identity but was silent about the meaning of blackness in a world of white supremacy. Malcolm X... 'put the word *black* in black theology.'"[34] Cone believed that King's commitment to integration and nonviolence involved a capitulation to the existing hierarchy, calling blacks to "turn the other cheek to white brutality, join the mainstream of American society, and do theology without anger and without reference to the history and culture of African Americans..."[35]

The foundation of Cone's theology was not Scripture or church dogma but, rather, the African-American experience of oppression. God, then, was seen as aligning himself with those who are suffering, to such an extent that God and his work are eventually reduced and radicalized (Cone might have preferred "contextualized") by this prism and viewed almost exclusively in terms of temporal and political liberation in the black experience.[d] This liberation becomes not just an implication of the gospel, but for all practical purposes the gospel itself as it applies to black reality.

For Dr. Cone, whites represented the evil against which God was conducting his saving work. He claimed that "theologically, Malcom X was not far wrong when he called the white man 'the devil.'"[36] Moreover, he condemned blacks who accepted a white theological paradigm: "There is no use for a God who loves whites the same as blacks.... What we need is the divine love as expressed in Black Power, which is the power of black people to destroy their oppressors, here and now, by any means at their disposal."[37/e]

Though black liberation theology made some headway in the rarified air of the academy, it was never broadly accepted in the pew. As one black pastor

---

[d] Though Cone's thought had much in common with the Latin American liberation theology that emerged in the 50s and 60s, he was initially unaware of the other version. The two theological currents have since established a rapport. See his preface to *A Black Theology of Liberation* (1986).

[e] Cone dialed back the vituperative rhetoric in more recent times, though his critique changed little with regard to its substance.

wrote in the Harvard Theological Review in 1971: "here and there black prelates and ecclesiastical leaders are one with Cone's thinking... [but] judging from pronouncements of older [church leaders], many have not caught up with Martin L. King Jr., much less the black Revolution."[38]

White Christians, for their part, responded by accusing Cone of reverse racism and by denouncing his lack of orthodoxy. Indeed, there is plenty that one could legitimately critique about black liberation theology. But James Cone did not create a God who legitimized oppression by the powerful or a gospel that was bad news for the poor or a spirituality that embraced haughtiness. Dr. Cone simply smelled a rat and decided to call it by name.

Though relatively few black people accepted the logical extremes to which Cone took his response, many did find something intuitively undeniable in his analysis. Black Liberation Theology recognized an enduring moral flaw in white identity itself. And it observed that black and white churches have situated themselves on opposite sides of a struggle—a struggle that no reconciliation effort can afford to ignore if it wants to remain coherent.

Black Liberation Theology reminded us that in a racialized society the way we relate to God and his work cannot be abstracted from our connection to the racial hierarchy. Many whites didn't take the hint, however, continuing to pursue a privatized and pietistic religion, while their black counterparts were concluding that achieving justice for the oppressed was an integral part of what God was trying to accomplish in the world.

With the advent of this distinctly black way of doing theology, there was no going back to the view that black Christianity was just an underdeveloped alternative to its white counterpart. Black Christians now had a spiritual worldview that resonated with their experience, and they were no longer content to occupy their "place" in a relationship defined by white haughtiness.

The American Church entered the Civil Rights Era divided along racial lines and emerged looking largely the same. But it was not the same; it was, if anything, less hopeful. The agapic conciliation of Martin Luther King Jr. did not heal Christian racial dysfunction, perhaps because it tiptoed too much around haughtiness. Others, like Dr. Cone, forcefully pointed out the weaknesses of whiteness but did not aspire to Christian unity. For their part, the relatively few whites who were interested in solving the problem didn't see themselves as part of the problem. So, they were not ready to lead and not ready to be led. Whereas it had once seemed as if the Church might be the key to racial reconciliation, it was beginning to look more like a lock.

Chapter 16

Political Backlash

In a case of history recycling, if not repeating itself, both Reconstruction and the civil rights era ushered in brief periods of euphoric optimism for black Americans. Unfortunately, the parallels did not end there. Just as Redemption delivered a historic white counterpunch to Reconstruction, a century later there was once again a price to pay for progress. In the wake of the Civil Rights Movement black ascendency once again posed a perceived threat to the racial hierarchy, stirring up white fears about a loss of power, privilege, and tangible advantages—and provoking "white backlash."

This backlash phenomenon is sometimes depicted as a late sixties/early seventies snapshot—a reflexive white power response to black power. As Neubeck and Cazenave argue, however, white backlash is more than an event; it is, rather, "a process of racial control by which white racial hegemony, when threatened and disturbed, is brought back into equilibrium."[1] In some ways the entire contemporary period of race relations has been a kind of thrust and parry in search of such an equilibrium.

Southern white society was never in a hurry to implement civil rights reforms. But as racial conflict erupted in Northern cities, even Northern whites began to get cold feet. A 1964 Gallup Poll found that 28 percent of Northerners thought the Johnson administration was moving "too fast" on racial integration. On the contrary, only 13 percent thought they were proceeding "too slowly." Gallup asked the same question again in 1966, after racial disorders had erupted in forty-three cities around the country. The transformation was remarkable. By that time a full *52 percent* of Northern whites were convinced that the government was moving too fast, whereas only 8 percent still felt that the pace was "too slow."[2]

Rather than examining governmental protagonism, pollster Louis Harris focused his research on black activism. His results paralleled Gallup's findings. In 1964, Harris asked about the pace with which blacks were pushing civil rights progress. Whites were evenly divided across the spectrum of responses: "too fast" (34%), "too slow" (32%), and "about right" (34%). But two years later that white response had changed dramatically. By that time 85 percent were saying, "too fast," and only 3 percent answered, "too slow."[3/a]

While many whites opposed government assistance to minorities, others tolerated it as a kind of "hush money," throwing blacks a bone in the hopes of placating them. These programs served to mitigate black disadvantage at arm's length, without requiring whites to personally interact with their racial other. The same could not be said for other government initiatives, however, some of which excited a far more passionate white reaction. Nothing, it seems, lit the backlash fire like school desegregation, including and especially the issue of busing. Let's look at how this white resistance evolved.

The Supreme Court established no time frame for implementing its 1954 *Brown* decision, other than to proceed with "all deliberate speed." The white Southern establishment conveniently overlooked the *speedy* part, however, and concentrated all its energies on being *deliberate*. As a result, school desegregation saw very little progress over the next decade. But in the wake of the 1964 Civil Rights Act and the 1965 Elementary and Secondary Education Act, Southern states finally found themselves forced to do *something* in the direction of desegregation.

Three-fourths of them opted for a strategy called "Freedom of Choice," a program that purportedly allowed students to attend any school in their system. However, for black families to attend white schools, they had to apply to officials who were almost universally committed to the status quo. With implementation resting in the hands of people who wanted the program to fail, it should come as no surprise that an informal system of impediments and coercion soon arose, making a mockery of both "freedom" and "choice."

Applicants regularly heard that white schools were already overcrowded, that buses did not run through their neighborhoods, or that they could not participate in extracurricular activities. They faced arcane requests for documentation, were told that their forms appeared forged, or that the school couldn't accept too many students from the same family. These complications were often accompanied by implicit and/or explicit threats, warning pushy parents that they could lose their homes or their jobs.[4]

As a result, by January of 1966, very few black pupils in the South went to school with whites (5.2 percent according to the Southern Regional Council

---

[a] For more background on Harris's polling about white backlash, see: www.scottgarber.com/was_notes.pdf, Note 16.1.

and 7.5 percent according to the Office of Education). In 1965-66 over one hundred "Freedom of Choice" districts granted *no* transfers whatsoever.[5] The superintendent of Alabama's Anniston schools declared them "desegregated" when only 216 of 3,200 black students were going to school with whites.[6]

By 1968, the Supreme Court had lost patience with the "Freedom of Choice" model and began to demand desegregation plans that yielded results rather than just vague opportunities (*Green v. School Board of New Kent County*). When the Nixon administration dragged its feet on implementation, Justice Black saw it as the President's "payoff to the South"[7] and decided to intervene. He called for a court order, not an opinion that could be parsed, demanding that unitary school systems must replace distinct black and white schools immediately. "All deliberate speed" was dead.

This order brought significant desegregation to some districts, but many holdouts remained. That recalcitrance led the Supreme Court (*Swann,* 1971) to rule that in school districts where de jure segregation had been practiced, the federal courts could order busing and redraw school zones, in order to eliminate "all vestiges of state-imposed segregation."[8] Nixon had opposed such a ruling, and even after the case was settled he instructed his secretary of Health, Education, and Welfare to "do what the law requires and not *one bit more.*"[9] By September of that year the House had proposed twenty-five different anti-busing bills. None of them made it through the Democrat-controlled Judicial Committee. The popular battle over busing was on.

Of course, busing in the South was nothing new. For nearly half a century every Southern state had funded such transportation in an effort to facilitate segregation, with some black students transported over forty miles to attend segregated facilities. There had been no white outcry—that is, until the purpose of busing changed—at which point whites began to object "in principle" to the notion of transporting students away from neighborhood schools. The sound and fury of this protest was considerable, fueled by fears of predatory black sexuality, criminality, and substandard educational levels.

Unable to change the new system, many white families simply circumvented it. The first line of resistance was subterfuge—giving fake addresses, setting up proxy residences, swapping houses with relatives, even giving over guardianship of their children to suburban families. A second strategy involved the vast expansion of private schools, sometimes referred to as "segregation academies." Attendance at such schools from pre-1964 levels to the 1971-72 school year increased twenty-fold. The third phenomenon was demographic, white flight from the cities to the suburbs. While the reasons for this shift go beyond race, the integration of urban school systems was a major factor, causing parents to look for housing in a district with "good schools."

Though busing was effective in achieving greater racial balance in the short term, the combined effect of these white backlash strategies proved enormous, leading to a de facto re-segregation of city schools. Minchin and Salmond, in *After the Dream*, observed that "by the late 1970s, many urban school systems were suffering from record levels of white flight. That exodus made busing less relevant, because most cities found that they no longer had enough white pupils to transport."[10]

For example, in 1970, Dallas had 160,000 students in its system. Seven years later more than 40,000 white pupils had vanished, with the percentage of black students soaring from 18 to 62 percent over a twenty-year span. In Richmond, Virginia the student population was 55 percent white in 1962; by 1978 it had become 82 percent black. During the 1970s the city of Atlanta lost an incredible 40 percent of its white population. Over 100,000 people headed to the suburbs, leaving the city's public schools about 90 percent black.[11]

By March of the 1972 election year, Gallup reported that "74 percent of southern whites were opposed to 'compulsory busing' and that 68 percent of Northern whites agreed with them."[12] Clearly, powerful social forces were at work, forces no politician could ignore. One of them, however, became a national spokesman for white backlash—Alabama Governor George Wallace.

Wallace had declared in his 1963 inaugural address: "In the name of the greatest people that have ever trod this earth, I draw the line in the dust and toss the gauntlet before the feet of tyranny, and I say segregation now, segregation tomorrow, segregation forever."[13] Sensing the mood of the country, he mounted a third-party bid for the presidency in 1968. By that time Wallace had traded in his overt, racially-charged rhetoric for an "anti-Washington" message that, while broader in its appeal, was sufficiently clear in its intent to galvanize an amazing share of the backlash vote. Running as an independent, Wallace won five Southern states outright, capturing 46 electoral votes. He got a total of 10 million votes nationwide, 13% of the total.

In 1972, Wallace changed tactics and entered the primaries as a Democrat. Still challenging Washington, standing up for law and order, and promising to end school busing, Wallace became the hero of the backlash movement. Had he not been shot and paralyzed in an assassination attempt in May of 1972, he would have been a force to be reckoned with at the

Democratic Convention. At the time he dropped out, Wallace held a sizable lead over both George McGovern and Hubert Humphrey in the popular primary votes cast, though he trailed McGovern in delegates.

Richard Nixon picked up the scent of Wallace's appeal to backlash voters, but his advisors differed over strategy. Daniel Patrick Moynihan wrote a memorandum (leaked to *The New York Times*), suggesting that "the time may have come when the issue of race could benefit from a period of 'benign neglect.[14]'" Moynihan thought Nixon needed to focus on black progress, "while seeking to avoid situations in which extremists of either race are given opportunities for martyrdom, heroics, histrionics or whatever."[15]

But then there was Pat Buchanan, an advocate of racial polarization politics. His plan was to rally African-American support for a black Vice-President by passing out bumper stickers in ghettos and trying to get a black person nominated at the Democratic Convention. By painting the Democrats black, he believed that Nixon could peel off white union supporters from the democratic ranks. Buchanan argued that that would "cut the Democratic party and country in half,"[16] leaving the Republicans with "the far larger half."[17]

In the racialized politics of that era, Nixon pursued what became known as the *Southern Strategy*, the brainchild of campaign guru, Kevin Phillips. In a 1970 interview with *The New York Times*, Phillips explained:

> From now on, the Republicans are never going to get more than 10 to 20 percent of the Negro vote and they don't need any more than that... but Republicans would be shortsighted if they weakened enforcement of the Voting Rights Act. The more Negroes who register as Democrats in the South, the sooner the Negrophobe whites will quit the Democrats and become Republicans. That's where the votes are. Without that prodding from the blacks, the whites will backslide into their old comfortable arrangement with the local Democrats.[18]

Nixon became adept at framing issues in ways that catered to white backlash. He began the charge for welfare reform, targeting "welfare cheats." This had not been a major concern until the vast expansion of the welfare rolls in the late 1960s, when African Americans were finally able to take advantage of government programs without the barriers they had faced in the past. As a result, the number of people receiving Aid to Families with Dependent Children (AFDC) benefits more than doubled between 1965 and 1970, during which time people of color became the outright majority of all recipients.[19] In a conversation with his advisors about welfare reform, Nixon "emphasized that you have to face the fact that the whole problem is really the blacks. The key is to devise a system that recognizes this while not appearing to."[20]

In a kind of cruel historic irony, Nixon ran as a champion of "law and order." In 1968, he warned that if the current rate of new crimes continued:

> ...the number of rapes and robberies and assaults and thefts in the United States today will double by the end of 1972[!]... If we allow it to happen, then the city jungle will cease to be a metaphor. It will become a barbaric reality, and the brutal society that now flourishes in the core cities of America will annex the affluent suburbs.[21]

As a result of the black-led racial disturbances of the late 1960s, law and order vaulted up the list of social concerns. Nixon's get-tough talk indirectly reassured nervous whites that black people would not get too far out of "their place" and that the racial hierarchy was safe.[b] On the other side of the ledger, Democrats were, in general, hampered by their commitment to the special interest groups that comprised their constituency. That left Republicans to take the lead in appealing to disaffected whites, and as LBJ had predicted, to take control of the South. It is no coincidence that between 1968 and 2008 the only Democrats to be elected President were themselves Southerners.

The first of these Democrats to find a winning formula was former Georgia governor, Jimmy Carter, who burst onto the national scene in 1976. Having grown up in the segregated South, Carter had learned the art of mixing moderate politics with an outsider, evangelical appeal that kept enough of the backlash crowd in his camp. After running for governor as a moderate against white supremacist Lester Maddox in 1966 and finishing third in the primaries, he mounted a campaign against former governor Carl Sanders in the Democratic primary of 1970. This time, however, he was running against a quasi-liberal, and Carter's campaign acquired a ring of Southern populism.

Carter's inevitable connections to the white south allowed him to emphasize the most expedient aspects of his persona. For instance, in 1965 his Southern Baptist Church in Plains voted to bar "all negroes and civil rights

---

[b] Despite his personal bigotry and reliance on race-baiting politics, Richard Nixon was a complex man with complex politics. His administration was not the disaster for African Americans that one might suppose. For more on this side of Nixon, see: www.scottgarber.com/was_notes.pdf, Note 16.2.

agitators" from membership. Some Carter biographies praise Jimmy and Rosalynn Carter for heroically casting two of the three dissenting votes in that decision. Others find it not so heroic that they remained members of the overtly segregated church, as the exclusionary rule was not changed until after Carter's presidential victory in 1976.

Historian E. Stanly Godbold, author of *Jimmy and Rosalynn Carter: The Georgia Years, 1924-1974*, maintains that though Carter was not a segregationist, "he did say things that the segregationists wanted to hear. He was opposed to busing. He was in favor of private schools. He said that he would invite segregationist governor George Wallace to come to Georgia to give a speech."[22] He ran far enough to the right in that 1970 gubernatorial race that the Atlanta Constitution labeled him an "ignorant, racist, backward, ultra-conservative, red-necked South Georgia peanut farmer."[23/c] To the surprise of some of his supporters, however, he announced in his inaugural address: "I say to you quite frankly, that the time for racial discrimination is over."[24] Carter went on to govern as a fiscal reformer who pursued a somewhat progressive social policy, though he did maintain his opposition to busing.

Carter never did invite George Wallace to speak, but the two squared off in the 1976 Democratic primaries. The now crippled Wallace soon folded and endorsed his opponent, claiming that he had "paved the way for a Jimmy Carter."[25] In November this moderate Democrat with a feel for Southern sensibilities nearly swept Dixie against the Northern Republican, Gerald Ford.

Once Carter became President, he expanded the federal civil rights agenda, albeit rather modestly. Though limited by a terrible economy (and his own commitment to austerity), he was nevertheless disinclined to pursue an agenda that would outpace the capacity of whites to assimilate it. Carter did enforce court orders for busing, but his administration took few new initiatives. Legal opinion was already moving toward a more restrictive view of busing, and popular sentiments were squarely against the practice.

For years civil rights advocates had pushed for a national right-to-work bill. After early vacillation Carter did eventually sign the 1978 Humphrey-Hawkins "full-employment" bill, though by that time it had been watered down and rendered more or less symbolic.[d] As for affirmative action, early in

---

[c] It seems that Carter was engaged in a feud with the newspaper back then, which may have contributed to the exaggerated nature of this characterization.

[d] For more on this bill, see: www.scottgarber.com/was_notes.pdf, Note 16.3.

his presidency Carter endorsed an ambitious bill to increase minority contracts in public works, but his administration generated hardly any other proposals of note until the end of his term, when he had already lost to Ronald Reagan.

Though Nixon and Carter both managed to connect politically with elements of white backlash, their administrations generally continued to enforce and even expand the Johnsonian civil rights agenda. As Yale Law Professor and former Assistant Attorney General Drew S. Days III put it, from Roosevelt to Reagan the nation had accepted "two basic premises: first, that America has yet to fulfill the promises of 'life, liberty and the pursuit of happiness' on an equal basis for large groups of its citizenry; and second, that the federal government should play a major role in vindicating civil rights."[26]

The first president to challenge those principles directly and unapologetically was Ronald Reagan. A congenial fellow who seemed to get along well enough with African Americans on a personal level, Reagan's approach to government dovetailed a bit too conveniently with the white backlash agenda—so much so that he found himself constantly fending off charges that there was a racial animus behind his political philosophy. Indeed, an ABC News-Washington Post poll taken in January of 1986 found that 56 percent of black respondents considered the President a racist.[27]

Whatever his personal attitudes toward black people might have been, Reagan's history with racial justice inspired little confidence. He originally opposed the Civil Rights Act of 1964 on what he called "constitutional grounds," because it infringed on personal rights. In the 1966 California gubernatorial race he declared: "If an individual wants to discriminate against negroes or others in selling or renting his house, it is his right to do so."[28] He called the 1965 Voting Rights Act a "humiliation to the South."[29] The launch of his 1980 campaign, proclaiming his support of "states' rights," took place in Philadelphia, Mississippi, a town famous for the 1964 murder of three civil rights workers.[30] In the 1984 campaign, while stumping in Georgia, Reagan—an inveterate name-dropper—invoked the legacy of Jefferson Davis.[31]

Reagan perfected the art of using coded racial language that appealed to the backlash vote. He hammered away on the concept of welfare, casting it as a giveaway to irresponsible and/or dishonest black people by his frequent anecdotal references to a pink Cadillac-driving "welfare queen." There was, of course, no need to mention the color of the queen in question.

An even more subtle outreach to disaffected whites was Reagan's anti-Washington rhetoric, a tactic straight out of George Wallace's playbook. In

1981, an interviewer questioned Lee Atwater, a Reagan advisor and his 1980 campaign manager (at the time responding as an anonymous administration official), about whether the President's policies and his coded language were designed to appeal to the racist element among Wallace supporters, without being so blatant as to offend the broad spectrum of whites. This is how Atwater explained what he called Reagan's "new southern strategy:"[32]

> You start out in 1954 by saying, "Nigger, nigger, nigger." By 1968 you can't say "nigger"—that hurts you. Backfires. So you say stuff like "forced busing," "states' rights," and all these things that you're talking about are totally economic things and a by-product of them is [that] blacks get hurt worse than whites. And subconsciously maybe that is part of it... because obviously sitting around saying, "We want to cut this," is much more abstract than even the busing thing and a hell of a lot more abstract than "Nigger, nigger."[33]

As president, Reagan set out to reinvent the federal approach to civil rights—with mixed results. He tried to undo Johnson's Executive Order 11246—thereby replacing affirmative action with a colorblind standard—but when he saw that it would meet with significant opposition, even from within his own party, he abandoned the plan. Reagan initially opposed a national holiday honoring Martin Luther King Jr., the renewal of the Voting Rights Act, and the expansion of the Fair Housing Act. Only when it became obvious that Congress was prepared to override his veto did he decide to sign each of those measures. In two other cases, the 1986 Comprehensive Apartheid Act (imposing economic sanctions on South Africa) and the Civil Rights Restoration Act of 1988, Congress actually did override a Reagan veto.

Though the President was unable to impose his legislative civil rights agenda, in keeping with Reagan's philosophy of federal non-intervention, his administration was decidedly less aggressive than those of his predecessors when it came to enforcement. For decades, the federal courts and the corresponding executive administrations had realized that voluntary compliance did little to eliminate racial discrimination, much less achieve racial parity. Therefore, with varying degrees of enthusiasm, they had gradually ratcheted up federal pressure against recalcitrant individuals and institutions. Eschewing that legacy, Reagan insisted on returning to a more voluntary approach—not because of any proof that coercion was no longer necessary but simply because of his categorical belief that it was illegitimate.

In his quasi-evangelistic promotion of colorblind justice Reagan went so far as to invoke Martin Luther King's dream that people should be judged by the content of their character rather than the color of their skin. Reagan and King may well have shared the rhetorical ideal of a society without racial discrimination—but to imply that King believed this goal could be accomplished by simply ignoring race was, to put it charitably, a leap of logic.

Far from colorblind, Dr. King was keenly color-aware. As he said in his 1964 classic, *Why We Can't Wait*:

> Whenever this issue of compensatory or preferential treatment for the Negro is raised, some of our friends recoil in horror. The Negro should be granted equality, they agree, but he should ask for nothing more. On the surface, this appears reasonable, but it is not realistic. For it is obvious that if a man enters the starting line of a race three hundred years after another man, the first would have to perform some incredible feat in order to catch up.[34]

In 1967 he added, "A society that has done something special against the Negro for hundreds of years must now do something special for him, in order to equip him to compete on a just and equal basis."[35] Clearly, King would have rejected Reagan's approach in favor of Judge Robert Carter's view that "racial parity cannot be achieved through the application of colorblind principles in an atmosphere of racism."[36]

While Reagan didn't convince hardly anyone that he and Martin Luther King were just two peas in a pod, he did manage to popularize colorblindness. Indeed, this may be his most important "contribution" to the notion of racial justice. The genius of colorblindness is its capacity to shore up white hegemony by endorsing an ostensibly egalitarian principle.

I do not mean to say that either Reagan or any other white proponent of colorblindness was/is *consciously* motivated to accept the colorblind principle because of its self-serving effect. But what I do mean to say is that, however subliminal its modus operandi, the self-serving effect does matter. Otherwise, it's hard to explain why the internal logic of colorblindness is so much more compelling to those it benefits.

Equality in the abstract might well be colorblind, but since we do not live in an abstract, context-free vacuum, such a notion of equality is also irrelevant. We do not live in a sinless world in which we can assume that the status quo is some guarantor of equality. Rather, we live in a sinful world in which people constantly create inequalities by using and abusing others for their own benefit. The result of "colorblind justice" is not the correction of existing inequalities but rather the protection of existing inequalities.

In an unequal world, if equality is the strategy, it cannot also be the goal. It's a matter of simple mathematics. Take any two unequal numbers. Add the same number to each. When you add equally to those unequal numbers, the result will be the same numerical disparity you began with. You merely maintain the status quo.

In order to achieve equality, there must be some compensatory mechanism to equalize the advantages that the oppressors have gained, either individually or as a class. If that inequality was created along racial lines, then any realistic rectification must also happen along racial lines. Colorblindness simply refuses to take race into account, instead opting to hit the reset button, as if the past had no enduring consequences. It trumpets a future full of "equal opportunity," as if opportunity had everything to do with the road ahead and nothing to do with one's starting point.

This notion of equality without equalization is a little like two brothers playing Monopoly. The older one, acting as the banker, amasses a huge fortune by cheating the younger, until he eventually controls all the major properties on the board. Finally, the younger sibling catches on and tells their mother. Mom scolds the older boy and announces, "If I hear of any more cheating by either of you, I'm going to put the game away." If both play fair from that point on, they will be playing by the same (equal) rules. Nevertheless, there will be no real equality, because the younger brother can never recover from his unjust disadvantage.

It should come as no surprise that the post-Reagan political landscape looked vastly different from the one he had inherited. The Gipper is remembered for restoring American pride, but that feel-good feeling was not built on a sense of ethnic inclusivity. Rather, he offered a celebration of traditional white identity, lending mainstream legitimacy to the white backlash mentality. Reagan also honed the use of a racial symbolism capable of communicating affinity in ways that were at once powerful and yet so subtle as to be opaque, sometimes even to their perpetrators.

George H. W. Bush inherited this new political climate from his predecessor. But he also inherited a campaign advisor named Lee Atwater— which meant that implicit racial messaging was likely to play a role in the 1988 presidential campaign. Needing a boost to help his candidate recover from a seventeen percent deficit in the polls, Atwater & Co. found the answer in a loose thread from the Democratic primary campaign.

Bush's opponent was Gov. Michael Dukakis of Massachusetts. On Dukakis's watch, a convicted murderer had been released on a weekend furlough, as part of an ongoing program. This time, however, he escaped to Maryland, where he brutally raped a woman after (non-lethally) assaulting and stabbing her husband. Al Gore, who eventually dropped out of the race, first brought up this prisoner release program in a primary debate, without mentioning any details. But the Bush team began to pull on that loose thread, and when they did, Dukakis's presidential aspirations unraveled.

The convict's name was William Horton. Horton was a big, black man with a menacing-looking mug shot. His victims were white, which made him the perfect boogey-man, the incarnation of age-old fears. Atwater, smelling blood, gave his secret weapon the nickname "Willie," a moniker that would live in political infamy. Referring to Dukakis, he vowed to "strip the bark off the little bastard" and "make Willie Horton his running mate."[37/e]

The attack began cautiously, with the Bush people circumspectly avoiding any overt mention of the perpetrator's race. But then a Bush-backing political action committee publicized pictures of Horton in a TV ad, and the story began to gain traction. The images were soon replayed over and over as the backdrop to TV news reports.

Then, one month before election day, the Bush campaign ran an anti-Dukakis spot in which a series of convicts trudge into a prison yard, through a revolving door, and immediately back out into the public. Only two of the fifteen or so inmates depicted are black. Horton is not mentioned by name, but only one prisoner looks up to make eye contact with the camera—a large black man with a bushy, Horton-*esque* afro.

Never mind the fact that the furlough program was similar to those that existed in other states, that it had been started by Dukakis's Republican predecessor, or that it was statistically successful. Dukakis's abstract defense stood no chance against the Republicans' nightmare narrative. With Dukakis tarred and feathered and the Bush team adopting their best "Who, *me?*" pose, the former Vice-President won by eight points, capturing nearly four times as many electoral votes as his opponent.

---

[e] Atwater, suffering from an inoperable brain tumor in 1991, apologized to Dukakis for his tactics.

After twelve years of being out-maneuvered by the Republicans, in 1992 Democrats finally took the advice offered them by pollster Stanley Greenberg in 1984. His research had led him to conclude that Reagan Democrats (traditional Democratic voters who jumped parties in 1980 and beyond) represented essentially the white backlash vote.

> These white Democratic defectors express a profound distaste for blacks, a sentiment that pervades almost everything they think about government and politics... Blacks constitute the explanation for their vulnerability and for almost everything that has gone wrong in their lives; not being black is what constitutes being middle class; not living with blacks is what makes a neighborhood a decent place to live.[39]

While far from anti-black himself, Bill Clinton understood this reality. According to Hillary, he had to figure out "exactly how 'angry white males' felt—he had to feel it himself."[40] While black constituencies generally found Clinton charming, on a policy level they were largely complicit in what political scientist Robert C. Smith calls *accommodationism*.[41] That is, black people accepted the fact that no liberal pro-black advocate could capture enough of the white vote to get elected. The candidate must somehow occupy the political center, and that required at least some sensitivity to angry white concerns. By 1992, African Americans were no longer looking for a champion, just a bulwark against white backlash.

Clinton de-emphasized special interests and focused on the economy, especially the middle class. He opposed racial quotas, promised to reform welfare, and took a tough position on crime. If a candidate wanted to reassure white voters that the racial hierarchy was safe, crime and welfare were the two most iconic issues, as black people were over-represented in both categories.

As President, Clinton followed through on his promises. He proposed and passed tough crime measures—including 100,000 more cops on the street and "three-strikes-and-you're-out" (life) sentencing for violent offenders. During his administration incarceration rates soared to record levels, and to match this surge, he expanded the prison system far more than his predecessors.[f] From

---

[f] State/federal incarceration rates at the end of Clinton's tenure were nearly 2x those at the end of the Reagan era and nearly 1.5x those of George Bush 41's final year. Source: Lisa Feldman, Vincent Schiraldi, Jason Ziedenberg. "Too Little Too Late: President Clinton's Prison Legacy," (Justice Policy Institute Policy Report; February, 2001), 8. www.prisonpolicy.org/scans/clinton.pdf.

1993 to 1999, while funding for many government agencies was in decline, the Justice Department received an increase of *seventy-two* percent.[42] Crime rates did go down significantly over Clinton's two terms, but the precise contribution of his initiatives remains a matter of debate.[g]

Clinton used these hierarchy-enhancing policies to balance out his more progressive agenda. Even though he had run against quotas,[h] in 1995 he surprised some observers by protecting affirmative action. *Time* magazine prefaced the announcement of his decision by saying:

> All year Bill Clinton has been hurrying toward political center on everything from balancing the budget to school prayer. So, it seemed a safe bet that his four-and-a-half-month review of federal affirmative-action programs would end with a decision aimed at placating 'angry white males' opposed to racial preferences.[43]

Even so, Clinton was forced to spin his "mend it, don't end it" approach to affirmative action as reform. Presenting his plan in a major address, he spent nearly as much time delimiting affirmative action as defending it, and he pledged to protect everyone's rights, even those of "white men."[44] The following year, in August of 1996, the President ended "welfare as we know it,"[45] replacing it with the far less generous "workfare." That November Clinton won handily, splitting the Southern vote with Bob Dole.

Four years later, a new southern voice appeared on the scene, this time a Texas Republican promoting voluntary progress on Civil Rights. George W. Bush echoed Reagan's colorblindness, but he rejected the dogma that our problems will disappear if government just gets out of the way. Instead, Bush proposed engaging with social issues through a grand, quasi-communitarian collaboration between the government safety net and charitable agencies.

He challenged people of faith (and, implicitly, Christians in particular) to unleash the power of their convictions. Mr. Bush invoked St. Francis of Assisi

---

[g] During Clinton's tenure the overall crime rate dropped for eight years in a row. Violent crime decreased by 30%, homicides by 38%. His approach also included a strong emphasis on prevention, as well as a significant gun-control provision, so it's hard to weigh the relative contribution of each element. In addition, he also oversaw an economic boom, which tends to reduce crime. See: http://clinton5.nara.gov/WH/Accomplishments/eightyears-06.html.
[h] For more on the evolution of judicial opinion and its relevance for running against quotas, see: www.scottgarber.com/was_notes.pdf, Note 16.4.

and called on Americans to sow love where there is hatred, to shed light where there is darkness, and to bring hope where there is despair. While insisting on the need for limited government, he also recognized the limitations of the free market, saying: "The invisible hand [of capitalism] works many miracles. But it cannot touch the human heart."[46]

Bush extended specific hope to those interested in civil rights, when, in his first inaugural address, he declared:

> While many of our citizens prosper, others doubt the promise, even the justice, of our own country. The ambitions of some Americans are limited by failing schools and hidden prejudice and the circumstances of their birth.... We do not accept this, and we will not allow it. Our unity, our union, is the serious work of leaders and citizens in every generation. And this is my solemn pledge: I will work to build a single nation of justice and opportunity. . .[47]

Unfortunately, President Bush proceeded to govern as if race were not a problem, so this purposeful volunteerism never rose to the level of its promise. Near the end of Bush's first term, the U.S. Commission on Civil Rights, a bi-partisan government panel comprised of four Democrats and four Republicans, issued a draft report on his civil rights record. Its executive summary stated that "President Bush has neither exhibited leadership on pressing civil rights issues, nor taken actions that matched his words."[48/i]

The Government Accountability Office also weighed in on the Bush administration's civil rights' record. Its investigators noted that Bush's Civil Rights Division (CRD) filed far fewer claims to protect voting and other rights than it had under Clinton[49] (even fewer than under Reagan). It found that many complaints were simply dismissed out of hand without proper follow up, an ethos of inattention that led to a "mass exodus of career attorneys."[50] (The Justice Dept. later confirmed that 70% of those in the CRD left between 2003 and 2007.[51]) The CRD also became highly politicized, amid charges of illegality for hiring career lawyers based on their political orientation.[j]

---

[i] For more background on the political chicanery that took place after the publication of this draft, see: www.scottgarber.com/was_notes.pdf, Note 16.5.

[j] A Justice Department investigation conducted during the Bush years found that improprieties and illegalities occurred in this politically-based hiring. See: Office of the Inspector General, Office of Professional Responsibility, "An Investigation of Allegations of Politicized Hiring and Other Improper

Even though "voluntary progress on civil rights" has always been something of a historical oxymoron, I'm not suggesting that Bush proposed it in bad faith. In fact, I think he believed it would work. But it did not.

Some of that failure was circumstantial. After September 11, 2001 the administration radically re-directed its focus to external threats. As a result, whatever the President's initial interest in racial justice might have been, it was quickly overwhelmed by competing interests. The real problem, however, was that Bush treated racial justice as ancillary to governing, and that practically guaranteed that it would be deprioritized by one crisis or another.

For a voluntary effort to have had any chance whatsoever, the cheerleader-in-chief needed to continually project empathy and highlight progress. But, instead, Bush ended up sitting quietly on his pompoms. After his inauguration, he rarely made any substantive mention of Civil Rights.[52] Furthermore, he never convinced African Americans that he cared. A CBS/New York Times poll, conducted in the aftermath of Katrina, asked African Americans, "How much does Bush care about the needs and problems of black people?" 76% replied, "not much/none." Only 1% said, "a lot."[53]

Bush's "see-no-evil" approach was also a fix-no-evil approach. Indeed, colorblind governance amounted to an implicit declaration of "Mission Accomplished" regarding government's role in race. But race wasn't resolved, and it wasn't going away. In fact, the biggest surprise in America's racial history was just around the corner, as we shall see in the next chapter.

Personnel Actions in the Civil Rights Division," (U.S. Department of Justice, July 2, 2008,64. www.usdoj.gov/oig/special/s0901/final.pdf.

Chapter 17

The Obama Phenomenon and How It Got Trumped

I never expected to see a black President of the United States—at least not until July 27, 2004, when Barack Obama delivered the keynote address at the Democratic National Convention. He was then just a state senator from Illinois running for a seat in the U.S. Senate. Four years earlier he had watched the Democratic Convention on a Jumbotron in the arena parking lot.

As he walked to the platform, I was wondering, "Who in the heck is this guy?" But as soon as he finished, even as he was still acknowledging the applause, I turned to my wife and said, "That man will be President of the United States." My rare prophetic utterance notwithstanding, I certainly didn't expect my prediction to come true in the next election cycle. But it happened—and not just once but twice.

Throughout our entire history white dominance has made such an accomplishment unimaginable. But now that the unimaginable has become undeniable, this historic shift must tell us something about white identity and its moral trajectory. The question is: *What* exactly is it telling us?

Given the historic resilience of haughtiness and the unlikely prospect of sin just getting tired of being bad, it would be hazardous to conclude that any one event could signal the demise of racial haughtiness. Of course, things can and do change. But sometimes they change in order to remain the same.

When my daughter was little, I held her hand as she crossed the street. Now that she's all grown up, I don't do that anymore. That doesn't mean that parental love is dead or even diminished. It just means that a constant attitudinal orientation may manifest itself in very different ways in the face of changing circumstances.

As we just saw, even before the celebration of civil rights had died down, haughtiness was regaining its vigor in the form of white backlash. And, as we shall see, Obama's ascendency did not vanquish this immoral tendency—though nearly a decade of Obama did present some adaptive challenges for white identity and for the look and feel of white dominance.

But let's go back to the fundamental question. Given the low regard in which whites have traditionally held African Americans, how could a black man rise to the nation's highest office—especially on the heels of a rather successful era of white backlash? To comprehend how Barack Obama became President of the United States, we must first explore several dynamics: how he diffused negative stereotypes, how America's demographics were changing, and how Obama as a symbol impacted the popular imagination.

What, exactly, does blackness mean in the case of President Obama? He is undoubtedly perceived as a black man—and has self-identified as such. But in important ways he is at least as white as he is black. Genetically, Obama is half and half. On the cultural side of the ledger, however, the influences are not so balanced. His Kenyan father was little more than a symbolic presence in his life, though in any case he would not have been a black *American* father figure. A young Barack was undoubtedly broadened by his time in Indonesia, the multiculturalism of Hawaii, and his adolescent contact with African Americans, but the most powerful influences during his formative years were his white mother and his white grandparents. His subsequent academic career reads like a *Who's Who* of establishment institutions—Columbia University, Harvard Law, the University of Chicago.

Nonetheless, partly because of society's insistence and partly because of his own determination, Obama embraced the African-American experience. He became a community organizer on Chicago's South Side. He joined Jeremiah Wright's church. He married a black woman. He even does an impressive Al Green imitation.

Not everyone remembers it now, but candidate Obama was once considered so un-black that it took him a while to gain acceptance in the African-American community. Despite his self-identification, Obama experienced and internalized many white influences. As a result, he doesn't exactly exude blackness. In fact, his ethnic reality is far too nuanced to be traced on a black/white axis. As he wrote in college: "Caught without a class, a structure, or tradition to support me, in a sense the choice to take a different path is made for me…The only way to assuage my feelings of isolation are to absorb all the traditions [and all the] classes; make them mine, me theirs."[1]

So, Barack Obama is not a black man who has adapted to white culture or assimilated the same. He's a black man who *is* white. Or a white man who is also black. Take your pick. The bottom line is that Obama does not relate to whites as a black man, and that helps to make him safe.

Despite his opponents' efforts to transform him into a black radical—*e.g.,* Rush Limbaugh's claim that "Obama's entire economic program is reparations"[2]— he was not a black advocate in the mold of Dr. King or Jesse Jackson. And that allowed him to capture the political center in a two-party race, defeating John McCain by eight points and garnering the lion's share of the electoral votes. Granted, he still lost the white vote by twelve points (55-43), but in the post-civil rights era no Democrat has ever won the white vote. Notably, however, in 2008 Obama bested Clinton's 1992 white vote spread.

Changing demographics also played an important role. Not only was Obama not as black as the average black American; importantly, America itself was not as white as it used to be. On May 17, 2012, *The Washington Post* announced: "For the first time in U.S. history, most of the nation's babies are members of minority groups, according to new census figures that signal the dawn of an era in which whites no longer will be in the majority."[3]

The electoral impact of this sea change is already being felt. The first election in which less than 90% of the voters were white was in 1976. Since then, white numbers have dropped rather dramatically. How does that affect election results? Consider that in 2012 Obama carried only 39% of the white vote, as opposed to the 43% he won in 2008. But the white share of the voting electorate had shrunk in those four years from 74% to 72%, allowing him to emerge victorious, despite the loss of white vote.

Even if we take into account these demographic changes in the electorate and Obama's unorthodox racial identity, it still seems surprising that a black man managed to convince millions of white people to count him worthy of the nation's highest office—and not just once but twice. Given everything we have seen about the power of haughtiness in this country, how was that possible? Was sin surreptitiously swept out to sea?

The Obama presidency did, indeed, pose a threat to the more antiquated versions of white superiority, but he represented less of a challenge to more recent incarnations of racial haughtiness. He seemed relatively safe, not only because of who he was, but because he didn't make too much noise about the racial legacy of white oppression or stir up white guilt. He embraced a broad swath of white values. And he knew how to play the game by white rules.[a]

---

[a] In its contemporary form white dominance is not maintained so much by outright exclusion as by controlling the rules of the game. So, more people may participate, but to avoid marginalization they must play the white way.

Columnist Leonard Pitts, Jr., writing on the (later aborted) 2012 presidential candidacy of Herman Cain, made the following observation:

> Modern social conservatives do not hate black people en masse. There are two kinds of blacks they love. The first is those, such as [Condoleezza] Rice, who are mainly mute on the subject of race, seldom so impolite as to say or do anything that might remind people they are black. The second is those, such as Cain, who will engage on race, but only to lecture other blacks for their failures as conservatives conceive them.[4]

Though this double-edged critique was not aimed at Obama, there are black critics who think it describes him a bit too accurately. Frederick Harris, a professor of political science at Columbia University, came down hard on the President, as well as the supportive black community, in a 2011 essay for *The Washington Post* entitled "Still Waiting for Our First Black President":

> Obama has pursued a racially defused electoral and governing strategy, keeping issues of specific interest to African Americans... off the national agenda. Far from giving black America greater influence in U.S. politics, Obama's ascent to the White House has signaled the decline of a politics aimed at challenging racial inequality head-on. And black Americans are complicit in this decline. Fearing that publicly raising racial issues will undermine the president in the eyes of white voters, African Americans appear to have struck an implicit pact with Obama.[5]

Professor Cheryl Harris of UCLA Law School agreed, claiming: "For the most part, President Obama has either avoided discussion of racial inequality or advanced the view that it is a problem best addressed by not attending to race."[6] She went on to conclude:

> Taken together, Obama's statements, policy initiatives, and legal arguments paint a picture of an administration that is not racially insentient but is seeking to avoid staking out any ground that might be seen as racially controversial.... Substantively the administration also seems convinced that race-neutral economic policy is both politically and materially more efficacious than race-targeted approaches.[7]

White hegemony continued to be an inescapable fact of life, even (and maybe especially) for a black president, who could ill afford to become the poster child for African-American interests.[b] Obama himself said from the very onset of his administration, "Keep in mind that every step we're taking is designed to help all people. But folks who are most vulnerable are most likely to be helped, because they need the most help... My general approach is that if the economy is strong, that will lift all boats."[8]

He also made himself more acceptable, as Pitts suggested, because he wasn't afraid to tell African-American audiences the kind of things that whites think blacks need to hear. President Obama was known for his sometimes-blunt appeals to black fathers to shoulder more responsibility.[c] He was even accused of evoking white stereotypes when, in a September 2011 speech to the Congressional Black Caucus, he challenged his listeners to: "Take off your bedroom slippers. Put on your marching shoes. Shake it off. Stop complainin'. Stop grumblin'. Stop cryin'. We are going to press on. We have work to do."[9]

Obama was, to no one's surprise, far more proactive in his defense of civil rights than his predecessor. In its first twenty months, Bush's administration filed only one employment discrimination case; Obama's filed twenty-nine.[10] In his second term he launched a program called "My Brother's Keeper," a modest joint venture between government and philanthropy designed to mentor minority youth. Toward the end of his presidency he targeted mass incarceration through the Justice Department. Obama himself commuted a record 1,715 prison sentences that he considered excessive, mostly those of non-violent drug offenders (85% of those in the last six months of his presidency, including 330 on his last day in office).[d]

---

[b] During the 2012 campaign, it was Joe Biden who addressed the NAACP one day after Mitt Romney. The President's spokespersons cited a "scheduling conflict," even though he was at home in the White House.

[c] Reacting to Obama's 2008 Father's Day speech, Michael Eric Dyson wrote: "Obama's rebuff of black fathers and his firm insistence on personal responsibility were calculated to win over socially conservative whites who were turned off by the Rev. Jeremiah Wright..." Michael Eric Dyson, "Obama's Rebuke of Absent Black Fathers," (*Time*, June 19, 2008). www.time.com/time/magazine/article/0,9171,1816485,00.html.

[d] By contrast, Obama granted fewer *pardons* than almost any other president. Overall, between pardons and commutations, only Truman, FDR, and Wilson granted clemency more often. Obama also received more petitions for clemency than the last nine presidents combined. See: John Gramlich and Kristin Bialik, "Obama used clemency power more often than any president since Truman," Pew Research Center, Jan. 20, 2017, www.pewresearch.org/fact-tank/2017/01/20/obama-used-more-clemency-power/.

Far from a black advocate, President Obama cast himself in the role of interpreter-in-chief on racial matters. In his first term, after black Harvard professor Henry Louis Gates was arrested for trying to enter his own house, Obama entered the fray, inviting the professor and the arresting officer to the White House for an ill-fated "beer summit." In his second term, however, in the aftermath of the Trayvon Martin verdict, the President spoke more personally and eloquently about the racial cross-currents involved, demonstrating genuine leadership on this issue. And he continued to ratchet up the sympathetic yet explanatory rhetoric, as the cases of racial violence against African Americans piled up during his administration.

The truth is that no politician can afford to stir up too much of the dust that settled after white backlash. Race-based policies have fallen into disfavor with both the courts as well as the general public. As a result, Barack Obama's program for overcoming racial inequities looked more like that of George W. Bush than that of Lyndon Johnson. Obama's governing philosophy was certainly more progressive than Bush's, but in many ways he simply delivered on the previous president's promises—protection against civil rights infractions, race-neutral policies that along the way disproportionately help minorities, and symbolic leadership from the White House.

The symbolic power that Obama possessed as the first black president should not be underestimated. For many African Americans, his significance was far more about who he was than what he did—an inspirational, identity-altering source of pride—Jackie Robinson to the tenth power. But Obama's racial identity also held a certain attraction for whites (even for some who didn't vote for him). Electing a black man who is not so terribly black helped a lot of white folks cast themselves in the reformer mold of Branch Rickey.

No, it was not that mythical Promised Land of which civil rights dreamers dreamed. But the election of a black President seemed to help at least some of us cross over into the white people's Promised Land—a land in which we could proclaim the ugliness of oppression a thing of the past, a land in which we no longer had to right the remaining racial wrongs, a land in which we could rightly revel in our colorblind virtue. For many, the Obama presidency was the living, iconic "proof" that we have arrived.

As important as the symbolic effect of an Obama presidency was for those it inspired and for those who co-opted it for their own reassurance, that symbolism was equally powerful for those who felt threatened by it. After more than two centuries in which presidential candidates not only needed to be white but pretty much needed an Anglo-sounding surname to get elected, all of a sudden, a black man named Barack Hussein Obama was sitting in the Oval Office.[e] And that was bound to make some people nervous.

For these folks, Obama's relative whiteness and low-key civil rights emphasis was either beside the point or simply cloaked some more sinister racial agenda. For them, he represented nothing less than the dethroning of white dominance. Few would say or perhaps even think this in such stark terms. Indeed, their antipathy was often presented as purely political. But the politics of white backlash and the preservation of white dominance have always been joined at the hip.

Some of the white reaction to Obama bordered on the irrational, including an impervious-to-fact campaign to discredit the President because of his place of birth. As late as 2010, a full twenty percent of Americans believed that Obama was born outside the U.S. Remarkably, five years later, twenty percent of Americans *still* believed that Obama was born outside the U.S.[11] Despite the President's oft-repeated affiliation with Christianity, nearly seven years into his presidency, almost 3 in 10 Americans believed that he was a Muslim.[12]

Anti-Obama backlash contributed to the rise of a political phenomenon known as the Tea Party. In 2010, those who self-identified with the Tea Party comprised somewhere between 10% and 20% of the population.[f] In that year's mid-term elections, however, Tea Partiers were more than twice as likely as other potential voters to cast a ballot, resulting in an electoral impact that vastly exceeded their numbers. Since the majority classified themselves as Republicans (joined by many independents who voted Republican), their influence in primaries and caucuses was particularly significant. Tea Party dynamism spearheaded a mid-term (2010) electoral revolt that President Obama described as a personal "shellacking."

---

[e] The only non-English/Celtic exceptions are Roosevelt, Van Buren, and Hoover (Dutch); and Eisenhower (German, *Eisenhauer*).

[f] This identification varied considerably, depending on how the question was asked. *The Blair-Rockefeller Poll* (cited below) identified 10.6% of the population as Tea Party "members." This is, of course, a loose designation, as there is no official affiliation. *The New York Times/CBS News Poll* found 18% who identified themselves as Tea Party "supporters." Only 20% or so of these people had ever attended a Tea Party event or donated money to the cause, so being a "supporter" appears to be mostly a matter of felt affinity.

Understanding what made the Tea Party tick provides a peek behind the mask of one of white dominance's more recent disguises.[13/g] In-depth polling conducted in 2010 reveals that the typical Tea Party supporter was white (91%), Christian (85%), over forty-five (63%); and male (58%). More than nine in ten thought that the country was on the wrong track, and more than half described themselves as "angry" about it.

Much of that dissatisfaction was aimed at President Obama, with nine in ten members of the Tea Party disapproving of him. They were far more likely than others to identify him as a Muslim. Three quarters of Tea Partiers said that Obama didn't share the values most Americans live by—and even more (84%) were convinced that their own views *did* represent mainstream America.

Yes, polls showed a certain affinity among whites, both inside and outside the Tea Party, concerning government intervention on behalf of minorities. But on other questions, including their view of Obama, Tea Partiers differed significantly from other whites. Perhaps their vision of "real" America did not extend beyond the Republican Party—or even that far. Or perhaps they simply believed that their perspective defined America by default.

This recent installment of white backlash altered the American political landscape, galvanizing the voice of the angry white male. Hardly any of this white reaction was ostensibly about race, but rather about political philosophy and tradition and religio-culture wars variously defined. It involved a lot of talk about saving our future, which inevitably involved preserving a white-dominated past. Colorblindness lent an air of plausible deniability to the whole affair, obliged, as it was, to avoid the *R* word, even if it represented the inescapable subtext of every potential threat to the existing hierarchy.

The Obama era may not have been a threshold event on the order of the civil rights era, but it did represent a significant pendulum swing in the ongoing dialectic that is racial tension in America. And the real proof of Obama's significance was not just his capacity to energize an ignored minority; it was his capacity to generate white backlash.

The white backlash against Obama included not only the aforementioned ad hominem attacks on his birthright and religion but an all-out campaign of Republican obstructionism against his governance. Seven Republican

---

[g] The Tea Party statistics that follow are culled from two different sources and interwoven here. For sources and methodology, see accompanying endnote.

senators informed Joe Biden, even before the inauguration, that party leadership was not going to let them support anything that Obama proposed for at least two years. "'If he was for it,' explained former Ohio Senator George Voinovich, 'we had to be against it.'"[14] This opposition eventually stretched well beyond the first two years and sought not only to block the President's legislative agenda but his judicial appointments as well.[15]

For some of Obama's opponents, however, obstructing the President in particular and the Democrats in general was not a vehement enough response. This cohort sought to outflank rank-and-file Republicans on the right, bringing about a fundamental change within the Republican Party and setting the stage for the unlikely candidacy of Donald Trump. Indeed, there could hardly be a more unambiguous demonstration of the persistent power of white backlash than the rise of Trump. After mounting an aborted primary campaign in 2011 (largely on the back of birther-generated publicity), this tycoon returned in 2015 to an even more polarized electorate and surprised everyone by winning first the Republican nomination and then the general election.

Seemingly obsessed with one-upping his predecessor at every turn, Trump has hyper-personalized the notion of backlash in the case of Obama, no matter how insignificant the point of comparison or how unfounded its factual basis. Comparisons range from drawing a larger inaugural crowd to outperforming Obama on any and every aspect of the economy—offering better health care; being "much tougher on Russia" (as well as ISIS, Iran, etc.); driving harder bargains and coming up with better deals; making the CPAC Conference more "exciting" than it was during the Obama years; working more frequently in the Oval Office; and being more attentive to military families who have lost loved ones.[h]

Apart from his "anything you can do, I can do better" personal crusade, Trump has shown himself to be, both implicitly and explicitly, a protector of the white hierarchy. His campaign theme, "Make America Great Again,"[i] picked up on an ascendant theme in conservative thought, the celebration of American exceptionalism, and took it to a new level.[16] Though most white

---

[h] Admittedly, Trump has engaged in similar one-upmanship with other individuals, but Obama appears to be his favorite foil.

[i] This phrase did not originate with the Trump campaign, though Trump did trademark it immediately after the 2012 campaign. Reagan used "Let's make America great again" as one of his campaign slogans. Bill Clinton also referred to the idea in speeches, though it never became a campaign slogan.

Americans may not process this notion in strictly racial terms, the values they associate with America's greatness (such as individualism) are values that they also associate with white identity. As a result, to the extent that people feel a loss of white hegemony, they feel a loss of greatness as well.

Just when was this golden age to which we must hearken back? It's not clear that there is a right answer to that question, as there is some evidence that, when asked, people tend to associate America's greatest era with their own coming of age.[17] The nostalgia in question, however, may not be for an actual moment or era at all, but for a sense of power, well-being, and social predictability. For Trump supporters this most certainly predates the Obama years and may go much further back. For African Americans, however, moving back in time connotes a rollback of their own power and wellbeing. So, many black people sense something sinister in the words, "Make America Great Again"—and many white people hear even more than they suppose.

Trump's racial rhetoric, couched in the context of his long history of (at best) racial insensitivity[18] and his white nationalist appeal,[j] has even attracted support from troubling alt-right elements, who see in him an opportunity to expand their influence. The president's pronouncements, often in the form of Tweets, include his extensive critique of black athletes and his take on the August 2017 violence in Charlottesville, Virginia.

After Mr. Trump suggested a moral equivalency between the white supremacists/Nazis and the counter-demonstrators in Charlottesville, the outcry, even from his own party, was such that he was forced to backtrack, offering a blanket denunciation of racism.[19] The following day, however, Trump once again defended his original remarks. In the end, the incident didn't make a dent in the President's approval rating.[20] Why? Perhaps because (as per a poll taken a week after the incident) when Trump voters were asked which group faces the most discrimination in America, 45% answered "white people" vs. only 16% who said "African Americans."[21]

It was always clear that this mentality existed in America. What was unclear was just how many people were affected by it. The conventional

---

[j] Trump's "equal-opportunity" variety of haughtiness denigrates not only African Americans but Latinos, Native Americans, Muslims—and people from what he characterized as "shithole countries." See: Darran Simmon, "President Trump's other insensitive comments on race and ethnicity," *CNN Politics*, Jan. 13, 2018. www.cnn.com/2018/01/11/politics/president-trump-racial-comments-tweets/index.html.

wisdom (to which I subscribed) was that the shrinking white demographic (down from 74% of the electorate in 2008 to less than 70% in 2016) would ensure the ultimate failure of such an appeal. And it probably will. But not quite yet.

Current efforts aimed at voter suppression and/or additional foreign election meddling could temporarily prolong this unexpected electoral majority. In the long run, however, Trump's political coalition looks like a loser. Even erstwhile conservative George Will called it the "kamikaze arithmetic of white nationalism." In a post-election editorial in *The Washington Post*, Will opined that "in 2016, Republicans won a ruinous triumph that convinced them that they can forever prosper by capturing an ever-larger portion of an ever-smaller portion of the electorate."[22]

But whatever the future may hold, the present is what it is. And "what it is" is nothing less than yet another iteration of white backlash on the heels of African-American progress—progress in this case represented by Mr. Obama.

The 2016 election was, no doubt, about far more than racial haughtiness. After all, Trump managed to win in places where Obama had twice carried the day. And he did so, even while Obama was still enjoying a 57% approval rating.[23] But make no mistake; without the re-imagining, re-packaging, and re-branding of historic white haughtiness, there could be no President Trump. Only after this current wave of backlash has washed ashore and back out to sea, will we be able to appreciate the net effect of the Obama/Trump legacy.

Chapter 18

The Dynamics of Modern Haughtiness

I have insisted throughout this volume that racial haughtiness is an embedded feature of white identity, part of a worldview that desperately desires a world that conforms to its view. In the last couple of chapters, we have reviewed the political history of modern white backlash. Some of the tactics we have observed were rather overt, others covert, and still others perhaps unintended yet effective.

In order to sustain the historic racial hierarchy in the contemporary era, however, political tools alone will not avail. While many whites are content to let politicians fight proxy race wars for them, individuals are uncomfortable engaging in overt racial discrimination. They may admit that racism still exists at some level, but nobody is anxious to be associated with it.

In order to maintain plausible deniability about racial haughtiness while preserving the racial hierarchy—without referring to either for what they are—increasingly subtler strategies[a] are necessary. In this chapter, we will explore the dynamics of haughtiness in our current context by examining the rise of symbolic racism, the racial respect gap, and the role of white revisionism.

Social and political psychologists have spent a great deal of time examining contemporary white reactions to the black pursuit of equality. These psychologists have focused on what has come to be known as "the principle-implementation gap"—that is, the incongruity of white support for equality in *principle* versus their consistent opposition to concrete policies that might promote equality in *practice*.[1] One of the most important theories that has emerged regarding this indirect perpetuation of the racial hierarchy is known as *symbolic racism*. According to David O. Sears, a pioneer of this perspective, symbolic racism has two main components—an emotional antipathy toward black people and an emphasis on certain traditional values.[2]

This anti-black affect does not typically rise to the level of actual hatred or even, perhaps, dislike. Rather, it is a kind of disapproval that results in

---

[a] By calling them "strategies" I do not mean to imply that they are intentional. Indeed, their effectiveness may be directly proportional to on their invisibility.

relational and social uneasiness. It is the sentiment that prompts statements like, "I don't have anything against black people, *but...*" This inevitable adversative serves to relegate African Americans to the status of "other," because many whites feel that black people do not share, or at least do not manifest, the values associated with white identity (or, as many whites see it, American identity). These values include individualism, self-reliance, hard work, obedience, discipline, thrift, punctuality, and delayed gratification.

Rather than positing some sort of inherent white superiority, symbolic racism abstracts that superiority from white *personhood* to the *values* that define white identity. These whites believe that their dominance springs from their adherence to these values—and that black people could achieve a similar level of success if they would only get with the program. Therefore, if whites denigrate blacks, it is not so much because of their color but because of their culture—a way of thinking and acting that keeps them from upholding their end of a social contract unilaterally defined by the dominant white society.

Symbolic racism theory makes an important contribution to our analysis, helping to explain the mechanism whereby haughtiness continues to define whiteness—i.e., the abstraction of superiority from something inherent in white *people* to values that historically correlate with white *identity*. But, while symbolic racism helps us to understand *how* the notion of white superiority has morphed in the post-civil rights era, this theory has no satisfactory answer for *why* these attitudes of superiority even exist or are so stubbornly bent on survival. In order to complete this picture, we need to recognize the sin of haughtiness and its creative obsession for a world that reflects its hierarchical worldview. Otherwise, discussions of symbolic racism end up mired in a superficial nexus between white superiority and conservative ideology, all too often conflating the two.

Contemporary conservatism does tend to affirm some of the same values that comprise symbolic racism, so there is ample evidence of correlation between the two. Correlation, however, is not the same as causation; even though some conservative values end up facilitating white dominance, conservatives may not be attracted to those values for that reason. Confusing conservatism and symbolic racism is unfair and unhelpful, not only because it leads to an unnecessarily broad and harsh judgment about conservatives' racial attitudes; it also mistakenly implies that non-conservative whites are somehow exempt from symbolic racism and the haughtiness that drives it.

Many of these more progressive whites are no more relationally attuned to African Americans than are their conservative counterparts. And they may be equally convinced about black inferiority vis-à-vis the values that define white identity. They simply externalize it differently. Instead of leaving African Americans to pull themselves up by their bootstraps, these whites are more likely to support a paternalistic attempt to improve the lot of black people by assimilating them into the "right" culture. Others will support programs that ameliorate the impact of the racial hierarchy—but without any real intention of dismantling the social structures that sustain it. They're not about to saw off the (elevated) branch they're sitting on.

Haughtiness is not merely a function of one's political ideology; it is a moral predilection in search of a coherent political expression. Whatever shape that political outworking takes, in our day it is likely be wrapped, either explicitly or implicitly, in the subterfuge of values—because blatant claims to racial superiority are now considered bad form. White *people* may lay claim to any number of values, but white *identity* relates especially to those values associated with symbolic racism, because those values define an ethic that differentiates whites from blacks, bolstering the white sense of superiority.

We could certainly debate the extent to which the values claimed by white identity correlate with actual differences between the two racial groups. What is clear, however, is that the *superiority* associated with those values is bogus. Some of these "white" values are more cultural than moral, even though whiteness tends to regard them as a matter of goodness. To imagine that one's affinity with this set of values adds up to moral superiority requires a judgmental spirit that flouts a whole host of Scriptural warnings.

Quite apart from the "judge not" problem, the values that are chosen to signify white superiority are the result of some pretty serious cherry-picking. There are many other values that could have been identified as morally and/or socially significant. So, why this set? I would submit that it is not because they are substantively more characteristic of uprightness but simply because they are perceived to be characteristic of white identity. Such circular logic is obviously designed to fulfill a need. Haughtiness needs to feel superior, so it takes a selfie and proclaims that image the standard of goodness.

Naturally, those who adhere to white values tend to be more successful at navigating the American social landscape. But this near tautology is akin to saying that a famous golfer who designed a course to suit his strengths has a competitive advantage when playing there. In a society historically defined by a dominant white majority anyone, regardless of their color, stands a better chance of prospering if they respect and reflect the established values.

Not only is this abstracted superiority problematic for the reasons listed above; there are also legitimate questions about the desirability of some of the values themselves. When viewed through the lens of Christian ethics, these defining elements of whiteness are not exactly the cultural equivalents of faith, hope, and love.

For example, take the vaunted American ideal of individualism and its corollary, self-reliance. According to Webster, individualism, when considered morally, holds that "the interests of the individual are or ought to be ethically paramount." As a social paradigm it focuses on "the political and economic independence of the individual and stress[es] individual initiative, action, and interests." The notion that our personal interests come first is clearly opposed to both the spirit and the letter of Scripture. And while the Bible holds us personally responsible for our actions, it does not call us to self-reliance but to a dependent relationship with God and an interdependent relationship with others.

Some of the other qualities associated with white identity may be more noble, but even whites would not have embraced them so readily had it not been for the practical benefits associated with them. Take, for example, hard work, a cultural value significantly sweetened by the practical promise of prosperity, a historically functional correlation for American whites. Not so for African Americans, who for centuries worked *really hard* as slaves, sharecroppers, and menial laborers (hence the expression "slaving away") without enjoying any appreciable upward mobility as a result.

What's at issue here, however, is not really the objective deficiency or superiority of one set of values versus another. It's not about the natural ethnocentric tendency to prefer one's own cultural values. The real problem is respect and its relationship to haughtiness.

Haughtiness was once enshrined in a system of unequal rights. Thankfully, that legal system has been dismantled. But haughtiness survived the demise of its social trappings and found a clever new way to redefine superiority. Indeed, the haughty can grant equal rights; what they cannot grant is equal respect. Because that would require not just a *redefinition* of superiority but its *renunciation*.

For Christians, of course, reconciliation means more than respect; it must embrace love as well. The problem is, real love requires respect. We white

Christians can never love black Christians as ourselves until we learn to respect them as ourselves. Without respect what we call "love" will never rise above pity for the inferior, or compassion for the downtrodden, or paternalism for the unenlightened, or warm, fuzzy feelings for the conveniently distant.

That is why haughtiness is so insidious. Real love demands respect, but haughtiness cannot abide it, because respect undermines our sense of superiority. Without respect the best we can manage is to "love" our brother as *other,* an attitude that spits in the face of the Trinitarian ideal and denies the dynamic of *we* that must rule in the body of Christ.

Why can't we get to respect, much less to love? It is a failure to deal with the sin of racial haughtiness. We don't want to face what history tells us about who we are. So, we re-imagine that picture, painting ourselves with pastels.

The Civil Rights Movement created a moral vulnerability in white society. But soon that open wound began to scar over, and whites grew weary of hearing about the unpleasant consequences of their attitudes and actions. At that point the temptation was to abandon the messy business of righting racial inequities and opt, rather, to simply control the narrative. As a result, in this contemporary era race relations are not so much about adjudicating the past or creating a just and brotherly interracial future. Rather, it's more about white people finding a way to justify themselves and their attitudes.

Many years ago, while living in a Europe, I took my car to the repair shop. When I went to retrieve the vehicle, I asked the owner of the one-man operation how much I owed him. Well, he must have thought that I was either a rich foreigner or a dumb foreigner or both, because the amount he quoted was enormous. As calmly as I could, I asked the mechanic if he could please break down the charges and show me why the bill was so high. "Sure," he replied, grabbing a blank bill and licking the end of his greasy pen.

Near the bottom of the sheet, next to the word *Total*, he recorded the amount he had just quoted me. Then he moved up the page to the block labeled *Labor*. After pondering the matter for a moment, he scribbled down a figure that seemed to please him. Then, right in front of my very eyes, he said, "Now, let's see…" That's right—he subtracted the arbitrary labor charge from the pre-determined bottom line to come up with the cost of the parts!

Dumbfounded, I stared at the page. But then I noticed that he had made a mistake. "You know what," I pointed out, "these figures for parts plus labor don't add up to the total." So, he re-calculated, this time beginning from the top and totaling the parts and labor. "You're right," he admitted, looking at a sum that represented a significant discount from his original price. "I guess you owe me only this much."

As absurd as it may seem, haughtiness operates in a similar fashion. It begins by deciding how we need to feel about ourselves and then fills in the blanks of history, white motivations, and black realities so that they add up to the pre-determined outcome. Not only does this kind of subjective arithmetic not add up; it also creates a significant roadblock to racial healing. As long as whites and blacks have a very different view of that bottom line—the benignity of white identity—real racial harmony remains a pipe dream.

The fact is that haughtiness has not disappeared; it's just gone undercover, camouflaged by a colorblind revisionism. The only people really fooled by this disguise, however, are those who wear it. African Americans have no vested interest in such make-believe, nor can they ignore their ongoing racial reality. However inviting it may feel for those ensconced in their white enclaves to say so, America is not a post-racial society. Not even close.

Chapter 19

Racial Justice on Trial

Today, two decades into the 21st century, there remains a significant and largely static gap between white and black socio-economic wellbeing. Though this divide is fueled by haughtiness, it is facilitated by societal structures, and both must be transformed if we are to move in the direction of racial justice and healing. The next two chapters focus on perhaps the single most far-reaching, hierarchy-enhancing institution in contemporary society—the American correctional system.

In order to improve my own grasp of this situation I spent months immersing myself in the dizzying dynamics of crime, anti-crime, and the nuances of the criminal justice system as it relates to race. The answer, as I have come to understand it, is neither as simple nor as straightforward as the racial injustices of the past. What is clear, however, is that an institutionalized prejudice does indeed permeate our criminal justice system, casting a long, discriminatory shadow over equal justice in this country in sometimes subtle, but nevertheless significant ways.

This chapter analyzes three key aspects of our system of justice and how these contribute to black disadvantage—legislative priorities, law enforcement, and the dynamics of the judicial process. In the following chapter we will examine the result of this institutionalized discrimination, the mass incarceration of black people in America. Our goal is to appreciate not only the sociological implications of this phenomenon for black well-being but also its spiritual implications as it relates to racial haughtiness.

Legislative Priorities

Our criminal justice system has its roots in the laws that are established and the penalties that are associated with them. These laws, of course, are not handed down from Mt. Sinai. They are written by powerful people, mostly to protect the status quo and often with very little sensitivity to or interest in the wellbeing of those who might end up on the wrong side of those laws. Because this topic is far too broad to tackle in just a few pages, I will focus on the single legislative priority that has most exacerbated black incarceration.

Much of the growth in the U.S. prison population over recent decades is directly attributable to the war on drugs, a war that has been fought disproportionately on African-American turf. In 1980, there were only 40,000 people incarcerated in the U. S. on drug charges. By 2010 that number had risen more than tenfold, to over half a million.[1] Currently, nearly half of all federal inmates are serving on drug-related charges.[2]

There can be no doubt that African Americans are disproportionately affected by this crackdown on illegal drugs. It is the single type of crime for which black people are most frequently arrested and jailed. Compared to whites, they are 2.5 to 4.5 times more likely to be arrested for drug-related offenses[3/a] and six times more likely to be imprisoned on such charges.[4]

Why is that? Are black people simply far more prone to engage in illegal, drug-related activities? If this were most any other crime, we wouldn't know how often it was actually committed—only how often people get arrested and processed for it. Fortunately for our current inquiry, drug crimes are different. The Substance Abuse and Mental Health Services Administration (SAMHSA) tracks drug usage, allowing us to compare illegal drug use with law enforcement outcomes. What does that comparison tell us?

SAMHSA has found that regular drug use among blacks is only slightly more frequent than it is among whites, by a ratio of 1.16 to 1.[5/b] That indicates

---

[a] This ratio is expressed as a range, because the FBI's national arrest statistics do not parse out race and ethnicity, lumping almost all Hispanics in the "white" category. Compared to (non-Hispanic) whites, however, Hispanics face a very different reality in the criminal justice system. Therefore, for the purposes of our black/white comparison, it's not at all useful to contrast black arrest rates with white arrest rates that include Hispanics in the "white" category. So, I calculated an alternative estimate of the arrest rate by disaggregating the Hispanic arrestees from the non-Hispanic whites. The lower number in the range expressed above represents the FBI figures, and the higher number, my estimates. For more information on how these arrest ratios were calculated, see: www.scottgarber.com/was_notes.pdf, Note 19.1.

[b] Comparison based on those 12 and older who have used illicit drugs in the *last month*. This is probably the most reliable measure of current drug use, but were we comparing *lifetime* drug use, the ratio would be virtually reversed (1.17 to 1, white use being more frequent than black use by this measure). See endnote for citation and compare Table 1.29B, p. 224, for lifetime use.

that blacks and whites are committing nearly the same number of drug crimes.[c] But, as black and white drug offenders interface with the criminal justice system, their experiences diverge significantly.

One of the principle reasons why so many African Americans are languishing in prison on drug-related charges has to do with the sentencing rules adopted in recent decades. Let's look at one example that we can track over time. In the throes of a drug-war fever, Congress overwhelmingly passed[d] and President Reagan enthusiastically signed the *Anti-Drug Abuse Act of 1986*, which, for the first time made a legal distinction between crack cocaine and powder cocaine. Powder was more expensive and far more often the choice of whites. Crack was cheaper and far more popular with black users. Because of the way they are ingested, these two forms of cocaine provide a somewhat different experience, but they are essentially the same drug.[e]

Crack use was growing rapidly during the 1980s, fueling a furious hype over the spread of drug violence and the threat it posed to American society

---

Several important caveats must be attached to this ratio. 1) Most convictions result from plea bargains, so the crime for which individuals are incarcerated may not be the same one for which they were arrested. 2) The stated reason for incarceration is based only the most serious crime involved in that conviction. 3) This ratio reflects only those in state or federal prison, where drug charges are more likely to be for trafficking. Possession charges are most often served in local jails, where demographic record-keeping is too inconsistent to trace the fate of those convicted on a specific charge.

While these caveats do introduce a measure of imprecision, I don't believe that imprecision skews statistically toward one race or another. As for my juxtaposition of this relatively equal drug usage rate with the widely divergent arrest/incarceration rates cited above—there may be some margin of error associated with these statistics, but my comparisons are on an order of magnitude that is unlikely to be substantively affected by such considerations.
[c] Though *prison* time usually results from trafficking (see footnote *b* above), I am assuming that the frequency of drug use and trafficking roughly coincide in a given population. Despite urban myths about white suburbanites buying drugs in black urban settings, research indicates that people normally buy drugs in the same social communities in which they buy other products.
[d] The House voted 392–16 in favor, the Senate 97–2.
[e] The essential difference is that crack cocaine is mixed with baking soda and baked into a crystalline form that produces a cracking sound when smoked. Though there are other means of ingesting cocaine, snorting powder or smoking crack are the most common. Crack enters the bloodstream faster, producing a quicker, more intense high of shorter duration.

and to the black community in particular. In 1986, the same year the Anti-Drug Abuse Act was passed, the American public found itself absolutely barraged by a media-fueled crack mania. Laura Gómez, Professor of American Studies and Law at the University of New Mexico, recalls:

> Within eleven months of the first mention of "crack" in a 1986 *New York Times* article, six of the nation's largest and most prestigious news magazines and newspapers had run more than one thousand stories about crack cocaine. *Time* and *Newsweek* each ran five "crack crisis" cover stories. ... The three major network television stations ran 74 stories about crack cocaine in six months.[6]

It wasn't just the fate of street punks and the respectable citizens who might get caught in their crossfire that ignited public sentiment. Headlines like "Cocaine Babies: Hooked at Birth," (*Newsweek*: July 28, 1986) and "Cocaine Claims Its Tiniest Victims: Babies Born Addicted" (*People*: September 8, 1986) helped transform a serious social issue into a tragi-pop phenomenon known as the "crack baby." Columnist Charles Krauthammer described the scenario in quasi-apocalyptic terms: "The inner-city crack epidemic is now giving birth to the newest horror: a bio-underclass, a generation of physically damaged cocaine babies whose biological inferiority is stamped at birth."[7/f]

Nearly everyone agreed that *something* had to be done, and Congress couldn't wait to come to the rescue. Bandwagon jumping aside, most lawmakers' intentions were probably far better than their understanding,[g] as their investigation into the true nature of the drug was cursory at best. Their response was to hyper-criminalize the possession of crack vs. powder cocaine.

As a result, mandatory minimum sentences would henceforth be handed down for crack amounts that were *only 1/100th* of the powder levels. Simple possession[h] of crack cocaine weighing as much as a nickel (5 grams) would

---

[f] Krauthammer's article was written in 1989, so it clearly did not influence the 1986 legislation. I offer it here to illustrate the enduring alarm of that era.
[g] A majority of black lawmakers supported the measure but soon changed their minds. By 1997, the Congressional Black Caucus called on President Clinton to eliminate the two-tiered sentencing arrangement. See: Steven A. Holmes, "Black Lawmakers Criticize Clinton Over Cocaine Sentencing," (*The New York Times*; July 24, 1997; www.nytimes.com/1997/07/24/us/black-lawmakers-criticize-clinton-over-cocaine-sentencing.html).
[h] The original 1986 bill specified this penalty for possession with intent to distribute, but the follow-up *Anti-Drug Abuse Act of 1988* made simple

put the offender away for five years, whereas the powder offender would need more than a pound (500 grams) of virtually the same substance to merit the same punishment.[8] At the time, crack was the *only* drug sanctioned by a federal mandatory minimum sentence for simple possession. Possession of any other controlled substance was punishable as a misdemeanor carrying a *maximum* sentence of one year in prison.[9][i]

There was no scientific basis for this calculation; it evidently just seemed like a number big enough to make a point. Rep. Dan Lungren (R) California, the proud owner of an unimpeachable "get-tough-on-crime" record, helped draft the 1986 law. In 2010, he admitted to his House colleagues that the 100:1 ratio was unjustified, saying: "We initially came out of committee with a 20 to 1 ratio [but] by the time we finished on the floor it was 100 to 1. We didn't have an evidentiary basis for that but that is what we did thinking we were doing the right thing at the time."[10]

Subsequent scientific research debunked much of the hype upon which this legislation was based.[j] More than thirty bills were introduced between 1993 and 2009 to address the unfairness of the 100:1 sentencing disparity and its disproportionate impact on African Americans. They went nowhere.[11] Likewise, the U.S. Sentencing Commission tried repeatedly to amend the sentencing guidelines. But it wasn't until 2010, when the vast majority of those responsible for this imbalance were no longer in Congress and

---

possession enough to trigger the mandatory penalty. Often overlooked but not insignificant is the fact that the 1988 law also considered anyone involved in the enterprise *at any level* a conspirator worthy of the maximum applicable penalty warranted by the quantity of crack in question. See: Stephen Murdoch, "The Debate Over Mandatory Minimums," (*Washington Lawyer*, DC Bar, November 2001). www.dcbar.org/bar-resources/publications/washington-lawyer/articles/november-2001-mandatory-minimums.cfm.

[i] This distinction was so exaggerated that only two states ever adopted the federal standard for their own correctional system (Kyle Graham, *supra*, 775). By 2007, even those two had joined eleven other states with less exaggerated formulas, usually not more than 10:1. The vast majority never changed their longstanding 1:1 ratio. See: Ricardo Hinojosa, et. al.; "Cocaine and Federal Sentencing Policy," United States Sentencing Commission, May, 2007; www.ussc.gov/sites/default/files/pdf/news/congressional-testimony-and-reports/drug-topics/200705_RtC_Cocaine_Sentencing_Policy.pdf.

[j] For more background on the research regarding the "crack baby" and the public safety hype, see: www.scottgarber.com/was_notes.pdf, Note 19.2.

methamphetamines had replaced crack in the headlines, that that body finally admitted that the 1986 bill had been ill-advised.

The Fair Sentencing Act of 2010 reduced the crack/powder ratio from 100:1 to about 18:1 (from less than an ounce to just over a pound for a five-year mandatory sentence). But even this new ratio was not based on a scientific assessment of the two forms of cocaine. Rather, some sort of face-saving political compromise was necessary to get the bill passed. And though the 2010 Act was at least a tacit admission that the 1986 bill was misguided, the 2010 legislation did not apply retroactively. That did not happen until the passage of the FIRST STEP Act, signed into law in December of 2018.[12/k]

No one knows how many other laws continue to exercise an adverse and discriminatory effect on African Americans, though the endurance of a blatantly prejudicial standard like the 100:1 sentencing ratio highlights the likelihood that other less exaggerated inequalities could easily avoid scrutiny. What this example does illustrate is just how easily even the ostensibly well-intentioned concerns of the majority can wreak havoc on minority interests— and just how difficult it is to challenge such institutionalized discrimination.

Law Enforcement

Within the African-American community there is a widespread conviction that justice is somehow peeking around its blindfold. This is particularly true when it comes to race-based targeting by the police, including the infamous charge of "Driving While Black" (DWB). Are black people really treated differently in traffic stops, or is this a matter of urban legend?

There is plenty of anecdotal evidence to support the discrepancy in stop rates that could be attributed to DWB. My own pastor, David Anderson, tells the story of his first day as a young black minister interning in a suburban megachurch in a wealthy white suburb of Chicago. That first day on the job he was stopped not once or twice, but *four* times by white police officers, because, he "fit the description of someone [they were] looking for."[13]

While this incident may be more dramatic than most, it is certainly not unique. But do such experiences represent the exception or the rule? Is there any statistical evidence that speaks more broadly to the DWB phenomenon?

---

[k] For more background, see: www.scottgarber.com/was_notes.pdf, 19.3.

In this century many studies have examined racial profiling in traffic stops. There are two sources for these studies. First, we have law enforcement itself. But we also have polls that ask the driving public about their interactions with police. The most well-known of these is produced by the Bureau of Justice Services (BJS), an arm of the U.S. Department of Justice.[14]

There are, however, important unknowns for which none of the existing studies can account. For instance, how many miles does the average black motorist drive per year vs. the average white motorists?[l] What is the density of the police presence in the areas in which the two racial groups do most of their driving? Are there differences in driving habits?

Despite the limitations inherent in these studies,[m] a broad survey of the available data does support certain conclusions. First, it seems that African-American drivers are, indeed, stopped at least somewhat more often than their white counterparts. The Open Policing Project at Stanford University is perhaps the most comprehensive collection of nationwide data. In a 2017 working paper a group of Stanford researchers analyzed the results of more than 60 million State Highway Patrol stops in 20 states between 2011 and 2015.[n] They found that blacks were stopped more often than whites in 80% of

---

[l] There is some evidence that black drivers drive fewer miles. Reliable data from more recent years is a bit hard to pin down, but black drivers drove more than 20% less than whites in 2009, according to "Chapter V: Personal Miles Traveled: Table 17. Driver Model of PMT, Excluding Licensing (1990, 2001, and 2009)," Federal Highway Transportation Administration, Office of Transportation Policy Studies. 2009 (*mrry*), https://www.fhwa.dot.gov/policy/otps/nextgen_stats/chap5.cfm#18a.

[m] In addition to the aforementioned limitations that are common to all such statistical studies, the BJS study presents some particular issues mentioned in the endnote above. Local studies based on data supplied by law enforcement are designed by different researchers for different purposes and measure different criteria. If racial bias affects police behavior during a traffic stop, it could also affect their reporting of those stops. Even in the Stanford study, which aggregates data from across the nation, inconsistent reporting is an issue. They rely on information from less than half of the states on any given question, as it is simply not collected in a uniform fashion or, often, not at all.

[n] Importantly, this data set contemplates only stops by *State Highway Patrols*. That makes the conditions under which stops occur somewhat more consistent from state to state, but it may also make the statistics less representative of urban population centers where African Americans are concentrated and where local police rather than Highway Patrols make most of the stops. Only

the localities from which they obtained data. Nationwide, the stop rate for African-American drivers was 1.4 times that of white drivers.[15]

Of course, police officers can sometimes ascertain the race of the driver before initiating contact, but often they do not have enough visual information to make a stop based on racial bias, even if they might be prone to do so. And that makes the post-stop results even more significant.

According to the Stanford findings, African-American drivers are 19% more likely to receive a citation once stopped. They are 75% more likely to be subjected to a search.[16] They are almost twice as likely (1.9x) to be arrested.[17/o] But in spite of the greater scrutiny to which blacks are subjected, the two races have about the same "hit rate" for contraband (drugs, alcohol, stolen goods, weapons, etc.).[18] The Stanford researchers found that the threshold for searching black drivers was lower than for white drivers in nearly every location they considered, about 20% lower in the aggregate.[19]

Keep in mind that the 75% greater likelihood of being searched and the nearly 90% greater likelihood of being arrested are *on top* of the 40% greater likelihood of being stopped in the first place. That means that the average black person driving down the street is *more than twice as likely* as the average white person to be searched or arrested.

Similar disparities show up in statewide studies. North Carolina has one of the most robust data collection procedures of any state, encompassing law enforcement at every level. In his 2018 book, *Suspect Citizens*, Frank Baumgartner of the University of North Carolina examined the results of 20

---

twenty states collected and provided sufficiently consistent and demographically relevant information for comparative statistical purposes.
o Sometimes a search results in an arrest, but on other occasions an arrest triggers a mandatory search. So, the U. of Cincinnati Policing Institute, in a study conducted for the Arizona Department of Public Safety, examined whether disproportionate criminal behavior by blacks was responsible for more legitimate arrests and, hence, for higher search percentages. Even when controlling for a wide variety of variables, the study still showed significant racial differences, echoing nationwide statistical trends. Given the same legal, vehicle, and stop characteristics, black drivers were significantly [1.9x] more likely to be arrested than whites and more than twice as likely to be searched. When those searches were prompted by police discretion rather than mandatory criteria (arrest, e.g.) the ratio climbed to 3:1. (Robin S. Engel, et. al., "Traffic Stop Data Analysis Study: Year 3 Final Report," University of Cincinnati Policing Institute, 2009, www.azdps.gov/ sites/default/files/media/Traffic_Stop_Data_Report_2009.pdf.)

million stops dating from 2002. He and his team found that "compared to their share in the population, blacks are almost twice as likely to be pulled over as whites... and [have] about four times the odds of being searched."[20] Though the "hit rate" for contraband in such searches is slightly lower for black people, they are still arrested 43% more often than their white counterparts.[21]

Missouri also collects very detailed statewide information. The state Attorney General's 2017 report indicates that African-American drivers were 1.85 times more likely to be stopped and 1.5 times more likely to be searched and arrested than white drivers.[22] In both Illinois[23] and Minnesota,[24] African Americans were searched at a rate 3 times that of whites, even though the contraband hit rate for white suspects was nearly 2 times that of blacks. What kind of public outcry might we expect if those numbers were reversed?

Ever since the Rodney King incident there has been a growing focus and concern surrounding police violence, lethal and otherwise, directed toward African-American detainees and suspects. The proliferation of cell phones with video capability, as well as police cameras, is increasingly illuminating the heretofore murky world of police encounters in minority communities. Beginning with the 2014 shooting of Michael Brown in Ferguson, Missouri, this issue has been the subject of intense media scrutiny.[p]

From 2010 to the present, the Justice Department (DOJ) has carried out investigations of police departments, not only in Ferguson but in New Orleans, Newark, Cleveland, Chicago, Baltimore, and elsewhere. These investigations show a strikingly similar pattern of unconstitutional policing that has a disproportionately egregious impact on African Americans.

For instance, the DOJ report on Ferguson, MO cites "unlawful conduct within the Ferguson Police Department that violates the First, Fourth, and Fourteenth Amendments to the United States Constitution, and federal statutory law."[25] In addition to "a pattern of stops that are improper from the beginning, it also exposes encounters that start as constitutionally defensible but quickly cross the line."[26] They found that the Baltimore Police Department "makes stops, searches and arrests without the required justification; uses enforcement strategies that unlawfully subject African Americans to disproportionate rates of stops, searches and arrests; uses excessive force; and retaliates against individuals for their constitutionally-protected expression."[27]

---

[p] As actor Will Smith commented on a July 28, 2016 *Tonight Show*: "Racism isn't getting worse; it's getting filmed."

After comparing citizen's accounts with official police reports, Chicago's own municipally-appointed task force concluded that the evidence gave "validity to the widely held belief the police have no regard for the sanctity of life when it comes to people of color."[28]

While such investigations revealed localized abusive patterns, in 2015, *The Washington Post* began to do what no official agency has ever done— tally the deadly police shootings of civilians nationwide. Since then, the overall annual numbers of fatal shootings by police have remained remarkably consistent at just under 1,000 people per year. The overwhelming majority of these police actions are justified, at least in the context of existing law enforcement procedures in a heavily armed society.

Part of what prompted this effort in the first place, however, was concern about the frequency with which lethal force was used against African Americans, particularly against unarmed African Americans. Indeed, in 2015 it seems as if they were disproportionately the victims of police shootings. In that year, African Americans died at the hands of police at about twice the percentage that they represent in the general population, and *unarmed* black people were killed at more than three times their population profile.[29]

Interestingly, however, the scrutiny focused on unarmed civilian killings seems to have had an effect. The overall number of such deaths dropped from 94 to 51 in just one year (2015-2016, 2018 = 47). The decline in shootings of unarmed *blacks* has been especially pronounced. In 2015, 32 unarmed whites (UW) were killed by police, compared to 38 unarmed blacks (UB). In 2016, however, the tally dropped to 22 UW vs. 19 UB (2018 = 23 UW vs. 18 UB).[30]

Based on demographics alone,[q] blacks are still over-represented in fatal encounters with the police, as there are 4.6 times as many whites as blacks in the general U.S. population.[31] Nevertheless, this significant statistical adjustment suggests both good and bad news. The good news is that awareness, responsibility, training (and whatever other factors may have contributed to the shift) can have a positive impact. The bad news is that any situation that could improve that much was clearly in dire need of improvement. Of course, it didn't get better by itself; it got better only under

---

[q] I say, "based on demographics alone," because other factors affect how often fatal shootings occur. For instance, if police have more (per capita) encounters with blacks than with whites, they could apply the same deadly-force criteria with both and still end up killing a disproportionate number of blacks.

intense pressure. Which tells us something about the reluctance of ingrained racial attitudes to evaporate on their own—and about the likelihood that there has been considerably less progress on less targeted forms of discrimination.

Judicial Process

As we have just seen, our legislative priorities and policing practices funnel disproportionate numbers of African Americans into the criminal justice system. But the problem doesn't end once they are in the system. The dynamics of the judicial process itself further exacerbate black disadvantage.

Frequently this discrimination begins with inadequate legal counsel. Granted, the quality of counsel one can afford is more a function of economic class than race. Nevertheless, since black people are overrepresented among the poor, the result is still the same—more blacks behind bars for longer terms.

Sometimes the quality of the defense counsel can be the key to a shorter sentence or even probation. Sometimes it is all that stands between a wrongful conviction and a finding of innocence. An examination of wrongful convictions in which the defendant was eventually exonerated found that one in eight such cases were the result of *severely* inadequate legal counsel. Furthermore, researchers estimate that improved legal counsel might have prevented a majority of wrongful convictions in the first place.[32]

The National Registry of Exonerations, a joint project of the University of Michigan Law School and the Center on Wrongful Convictions at Northwestern's School of Law, has recorded 2,215 exonerations since 1989.[33] This is only the tip of the iceberg, however, as they can catalogue only those that are brought to their attention. The Registry recognizes that they have inevitably "missed the vast majority of low-visibility exonerations."[34/r]

Even though the data on exonerations are unavoidably partial, it seems safe to say that black people are at least somewhat more likely to be the victims of wrongful convictions. Nearly three in eight incarcerated persons are black, but about half of all those exonerated are black. These eventual

---

[r] The number of exonerations is necessarily small, not for lack of cases that might be overturned but more on account of the time-consuming nature of the exoneration process, which averages 11.9 years from conviction to exoneration. According to Gross and Shaffer (*supra*, 4): "Most innocent defendants with short sentences probably never try to clear their names."

exonerations are not likely to occur because of the extraordinary diligence of the inmates' top-notch defense teams, so the rate of wrongful conviction for black people might even be somewhat underrepresented by their rate of exoneration.[s]

One of the most common sources of wrongful conviction is erroneous eyewitness identification. This is particularly the case in certain cross-racial crimes for which blacks are frequently misidentified. For example, "53% of all sexual assault exonerations with mistaken eyewitness identifications involved black men who were accused of raping white women"— an enormous racial disproportion of about 10 to 1.[35]

The disproportionate black reality that is mass incarceration has no single cause. It is not sustained by one giant taproot but by a diverse series of capillary roots that permeate the criminal justice system. No one of them alone is sufficient to explain the entire phenomenon, but their cumulative contribution both anchors and nurtures the visible growth. In addition to inadequate counsel and wrongful convictions, there is another important tendril in this root structure—racial disparities in sentencing.

The chart below compares the prison terms to which non-Hispanic black and white convicts were sentenced in federal courts in 2014.[36] The vertical bars show the relative number of convicts, by race, who received sentences in the time range indicated at the base of the chart. The distribution of sentences is visibly skewed along racial lines, with whites more likely to receive a shorter sentence—especially in the "none" category, which means that these convicts received probation and/or a fine. Whites receive such sentences at a ratio of 1.8 to 1, compared to African Americans. On the other end of the spectrum, the relative number of blacks goes up as the sentences get longer. Blacks are 1.5 times as likely to receive a sentence of ten years or longer.[t]

---

[s] There are, of course, other possible factors here, such as whether the organizations that offer help to people in seeking exonerations give preference to minorities. However, in a perusal of the requirements for seeking help from The Center on Wrongful Convictions, I found no explicit mention of such a preference. Two of the 83 affiliated agencies listed on their website do make indigence a requirement, but prisoners of any race tend to be poor.

[t] It is impossible to meaningfully compare the *raw number* of whites and blacks in each category, because there are so many more whites in the general population. Therefore, my chart reflects the *rates* at which the two racial groups received sentences in the ranges expressed. To make the chart more readable, I reorganized the number of Bureau of Justice Statistics sentencing

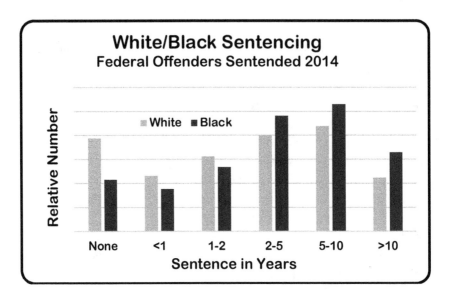

The U.S. Sentencing Commission (USSC), the bipartisan agency located in the judicial branch that tracks sentencing statistics and makes recommendations to both lawmakers and judges, confirms the existence of a racially discriminatory impact at the sentencing level. The USSC reports that from 2012-2016 black men received 19.1% harsher sentences[37] —even after taking into account the nuanced facts surrounding the cases.

Note, however, that this statistic applies only to *men*.[u] For while there is a racial disparity in the sentencing of male convicts, it turns out that there is also quite a disparity in the sentences handed down to men and women respectively. According to the USSC, from 2012-2016 "female offenders of all races received shorter sentences than White male offenders,"[38] as they had in previous reporting periods. Black women and white women receive very similar sentences. So, the problem, it seems, is not just color but also the historic prejudices of white society against black men.

---

ranges from 19 to 6. This does not alter the total number of convicts accounted for, only the way the sentence-length categories are organized.
[u] Men represent 85.3% of those sentenced in the federal system (2014) and, due to their longer sentences, an even higher percentage of those subsequently in prison. Source: BJS' Federal Justice Statistics Program website (http://bjs.ojp.usdoj.gov/fjsrc/).

Focusing only on this black/white male cohort, some statistical models show the sentencing gap decreasing rather dramatically in recent years. This would be a welcome development, but the USSC sounds a note of caution.

> The narrowing gap between Black and White male offender sentence lengths is due, in large part, to sizeable reductions in penalties for crack cocaine offenses, in which Black offenders constitute the large majority of the offenders. Despite these apparent changes in sentencing outcomes, the Commission's… analysis shows that when other relevant factors are controlled for, the gap in the sentence length between Black male and White male offenders did not shrink but, in fact, remained relatively stable.[39]

It's quite clear, then, that the sentencing results follow a racialized pattern. But just *how* does this disparity occur? Let's examine two aspects of the sentencing process[v]—the criteria employed in the sentencing guidelines and Congressionally-mandated minimum sentences.

A sentencing table[w] directs the judge to a range of appropriate sentences by cross-referencing two different considerations, the criminal history of the convicted person and the seriousness of the offense. There are forty-three different levels of seriousness assigned to the continuum of possible offenses. The differences between the offense levels assigned to whites and blacks are not great, though whites are somewhat more likely to be associated with less serious offenses and blacks with more serious offenses.[x]

The other part of the equation is the criminal history axis, comprised of six different categories. Here we find a more dramatically racialized picture. As illustrated by the chart below,[y] over half (56%) of all whites are in Criminal

---

[v] The following refers to the federal sentencing guidelines. A number of states also have guidelines, and they tend to operate on similar principles.

[w] See: www.ussc.gov/Guidelines/2012_Guidelines/Manual_PDF/Sentencing_Table.pdf.

[x] If we were to divide the offense levels into four groups, the lowest fourth would be comprised of 18% whites (w) and 15%, blacks (b). The second quarter breaks down 38% (w) vs. 34% (b), the third quarter 34% (w) vs. 39% (b), and the uppermost quarter 9% (w) vs. 11% (b).

[y] As in the case of the sentence length chart above, the "relative number" depicted here compares the *rate* at which whites and blacks are assigned to these various categories. See the footnote above for further explanation of how the values for these charts were calculated.

History Category I, whereas blacks increasingly predominate in the higher categories. The disparity is most notable on the two extremes. The ratio of whites to blacks in Criminal History Category I is 1.8 to 1, whereas the black presence in Criminal History Category VI is double that of whites.[40]

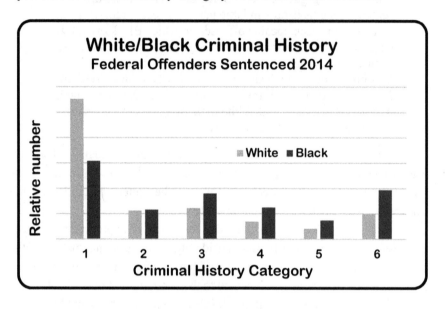

These differences in criminal history exert an enormous influence over sentencing. A person in Criminal History Category I could commit a crime with an offense level up to eight (out of 43) and still stand a chance of being sentenced to probation. The sentencing table works on a sliding scale, however, so that those on the other end of the spectrum—Criminal History Category VI Criminal Record holders, who are overwhelmingly African American—are essentially ineligible for probation. They can expect to receive about twice the prison time of those in Criminal History Category I for the same offense across the whole range of the sentencing table.

If we compare the distribution of blacks and whites across the two charts above (Sentencing and Criminal History), a striking similarity emerges. Whites predominate in the left-hand portion of the chart with blacks becoming relatively more numerous as you move to the right—toward higher criminal history levels and longer sentences.

What does this parallel tell us? It tells us that the sizable disparity between black and white prison terms is not primarily the product of prejudice on the part of judges or juries. However much race may have influenced sentencing in the past (either in individual cases or in the aggregate), sentencing guidelines have homogenized this process. So, now, if there is discrimination to be found, it is far more likely to be systemic than personal in nature.

There is, however, another systemic factor to consider here—mandatory minimum sentences, which have exerted considerable influence over the fortunes of African Americans. In order to combat certain crimes (or to at least create the appearance of doing so), Congress has mandated[z] minimum sentences that are anything but minimal. The result is a schizophrenic approach to punishment—on the one hand a nuanced and graduated system of sentencing guidelines; on the other a blunt instrument that assigns draconian penalties for relatively arbitrary levels of culpability. It's a little like two parents who can't decide how to discipline a child—or maybe a single inconsistent parent whose corrective measures vacillate incoherently.

For instance, imagine two criminals who are tried for possession with the intent to distribute crack cocaine. One was caught with 28 grams and the other with 27.99 grams—essentially the same crime.[aa] Because of a mandatory minimum, the first will receive a minimum sentence of five years (and perhaps considerably more), along with all "conspirators," regardless of how serious/minor their role in the crime. The second, in accordance with the sentencing guidelines, will receive no more than a year of incarceration. And their "conspirators" will be sentenced according to their involvement.

As it turns out, drug crimes are the type of offense to which mandatory minimum sentences are most commonly applied, "in recent years... [accounting] for approximately two-thirds of the offenses carrying a mandatory minimum penalty."[41] 39% of all African Americans sentenced to federal prison in 2014 were sentenced for drug crimes,[42] and 63% of black offenders in prison at the end of 2016 had been convicted of an offense carrying a mandatory minimum penalty.[43/bb]

---

[z] Most state legislatures also impose mandatory minimum sentences. Drug crimes are often the target, but the specifics vary from state to state.
[aa] This is according to the scale established by the Fair Sentencing Act of 2010. From 1986-2010 the 5-year-minimum trigger was only 5 grams.
[bb] The 39% cited here for blacks compares with 33% for whites. The 63% cited here for blacks compares with 55% for whites. This gap, while still significant, has shrunk since the Fair Sentencing Act of 2010. In part, that's because the number of whites convicted of an offense involving a mandatory

This situation is further exacerbated by the fact that black offenders are far more often convicted on a drug charge with a weapons enhancement (18 U.S.C. § 924(c)). In fiscal 2016 blacks accounted for 53% of such convictions, whites only 16%.[44] In cases involving multiple counts of 924(c) violations, African Americans represented 71% of such convictions, whites just 6%.[45]

Why does this matter? Because using or carrying a weapon during a drug crime carries a five-year minimum. Subsequent convictions incur a penalty of 25 years. And 924(c) sentences are consecutive to the primary offense.

Here again, the question is not just about the discriminatory *application* of the rules but about the discriminatory *effect* of the rules themselves. Why, exactly, do these classes of crime merit especially harsh sentencing? Perhaps arguments could be advanced concerning their special seriousness, but, if so, why not simply tweak the sentencing guidelines, rather than imposing mandatory minimums to supersede the guidelines? Why elevate certain crimes—committed disproportionately by African Americans—to whipping boy status? Would mandatory minimum sentences, a strategy whose public safety and law enforcement benefits are dubious at best,[cc] remain in place if they contributed to locking up whites at five times the rate of blacks?

Sentencing guidelines represent a far more reasoned and proportional approach to criminal punishment than that imposed by mandatory minimum sentencing. But even this more judicious approach results in seriously disproportionate results for black convicts. So, we must ask the following question: Do black people, in fact, commit more serious offenses or does our system simply attach greater seriousness to the offenses blacks commit? After all, the determination as to which crimes are worse than others, just how severely they should be sanctioned, and under what conditions—that is a judgment made by people, people who are products of a racialized society.[dd] As such, these judgments should be regularly and critically reviewed.

---

minimum has gone up since methamphetamines became a legislative target. That may shrink the racial differential, but applying exaggerated penalties that disproportionately impact whites does not amount to moral or judicial reform.
[cc] For a more detailed evaluation of these supposed benefits, see: www.scottgarber.com/was_notes.pdf, Note 19.5.
[dd] Interestingly, drug and weapons crimes are not included in the FBI's Part I crimes, the crimes generally considered most serious. Nevertheless, the penalties attached to drug and weapons crimes are among the most draconian.

The U.S. Sentencing Commission, in their review of sentencing disparities, observed that the guidelines are based on "legally relevant factors,"[46] such as criminal history[ee] and weapons involvement. At the same time, however, they seem concerned about the possibility that demographic disparities "may result from disproportionate processing by the criminal justice system"[47] and that "mandatory minimum penalties... are being applied most frequently to a population that is not necessarily representative of all persons violating such laws."[48/ff]

This "disproportionate processing" to which African Americans are subjected (more vigilance, searches, arrests, etc.) sweeps vast numbers of young black men into the criminal justice system and one step closer to a criminal career. If the resulting conviction is for a felony offense the future consequences are grave both in and out of the criminal justice system. A criminal background translates into a higher Criminal History Category and leads to harsher sentences in the future. In addition, "safety valve" relief for mandatory sentences is unavailable to those with felony convictions.[gg]

Most convictions, however, do not occur in the relatively well-regulated context of felony courts. An estimated eight out of ten criminal cases take place in the far murkier world of misdemeanors. Though in theory a defendant is always innocent until proven guilty, when it comes to misdemeanors, things work just about the opposite way around. Arrests lacking probable cause are not likely to be screened out. Many defendants can't make bail, and the time they would spend in jail awaiting the adjudication of their case might exceed the jail time they would receive if convicted at trial. Even if they do go to trial, it's likely to be their word against that of the arresting officer, and the penalty is almost certain to be considerably worse than if they just plead out. So, more often than not, that's exactly what they do.

[ee] For a more detailed explanation of the impact of criminal history in the sentencing process, see: www.scottgarber.com/was_notes.pdf, Note 19.6.
[ff] For more of the Commission's evaluation of this problem see www.scottgarber.com/was_notes.pdf, Note 19.7.
[gg] Due to the harshness of the mandatory penalties, the system has evolved over time to give relief to people with minimal criminal records. This "safety valve" provision, while used extensively, applies only to people in Criminal History Category I, which automatically excludes felons. While the safety valve helps mitigate the impact of mandatory minimums, it exacerbates the relative racial impact of these sentences, because black convicts are far less likely than whites to have the Category I classification (see chart above).

Such convictions, while almost automatic, are not at all inconsequential. A misdemeanor drug conviction results in ineligibility for federal student loans and (in some areas) for public housing. Even one misdemeanor (depending on the jail time served) can increase one's Criminal History Classification from I to II, creating a criminal record that reverberates throughout each future contact with the justice system.

The picture that begins to emerge is that of a black population that interfaces with the criminal justice system, not at a single point at which they might find themselves at a disadvantage, but rather in in a multi-tiered system in which the discriminatory impact is likely to be iterative. There are many situations in which black people can find themselves disadvantaged—which neighborhoods are targeted for policing, who is stopped, who is searched, who is arrested, who is charged and with which counts, who has access to qualified counsel, who is arrested for crimes deemed most serious, who has been here before, and who receives longer sentences. Of course, the vast majority of those arrested, convicted, and sentenced have indeed committed a crime. Still, the scale of the incarceration disparity (blacks incarcerated at five times the rate of whites) should make us wonder about the impact of the system itself—especially when a similar incarceration disparity exists for drug crimes that we know whites and blacks commit with approximately the same frequency.[hh]

With so many potential points of disadvantage, the discriminatory impact of each one does not have to be large in order for the cumulative effect to be considerable. To illustrate how such iterative impacts can add up,[ii] let's imagine a new extreme sport, slalom rollerblading, in which contestants plummet down a steep and winding course that includes jumps and obstacles. Not surprisingly, this exciting but dangerous activity results in quite a few injuries, some so serious that the competitor misses the rest of the season.

There is a problem, however. This sport has both a North American and a European circuit, and season-ending injuries are not occurring at the same rate on both circuits. Though the overall casualty rate for the entire

---

[hh] Sometimes I refer to a 6:1 ratio and other times a 5:1 ratio, depending on whether I am talking about incarceration for drug crimes/mandatory sentences or overall incarceration rates.

[ii] This illustration was inspired by a similar one that appears in Mahzarin R. Banaji, Anthony G. Greenwald, *Blindspot: Hidden Biases of Good People*, (New York: Delacort Press, 2013), 203-204.

competition is around 5% per round, it averages out to only 3% in Europe and 7% in North America. To put it another way, 97% of the Europeans escape injury each round, compared to 93% of the Americans.

As the injuries affecting key competitors build up, commentators notice this continental disparity but are at a loss to explain it. Some chalk it up to bad luck or, perhaps, the more rambunctious style of the North Americans. It turns out, however, that there are some subtle differences in the courses. The American runs have just slightly more precipitous drops, barely tighter turns, less forgiving barriers, and a slicker composite course surface. In a sport played so close to the edge, these differences, invisible to the naked eye, are largely responsible for the injury disparity.

What, then is the overall impact of this iterative disadvantage over the course of ten rounds of regional competition? As the two teams prepare to meet at the world championship, of the 100 competitors who began on each side, about one quarter of the Europeans (26) have been forced to withdraw on account of injury. On the American side, however, more than half (52) are physically unable to compete.

So, we see that seemingly small inequalities can add up to big disparities when repeated often enough. And this is precisely what African Americans experience as they interface with the American justice system. Even when black disadvantage is not the intended consequence, it remains, nonetheless, a very real and very significant consequence—and a continuing contributor to America's racial divide.

Chapter 20

Mass Incarceration and the Moral of the Story

Having outlined some of the sources of inequality in the American justice system, it's now time to drill down into the consequences of those disparities. My primary focus in this chapter is mass incarceration, but I also want to examine the broader social consequences of this phenomenon—and what it tells us about racial haughtiness in contemporary America.

The elevated level of black incarceration is nothing new. Ever since the post-Civil War period blacks have consistently been imprisoned at a rate far exceeding that of whites. During the middle of the 20th century, however, while the overall incarceration rate in the U.S. remained relatively steady,[1] the ratio of blacks to whites in the correctional system began gradually increasing (1926 = 2.5:1, 1975 = 4.5:1).[2] By 2010, this ratio stood at 6 to 1.[3]

By the beginning of 2017 about 1 in 38 persons in the United States were under some form of correctional supervision.[4/a] For African-American men, however, that figure was nearly 1 in 8.[5/b] More than three percent of black male adults were in state or federal prison.[6/c] Black males under the age of twenty were nearly twelve times as likely as whites of the same age to find themselves in prison[7]—a good way to get a bad start.

During the 1960s and 1970s rapidly rising crime rates seemed to justify the emerging law-and-order mantra in American politics. The eighties saw a more modest (12%) but nevertheless far more publicized increase in violent crime. This heightened the fervor for long mandatory sentences, three-strikes-

---

[a] "Correctional supervision" includes state or federal prison, local jails, parole, and probation.

[b] This composite calculation totals the black male correctional population from Bureau of Justice Statistics documents and compares them with U.S. Census figures for black males 18 and older. For more information on this calculation see: www.scottgarber.com/was_notes.pdf, Note 20.1.

[c] This percentage may differ from those reported in some government publications, because those often compare the number of people in prison (by demographic) to the overall population for that demographic (all ages). But since the number of minors in the prison system is so miniscule as to be negligible for statistical purposes, it seemed more relevant to compare the number of black men in prison with only the black male *adult* population.

and-you're-out rules, and other adjustments that channeled more and more convicts into the correctional system for increasingly longer sentences.

Over the subsequent two decades (1990-2010) both violent crime and property crime rates plummeted by more than 40%.[8] But whether the symptom was increasing or decreasing crime rates, the medicine turned out to be more of the same—mass incarceration.[d] So much so that the number of people under the supervision of correctional authorities in the United States nearly quadrupled in the three decades between 1980 and 2009.[9] As a result, 21st century America now has the highest (official) incarceration rate of any major nation,[10/e] upwards of one percent of the entire adult population.[11/f]

An estimated one quarter of all black males born in 2001 will go to *prison* (serious state or federal facilities, not just local jails) during their lifetimes,[g] a circumstance that signals a full-blown crisis for African-American society. At some point, the loss of so many (mostly young) men in a given sub-population reaches a tipping point of social and economic dysfunction, beyond which that group simply lacks the wherewithal to independently right itself.

Whereas a college education is one of the most reliable predictors of black economic and social progress, incarceration is one of the most reliable predictors of black social disadvantage. In 1980, for every 100 black men in college 45 were incarcerated; by 2015, for every 100 in college 71 were

---

[d] The term *mass incarceration* strictly refers to those who are in jail or prison, but the causes and consequences of this phenomenon generally apply to all those who are under correctional supervision, including those on probation or parole, who are convicts despite not actually being behind bars.

[e] Only incarcerated persons can be considered for the purposes of international comparison, as probation and parole systems in different countries vary widely. The Seychelles (population < 100,000) is the only country with a higher rate than the U.S. Canada incarcerates people at only 15% of the U.S. rate, Russia 64%. The worldwide average is 21% of the U.S. rate, but that includes the U.S., which has over 20% of the global incarcerated population. If the U.S. incarcerated population is excluded from the worldwide total, the rest of the world incarcerates at only 16% of the U.S. rate.

[f] The actual percentage is 0.86%, with 2,162,400 incarcerated out of a total adult population of 249,485,228 people.

[g] The original Justice Department projection of 1 in 3 black males was based on the 2001 black male prison incarceration rate. Sine then that rate has declined significantly, so a 1 in 4 ratio now seems more realistic. See: Thomas P. Bonczar, "Prevalence of Imprisonment in the U.S. Population, 1974-2001," (U.S. Department of Justice; Office of Justice Programs; August 2003), 8.

incarcerated.[12/h] With this key historical factor moving in exactly the wrong direction, it's not difficult to understand why there hasn't been more progress in overcoming historic social disparities relative to the white population.

To put this level of incarceration in perspective, consider the five largest countries of Western Europe: the UK, Germany, Spain, Italy, and France. Their combined population is roughly equivalent to that of the U.S. But their total incarcerated population—for all ages, ethnicities, and genders—does not amount to *even half the number of black men* behind bars in the U.S.[13/i]

The corrosive effect of mass incarceration is accentuated by the fact that it is invisible, cumulative, and intergenerational.[14] The incarcerated population is, by design, hidden from view. But those who get hidden tend to stay that way, as incarceration is more often a destiny than a detour. Nearly half (46%) of black prisoners are re-arrested within one year of their release. Seven out of eight are re-arrested within nine years.[15/j]

This effect is cumulative as well, because once people have been incarcerated, even when they do avoid returning, their chances of finding employment diminish considerably. Research conducted by Devah Pager of Princeton University highlights the impact of a prison record for those seeking employment, especially for black people.[16] The study, conducted in Milwaukee, Wisconsin, featured two black and two white participants, college students who pretended to be high school graduates with no college education. They took turns presenting themselves as having or not having a felony record for drug possession with intent to distribute, for which they had served eighteen months in prison. Their qualifications were otherwise identical, and they were also deemed to have equivalent presentation skills. The only real variables were the presence or absence of a record—and, of course, their color. The goal of the study was to discover how often the various applicants received callbacks from an employer.

---

[h] During the 2015-16 school year, 997,700 black men were enrolled in college, while 703,990 were incarcerated. For more background on the history of this comparison, see: www.scottgarber.com/was_notes.pdf, Note 20.2.
[i] Total for the UK, Germany, Spain, Italy, France (2015) = 335,125 = 48% of 703,990 black men incarcerated in the U.S. See: Roy Walmsley, "World Prison Population List, 9th ed."; (London, International Centre for Prison Studies. www.idcr.org.uk/wp-content/uploads/2010/09/WPPL-9-22.pdf) *with* E. Ann Carson, "Prisoners in 2015" and "Jail Inmates in 2016," *supra*.
[j] This statistic measures only the first arrest after release. Whites were re-arrested at a rate of 40% (1 yr.) and 81% (9 yrs.) See endnote citation.

Despite fair employment regulations (ostensibly) protecting ex-convicts from job discrimination, having a record nevertheless made a difference.[k] White applicants without a criminal record got *twice* the number of callbacks as whites with a criminal record (34% vs. 17%). But the effect was even more dramatic for black applicants. Those without a criminal record received nearly *three times* the callbacks as those with a criminal record (14% vs. 5%). So, while a criminal record put a major dent in both black and white job prospects, the impact was 40% greater for blacks than for whites.

If a criminal record mattered, however, race mattered even more. White applicants *with* a criminal record still got more callbacks than black applicants *without* one—17% vs. 14%! And white candidates *without* a criminal background were *seven times* more likely to get a callback than equally qualified blacks with a record. Black ex-cons clearly got the double whammy.

Not only can the consequences of mass incarceration be largely invisible and cumulative in nature; the consequences of mass incarceration are unavoidably intergenerational as well. By the age of 14, one in four African-American children have had a father go to prison. For whites that number is only 1 in 28.[17] A report for the Pew Charitable Trust cites one study which "found that 23 percent of children with a father who has served time in a jail or prison have been expelled or suspended from school, compared with just 4 percent of children whose fathers have not been incarcerated."[18]

Along with all this bad news, however, there is a measure of good news, or at least better news. Sadly, a generation of mass incarceration has ravished black America. But incarceration is becoming at least somewhat less massive.[l]

The most recent data from the Bureau of Justice Statistics indicate that the incarcerated population has dropped every year from 2009-2016. The overall number of people in the correctional population (including probation and parole) also declined during this period.[19] This is the first actual *decline* in the incarcerated population since BJS began reporting this figure in 1980.[20]

---

[k] In Milwaukee, employers are not allowed to discriminate against those with criminal records, unless that status is germane to the job. Such jobs were excluded from the study, as were those that mentioned a background check or gave any explicit signs that a criminal record would raise concerns. Not all employers ask explicitly about a potential criminal background, so to ensure that this information was noted, the participants included work they had done in prison on the application and listed their parole officers as references.

[l] This has been the case through the most recent reporting year (*mrry*) of 2016.

Wherever this overall incarceration trend might go from here, the decrease in mass incarceration that has already occurred represents a positive development for African Americans. The nationwide arrest rate for blacks peaked in 1989 and then declined steadily to just *half* that highest rate in 2014.[21] In addition, from 2008-2016 black incarceration *decreased* by 19%.[22/m]

So, what's going on here? It would be nice to think that the decline in black arrests represents a greater sensitivity to overt discrimination and better training for police forces. It would be nice to believe that the decline in incarceration means that we've reached the logical limits of a failed approach and entered a more enlightened era of criminal justice. To whatever extent such forces are at work, that is certainly cause for celebration.

Let's stop and consider these recent trends in a larger context, however. This isn't some sort of utopian leveling of the playing field but a long-overdue adjustment to an enormous disparity. Recent improvements notwithstanding, everything I've said above is still true. The black incarceration rate is *still* five times that of whites, an embarrassment of historic proportions that remains both morally indefensible and socially unsustainable.

True, the Obama administration was more civil rights-sensitive than its predecessors, but it's not clear how much of this reduction in incarcerations (which came quite quickly on the heels of the 2008 election) is attributable to actual policy and enforcement changes. It's also unclear just why there has been such an exaggerated lag time between the reductions in crime/arrests and the eventual decline in the prison population. The evidence seems to suggest that the decrease in black incarceration rates is due more to circumstantial changes than to a psycho-spiritual transformation among whites.

One of those changing circumstances has been a dramatic, across-the-board decrease in serious crime.[n] According to the FBI's Uniform Crime Report, between 1991 and 2014 (the most recent reporting year, *mrry*) the rate of both violent and property crime fell by almost exactly half, reaching their lowest levels since 1970 and 1966 respectively.[23/o] With less crime being

---

[m] This includes both black prisoners and jail inmates. See endnote for sources.

[n] For more background on how the FBI categorizes serious crime, see: www.scottgarber.com/was_notes.pdf, Note 20.3.

[o] Note that the Uniform Crime Report tool furnishes data only through 2014, but 2015 and 2016 saw a spike of 3.9% and 4.1% respectively in violent crimes, driven by a spike in homicides (+10.8% in 2015 and +8.6% in 2016). The reasons for this sudden phenomenon are not entirely clear, though some

reported and investigated, the result was a trickle-down effect on arrests, convictions, and incarcerations. Curiously, the black prison population declined by only 19%, even though overall crime and black arrests both dropped by 50%.

Changing circumstances also led to a change in our perceived threats. After 9/11, the fear/panic factor that drives our political priorities shifted from domestic crime to external threats and then eventually to financial meltdowns and their aftermath. According to *The Washington Post*, "In 1994, more than half of Americans called crime the nation's most important problem; by 2012, only 2 percent of those surveyed by Gallup said so."[24]

In addition, the "solution" of mass incarceration was itself creating new problems. Since we couldn't build facilities fast enough to keep up with the influx of prisoners during this era, overcrowding became a serious issue. So much so that by 2010, the federal system was at 136% of capacity, with 19 states at more than 100% of capacity.[25] The problem in California prisons became so acute that in May, 2011 the U.S. Supreme Court ruled that the overcrowding constituted "cruel and unusual punishment" and ordered the state to reduce its prison population by more than 30,000.[26]

In the wake of the economic downturn that began in 2007, there was neither enough money to fund new facilities nor the political will to spend more than $30,000 per year, per prisoner on an ever-increasing number of inmates.[27] According to the U.S. Department of Justice, "In 2010 alone, state and federal governments spent $80 billion on incarceration."[28] Having created a monster too big to feed, authorities had to reconsider the wisdom of locking up so many low-level offenders for extended periods of time.[p]

---

criminologists suggest that the increase among blacks is a post-Ferguson reaction, while among whites it is driven by the opioid crisis. According to a report from the Brennan Center for Justice and NYU Law School, violent crime *decreased* in 2017 by just over 1%. See: Timothy Williams, "Violent Crime in U.S. Rises for Second Year in a Row." *The New York Times*, Sept. 25, 2017. www.nytimes.com/2017/09/25/us/violent-crime-murder-chicago-increase-.html. Also: Ames Grawert, James Cullen, "Crime in 2017: An Updated Analysis." The Brennan Center for Justice, Dec. 19, 2017. www.brennancenter.org/analysis/crime-2017-updated-analysis.

[p] Overcrowding has lessened but remains a problem. In 2016 the Federal prison system was at 114% of capacity and 14 states were at more than 100% (vs. 19 states in 2010, though those 14 were mostly at less egregious levels of overcrowding). See: "Prisoners in 2016," cited in endnote 22 above, p. 14.

In an August 12, 2013 speech, Attorney General Eric Holder reported that he was directing the U.S. Attorneys to stop charging low-level drug offenders with crimes that carried draconian mandatory sentences—an approach dubbed "Smart on Crime." In March of 2014 Holder proposed a change to the Federal Sentencing Guidelines that would reserve the harshest penalties for the most serious drug crimes and most violent offenders but reduce sentences for up to 70% of all drug offenders by an average of 18%.[29] The following month the administration announced a clemency route for non-violent offenders who had served ten years of their sentence, didn't have a significant criminal history, and would likely have received a shorter sentence under current sentencing rules.[30]

Back then it looked as if we might be on the verge of a bipartisan re-thinking of our criminal justice approach. Some legislators wanted to offset racial disparities in sentencing and combat the destabilizing and counter-productive effect these laws have on minority communities. Others wanted to shrink the criminal justice system as part of an overall plan to pare down the reach of government. The overriding motivation, however, was to save money. While that reasoning has its own merits, in terms of our primary focus, racial haughtiness, it is disappointing when reform benefitting African Americans becomes viable only as an unintended consequence of a strategy designed primarily to protect the economic interests of the dominant.

In the Trump era this push to save money has certainly continued. On the one hand, the President supported the bipartisan FIRST STEP Act, which includes significant sentencing reform and his promise that it would "SAVE tremendous taxpayer dollars."[31] On the other hand, "smart on crime" talk is out, and "tough on crime" talk is back, confounding the overall message about where criminal justice is headed.

Attorney General Jeff Sessions rescinded significant portions of Holder's "Smart on Crime" initiative.[32] In a June, 2017 op-ed in *The Washington Post*, Sessions argued for *increasing* our reliance on mandatory minimum sentences as a way to "get tough" on crime again.[33] If, as we have seen, reliance on mandatory minimums contributed significantly to mass incarceration in the first place, it's hard to see how a return to this strategy could have a different outcome this time around.

Trump likes to wield the enduring popular myth of rising crime rates. Weeks after taking office, the President summoned county sheriffs to the White House to announce his hard-hitting approach to criminal justice. Why the crackdown? Because, as he said, "The murder rate in our country is the highest it's been in 47 years, right? Did you know that? Forty-seven years. I used to use that — I'd say that in a speech and everybody was surprised, because the press doesn't tell it like it is."[34]

Of course, his claim wasn't even remotely true. But for the purpose of propaganda, that doesn't matter if people are inclined to believe it—and polls show that many people are indeed inclined to believe it. From 1991-2017 (*mrry*) crime consistently *decreased*—between 50% (FBI) and 70% (BJS).[35] Nevertheless, when Gallup asked Americans if there was more or less crime in the U.S. than the year before, from 1993-2018 a majority consistently told Gallup that crime was on the rise. For much of that time more than *two-thirds* of Americans held this contrary-to-fact opinion.[36]

Of course, supporters of mass incarceration sometimes point out that crime *decreased* significantly during the very period in which the use of incarceration *increased*. So, before we leave this topic, let's address that issue.

Correlation (that the increase in incarceration was accompanied by a decrease in crime) does not prove causation. Some, therefore, refuse to assign any efficacy to incarceration at all. But while it's important to qualify what it means to say that incarceration "works," it seems that there is sufficient evidence to conclude that incarceration did indeed *contribute* to this historic decline in crime. But whether that means that more incarceration is always more efficacious and/or justified—that is a very different question.

Incarceration, when properly designed, reduces crime by physically isolating the criminal element and by providing a deterrent. So, taking the most frequent and violent offenders off the streets makes an initial difference. But super-*sizing* the system doesn't make it super-*productive*. Resources expended on less-dangerous criminals don't seem to provide similar crime-reduction benefits. Some experts contend that the optimum incarceration level for crime reduction may be only about half of the current U.S. rate.[37]

The same principle applies to deterrence. The possibility of incarceration does make people think twice about committing a crime, but the possibility of relatively longer incarceration seems to make little difference. According to a report by the Pew Foundation: "Today, it is widely agreed that deterrence is more a function of a sanction's certainty and swiftness than its severity. This means that the 36th month of a three-year prison term costs taxpayers just as much as the first month, but its value as a deterrent is far less."[38]

At the very least, it's clear is that mass incarceration is not a silver bullet. Increased incarceration and crime reduction don't necessarily move in tandem. Keep in mind that the prison population had been exploding for more than a decade *before* crime even began to wane in the early nineties. In a seven-year period beginning in 1984, during which the rate of incarceration increased by an astounding 65%, the crime rate nevertheless *rose* 17%, reaching its highest level ever in 1991. In the next seven years, from 1991 to 1998, the rate of incarceration increased at the robust but somewhat less dramatic pace of 47%. During that period, however, crime *decreased* by 22%. So, over a fourteen-year period, the incarceration rate more than doubled, but crime fell less than 10%. That suggests that imprisonment is, at best, a rather blunt instrument.[39]

Even during 1991-1998, when falling crime rates did accompany rising rates of incarceration, the causal connection is far from straightforward. During that period, Texas managed a crime reduction of 35% while locking up 144% more inmates. But New York achieved an *even greater* reduction of 43% while locking up only 24% more. When it came to cutting crime, and especially violent crime, the thirty states whose incarceration growth rates were below the national average *outperformed* the twenty whose rates were above the national average.[q]

Any consideration of whether mass incarceration "works," must also consider what constitutes effectiveness in the broader social and spiritual sense. If reducing crime were the only goal, we could just summarily execute all criminals—low cost, zero recidivism, high deterrence. But we don't do that, in part because of the kind of society we aspire to be. Before alienating people from their "inalienable" rights, our notion of justice demands a compelling and proportionate rationale. And we hold out the hope that at least some offenders can be rehabilitated.

Furthermore, it is impossible to address the question of incarceration's effectiveness by looking only at its impact on crime and ignoring its impact on people. What about the individual lives and futures that are sentenced to confinement? What about the families and communities that suffer because so many of its members are absent? What about the interracial relationships

---

[q] For more information on the possible reasons for crime reduction other than incarceration, see: www.scottgarber.com/was_notes.pdf, Note 20.4.

that are frayed by a hierarchy-enhancing institution that hearkens to the concerns of the majority while turning a tin ear to minority wellbeing?

I have dedicated considerable space to this subject of mass incarceration, in order to demonstrate the important role that this institutionalized phenomenon has played in perpetuating America's racial hierarchy in recent decades. In support of this thesis I have unpacked just *how* these racialized disparities operate. But that is not enough. We must now proceed to the even more uncomfortable subject of *why*. If mass incarceration reflects badly on our society, if it costs us dearly, if it is an inefficient method for ensuring public safety, if it wastes the lives of those behind bars, if it generally makes them less productive citizens, if it drains the human capital necessary for black progress, and if it reinforces racial division—then why have we been so enamored with it?

Some point to the influence of Scripture itself, the notion that the state is God's instrument tasked with dispensing justice. But for this justice to be just, it must also be impartial. So, why has the white-dominated power structure been so much more zealous in its prosecution and punishment of people who don't look like us? Is this really a hunger and thirst for righteousness, or perhaps something far less noble?

But aren't criminals free moral agents who need to be held accountable for their choices? Certainly. The fact of free moral agency has more than one implication, however. Yes, it means that we should hold people accountable for their actions. But if they are, indeed, free moral agents, then we must recognize that they could be persuaded to make different choices.

Why, then, do we put all our eggs in the basket of retributive punishment and its negative deterrent, when we could be changing those criminal choices by offering more appealing alternatives? If we have been the architects of an environment that makes criminality more likely, we must also have at least some capacity to alter that environment in ways that make criminality less likely. And, I would argue, we have a moral responsibility to do so. The question is: "Do we have the *will*?"

Overall, the answer seems to be, "apparently not." Changing the context out of which criminality arises seems too much like a job for big government, and many whites reflexively believe that big government is, by definition, bad government—categorically inept, profligately wasteful, and perversely dedicated to robbing resources from the deserving and bestowing them on the undeserving. Mass incarceration, however, seems like an ironic exception to this distaste for big-government, because our response to criminality is a governmental apparatus big enough to make Stalin proud—or at least envious.

Since government intervention is not a real option, then perhaps the Church could help. But the Church isn't really the ideal institution either, because its only real unity is pretty much invisible. So, what we're really talking about are churches, plural, who don't have the common vision or infrastructure to tackle something so massive—even if they were so inclined.

Having conveniently precluded any sort of constructive institutional engagement, many whites are content to curtail criminality through mass incarceration and leave the underlying issues to individual initiative. Not their own individual initiative, mind you, as they live on whatever side of town is as far away from criminality as they can get. What's needed is someone closer to the action, someone who might derive enough personal benefit from such changes to work sacrificially on their behalf. Which brings us to the obvious choice—black people themselves.

Insisting that the people on the short end of the lever must do the heavy lifting just because we on the long end have encumbered them with a self-interested motivation to do so is, of course, a perversely disingenuous bit of moral reasoning. Especially when the encumbrances in question are not mere historical artifacts but, rather, ongoing realities. Nevertheless, this is precisely where a lot of white people find themselves today, not a few of whom are committed Christians. We've outsourced loving our black neighbors—by encouraging our black neighbors to love themselves.

There is, however, another reason for which whites might perpetuate or at least tolerate mass incarceration—a sense of superiority rooted in racial haughtiness, the same sense of superiority that has, for centuries, justified the rightness of the racial hierarchy. Whether we're talking about overt forms of white-over-black hierarchy like slavery and Jim Crow, or more subtle forms of discrimination, like locking up blacks at five times the rate of whites, the moral animus is eerily similar. Such inequities endure only because at some level we believe that people are getting what they deserve.

Consider the possibilities. Either blacks and whites are equally human—equally created in the image of God and therefore moral equals—or they are not. If we hold that the races are *not* moral equals and that black people are morally inferior and, therefore, more given to criminality, then mass incarceration might be a reasonable, even humane option for controlling this built-in brutishness. If, however we *are* moral equals, then there is something massively distorted about a color-coded system of mass incarceration.

I suppose that, if asked, most whites would heartily affirm the moral equality of all people. Christians have particularly robust theological reasons for doing so. Note, however, that the correlation between principled commitments (theological or otherwise) and implicit attitudes is frequently tenuous, with the latter generally exercising a greater influence over behavior. It seems that somewhere between theory and praxis, haughtiness has somehow moved us to approve, or at least accept, a system that makes sense only if whites are morally superior and, therefore, more deserving.

Because racial haughtiness is foundational to racial injustice, in order to right the wrongs in our criminal justice system, we whites must experience a spiritual change—moving from the insular deservedness of a haughty other to the empathetic solidarity of a humble brother. In the case of mass incarceration, one test of that spiritual change will be our willingness to line up on the side of not only justice but of black wellbeing as well. For as long as there are twice as many black men under the mastery of the correctional system as there were under the mastery of slave owners at the onset of the Civil War,[40/r] none of us can claim to be "free at last."

---

[r] There were 1,981,389 male slaves in 1860, 1,018,602 of whom were minors, yielding an adult population of 962,787. Compare that with an estimated 2,009,721 black men under some form of correctional supervision in 2016. "Correctional supervision" includes state and federal prison, jail, probation, and parole. Note: BJS does not break down jail, probation, and parole populations by race and sex, so I had to extrapolate those male populations, based on gender demographics for all races. I believe this result to be a generally reliable estimate. See endnote for statistical source citations.

Chapter 21

Racial Reconciliation and Contemporary Christianity

In the aftermath of the Civil Rights Movement, there was a window of opportunity for churches to seize the moment and coalesce around a vision of Christian unity across racial lines. But Christians, white and black, missed that moment. Rather than casting a vision of what could be, churches bowed to the pressures of the ecclesiastical marketplace and doubled down on their longstanding racial conservatism.

By "doubling down," I mean that not only did churches remain just as segregated as they had been; many actually discovered a new justification for it. During the 1970s and 1980s church-growth gurus were hawking the "homogenous unit principle,"[a] convincing happy-to-hear-it leaders that cultural likeness, rather than diversity, was the key to building a successful ministry. The homogenous unit principle held that people will more readily participate in a congregation that reflects their own cultural preferences.

The popularization of this notion coincided with the expansion of the automobile-based society, which allowed people to choose a place of worship outside their community of residence. As a result, newer suburban churches, some of them mega-churches, began to proliferate. Meanwhile, white urban congregations in "changing neighborhoods" generally fell upon hard times, sometimes relocating, sometimes withering away. Not surprisingly, making the church more welcoming to people who were the same often had quite the opposite effect on those who were different. The unspoken distinction between *we* and *they* became even more obvious, and relatively few churchgoers crossed the color line.

---

[a] See: Donald A. McGavran, *Understanding Church Growth*, (Grand Rapids, Wm. B. Eerdmans, First Edition 1970). McGavran developed this concept as a missiological principle, reacting to the imposition of outside cultures on indigenous populations. But it was soon applied as a strategy for church growth in America and as a rationale for congregational ethnocentrism. To better understand how Christian leaders of this period grappled with the ramifications of this principle, see: "The Pasadena Consultation," part of the Lausanne Movement in 1977 (www.lausanne.org/content/lop/lop-1).

Apart from a few black megachurches whose charismatic leaders attracted a small white following, black churches remained the Afrocentric counterpart to white Christianity. Their natural interface with the African-American community kept black congregations far more engaged with social issues. But while the Civil Rights movement continued to receive reverent lip service, a passion for the prosperity gospel was rapidly replacing the mantra of justice for the oppressed. Meanwhile, in the white Christian world, racial inequality had become somebody else's homogeneous unit problem.

This radical and intentional separation along the lines of race/culture clearly ran counter to Martin Luther King's vision of a beloved society. Dr. King had traced only the broadest outlines of ecclesiastical integration, but he clearly had in mind an *inclusive* dynamic, bringing the racially alienated together into loving community. In this era, however, Christians gravitated toward an *exclusive* dynamic—loving those who were most like them already.

In the long run this racialized ecclesiastical landscape was simply not sustainable. Not because it wasn't comfortable, for most whites and most blacks felt right at home. It was unsustainable because it was so diametrically opposed to the message of the New Testament. American Christianity had opted for the one solution that the Apostle Paul had refused to contemplate for differences between first-century Jews and Gentiles—division.

During Jim Crow there was no external societal pressure in the direction of an integrated church. Quite the opposite, in fact. But now, as other social institutions were becoming more inclusive, the Church, which had the wherewithal to be a locomotive for change, was quickly becoming the caboose. That was bound to create some cognitive/theological dissonance for somebody, somewhere. And it did.

Pioneers of Christian Racial Reconciliation

In the midst of the generalized race fatigue and post-racial pretensions that characterized the post-Civil Rights era, there arose a small but vocal prophetic counter-movement, challenging the status quo and pursuing a pathway to reconciliation.[b] The early protagonism came from black

---

[b] For an excellent summary of this period on which I have relied heavily, see: Michael O. Emerson and Christian Smith. *Divided by Faith.* (Oxford: Oxford Univ. Press, 2000), 52 ff.

evangelicals like John Perkins, Tom Skinner[c], and Samuel Hines; leaders who took up the theme of Christian racial reconciliation that was once a key ingredient in the message of Martin Luther King Jr.

John Perkins was the product of rural Mississippi, where he learned to despise both white oppression as well as black submission, not to mention the religion that served to normalize that dynamic. But after running away to California in search of personal prosperity, God got ahold of him, and he returned to Mississippi to begin a ministry dedicated to a holistic form of racial rapprochement, including an intentional community in which black people and white people lived and worshiped together.

Perkins consistently reached out to white fellow evangelicals, but his pathway to reconciliation was not an easy one. Perkins insisted that the definition of sin must "include every wrong, corporate or individual, that threatens the dignity of man."[1] He did not gloss over the difficulties whites encountered when working under black leadership, observing the power of "the often unconscious assumption that the historical dominance of whites over blacks in America has some inherent validity."[2]

Rev. Perkins insisted that fixing Christian racial dysfunction required far more than a cathartic moment of repentance or interracial handholding. His mantra was "relocation, reconciliation, and redistribution."— a reality worked out in the challenging crucible of sharing life together.

Christian sociologist George Yancey has distilled the message of the early black pioneers of Christian reconciliation into four principles: 1) Intentionally create primary personal relationships across racial lines. 2) Work together to dismantle structural and institutional racial inequality. 3) White repentance not only for personal sins but for historical and structural sins that are corporate in nature. 4) Black forgiveness for the white legacy of abuse.[3]

---

[c] Skinner was a Harlem gang leader and hater of all things white. After his conversion, however, he became a powerful voice for Christian racial reconciliation. His radical vision for Christian race relations was that believers be "the live expression on earth of exactly what is going on in heaven, where Jesus is Lord and God is in control." (See: Barbara Williams Skinner, "The Black Church and the Promise of Racial Reconciliation," *Seattle Pacific University Response*, Winter 2009, Volume 32, Number 1). In 1964, Skinner became a founding member of the National Negro Evangelical Association, in order to address social issues that National Association of Evangelicals was ignoring. He remained engaged with white Christians, working as a bridge between the two communities until his death in 1994 at 52 years of age.

In the early years of the post-Civil Rights era this message got a lot of attention but saw very little application. Church life continued its apartheid pattern, though a few more progressive white evangelical voices like Jim Wallis, Ron Sider, and Tony Campolo began to point out the necessity of personal and institutional change. Billy Graham laid an important foundation by symbolizing unity in his crusades. And *Christianity Today* paid enough attention to the issue to keep it in front of the broader evangelical audience.

After a lull in the early eighties, toward the end of that decade a new set of leaders began to emerge, both white and black, for whom Christian racial reconciliation was a primary focus. The following years saw a flurry of activity—publishing, conferences, denominational pronouncements, a nascent theology of reconciliation, and the founding of intentionally multiracial churches, along with the integration of existing congregations. Evangelicals supplied much of the energy for this movement, but intentional efforts to bridge historic gaps gained momentum in Roman Catholic and mainline churches as well. As a result, the share of congregations that can be considered multiracial increased from 7.4% in 1998 to 13.7% in 2010.[4/e]

Catholic congregations have long been more integrated than those of Protestants,[f] though differing dynamics make it difficult to compare apples with apples. Protestants gravitate to wherever they feel most comfortable, whereas Catholics are more prone to associate with a parish based on geography. As a result, Catholic racial mixing can sometimes be more visible but less intentional. Also, some "multiethnic" parishes feature multiple language groups that worship in the same place but not at the same time.

Mainline Protestantism has historically been more attuned to social issues than has its conservative counterpart, but it has nevertheless been slower to generate racial diversity within its congregations (7.4% vs. 14.4%, multiracial mainline vs. multiracial evangelical congregations).[5] Evangelicals, who tend to view reconciliation as interpersonal, have been more successful at integrating the pews, aided by a closer affinity with minority congregants in terms of worship dynamics and theological emphases.

---

[e] These figures include congregations from all faith traditions in which the principle racial group does not constitute more than 80% of the congregation.
[f] Dr. Scott Thumma, Professor of Sociology of Religion at Hartford Seminary, citing the 2010 Faith Communities Today Survey, puts the figure at 27.1% of Catholic/Orthodox congregations that have no more than 80% of one race vs. 12.5 % of Protestant congregations. See the citation in the following endnote.

Denominational Reconciliation

On the denominational level there have been several significant developments in the direction of racial unity in recent decades.[g] Perhaps the most poignant became known as the "Memphis Miracle." As recounted earlier, at its inception in the early 20th century Pentecostalism was heavily integrated, but within a few years longstanding cultural patterns re-asserted themselves, and congregations segregated. This culminated in the formation of the all-white Pentecostal Fellowship of North America.

When Bishop Bernard Underwood was elected head of the PFNA in the early nineties, he already had a close personal and working relationship with Bishop Ithiel Clemmons of the black Church of God in Christ and was determined to end the racial divide. A series of meetings culminated in a joint Congress in Memphis in 1994 that featured frank theological exchanges, prophetic words, tearful apologies, and an impromptu act of foot washing that a white pastor performed on Bishop Clemmons.

That afternoon the PFNA dissolved and the following day a new body was formed, the Pentecostal and Charismatic Churches of North America (PCCNA). Its board was comprised of an equal number of black and white leaders, and Bishop Clemmons was named its first chairman. They pledged to vigilantly "oppose racism in all of its various manifestations,"[6] pursue partnerships, and share pulpits.

The following year, 1995, the Southern Baptist Convention approved a resolution owning up to its history of racism and support of slavery. In addition, they apologized to "all African-Americans for condoning and/or perpetuating individual and systemic racism in our lifetime" and pledged "to eradicate racism in all its forms from Southern Baptist life and ministry."[7] Rev. Gary Frost, the second vice-president of the Convention and the first African American to hold that position, accepted the apology on behalf of

---

[g] In addition to individual denominational responses, in 2018 the National Association of Evangelicals included a theological critique of racism in its booklet, *For the Health of the Nation: An Evangelical Call to Civic Responsibility*, https://www.nae.net/for-the-health-of-the-nation/, 40-43. The National Council of Churches has a book-length guide for understanding and combating racism: *United Against Racism: Churches for Change*, (Washington, D.C., Friendship Press, 2018).

other black people. In 2012, Rev. Fred Luter became the first black president of the Southern Baptist Convention.

In the year 2000, officials of the United Methodist Church literally donned sackcloth and ashes in repentance for its legacy of racism toward both the blacks they had driven away from their church body, as well as toward those who had stayed. Representatives of black Methodist denominations that had split from white Methodism over their second-class status were in attendance for the apologies. Though they were moved by the gesture, they also wanted to see that apology translate from style to substance. AME Bishop McKinley Young commented: "The true measure of repentance will come when the lights are down and everyone has gone home."[8]

2006 saw the Episcopal Church come to terms with its own history. They passed a resolution expressing their "most profound regret that (a) The Episcopal Church lent the institution of slavery its support and justification based on Scripture, and (b) after slavery was formally abolished, The Episcopal Church continued for at least a century to support de jure and de facto segregation and discrimination." They then proceeded to apologize and repent for their "complicity in and the injury done by the institution of slavery and its aftermath."[9] They further resolved to hold a service of repentance at the National Cathedral (encouraging each diocese to do the same), make a full accounting of their history, and determine in their next convention how they could both materially and relationally become "the repairer of the breach."

The Catholic Church, too, has revisited past errors in the post-Civil Rights era. In 1985, Pope John Paul II apologized to Africans for slave trafficking perpetrated by people from Christian nations.[10] In the year 2000 he offered a broad apology on behalf of the Catholic Church for racism committed or condoned by Catholics over the course of the Christian era.

Perhaps more relevant to the specific American context, in 1979, the United States Conference of Catholic Bishops published a detailed Pastoral Letter on Racism, entitled "Brothers and Sisters to Us." That document served as a robust condemnation of racism and, to a lesser degree, as a mea culpa. At the 2002 National Black Catholic Congress, Msgr. Leonard Scott, a canon lawyer, called the document one of the Church's "best kept secrets."[11]

This pastoral letter noted that legal victories and the anecdotal success of certain minorities have lulled many into believing racism is a thing of the past. Nevertheless, they insisted, "the structures of our society are subtly racist, for these structures reflect the values which society upholds. They are geared to the success of the majority and the failure of the minority." [12] Given the social nature of this sin, they conclude that "each of us, in varying degrees, is responsible"[13] and call Christians to a "radical transformation in our own minds and hearts as well as in the structure of our society."[14]

While much of their analysis was commendable, the Bishops' prophetic finger did not wag so forcefully in their own direction. The best they could muster was to lament that racist Catholics weaken the witness of the Church, that the Church's representatives entrusted with minority problems were overwhelmingly white, and that they had not managed to overcome the popular perception of being a "white Church."

Though each of these denominational contexts is different, some common themes do emerge. The Protestant groups that expressed penitence each rightly recognized their responsibility for historical, personal, and corporate sin. In some cases, their repentance resulted in the elevation of black leadership, also an important development. These are certainly milestones in a racial history that has very few highlights.

Additionally, the apologies appear to be motivated by genuine contrition more than simply by the winds of political correctness. And there seems to have been little or no serious resistance to these initiatives. That, of course, does not preclude some sort of sincerity continuum, beginning with those who led the charge to those who supported it to those who were influenced by it to those who simply chose not to oppose it.

As proper as it was to issue such apologies and as helpful as they might have been for clearing white consciences and historically toxic ecclesiastical landscapes, they did not "solve" the problem. Nor could they have done so. The results obtained in each case were commensurate with the nature of the repentance—not because the white people involved didn't mean what they said, but because they didn't necessarily know what they were talking about. The haughty do not see themselves as such, so when they self-design their own repentance, it's a little like a blind man giving himself a haircut.[h]

To the extent that white Christians recognize their own racial sins, they tend to see them as anomalous and episodic. We might admit that we have collectively excluded black people or even hurt or defrauded them. But such behavior represents a departure from the kind of people we perceive ourselves

---

[h] For more background on the dynamic of black input in white church bodies, see www.scottgarber.com/was_notes.pdf, Note 21.1.

to be. So, once we recognize the activity as wrong, ask for the appropriate forgiveness, and determine to do better in the future, we figure that we've done our moral duty and that we can move on to the real mission of the Church.

It does not readily occur to us that the problem might be not only what we *have done* but fundamentally who we *are*—the heirs of a white racial identity defined by haughtiness. Nor does it easily occur to us that because of who we are, by default we tend to pursue and/or protect dominance—not just out of meanness or greed but because such a world is invisibly essential to our sense of self.

Repenting of bad behavior that is just a manifestation of a far more fundamental problem is like trying to rid your yard of dandelions by clipping the blossoms. Sin, however, is far more insidious than weeds. If you don't pull out dandelions by their roots, they'll come back, but they'll still look like dandelions. Future manifestations of haughtiness may look very different than earlier iterations. Getting it out by the root requires more than broad statements or power-sharing or even formal unity. While these are all important elements of reconciliation, the root of the problem goes far deeper.

Thinking back to the four principles of reconciliation promulgated by the early pioneers of racial reconciliation, we note that the first one has received short shrift across Protestant denominations. That is to "intentionally create primary personal relationships across racial lines." Indeed, some of these denominational initiatives themselves were the result of strong interracial ties between certain leaders. But you can't vicariously transfer that dynamic to individual church members; they must experience it for themselves. Multiplying the number of color-coded congregations huddled under the same denominational umbrella does not qualify as racial reconciliation. It's just a more evolved form of "separate but equal."

Parachurch Reconciliation

With denominations laboring under the weight of history and institutional inertia, much of the modern impetus toward racial reconciliation has come from parachurch organizations. Perhaps the two that have drawn the most attention to this issue over these decades have been the Billy Graham Evangelistic Association and, somewhat later, Promise Keepers.

Compared to individual congregations or denominations, such organizations benefitted from several distinct advantages when it came to challenging existing racial paradigms. First, rather than battling against consensus and tradition, they took their cues from a charismatic leader who wielded enormous ideological influence over the organization. Second, these ministries were high-profile, touching many people at once across denominational lines. And last but certainly not least, they were event-oriented, making them capable of projecting racial harmony in a very focused way without having to deal with all of the nitty-gritty, everyday issues of cultural disharmony that might affect a congregation.

Promise Keepers (PK) is a particularly interesting case, because racial reconciliation became part of its core mission. Bill McCartney, former head coach of the University of Colorado football program, founded this ministry in the early nineties to focus on Christian men and their personal integrity. By 1994, PK had become a national phenomenon, drawing more than a quarter of a million men to six stadium-style conferences around the U.S. That same year they published their manifesto, *The Seven Promises of a Promise Keeper*, one of which specifically committed PK participants to demonstrate the power of biblical unity by reaching across racial barriers.

Racial reconciliation became a dominant emphasis in the 1996 ministry year with the theme, "Break Down the Walls." Many events featured moving public acts of contrition, demonstrations of forgiveness, and high levels of symbolic unity. To overcome racial estrangement among Christians, they encouraged interracial personal relationships. All this brought positive media attention to the movement, and attendance topped one million.

Despite their emphasis on racial reconciliation, PK events remained largely white affairs (only 10%-15% minority participation in 1997). At a 1999 rally in Philadelphia half of the speakers were African American, but, even so, the minority response was underwhelming. In Hartford, after five years of interracial relationship building by PK's area manager, the percentage of minority participants still languished in single digits.[15] An overwhelmingly white turnout for a 2005 PK conference in Grand Rapids prompted Regional Director Fred Ramirez to call racial reconciliation, "the promise where we've had the least success and the greatest battle."[16]

True to his commitment and doubly burdened by the recalcitrance he encountered on this issue, McCartney went on the offensive, a speaking tour advocating for Christian racial reconciliation. He met with a devastatingly consistent response: "wild enthusiasm as I was being introduced, followed by a morguelike chill as I stepped away from the microphone. It was as if God had commissioned me to single-handedly burst everyone's bubble."[17]

On the positive side, Promise Keepers did raise awareness of the need for racial reconciliation, presenting racial unity as a desirable and even beautiful arrangement. Whereas denominations had largely ignored the importance of creating personal relationships and translating their corporate contrition to the individual level, Promise Keepers' approach put almost all of its apples in the individual basket. But once the cathartic, transactional repentance was complete, that was about all the reconciliation and racial unity most white participants were prepared to tackle.

Thinking back to the four principles of racial reconciliation promulgated by its modern black pioneers, we find that two of them were notably absent in the PK approach: 1) white repentance not only for personal sins but for historical and structural sins that are corporate in nature, and 2) working together to dismantle structural and institutional racial inequality. Once individuals had cleared their consciences of their own personal racial sins, for many whites there simply was no broader agenda to be addressed.

The Promise Keepers movement both fueled and reflected a broader trend among evangelicals. As the message of racial reconciliation evolved from its black roots to the broader white audience, its agenda shrank considerably. As Emerson and Rice explain, this is due in part to white America's individualistic, antistructuralist orientation—a tendency particularly common in the evangelical camp.[i] To even contemplate collective moral responsibility or to recognize the role of institutionalized racial inequity requires whites to step outside the fundamental paradigm through which they view the world and to employ tools that simply don't exist in their religio-cultural toolbox.

As the saying goes, if the only tool in your toolbox is a hammer, then every problem starts to look like a nail. And, so, as whites became the dominant force in the racial reconciliation movement, both the problem and its solution were bound to be re-defined in individualistic terms. The voices of the movement's black pioneers were either fading into history or being drowned out by the white sound and fury, leaving no one with the leverage to force whites to think outside their toolbox.

---

[i] For an insightful discussion of this issue, see: Emerson and Smith. *Divided by Faith. supra*, 76 ff.

Chapter 22

The Multiracial Church

While the widening of the racial reconciliation movement led to its whitening, the whitening of that movement also contributed to its widening. And despite the downsides associated with that evolution (as detailed in the last chapter), there has been an upside as well—the proliferation of multiracial[a] churches. This new wineskin is, I believe, one of the most significant and promising developments for Christian racial reconciliation in the contemporary era.

A smattering of multiracial churches, like the Brooklyn Tabernacle, arose in the 1970s and 1980s. But the real wave of change began with a new generation of leaders in the 1990s, a wave that has really come ashore in the 21st century. Multiracial church pastor and author, Mark DeYmaz, marks the beginning of this era, which he terms the "Pioneer Stage," with the publishing of *Divided by Faith* in 2000.[1]

One of the authors of that book, Michael O. Emerson, comments on how the multiracial church movement has exploded since that time:

> Since 1998, an explosion of materials, networks, and organizations has appeared claiming the need for, rightness of, and necessity of multiracial, multi-ethnic, multicultural churches. As best I can tell, in 1998 there were perhaps ten books on the topic (scattered across fifty years and multiple religious traditions) and a couple of denominational offices that tangentially had some materials on becoming more inclusive congregations. Today there are literally thousands of

---

[a] The terms *multiracial, multicultural,* and *multiethnic* are all used to refer to churches that are attempting to bridge racial divisions, including but not limited to the historic black/white divide. While some writers use the terms interchangeably, others insist on distinct meanings for each, distinctions that are not necessarily recognized by everyone else. I have opted for the term *multiracial* to refer to the entire movement for two reasons: 1) My focus is on the black/white racial divide, and 2) Sociologist Michael Emerson, perhaps the most recognized expert on this subject, uses *multiracial* to refer to the broad mix of such churches. His statistical analyses also use this terminology, regardless of the language employed/preferred by the reporting congregations.

materials on the topic, including books, articles, blogs, workbooks, denominational offices, conferences, undergraduate and seminary courses, workshops, websites, podcasts, Facebook pages, networks, and formal organizations.

I have a significant personal history with this phenomenon. My first foray into multi-racial ministry took place in the context of a church plant in the early eighties. This led to more than seven years working in traditional African-American churches (in two distinct eras, sandwiched around a fourteen-year missionary career teaching theology in Europe). Then, from 2003-2008, I served as the Senior Pastor at Washington Community Fellowship on Capitol Hill in Washington, D.C.—a multiracial, multi-denominational congregation begun by Myron Augsburger in 1981. I am currently a Pastor-At-Large at Bridgeway Community Church in Columbia, Maryland, one of the flagship multiracial churches in America. Dr. David Anderson, who founded the church in 1992, has become a leading voice in the multiracial church movement.

So, call me a true believer. I have watched this movement from its infancy. I am convinced that it has already made a significant contribution to Christian racial reconciliation, and I remain bullish on its future prospects. But if the multiracial church movement is to continue to fan the flames of reconciliation, it must not only build on its strengths; it must also come to grips with its limitations. And some of those limitations are directly related to the problem of racial haughtiness.

As the early black trailblazers of racial reconciliation insisted, real racial unity must be built on primary relationships between believers of different races. But where can such relationships be cultivated? Where can Christians from diverse backgrounds find a platform for mutual discovery, meaningful (not just artificial) shared experiences, and a cohesive bond that forces them to work through their differences in search of a truly multiracial reality?

I believe that the multiracial church can be such a crucible of change. Indeed, it is difficult to envision anything that could be called *Christian racial unity* without a significant manifestation at the congregational level. Absent this familial dynamic, theoretical talk about oneness soon wears thin, leaving the willing wondering, where do we go from here?

This is not to denigrate steps toward reconciliation and unity that are more limited and/or more broad-based in scope. They are necessary and helpful stages along the pathway from here to there. But they must be understood and undertaken as such, not as ends in themselves. Without some venue in which those budding relationships can grow, it ends up looking like a society in which men and women are allowed no further contact beyond a first date. Relationships can be established, but there's no way for them to flourish and become all they were meant to be.

The local congregation also functions as an ideal ideological home for the New Testament emphasis on unity across ethnic (and by extension, racial) lines. Here, the congregation is free to live out its multiracial identity as part of its core mission, not simply as an elective to be pursued only when it conveniently dovetails with more fundamental commitments. While it might be theologically untenable and practically suicidal to treat racial unity as the *sine qua non* of success to which all other emphases must bow the knee, by the same token, if it is undertaken only to the extent that it promotes church growth or evangelism or doctrinal purity or fellowship, it's not likely to occur in a very meaningful way.

The thing is, creating a truly multiracial environment is really hard work. When I first got involved with multiracial ministry, I thought that as soon as people saw the how beautiful it was and how perfectly it fulfilled God's vision for his people, they would flock to it. But it did not and does not work quite that way. The homogenous unit principle people were right about one thing— folks gravitate toward that which is comfortable and familiar.

Let's look at what is happening and not happening in this movement. The widely accepted definition of what makes a church multiracial is that no more than 80% of the regular attenders belong to a single racial group.[2] According to that standard, the percentage of people attending multiracial churches increased from 15% in 1998 to 20% in 2012.[3] That is certainly significant, but it also means that 80% of churchgoers (representing 86% of congregations) are still worshiping in settings defined by a single racial identity.[4] So, despite the promise and progress of multiracial churches, Christianity in America is still overwhelmingly color-coded.

In spite of the fact that evangelicals have supplied much of the energy for this movement, the percentage of evangelical congregations that can be classified as multiracial is barely above the norm for all faith traditions (14.4% vs. 13.7%).[5][b] At least that was the case in 2012, when the National

---

[b] Compared with only 7.4% of mainline Protestant congregations.

Congregations Study published the most up-to-date national survey information available. One would hope that further progress may have been made since that time. In recent years, however, there has also been a chilling, but as yet unquantified development that threatens this growth pattern.

After the 2014 police shooting of Michael Brown in Ferguson, Missouri and the spate of similar incidents that followed, an increasing number of African Americans who had gravitated to predominantly white congregations began to grow increasingly anxious. Their pastors, it seems, were all too often turning a colorblind eye to matters of racial justice. Even so, such straws rarely broke the camel's back. But then came the 2016 election, which saw white evangelicals support Donald Trump in record numbers.

Chanequa Walker-Barnes, a professor of practical theology at the McAfee School of Theology at Mercer University in Atlanta, had joined the staff of a majority white church. But after the outpouring of enthusiasm for Trump, she concluded that "something is profoundly wrong at the heart of the white church." Speaking for many others, she said, "We were willing to give up our preferred worship style for the chance to really try to live this vision of beloved community with a diverse group of people. That didn't work."[6]

She left, and she's not alone. In March of 2018, Michael O. Emerson, one of the architects of the multiracial church movement, was asked to comment on this growing crisis by *The New York Times*. He called the election of Trump "the single most harmful event to the whole movement of reconciliation in at least the past 30 years." He even expressed his fear that "it's about to completely break apart."[7]

Political divisions are not the only problem faced by the multiracial church movement. Though more and more congregations have crossed the 80/20 threshold to become quantitatively multiracial, from a qualitative point of view, not all these multiracial churches are created equal.

The authors of *United by Faith* divide multiracial congregations into three functional groups: 1) assimilated, 2) pluralist, and 3) integrated. *Assimilated* congregations are those in which one racial group is dominant, and the outgroup members are simply assimilated into that ethos. In *pluralist* congregations those of different races are all members of the same body and may gather together formally but lack any significant integration of their social networks. In *integrated* congregations no individual racial culture dominates. Rather, they have developed a "hybrid culture [that] is an expression of the congregation's unified collective identity."[8]

Of these three varieties of multiracial congregations, only one of them, the *integrated* congregation, provides a platform for *significant* racial reconciliation. The other two either lack the critical mass of personal interaction or impose cultural conformity with the congregational majority. Integrated churches, then, are the most authentic type of multiracial environment—but they are also the rarest of the three.[9]

Consider, too, that the multiplication of multiracial churches in recent years is partly due to increased involvement of Hispanics and Asians, who are *far more* likely than blacks or whites to participate in multiracial churches.[c] The bottom line, then, is that whites and blacks are experiencing significant racial reconciliation in only a fraction of "multiracial" churches.

It certainly sounds impressive to hear that the percentage of congregations considered to be multiracial nearly doubled between 1998 and 2010 (7.4% to 13.7%).[10] But given the aforementioned asterisks that we must attach to those figures, it's hard to imagine that the multicultural church is on the cusp of resolving the historic black/white rift within the Christian community.

Keep in mind that this black/white racial relationship is by far the most iconic. It has the most interrelated and hostile history. It is the primary stage upon which racial haughtiness has played out. So, for the multicultural church to be successful, it must bring black and white Christians together. If it does, I believe other racial relationships will follow suit. But we're not there yet.

Even in the best-case scenario—an *integrated* multiracial church in which blacks and whites truly interact—my experience is that there is often a degree of superficiality in what passes for "reconciliation." Most people who attend an intentionally multiracial church find *something* attractive about that emphasis, but that doesn't mean that they are all at the same place on the reconciliation continuum. Some are simply taken with the ideal represented by such a congregation but have never dealt with the hard realities of healing the past or sharing life together. Some believe that just participating in such a congregation makes reconciliation a reality. Others want to be stretched in this area, but there are distinct limits to what they can or will tolerate/assimilate in a given period of time. A relative few are "all in" for whatever it takes to live up to a biblically thorough and relationally fulfilling reconciled reality.

---

[c] Dr. Michael O. Emerson (cited above) shared this observation with me in personal email correspondence. The *"far more"* emphasis is his.

In general, whites who participate in such churches are not frequently challenged to think about their own solidarity with historic wrongs or about addressing institutional racial inequities—much less with the notion of racial haughtiness. Indeed, because of their connection with a multiracial church, they may well see themselves as exempt from whatever is wrong with whiteness. Any ministry that pressures members of the majority race to think too far outside of their individualist/anti-structural mindset may be hard-pressed to attract/keep much of a white crowd.

In their research for an article in the academic journal *Sociology of Religion*, sociologists found that, in the case of white people, participation in a multiracial congregation does not alter their views about the reasons for racial inequality. When it comes to African Americans, however, those:

> who attend multiracial congregations are actually less likely to affirm structural explanations for Black/White inequality than Blacks in nonmultiracial congregations... We find little evidence that multiracial congregations promote progressive racial views among attendees of any race or ethnicity. Rather, our findings suggest that multiracial congregations (1) leave dominant White racial frames unchallenged, potentially influencing minority attendees to embrace such frames and/or (2) attract racial minorities who are more likely to embrace those frames in the first place.[11]

This perspectival homogeneity undoubtedly promotes harmony in some superficial fashion. In the end, however, it robs whites of a corrective to their own majority myopia and their natural aversion to recognizing their collective failings. It's not enough to just agree; there can be no thoroughgoing reconciliation without an appreciation of the true nature of the problem—one that does not ignore the structural and systemic consequences of racial haughtiness. If whites don't get that truth from their African-American brothers and sisters, they're not likely to get it at all. What's worse, if their black counterparts go so far as to affirm the individualistic white mentality, whites will take that as an iron-clad confirmation of their own rightness.

When a black majority took over the government in South Africa, they recognized the central importance of telling the truth about the reality of apartheid. That led to the establishment of The Truth and Reconciliation Commission, chaired by Archbishop Desmond Tutu. He stated in the Commission's report: "However painful the experience has been, we remain convinced that there can be no healing without truth."[12] U.S. Representative John Lewis echoed this conviction when he observed that "confronting the truth... leads to liberation from our past."[13]

In this country, however, the white majority controls the conversation about race. Not surprisingly, then, there has been no rush to candor. But any white "repentance" based on a selective accounting of the facts is like washing up with soap and water after using oil-based paint. It may feel like a cleansing *process*, but because that process does not recognize the true nature of the problem—which requires a different solvent—not only do the stains of haughtiness remain, but those who are still stained walk away convinced that they are clean.

Black forgiveness, the flip side of this relational equation, is also diminished by this white inability and/or unwillingness to take a hard look in the mirror. If forgiveness extends only as far as white repentance, it will certainly be incomplete, limiting its conciliatory effect. And even if the scope of forgiveness graciously extends beyond the scope of repentance, in the long run reconciliation cannot do an end run around the truth.

When whites understand the nature of the offense as they choose to construe it rather than through the eyes of those who have been offended, a trust deficit is unavoidable. Forgiveness can be granted by an act of the will, but trust must be earned. If the offending party does not recognize their behavior as part of an ongoing pattern of haughtiness, then there is no reason to suppose that future interactions will be driven by anything other than the same old pretensions of superiority dressed in a new season's style.

There simply is no path to racial unity that doesn't take racial haughtiness seriously. But even when we do face up to our original sin, we still need a platform on which to build a new reality of racial harmony. And that is why we need the multiracial church. It is the only institution that possesses both the prophetic and therapeutic potential to cultivate the beloved community. But we not only need the multiracial church because it *possesses* that potential; we also need the multiracial church to *fulfill* that potential— providing a safe space to tell the truth and hear the truth, to work through the past, and to walk together into a transformed future.

Chapter 23

Alive and Well in the Here and Now

We have come a long way in our historical examination of America's original sin, observing the history of our racial dysfunction and how it has been driven by racial haughtiness. That connection was not so terribly hard to make or to accept—when we were looking in the rear-view mirror. After all, who can deny the reality of white social dominance based on racial distinctions? Or that for most of our history we have rationalized our dominance by appealing to a supposed superiority—essentially an admission of haughtiness?

But now that whites no longer rationalize their dominance by an overt appeal to superiority, we may be tempted to retract that confession. Okay, perhaps back in the day white Americans were, indeed, haughty. But if they were deemed haughty because they espoused superiority, then what should we conclude about contemporary whites who embrace racial equality?

It's not as if I haven't mentioned this issue of contemporary haughtiness already, but at this point in the book it becomes *the* crucial question. Our very next chapter begins to unveil the solution to racial haughtiness. And if haughtiness is *not* driving contemporary racial dysfunction—that is, if my diagnosis is mistaken—then my proposed fix will not fix anything at all.

Moreover, the current vitality of haughtiness matters to race relations in America and to Christian race relations in particular. We can reform our laws, our institutions, our on-ramps to opportunity. We can reform our ethics and even our interracial relational skills. But even if we do all these things far better than we have done them up to this point, if haughtiness is still alive and well, then we ourselves are still in need of reform. Until we are willing to challenge the very benignity of white identity in general and of our own in particular, racial reconciliation will remain an elusive dream.

In this chapter, then, I will supplement the considerable inductive evidence already presented with three additional arguments that are more deductive in nature. In order to demonstrate that haughtiness continues to define racial reality in our time we'll consider a psycho-sociological argument, a moral argument, and, finally, a personal argument.

The Psycho-sociological Argument

Newton's first law of motion states that every object in a state of uniform motion tends to remain in that state of motion unless an external force is applied to it. Interestingly, a similar dynamic can be observed in our attitudes, which also tend to maintain their current orientation unless acted upon by another force. I have dubbed this phenomenon the *Law of Attitudinal Inertia*.

Whether we're talking about the external world of physics or the internal world of our psyche, inertia represents a resistance to change. I am not suggesting that attitudes can't or don't change; they do, and with some regularity. I would submit, however, that they don't change simply because such change is intrinsic to their nature. Rather, the very opposite is true. Attitudes can be quite stubborn unless acted upon by a sufficiently influential external force.

Just as in the case of material inertia, the external force required to effect attitudinal change is directly proportional to the mass of the object. And that "mass" is largely dependent on the embeddedness of the attitude. An attitude becomes embedded when it is widely held by the group to which one belongs and/or when it persists for long periods of time and/or when it is associated with some benefit that accrues to those who hold it and/or when it is bolstered by rational justifications. These circumstances serve as mass multipliers, increasing attitudinal inertia. The greater the mass, the more embedded the attitude, and the greater the external force required to change it.

How does attitudinal inertia affect the present discussion? Well, the attitude of white superiority/racial haughtiness has clearly been around a long time and has been widely held by the group in question. Just as clearly, it has become enmeshed with benefits that accrued to whites and has been bolstered by a variety of rational justifications. Given that level of embeddedness, a superior attitude that has remained constant over the centuries is likely to be highly resistant to change.

That said, any attitudinal inertia can be overcome. It just requires a potent enough external force. So, then, has such an overwhelming force acted upon attitudes of white superiority in recent history? If so, it should not be hard to identify. If not, then the Law of Attitudinal Inertia would suggest that racial haughtiness is still present and still obstructing racial reconciliation.

The most formidable external force to be arrayed against attitudes of white superiority was the Civil Rights Movement. And it did, indeed, move the needle on white racial attitudes; altering our intellectual, social, ethical, and legal perspectives. Here, however, the plot thickens, because the impact of a social phenomenon on the human psyche is considerably more nuanced than, say, the impact of two marbles colliding on a table. In the wake of the Civil Rights Movement, the historic white sense of superiority would never again be what it had been. But it was not obliterated; it was merely bifurcated.

As Dr. Richard Scholl of the University of Rhode Island explains: "Attitudes contain four separate, but related, components: Cognition, Affect, Evaluation, and Behavioral Intention."[1] The first two of these are primary, and the latter two more derivative. *Evaluation* is an overall positive or negative orientation. *Behavioral intention* refers to how we are prone to act toward the object of our attitude. So, it's easy to see how these last two attitudinal elements could depend on other factors. Let's see how the primary controlling aspects of *cognition* and *affect* operate and what happens when they are bifurcated.

Of the two, the greater attitudinal inertia belongs to our affective sensibilities. Scholl notes that "while [cognitive] attitudes are relatively stable, they are subject to change based on changing information and perceptions of facts."[2] On the flip side, however, "attitudes that are based on strong positive or negative feelings (affect) are often very difficult to change."[3] Not only that, but our feelings may not be influenced by changes in thinking.

So, yes, the Civil Rights Movement did bring about change. But, as is often the case, racial *thinking* changed more readily than racial *feelings*. Prof. Scholl suggests that when these two attitudinal perspectives are not in sync, the mind sometimes invents what he calls "a more complex mental model that allows the individual to hold both beliefs."[4]

This helps us to understand what has happened to white attitudes of superiority in recent decades. We no longer (in general) *think* we're superior. But that doesn't keep us from *feeling* superior. This bifurcation is our "more complex mental model that allows us to hold both beliefs."

This bifurcation between our cognitive and affective attitudes helps to explain certain incongruities: a society that sounds evermore progressive on race, when in fact black people are making relatively little progress; a society that would elect a black president, while still expecting so little from the average black young person; a society that praises equality, while resisting the kinds of change that could lead to more substantive social equity.

Caught up in a post-game celebration of our own enlightenment, we didn't notice our affective attitudes quietly morphing from overt to covert. And, as a result, white feelings of superiority not only survived but became in some sense even more insidious by virtue of their greatly exaggerated demise. After all, what could be more dangerous than an invisible enemy?

The Moral Argument

As the Law of Attitudinal Inertia reminds us, attitudes are resistant—and affective attitudes are especially so. As a result, the psycho-sociological argument provides at least a partial explanation of how haughtiness has evolved and, in doing so, managed to survive. But does that argument alone constitute an adequate explanation for the resilience of superior white pretensions? When you consider the sheer hypocrisy of this bifurcation— advocating equality while harboring feelings of superiority and enjoying dominance—it seems like a pesky enough psychic dissonance that we might have at least recognized, if not resolved, it by now.

Here, however, the moral argument comes to our aid. As I have insisted throughout this book, haughtiness is more than just socially unacceptable; it is sinful.[a] And sin is pernicious. If we understand the nature of sin, we can begin to understand how haughtiness can surreptitiously infect white identity, even as the afflicted remain unaware.

In order to examine the dynamic of sin—to find out where bad behavior comes from and how it exercises control over us—we must go beyond psychology and sociology—we must appeal to theology. That's because sin is more than a designation of disapprobation that we attach to an existing behavioral phenomenon. Theologically speaking, sin is a dynamic cause capable of producing and sustaining that very phenomenon.

---

[a] In the previous (psycho-social argument) section I wanted to emphasize the psychological and sociological dynamics of the attitude apart from its moral/spiritual overlay. Therefore, I regularly referred to haughtiness as an attitude of *superiority*. In this section my goal is to emphasize the spiritual aspect of the problem, so I have opted to feature the term *haughtiness*.

Christian theology holds sin to be not just a social deviation but an active moral predilection that is endemic to the entire human race. In other words, we are not just sinners just because we sin; we also sin because we are sinners. Sin is not an extraordinary human response that requires some extraordinary prompting in order to manifest itself. It is, rather, an innate spiritual appetite that must be controlled in order to keep it from manifesting itself. And, while many sins are committed in the pursuit of some practical personal advantage, sin can provide an intrinsic satisfaction that does not require an identifiable extrinsic benefit to explain why someone would engage in it.

The Apostle Paul discusses the dynamic of sin in greater depth than any other biblical writer. He presents sin as just such an active principle, one that exerts an influence on the human psyche. His epistle to the church in Rome is particularly focused on this subject.

Though Paul insists that all people are "under the power of sin," (Romans 3:9) he nevertheless teaches that the recipients of God's grace are capable of resisting and overcoming that influence. Otherwise, he could not demand, as he does in Romans 6:12-14: "Therefore do not let sin reign in your mortal body so that you obey its evil desires… For sin shall not be your master…"

So, yes, we are capable of resisting sin's attraction, but that doesn't mean that when we do so our sinful condition just withers away or somehow goes into remission. Sin remains a potent, malignant threat that must be constantly resisted by appropriating God's grace with the help of the Holy Spirit. Paul pictures sin like a cancer on the spirit, something foreign and destructive to the spiritual self with which we identify and, yet, at the same time an unwelcome and malignant part of that same spiritual self.

The apostle says:

> I do not understand what I do. For what I want to do I do not do, but what I hate I do… As it is, it is no longer I myself who do it, but it is sin living in me… I have the desire to do what is good, but I cannot carry it out. For what I do is not the good I want to do; no, the evil I do not want to do—this I keep on doing. Now if I do what I do not want to do, it is no longer I who do it, but it is sin living in me that does it. So I find this law at work: When I want to do good, evil is right there with me. For in my inner being I delight in God's law; but I see another law at work in the members of my body, waging war against the law of my mind and making me a prisoner of the law of sin at work within my members. (Romans 7:15-23)

We see, then, that there exists a universal human inclination to deviate from God's character and/or his standards for human behavior. This is sin as *sinfulness*. Of course, the term *sin* is also applied to activities that are likewise out of conformity with God's character and standards, but such sinful activities are just the outworking of this fundamental sinful propensity.

As one of the sins identified in Scripture, haughtiness, too, springs from the need to satisfy this inner sinful proclivity. Like a junkie who finds relief by feeding his addiction, the haughty find gratification in the mere sensation of superiority. And that property of sin allows haughtiness to function as its own rationale and reward.

Don't get me wrong; haughtiness desperately desires a world that reflects its pecking order. But if circumstances diminish that dominant status, the haughty—rather than deciding that they no longer want to feel superior—are more likely to redefine dominance, re-assert themselves in more creative ways, or stew about the unfair loss of their rightful hegemony (all of which have occurred in our time).

Haughtiness not only craves a complementary social order; it is most at home when bolstered by a rationale for superiority. Armed with such a justification, the haughty feel free to disregard their intuitive moral dissonance and instead regard their superior status as a positive good. When this occurs, social stratification starts to look less like an oppressive hierarchy and more like everyone occupying the social position that best corresponds to them.

Even if its rationale is discredited, however, sin still finds a way to soldier on. Haughtiness can outlast its logical foundation—because it is not built on logic. Like other sins, haughtiness does not originate in a rational calculation. Rather, it is a projection of our fallen moral nature, our sinful propensity. The historically handy logical foundation known as white superiority is really an a posteriori logical backfill—more of a rationalization than a rationale. Reason may buttress our concupiscence, but it is not logically prior to our desire to elevate ourselves above others.

The sin of haughtiness functions like an immoral appetite, providing its own intrinsic rationale and reward. But not only is sin capable of producing bad behavior; it sustains itself by exercising an addictive influence over its regular practitioners. Hence, bad habits are harder to change than good ones. And the more entrenched the bad habit, the more of a stronghold it becomes.

Scripture often refers to the deceitfulness of sin. Sin passes itself off as something far more benign than it really is—a pathway to satisfaction, even a positive good. In Genesis 3:6 Eve "saw that the fruit of the tree was *good* for food and *pleasing* to the eye, and also *desirable* for gaining wisdom." After she had eaten that forbidden fruit, God confronted her. Eve's excuse? She had been deceived by something that looked far better for her than it was.

Like Eve, we can be fooled by sin's clever disguises, but sometimes sin operates in a different sort of stealth mode—what the Bible refers to as *blindness*. Blindness may find its origin in the spiritual darkness that surrounds sin itself (1 John 2:11). Or it may spring from the false light of self-righteousness: "If we claim to be without sin, we deceive ourselves and the truth is not in us." (1 John 1:8). The unseeing may even be blind to spiritual blindness itself. John writes to the Church of Laodicea: "You say, 'I am rich; I have acquired wealth and do not need a thing.' But *you do not realize* that you are wretched, pitiful, poor, *blind* and naked." (Revelation 3:17)

Jesus directed his harshest denunciations against the self-righteous Pharisees of his day for their self-induced blindness. Apropos of our current discussion, they were more concerned about the *appearance* of moral rectitude than about the actual attitudes of the heart. (Matthew 23:3,5). Christ criticized their obsessive conformity to the external law in giving a tithe (10%) to God, even of their spices, but neglecting

> the more important matters of the law—justice, mercy and faithfulness.... Woe to you, teachers of the law and Pharisees, you hypocrites! You clean the outside of the cup and dish, but inside they are full of greed and self-indulgence. Blind Pharisee! First clean the inside of the cup and dish, and then the outside also will be clean. (Matthew 23:23, 25-26)

So, given the fact that: a) haughtiness is sin; b) it is an entrenched and enduring component of white identity we don't have to opt into; and c) sinners are slow to acknowledge the presence or extent of their own sin—before we blithely assume that cognitive adjustments to our racial attitudes represent a corresponding inward transformation, we'd be wise to double-check that rosy self-diagnosis. Though the ideological renunciation of racial superiority has led to welcome social reform, as long as the heart harbors haughtiness there can be no true reconciliation, for racial haughtiness and racial harmony are fundamentally incompatible. Unless and until the dominant internalize equality, society will not realize equality.

So, then, how do we know whether a change in our cognitive ethic—from racial elitism to racial egalitarianism—represents a corresponding spiritual transformation from haughtiness to humility? Ethical change and spiritual transformation could, of course, go hand-in-hand. Indeed, a change in our ethics would seem a necessary precursor to affective, attitudinal change. But a changed ethic does not necessarily result in changed feelings. Affective attitudinal change could lag behind its ethical counterpart or could even take cover behind it. Moral standards can change with little or no impact on the heart, especially if we just blithely assume that cleaning up the cup on the outside will automatically sanitize the inside as well.

This sort of sinful self-deception is particularly prevalent among the haughty, who suffer from the proverbial carrot-in-the-ear syndrome. Even when confronted with the evidence, a haughty spirit categorically resists self-indictment. As a result, our subjective confidence that we are not under the influence of haughtiness is not a reliable predictor of our moral condition.

The Personal Argument

Understanding the dynamics of attitudes, especially *sinful* attitudes, helps us to understand how and why racial haughtiness is still alive and well today. There is no reason to conclude that an up-to-now permanent characteristic of an entire people has disappeared, unless we can forensically identify a clear process by which it was dismantled. That's the big picture. But now we turn from that panorama and zoom in for a close-up—to a wallet-size photo of me.

I began this book with the goal of changing race relations by shining a light on racial haughtiness. My starting point, however, was the lofty perch of moral enlightenment—always a precarious position. By virtue of being the one pointing out the problem and its solution, I saw myself as somehow exempt from the soul-searching I was advocating.

My "been there and done that" attitude was no doubt exacerbated by my history with Christian racial reconciliation. My wife and I have integrated three African-American neighborhoods by buying a house and living there. Directly out of seminary, with no visible means of support, we began planting a church in one of those neighborhoods in Dayton, Ohio. That was in 1981, when multi-racial ministry was practically unheard of in the Midwest.

I have also spent seven years as an associate minister in two black congregations affiliated with the National Baptist and Christian Methodist Episcopal denominations respectively. Then, from 2003-2008 I pastored a multi-racial church on Capitol Hill in Washington, DC. In the middle of all that, I dedicated many years to a missionary career in Europe, teaching theology in a cross-cultural setting and living as a cultural minority.

Over these decades, I've often written and spoken about the intersection of Christianity and race. Now I've poured several years of my life into this book. Clearly, this is more than a passing interest; it is a consuming passion.

So, imagine my surprise when, in the middle of my indictment of white haughtiness, it suddenly dawned on me that I, too, was white. This was not exactly an *aha* moment but more like a *duh* moment. How could I have missed the fact that a quasi-universal condition might affect me as well?

In the process of indicting my own race, I had inadvertently been sawing away at the branch on which I was sitting. Fancying myself a bold (or at least a somewhat annoying) champion of racial justice, it didn't occur to me that I might also be, at one and the same time, a perpetrator of racial haughtiness. Or that becoming part of the solution didn't mean that I had ceased to be part of the problem. I felt a paradigm shift coming on.

Once I began looking at myself through a different prism—as more likely implicated than innocent—certain things began to come into focus. Like my early, paternalistic efforts at multiracial ministry. Like my tendency to evaluate developments in the black church in terms of their assimilation of white church dynamics. Like the fact that, even as I wholeheartedly renounced stereotypes of racial superiority and inferiority that I consciously knew to be false, somewhere deep within me those very lies sometimes still resonated in an altogether discomfiting way—like the unnerving tug of temptation toward some sin you don't think you'd actually commit, but you're nevertheless troubled by the fact that it crossed your mind.

This, then, is my personal argument for the continued pervasive impact of haughtiness on white Christians today. I am the beneficiary of parents who consciously sought not to pass their prejudices on to me. I have no history of negative experiences with African Americans that would cause me—either consciously or subconsciously—to think poorly of them. (If anything, they have treated me far better than I deserve.) I have lived for decades with a heightened consciousness of these issues, dedicating significant time and energy to the cause of racial reconciliation. And along the way I have learned to value black contributions and to submit to black leadership.

To my mind, this unquestionably uncommon personal trajectory has only one explanation—the grace of God enabling me to fulfill his calling on my life. But, in spite of grace and destiny, in spite of my awareness of this issue and my commitment to it, it has been a struggle to purge my own heart of racial haughtiness. So, I can't help but suspect that I have some company. And that those who don't think they have a problem may not be, as they suppose, unaffected by haughtiness but simply unaware of its influence.

What, then, have we seen in this chapter? The psycho-sociological argument is based on the Law of Attitudinal Inertia, i.e., the natural resistance of our attitudes to change. Unless some external force has acted effectually upon these deeply embedded attitudes of racial superiority, there is no reason to suppose that they have lost their vitality.

The Civil Rights Movement did, indeed, have an impact on recalcitrant white attitudes. Rather than turning them around 180°, however, it simply bifurcated the cognitive and affective aspects of those attitudes. That did alter our *thinking*, but our *feelings* of superiority took a different tack, going underground. As a result, we may not have changed as much as we suppose.

Turning to the moral argument, we found that when sin's energy is added to the mix, our active resistance to change increases exponentially. Sin is strategically malevolent—deceiving, blinding, and addicting. It masquerades as light, as reason, as right. It aligns itself with the respectable and religious. When identified, sin simply shape-shifts, becoming invisible once again.

Sin never gives up, never goes out of style. It is impervious to social progress or sophistication. It doesn't go away simply because we ignore it or re-classify it. Sin creates strongholds that are difficult for the sinner—especially the haughty sinner—to perceive, let alone to overcome.

So, then, this centuries-old sinful stronghold is still part and parcel of white identity—even my own. We have largely failed to recognize this immoral condition for what it is—not just something we have *done*, but what we *have been* and, therefore, what we *have become*. No generation of white Christians has so much as acknowledged this moral pox on its own house, much less repented of it and engaged in the hard work of transformation.

It would seem, then, that the odds are stacked against us. But, thankfully, God specializes in the seemingly impossible. By his grace, not only is personal transformation possible, but so, too, is genuine racial healing. It is to that spiritual solution, and ultimately to that beloved community, that we now turn.

Chapter 24

From the Inside Out

Throughout this book I have been keenly interested in the ways in which social dynamics like power, perception, politics, and economics influence racial haughtiness and its manifestations. This attitude, however, is more than just the product of these psychological and social influences. It is, at its core, a spiritual problem. And, to the extent that the problem is spiritual in nature, the solution must be spiritual in nature as well.

By calling this solution "spiritual," I am not trying to limit our response to a private religious experience devoid of broader implications. The sin of racial haughtiness affects not only the world within us but also the world around us. As a result, its moral antithesis must address the full scope of its destructive impact. Hence, the title of this chapter, "From the Inside Out."

Moral transformation typically involves several steps, which, taken together comprise an *arc of becoming*. This intentional process of becoming somehow different than we are today might be accomplished rather quickly or play out over a long period of time, depending on the scope and scale of the change in view. It is not so critical to *distinguish* each stage as a discreet chronological experience. What is critical, however, is that we *complete* the transformational process. If we try to take a shortcut across the arc by skipping aspects of the change process that we find unattractive or intimidating, the result may be more of an adjustment than a transformation.

This progressive approach to moral transformation arises, I believe, from a biblical understanding of change. Its constituent elements can be found in the pages of Scripture, though they typically appear in an anecdotal and diffuse fashion. So, an integrated, ordered process like the one I outline in the upcoming pages is not a matter of chapter and verse. Nevertheless, I believe it to be faithful to the spirit of Scripture.

The actual process by which we change from the people we are into the people we aspire to be can be divided into six identifiable stages: 1) recognizing our sin, 2) sorrowing over our sin, 3) turning from our sin, 4) confessing our sin, 5) redressing our sin, and 6) replacing our sin. The first three steps are focused inward, and they are the subject of this chapter. Future chapters will flesh out the remaining steps. In the fourth step, confession, we externalize to both God and others what has happened inside of us. Finally, we will examine what change looks like in relation to those we have offended. That change focuses on both the past (redress) and the future (replacement).

Recognizing our Sin

There are two principle reasons for which we fail to recognize the truth about ourselves: either we're in denial or we're in the dark. Those two possibilities might appear to be mutually exclusive, but that's not necessarily the case. The fact is that we're more likely to remain in the dark about truths that we would want to deny if we knew them. The difficulty of diagnosing our own haughtiness is a case in point.

How, then, can we hope to see through the haze of haughtiness? Several possible strategies come to mind: 1) listening to other voices, 2) resetting our working assumptions, 3) reviewing our behavior, 4) taking stock of our attitudes, and 5) reconsidering the implications of corporate haughtiness. Let's see how these might help.

1) Listening to other voices: Robert Burns reminded us what a gift it is to see ourselves as others see us. We may be blissfully ignorant of our offenses, but those affected by our haughtiness are likely to know that something is awry, even if they can't articulate it. If we could just see what they see, feel what they feel—what a wonderful window on the truth about ourselves.

When it comes to haughtiness, however, there is a problem with this diagnostic tool. While it's potentially useful to listen to other voices, it's practically inaccessible—because most white people don't know black people well enough to have such a conversation.

Though honest interracial dialog on a peer level may be a rare commodity, there have always been a few high-profile black voices willing to address the issue of whiteness for anyone willing to listen. Take, for example, Michael Eric Dyson's socio-historical exposition of whiteness as identity, ideology, and institution.[1] Couched as it is in Dysonic erudition, his insightful analysis is not exactly popular reading—though it's hard to imagine that making it more easily understood would make it any more popular with whites.

A more visceral voice is that of Nation of Islam leader, Louis Farrakhan. He once indicted whites for having imposed themselves on all the other peoples of the world, making themselves the "center." He denounced our "proud, arrogant, haughty, self-conceited, boastful, mischiefmaking, bloodshedding manner [not to put too fine a point on it]."[2] Farrakhan went on to insist that we had usurped a position reserved for God, admonishing us to instead occupy our rightful place.

This sort of moralistic censure is likely to be dismissed as enemy fire. Too bad. As the 17th-century English Poet Laureate, John Dryden, advised: "Be industrious to discover the opinion of your enemies; which is commonly the truest; for you may be assured, that they will give you no quarter, and allow nothing to complaisance."[3] Minister Farrakhan may be wrong about a lot of things; but he's not wrong about everything. You don't have to accept someone's solutions to benefit from their analysis.

2) Resetting our working assumptions: Since our presuppositions often go a long way toward determining our conclusions, sometimes the only way to refresh our thinking is to hit the reset button on our working assumptions. For instance, we tend to suppose that we are innocent until proven guilty. Such a posture might be useful in the courtroom, but soul-searching is not a trial. It is, rather, an investigation. It's hard enough to see our own faults; there's no need to add a blindfold to our natural moral myopia.

When examining oneself, there is, of course, no such thing as objectivity. But there is always some starting point, some working assumption. The question is: what kind of working assumption is likely to direct us toward the truth? An across-the-board presumption of innocence is theologically untenable, given our human condition. That said, the fact that we are sinners by nature does not mean that we are guilty of every possible sin under every possible circumstance, much less of this particular one.

Keep in mind, however, that sinful patterns of behavior are learned— typically learned from the collectives to which we belong. So, those collective patterns can be good predictors, reasons to proceed with suspicion or not. For instance, the chances of a Pharisee being pharisaical would seem to be well above average. And if you hailed from the Kentucky-West Virginia border in the late 19th century and had a last name like Hatfield or McCoy, there's a good chance you might turn out to be the vengeful sort.

When it comes to self-examination, we tend to find what we're looking for. And what should we be looking for? Given the abundant evidence showing a correlation between racial haughtiness and white identity, we simply must allow that reality to inform our working assumptions. Otherwise, we may not recognize our own reflection in the moral mirror.

Without a self-skeptical working assumption, you're likely to be misled by the sparkle of exculpatory evidence. Maybe you don't hate black people the way a real racist would. Maybe you have a cordial relationship with certain black people. Maybe you don't use racial slurs. Maybe your church holds an occasional joint service with a black congregation. Maybe you like Oprah or you voted for Obama. Maybe you even laughed at "The Help." The problem is, not one of these circumstances is incompatible with haughtiness.

Since we all have a knee-jerk tendency to confirm our own self-righteousness, it's helpful to adopt a more detached point of view. In this case, that means seeing ourselves as part of a historical/cultural whole, heirs to the legacy of white identity. It is a legacy that has been passed from generation to generation—without any of those generations, including our own, ever addressing this fundamental moral flaw.

If haughtiness were some anomalous condition, a trap that ensnared only the occasional unwary and unsavory white person, it might make sense to presume one's own innocence. That is, in order to conclude that I am a haughty member of a generally non-haughty collective, I would need to find solid evidence that I am an evil exception to the rule. On the other hand, if white identity has long been and continues to be home-sweet-home to racial haughtiness, then the more reasonable course is to begin with the opposite assumption—that we have all been exposed and are likely infected.

It's a little like head lice. No parent wants to think that their own child has lice. The little critters are icky and embarrassing. Their very presence even seems to imply a certain hygienic failure. So, naturally, *my* kid couldn't be affected. But eventually we come to terms with the fact that if every other student in his or her class has head lice, we'd better check. And guess what?

Racial haughtiness is like moral head lice; it's shameful and repulsive. So, it's hard to even contemplate the possibility that I'm affected by it. Not me. But think about it. If haughtiness is part and parcel of the group to which I uncritically belong…

3) Reviewing our behavior: But what if—in spite of being exposed to haughtiness and even infected by it—we've been cured? People can and do change. Moral progress is part and parcel of Christianity, right? The question, however, is not whether we have the resources to change; the question is whether we have, in fact, actualized that potential and to what degree. In order to answer that question, let's consider the following three tell-tale behavioral

indicators of racial haughtiness—direct oppressive action against African-Americans, passing judgment, and hierarchy-enhancing inaction.

No white Americans living today have ever personally owned slaves (at least in the 19th century historical sense). Hardly anyone has participated in a lynch mob. Only a limited number have ever advocated white supremacy as a social option. Nevertheless, we still occupy a place at the top of a racialized social hierarchy. And that status affords us relatively more opportunity to take advantage of others, while at the same time rendering us relatively less sensitive to having done so.

So, we must ask ourselves: "Have there been times when, based on race, I have personally deprived particular African Americans of wealth, goods, opportunity, respect, protagonism, social standing, justice, etc.?" Regardless of whether we are motivated by our own sense of rightful superiority, anti-black sentiment, or are simply taking advantage of our relatively privileged social status, such acts of racial oppression (though perhaps more benign than those of earlier generations) continue to constitute a projection of haughtiness.

Many will hastily, perhaps even dismissively, deny that they have ever personally perpetrated this sort of racial injustice. Indeed, the fact that most whites have little social contact with individual blacks limits the opportunities for individualized discrimination. But though such offenses are not as common as they could be, they are more common than whites are likely to realize. If black people were polled as to the frequency with which they suffer such personal discrimination, we would see that the number of whites committing these offenses far exceeds the number who admit to doing so.

While such overt forms of domination may be currently less common, whites nevertheless play an ongoing role in perpetuating the established racial hierarchy. There is good evidence that equally qualified black people still find themselves disadvantaged with respect to whites in housing, employment, credit, and criminal justice. Yes, in most of these cases there are laws that protect minority rights, but within the parameters of those laws, people still make decisions that are not always legally reviewable but nevertheless consequential. And the slant of those decisions suggests a bias based on notions of racial worthiness.

Acting from a position atop the racial hierarchy, *somebody*, and with some frequency, is still taking advantage of African Americans. And chances are good that the majority of such people are unaware, either of their biases or of the consequences of those biases. So, before we simply assume that it couldn't be us, it's worth a closer look.

One sure sign of a haughty spirit is the habit of passing judgment. Jesus warns against this practice (Matthew 7:1), which is objectionable on several fronts, not the least of which is the attitude that often prompts it. The Oxford English Dictionary defines "passing judgment" as to "criticize or condemn someone from a position of assumed moral superiority." That "position of assumed moral superiority" constitutes a pretty accurate description of haughtiness.

If you want to know what we really think, just follow the trail of our criticism. White valuations regarding black people and blackness tend to follow a familiar, negative pattern. In fact, I'm not sure I've ever heard a complimentary generalization made by whites about blacks —unless you count the "Boy, those people sure can sing/dance/run/jump" variety of stereotypical credits.

White assessments of African-American culture, habits, values, morality, etc. inevitably involve an implicit comparison. Naturally, this juxtaposition with the white (right) way of being/doing is rarely articulated. But, then, there's no need to say aloud what everyone already knows intuitively.

Once a racial disadvantage exists, in order to perpetuate that injustice, the only thing we have to do is nothing at all. So, sometimes the most significant sign of haughtiness is our inaction. Satisfaction with an advantageous status quo comes quite naturally to the haughty, who are easily convinced that we have reached an equilibrium in which everyone is getting essentially what they deserve. But when that stasis amounts to entrenched inequality, such an equilibrium can be considered equitable only if whites are more deserving.

Closely related to doing nothing is doing something ineffectual. Over the last half century we as a society have dedicated untold billions of dollars, directly or indirectly, at the disparity between black and white wellbeing. Whether we think the size of the response has been too grandiose or too meager, the simple fact is that it hasn't worked. That is, if the goal was to achieve equality it hasn't worked. If the goal was to assuage white consciences and to ameliorate some of the effects of inequality while leaving the racial hierarchy intact, then I guess it's worked pretty well.

4) Taking stock of our attitudes: Our self-examination tends to focus on specific sinful acts, in part because this is the easiest type of sin to identify. And we have just mentioned a variety of behaviors that can be indicative of

haughtiness. It's important to keep in mind, however, that haughtiness itself is not an act but an attitude. Therefore, if we are to recognize this sin for what it truly is, we must be willing to look beyond the kind of overt oppression and discrimination usually associated with it.

Jesus himself was keen to point out the correlation between sinful activities and sinful proclivities. He explained, "For *out of the heart* come evil thoughts—murder, adultery, sexual immorality, theft, false testimony, slander." (Matthew 15:19) His Sermon on the Mount emphasized the nexus between anger and murder, as well as the link between lust and adultery.

That is not to say that every sinful attitude automatically translates into sinful actions. Or even that there is a strict moral equivalency between the two. But *both* are serious moral offenses. Even if we've never caused personal harm to anyone across racial lines based on some sense of superiority, nursing a haughty attitude remains a moral affront.

This is first and foremost an issue in our relationship with God, who resists such an attitude and is determined to bring the haughty down a few notches (or more like completely). So, even if our haughtiness had zero fallout on the horizontal plane, it would still be a significant spiritual matter. But the downside of haughtiness doesn't stop there. It inevitably skews our human relationships as well.

We're tempted to think that unspoken judgments and unrevealed attitudes, however inappropriate they may be, have little influence on race relations. After all, if it doesn't erupt into discriminatory behavior, how's anyone going to know what's buried deep in your psyche? Well, it's not as easy as you might think to mask a superior attitude. Even when others can't identify the marginalizing vibe, they may still feel it. Moreover, even if your haughtiness were to somehow remain so secret that it didn't alienate others from you—and this is critical—it would still alienate you from others.

Some whites can't imagine themselves as the purveyors of racial haughtiness, because they don't harbor anti-black sentiment. What's more, they may be critical of the racial hierarchy; they may work on behalf of racial justice; they may be advocates of racial reconciliation. But these same people may be surprised to find (as was I) that their kindly concern can be laced with paternalism. Haughtiness can appear benign, even "loving." But it is not a peer-to-peer affection. One person is the beneficiary; the other is the benefactor—the (white) knight in shining armor.

5) Reconsidering the implications of corporate haughtiness: Discovering the pervasive reach of haughtiness is like peeling back the layers of an onion. Up to this point we have focused on the personal and individual aspects of haughtiness, both as an attitude and as a way of relating to others. But that is not the only level at which haughtiness operates, and we must recognize this sin wherever it resides if we aspire to true transformation at both a personal and a relational level. That means confronting the reality of corporate racial haughtiness and our relationship to it.

Corporate haughtiness is a synergistic phenomenon in which the whole is actually bigger than the sum of its parts—because racial dominance is something we do together or we don't do at all. Isolated racial haughtiness simply cannot sustain a hierarchy. Isolated racial haughtiness would more likely to lead to the marginalization of certain haughty individuals than the marginalization of their supposedly inferior other. Just look at how contemporary society regards self-proclaimed racists.

For a racial hierarchy to function on a large scale—that is, for one race to establish and maintain its hegemony over another for centuries—there must exist a social compact in which nearly the entire dominant group is complicit. If that was true during a quarter of a millennium of slavery, it is even truer today, when there is far less overt, external support for racial dominance.

Back then, whites may have disagreed about slavery but were very much in agreement about racial superiority. This explicit and almost universally accepted groupthink was so mainstream that it was accepted as science rather than decried as sin. Now, however, the "fact" of white superiority has been all but banished from our visible ideological landscape. This development increases the relative role of that invisible, affective sensibility called haughtiness as the glue that holds the hierarchy together.

Never mind that an evolving white ethic sentenced slavery to the Hades of history—and eventually Jim Crow along with it. Racial haughtiness has never joined the Beast and the False Prophet in that Lake of Fire.[a] And that's because racial haughtiness is not indexed to an evolving white ethic but to a far more constant white identity.

---

[a] I realize, of course, that there is a distinction between Hades and the Lake of Fire. And, of course, that slavery, Jim Crow, and haughtiness are not in view in Revelation 20:10. This literary metaphor is intentionally based on popular conceptions rather than exegetical precision.

The problem, then, goes beyond what I, as an individual, do or think, or even what I feel. It is connected to who *we* are—and how *I* relate to that collective sense of self. Recognizing the sin of haughtiness requires us to address whiteness and our relationship to that racial identity. That's because racial haughtiness is a byproduct of belonging, of identification with a supposedly superior group.

White people can't help but be exposed to white identity, and they are inclined to regard it as benign. Indeed, some of that identity is benign—a matter of preferences, cultural patterns without much in the way of moral overtones. Within that legacy there are even admirable elements.

But it is not all goodness or innocence. As we have seen throughout this book, white American identity is also defined by a sinful predisposition toward racial haughtiness. And unless we whites consciously and critically confront this aspect of our collective white identity, how can we not be under its influence in one degree or another?

Sorrowing over Sin

The Apostle Paul wrote in 2 Corinthians 7:10: "Godly sorrow brings repentance." There is, then, a correlation between your emotional reaction to the sin you've recognized and the likelihood that you'll proceed in the direction of transformation. You must recognize your sin before you *can* do something about it, but recognizing your sin doesn't mean you *will* do anything about it. If you can contemplate racial haughtiness dispassionately, you're unlikely to experience meaningful change.

The classic biblical example of sorrowing over sin is Psalm 51, where David expresses his anguish over his adultery with Bathsheba and his cover-up murder of her husband, Uriah. As that psalm illustrates, sorrow is more than a fleeting, superficial rush of regret. Inner distress typically erupts in some sort of outward display of emotion, but it cannot be reduced to a facile measure of tears per minute. There is no necessary correlation between a given overt expression of grief and the authenticity of one's sorrow. But, absent a sense of mournful regret, transformation will remain elusive.

Compared to sadness, this sorrow is necessarily profound. And sorrow over haughtiness ought to be particularly profound, because haughtiness is not a one-off or even an episodic transgression. It is by nature habitual, an enduring and impenitent affront to a loving and holy God. Adding to the gravity of the offense itself is the inevitable relational estrangement such an attitude produces on the horizontal plane. If we *get* that, if we truly recognize the havoc our haughtiness has wrought, the only possible result is brokenness.

It follows, then, that any admission of haughtiness that is devoid of emotional overtones must be somehow deficient. Insufficient sorrow could be the result of minimizing the transgression. Perhaps because we simply haven't considered its seriousness or its shame. Or because this original sin is, by definition, common; everybody does it. Or because we excuse ourselves as the victims of whiteness. Or because our haughtiness hasn't given rise to overt discriminatory behavior—a kind of "no harm, no foul" rationalization.

Even when others don't notice or can't identify our attitudes, those inner sensitivities are no more of a mystery to God than the most overt transgression. And attitudinal sins clearly grieve the Spirit of God. When Paul instructs us not to "grieve the Holy Spirit," he includes in the list of possible grievances two attitudes, bitterness and malice (Ephesians 4:30 ff.). There's no reason to believe that this is an exhaustive list, so I would understand haughtiness and other attitudinal sins to be implicitly included. If racial haughtiness breaks the heart of God, shouldn't it break ours as well?

God's reaction to this specific sin of haughtiness goes beyond grief, however. He actively opposes those who embrace pride (Proverbs 3:34, James 4:6, 1 Peter 5:5) and is determined to bring down those who have elevated themselves above others. As 2 Samuel 2:28 tells us, "You save the humble, but your eyes are on the haughty to bring them low." Haughtiness doesn't just leave the Lord a bit bummed out. It doesn't just exclude us from potential blessings. Haughtiness turns us into targets of God's displeasure.

When it comes to earthly relationships, "hidden" haughtiness may seem somehow more benign and, therefore, not so worthy of sorrow. Some seem to think that if they don't *act* in an openly haughty fashion, they're not constructing relational barriers. But reconciliation means far more than not making things worse. Racial barriers already exist. And we are responsible to be reconcilers. Therefore, when we fail to tear down those walls, we cast our moral lot with those who erected them in the first place.

Harboring haughtiness in our hearts, even if it "stays" there, not only keeps *us* from being repairers of the breach; it actually keeps the breach from being repaired. The "secretly" haughty, whether they know it or not, lend their passive approval to an unacceptable status quo, standing in tacit solidarity with the cumulative injustice of our unhappy history and aligning themselves with the abusers rather than the abused.

If these very real consequences of haughtiness do not move us emotionally, if they do not at some level pierce us, then we need to go back to step one and/or prayerfully wait on God. Though we may have recognized that something was wrong, we certainly haven't recognized the moral urgency of that something. Until we grieve over the evil within us, we are simply not in a position to change it.

Turning from Sin

The third step in the process of moral transformation is that of turning from sin. There is, of course, a familiar theological term that relates to this dynamic—*repentance*. The problem with this terminology is that its popular use is rather imprecise, and scholarly attempts at precision end up disagreeing about the exact semantic and theological territory the term should encompass. Given the futility of trying to settle that question in these pages and the distraction that it would suppose for our central concern, I've opted instead to use the descriptive term, *turning from sin.*

Since, however, *repentance* is both a familiar term and one that is relevant to this discussion as well, it might be helpful to at least differentiate my categories of moral transformation from some common understandings of *repentance*. When we think of repentance, our focus might naturally be drawn to Christian conversion. Not only is this a perfectly legitimate use of the term; it is the one most frequently found in Scripture, describing one's initial turning from sin toward God.[b] The dynamic of repentance does not end at conversion, however. Rather, it begins there. As we progress in our spiritual journey, we must learn to live penitently, becoming sensitive to particular sins for which repentance is required.

Sometimes we also refer to *repentance* in an *über*-comprehensive way to denote the entire process of moral transformation.[c] Whether it is ever used

---

[b] Though this is the most frequent use of this word group, there are other passages in which repentance is applied to an ostensibly Christian audience. (2 Cor. 7:9, 2 Cor. 12:21, several times in Revelation 1-3).

[c] This is true not only in Christianity, but also in Judaism. See: Louis E. Newman, *Repentance: The Meaning and Practice of Teshuvah*, (Jewish Lights Publishing; Woodstock, Vermont; 2010). This Jewish ethicist suggests

quite so broadly in Scripture is debatable, but it is nonetheless perfectly natural to do so, given the fact that repentance serves as a kind of pivot point for the entire process—hence the idea of turning. The prior steps bring us to the point of repentance, and the subsequent steps flow from it.

The final use of *repentance* that I'd like to distinguish from what I'm labeling *turning from sin* involves an overly restrictive use of the term. It stems from a Greek word that has the basic meaning of "to change one's mind." That word, *metanoia* (or *metanoeō* in its verbal form), is consistently rendered in most English versions as *repentance/repent*.

The Greeks, who did not contemplate the possibility of moral transformation, often used this term to refer to mere changes of opinion. The radically different moral framework of the New Testament, however, ensures that *metanoeō/metanoia* do have moral and volitional connotations when they appear in the Sacred Text.[4] This distinction is important, because if Christian repentance can be construed as a mere change of opinion (or if this cognitive brand of repentance were necessarily indicative of a broader moral transformation) then those who have adjusted their formal ethic regarding white superiority might have greater reason to believe that their inner attitude of haughtiness has been automatically altered as a result.

If the spiritual dynamic that I am proposing does not align with any of these three interpretations of repentance, to what does it refer? *Turning from sin* describes an act of the will by which we reject our current sinful pattern, reorient ourselves toward a righteous alternative, and determine to move in that direction.[d] It is both a turning *from* as well as a turning *to*, although the sin we are turning from may be understood more clearly at first than the exact nature of the alternative, which may come into better focus over time.

To call this step an act of the will does not mean that there is not also an element of cognitive change involved. Perhaps at one time I did not understand the nature or the seriousness of my sin, but now I do. Perhaps I knew it was wrong but wasn't aware that I was guilty of it. Of course, it's also

---

seven steps to *teshuvah* (repentance) that roughly mirror my own list. He says on p. 78: "I would suggest that *teshuvah* as it traditionally been understood, comprises seven distinct steps: culpability, remorse, confession, apology, restitution, soul reckoning, and transformation."

[d] The term *repentance* is, of course, often legitimately employed in just this fashion as well. But since it is also legitimately used in other ways (as noted above), I have not used the term to designate this third step.

possible that I was aware of the nature of the sin but was simply unwilling to admit my own guilt, in which case the cognitive aspect of the change would be minimal.

Depending on my starting point, I may indeed need to come to a different understanding of my situation in order to do anything about it. It is important to note, however, that merely changing my *opinion* about the ethics of racial haughtiness—coming to see it as wrong or even as far more terrible than I had previously imagined—is not the same as turning from sin. It is not enough to see racial haughtiness as *a* sin; I must own it as *my* sin.[e]

Turning from sin also requires an acknowledgement of its deleterious impact on our relationships on both the vertical and horizontal planes. But acknowledgement alone is not enough. If I am morally torpid or lulled into complacency by the social acceptability of my sin, I could be conscious of it, even sorry for it, and yet do nothing in response. Turning goes beyond the cognitive and emotional to the volitional. I must *determine* to forsake haughtiness and intentionally reorient myself toward a righteous alternative.

I need to say a specific word about what it means to turn from our involvement in *corporate* haughtiness. As noted earlier, the individual and corporate aspects of this sin are inextricably linked. Racial haughtiness requires the complicity of the race. But individuals cannot control the behavior of the collective. So how do you turn from this collective sin? The fact that one person jumps ship does not turn the entire ship around.

Let's think first about how we react to our place in the larger picture and then consider how our individual actions might affect that larger picture. If you're white you can't simply decide not to be white any more. Turning from haughtiness is not a matter of racial self-loathing. Adopting an anti-white attitude is like throwing the baby out with the bathwater.

The bathwater, however, does need changing. Turning from the sin of corporate haughtiness requires a renunciation of the attitudinal reality of haughtiness that defines white identity.

It is much easier to pursue such a moral metamorphosis within a community of like-minded people. In the many years I lived in Europe I was

---

[e] It would, of course, be possible to recognize that an activity or attitude that we had previously considered to be licit was, in fact, illicit, even if we were not personally guilty of committing it. Nevertheless, I would distinguish this sort of moral *enlightenment* from the moral *transformation* in view here, a process that presupposes personal guilt.

often encouraged by contact with other Americans who were facing the same adaptations I was. In some cases, I would have had little in common with these people had we met in the U.S. And, yet, our common expatriate experience somehow bound us together. In a similar fashion, connecting with like-minded souls who are also battling haughtiness can provide a sense of belonging on what can otherwise be a rather lonely path.

Be advised that when you reject this defining element of white identity, other whites are likely to see you as abandoning and/or indicting them. This situation is not totally avoidable, but here are three tips for navigating this dynamic: 1) When you talk with other whites about racial haughtiness, try to focus on how it has affected you more than on blanket indictments. Referencing your own personal contrition will make people less defensive than casting general aspersions. 2) Monitor your own motives to avoid spiritual one-upmanship. There's not much point in replacing racial haughtiness with self-righteous haughtiness. 3) If you decide that it is, in fact, your job to make other whites aware of this issue—hold onto your hat.

While personal spiritual transformation has obvious value for the individual involved, it may seem as if your personal determination to turn from the sin of racial haughtiness will have little impact on an age-old social pattern, that it won't make much of a dent in the broader socio-spiritual problem. Keep in mind, however, that moral movements depend on a cumulative effect. Taking a cue from the natural world, we observe that as polar glaciers melt, ocean levels rise. That melting, however, takes place one drop at a time. None of those drops would have any individual reason to believe that they are having a significant impact on sea level. Nevertheless, as part of a broader movement they are, indeed, agents of change.

Also, consider the phenomenon of tipping points. Much of the power of contemporary racial haughtiness derives from its invisibility. If people recognized it for what it is and what it does, many of them would be alarmed, if not appalled. Just how many whistle-blowers would it take to unravel the complicity of this dominant moral compact and to point out the emperor's wardrobe malfunction?

I don't know just how many it would take. But here's what I do know: the public penitence of a single individual is not a single vote but a single voice. A vote, while significant, operates at the discreet power of one. But a voice, once heard, has the potential to multiply its power exponentially and even to change the direction of a generation.

Chapter 25

Confession: A Bridge to Reconciliation

In the previous chapter we began the transformational process with our inner selves, precisely where it should begin. We chose that starting point, in part, because the white psyche is the ultimate locus of the problem. But that starting point is also strategic, because our own consciousness is the reality over which we exercise the most immediate personal control. In our effort to come to terms with haughtiness, that inward focus has thus far led us through the private steps of recognizing sin, sorrowing for sin, and turning from sin.

The sin of racial haughtiness, however, poisons far more than our private personal piety. Its impact is relational and societal as well. Therefore, in order to achieve the necessary moral metamorphosis, we will have to move beyond our discreet, self-conscious bubble. True transformation cannot begin and end with us just being different or even doing differently than we used to. It must ultimately alter the moral fabric of our relationships—repairing and renewing our interactions with others across racial lines.

Transformation, then, requires both an *inner* personal response as well as an *inter*personal response. But how do we traverse the existential distance between *inner* personal penitence and *inter*personal healing? This chapter focuses on confession, the bridge between these two worlds.

The Essence of Confession

The biblical term *confession* comes from the Greek *homologia*, a compound word comprised of *homos* (same) and *logos* (word). In its verbal form it means "to say the same thing, to agree." In Greek, *homologia* need not imply an admission of wrongdoing, as it often refers to an affirmation or recognition. For example, in Romans 10:9 it is used for *declaring/confessing* that Jesus is Lord. And in 1 John 4:15 it speaks of *acknowledging/confessing* that he is the Son of God. In fact, the semantic range of *homologia* is so broad that it can be understood as a confession of sin only when the context specifically indicates such a meaning.

Our modern English notion of *confession* still adheres to the idea of agreement, but our usage of the term has become considerably more focused. When we hear the word *confession*, we automatically think in terms of owning up to some moral or legal transgression. Though *confession* occasionally indicates a different kind of agreement (e.g., *confession* of faith), we now understand it that way only when the situation so dictates.

Confession in a relational context is somewhat different than confession in a legal context. Confessing to a crime is an admission of guilt before the impersonal bar of justice (even if a judge or other individuals are there to represent justice in principle). Though such a confession may involve penitence, any sense of regret is quite secondary to the fact of the transgression itself. Indeed, some people who confess to a crime may feel morally justified or even quite proud of their actions.

By contrast, Christian interpersonal confession (whether to God or to others) does have a significant moral/emotional/relational dimension. It goes beyond simply admitting that we did something we should not have done. It expresses regret for the wrongness of that action and the offense/harm it has caused others.

Christian confession is more than just the confession *of* a wrong; it is confession *to* those we have wronged. We not only factually agree that we have sinned; we empathetically agree that our sin has hurt others and damaged the fabric of our relationship with them. That empathetic agreement reflects the fact that when we confess to others, our ultimate purpose in doing so is not merely to adjudicate a wrong but to restore a relationship.

Confession and Truth

As we discussed above, confession involves agreement. And agreement implies the participation of more than one party. A "confession" that agrees only with our own self-assessment but not with our counterpart's view of the offense will not resolve anything. In fact, it might even make matters worse.

To be genuine and effective, a confession must agree with the truth. The problem is that the truth about us and our sin is notoriously hard to identify— and even harder to accept. In fact, moral subjectivity is such that, left to our own devices, it's nearly impossible to establish the objective truth about who we are and how we have impacted others.

That's the bad news. The good news, however, is that we are not left to our own devices. By triangulating multiple perspectives on the same reality, we can arrive at a vision of the truth that is sufficiently clear to generate agreement and to allow for meaningful confession.

What is this multi-perspectival truth? First, there exists a truth about our sin as we perceive it. Then, there exists a truth about our sin as God perceives it. And, finally, there exists a truth about our sin as the offended perceive it.

While, at first blush such an approach to truth might seem overly relativistic, it corresponds quite neatly to the demands of confession. Again, we are not just adjudicating an offense; we are attempting to reconcile the alienated parties. For that purpose, mutual agreement on the nature of the offense—not only as perpetrated but as experienced—is more relevant to reconciliation than some "objective" accounting of what happened to which the parties may or may not subscribe.

Let's see what each point of view contributes to our overall appreciation of the truth, beginning with our own. We are, of course, intimately in touch with our own thoughts and feelings. The truth as we perceive it in our own conscience/consciousness has the advantage of being the most accessible of these three avenues to the truth. After all, without some self-conscious recognition of sin there can be no sorrow for sin, no turning from sin, and therefore no genuine confession of sin.

As valuable as this inner-personal truth may be, however, such subjective clarity does not necessarily translate into a clear and complete vision of who we are and what we have done. It merely defines how *we* feel about who we are and what we have done. Therefore, before we begin to confess/agree with that truth, we need to broaden its scope.

If we really want to know the truth about ourselves, we need God's perspective, for he knows us as we really are. And God graciously grants us access to his divine perspicacity—but he does not automatically download it to our consciousness. To benefit from that his perspective, we must, like David, ask God to search us and know our hearts, to test us and know our thoughts, thereby revealing if there is any wicked way in us (Psalm 139:123-124).[a] As the Holy Spirit enables us to grasp God's truth about ourselves, that truth can emend our own perspective and bring it into sharper focus.

---

[a] David's request is not, of course, for the benefit of God's further understanding but a petition, seeking access to God's perspective.

Which brings up the question: If God knows the *real* truth of the matter, then why do we need any other perspectives at all? After all, how can you improve on perfection? Here we need to distinguish between what God knows and what we know about what God knows. God knows the absolute, objective truth of the matter, but our only means of grasping that knowledge is constrained by finitude and blurred by the haze of sinful subjectivity. What we think we know about our sin may be the result of God's perspective editing our own. Or of our perspective editing his. Or some combination of the two.

Under the best of circumstances, we still "see through a glass darkly." That's why a third perspective can be so helpful when it comes to triangulating the truth. I'm talking about the truth as perceived by the offended party, in this case the truth about white racial haughtiness as perceived by African Americans. Like any human viewpoint, this one is also skewed by subjectivity. In this case, however, I would argue that this subjective slant does not diminish its usefulness; rather, it enhances it.

The perpetrators of haughtiness have, by definition, a natural tendency to overestimate their own virtue. The targets of haughtiness, however, have no vested interest in such illusions and can therefore serve as a subjective counterbalance. Beyond this corrective bias, however, the African-American take[b] on racial haughtiness is important for another reason. Only those who have been on the receiving end of haughtiness can speak to its personal and collective damage. Whites must come to appreciate and to grieve over that pain, if confession as empathetic agreement is to mean anything at all.

When South Africa embarked on its great national quest for racial harmony under the leadership of Bishop Desmond Tutu, they understood very clearly the need for both parties to agree about what, in fact, had happened—to look injustice in the eye. That's why they established *The Truth and Reconciliation Commission*. Originally, this was supposed to be simply a *truth* commission, but the white political establishment pushed to add the word *reconciliation*. Now, at first blush that might seem downright Christian of them. But many black people feared that the white version of "reconciliation" would come at the expense of truth, making a mockery of racial harmony.

---

[b] "The African-American take" is not meant to imply that black sensitivities are monolithic. Nevertheless, the continuum of sensitivities on this subject within the black community tends to cohere in a way that differentiates itself from the continuum of sensitivities within the white community.

Allen Aubrey Boesak and Curtiss Paul DeYoung discuss this tension in the introduction to their book, *Radical Reconciliation: Beyond Political Pietism and Christian Quietism*:

> We have discovered how often reconciliation is used merely to reach some political accommodation that did not address the critical questions of justice, equality, and dignity that are so prominent in the biblical understanding of reconciliation. Such political arrangements invariably favor the rich and powerful but deprive the powerless of justice and dignity.... This "reconciliation" employs a language that sounds like the truth but is, in fact, deceitful.... When we discover that what is happening is in fact, not reconciliation, and yet for reasons of self-protection, fear, or a desire for acceptance by the powers that govern our world seek to accommodate this situation, justify it, refuse to run the risk of challenge and prophetic truth telling, we become complicit in deceitful reconciliation.[1]

It is because of the indispensable role of truth in reconciliation that I have gone to such great lengths in this book to detail the pernicious reality of haughtiness—its fundamental ugliness, its cruel consequences, and its demeaning presumption. Truth be told, many whites would very much prefer a deceitful reconciliation—one that trivializes the hurt caused by haughtiness, one that tires after ten steps in someone else's shoes, and, above all, one that avoids any admission of moral solidarity with the past.

Arriving at the truth is critically important, but *how* we arrive at the truth is also important. *White as Sin* presents abundant evidence of white racial haughtiness, but convictions obtained by a preponderance of the evidence do not lead to reconciliation. When the goal is relational healing, only a confession will do. Confession, this fourth step in the process of transformation, takes the truth we recognize in step one, the sorrow we experience in step two, and the change of direction we experience in step three—and communicates our penitence to the people we have wronged. And that act of communication catalyzes our own transformative process and creates a bridge to authentic reconciliation.[c]

---

[c] Some might react to the use of "reconciliation" here, as the "re" prefix seems to imply the restoration of a previously existing harmony. While it's true that America has never enjoyed any state of racial harmony worth recovering, the term *reconcile* has come to refer not only to the restoration of harmony but also to the simple establishment of a harmonious relationship between parties

Agreement with the truth about our sin is essential to reconciliation. Even God, who loved us while we were still sinners and made the supreme sacrifice for our justification, still requires something from us as a condition of forgiveness. He requires an agreement regarding the truth. "If we *confess* our sins, he is faithful and just and will forgive us our sins and purify us from all unrighteousness." (1 John 1:9) As Proverbs 28:13 reminds us, if we want to find mercy we have to "confess and renounce" our sins.

Unilateral Forgiveness

It can be a long, hard road to bring white people around to this place of confession. But what if there were a shortcut? What would happen if black people simply forgave them, individually and collectively and absolutely, quite apart from an adequate confession?[d] Wouldn't that solve the problem?

Unilateral forgiveness is certainly a noble gesture and one that could well prove liberating for the forgiver. But unilateral forgiveness has its limitations. The first limitation is its potential scale. There are simply not many people willing to extend forgiveness without some show of penitence from the offender. How, then, could unilateral forgiveness granted by only a few function as a catalyst for broad-based racial reconciliation?

Second, unsolicited absolution implies an unsolicited indictment. For an offense to be forgiven, some very real wrongdoing must have occurred, at least in the mind of the forgiver. When the offended party extends unsolicited forgiveness to an offender who does not even acknowledge the existence of the transgression, there's a good chance the implicit indictment will actually exacerbate the relational rift. Of course, one can grant forgiveness without communicating it at all, but in that case its value is limited to the forgiver.

Third, there is an important distinction between forgiveness and trust. As noted in Chapter 22, forgiveness may be granted by an act of the will, but trust

---

in conflict. There is no English verb for *concile* (without the *re*) and *conciliate/conciliation* may refer to one party achieving greater favor with another, rather than a mutually harmonious relationship. Therefore, I use *reconciliation* here to denote the establishment of relational harmony, without reference to the recovery of any former condition.

[d] For further discussion of various forms of forgiveness and their relationship to confession, see: www.scottgarber.com/was_notes.pdf, Note 25.1.

must be earned. That repair can take time and effort under the best of circumstances—and trying to re-establish trust with an impenitent offender does not qualify as the best of circumstances.

Both forgiveness and trust are necessary for genuine reconciliation. Unfortunately, by its very nature racial haughtiness creates a serious trust deficit. That's because haughtiness is not just a momentary lapse that goes against our normal tendencies; haughtiness is a moral flaw that resides in that default tendency itself. Therefore, until the offended party knows that the offender at least "gets it," the likelihood that the sinful pattern will be repeated is going to undermine the trust necessary for racial harmony in the real world.

So, even if racial haughtiness and all its historical manifestations were unilaterally forgiven, the lack of a confession from the perpetrators would continue to poison the well of race relations. Racial healing and harmony can never become a reality among American Christians until racial haughtiness ceases to define that reality. And that will require whites to demonstrate a spirit of penitence and confession based on an agreement about the truth.

The Nuts and Bolts of Confession

While agreeing to the truth about ourselves is hard, vocalizing that agreement to others is even harder. In part, that's because of the humility required to do so. But confession is also hard, because it's a specialized and relatively rare kind of conversation. And when it involves race, it becomes even more specialized and even more rare. So, just how do we go about making such a confession, and to whom?

Confessing to God, whose Spirit we have grieved and whose holiness we have offended, is, of course, critical. Haughtiness disrespects God by violating his righteous standards and his design for human interaction. At its most basic level, racial dysfunction is not the result of poor people skills that we can somehow grow out of. It is the result of a moral failure that must be confessed. Keeping God in the picture helps to remind us of that fact.

Keeping God in the picture also motivates us to keep confession honest. When dealing with other people, we may be tempted to confess only the sins we think they're aware of, the ones we think they're holding against us. But, since God knows all the ugly details, in his presence we are far less likely to play such games. In the end, a God-size moral accounting will provide a healthier blueprint for dealing with others as well.

Haughtiness is a sin that must be confessed before God, because, like any sin, it is a transgression against him. But though God is rightly upset by this injustice, the actual pretensions of haughtiness—superiority, condescension, and disdain—are not focused upward but outward, toward our racial *other*. And they, not God, are the victims of its social consequences. So, while our confession must begin with God, it must not end with him.

What would it look like for white people to confess to their black counterparts? Well, let's begin with the most obvious case. If we can identify particular human targets of our haughtiness—if we have discriminated against others across racial lines, depriving them of wealth, goods, opportunity, respect, social standing, justice, or anything else—confession is in order. Likewise, if we have entertained a haughty attitude directed against a particular individual or if our general haughtiness has negatively impacted a particular relationship, that, too, is worthy of confession.

Though confessing to people and confessing to God are in some ways similar, there are important differences. The first difference has to do with confession as an agreement regarding the nature of our sin.

Since God understands our sin far better than we do, when confessing to him we seek to understand the nature of our wrongdoing from his omniscient perspective. Hopefully, the notion of haughtiness that we have been discussing throughout the book will provide a helpful handle for identifying some of the basic motivations behind racial sin. Still, we must be careful not to convert this insight into a reductionist shorthand that keeps us from contemplating the actual depth and breadth of sin's reach. Any form of moral know-it-all-*ism* tends to short-circuit repentance.

People, on the other hand, tend to identify our sin based on a subjective sense of how it has impacted them. They may never have identified our attitudes/actions as a manifestation of haughtiness. They may not even be able to parse out our individual participation vis-à-vis the entire white collective. They probably can recall, however, when and how those racial relationships have felt demeaning or discriminatory. So, confession may involve listening as well as talking, taking responsibility not only for what we know we have perpetrated but also for how it has resonated.

Others are unlikely to subject us to a psycho-spiritual analysis, and in any case, they cannot see inside our hearts. So, it's possible that their assessment of our culpability may be somewhat more limited than our own. In addition, when we approach someone in a spirit of contrition, a certain sense of propriety may lead that person to minimize the nature/seriousness of the offense. That should be understood as an olive branch, a welcome mat to relational healing, but it should not lead us to believe that our sin is, indeed, less egregious than we thought. Though others may know things about our wrongdoing that we do not, we also know things about ourselves that they do not. Therefore, we dare not limit our confessions to fit their perceptions.

Still, you might wonder, why make myself look worse than I need to? Well, it's not really making yourself look worse than you need to if you understand that truth is the thing that sets you free. It's not really making yourself look worse than you need to if you understand that sometime others play down the seriousness of our offense as an act of kindness—but they may nevertheless be waiting for you to disagree with their assessment rather than agree with it. Admitting to more than you need to does not make you look worse. Rather, it demonstrates how much you value your own integrity, the wellbeing of the other party, and your relationship with them.

How does this act and attitude of confession differ from apologizing? Granted, in popular parlance these terms may be used somewhat interchangeably or take on a variety of nuances according to a given context. My usage here conforms more to what Susan Wise Bauer explains in her book, *The Art of the Public Grovel*. She says: "Apology and confession are not the same. An apology is an expression of regret: *I am sorry*. A confession is an admission of fault: *I am sorry because I did wrong. I sinned*."[2]

So, an apology does express remorse, but it may not recognize the objective wrongness of our behavior. It may focus only on our regret that the other party *feels* offended. Or it may allow for the possibility that they bear part of the blame. Or maybe they misunderstood or they're just overly sensitive. Clearly, such an apology does not qualify as a "confession" in the sense that I am using the term.

Because of these differences between an apology and a confession, Bauer maintains: "Confessions are harder. Confessions require that the accused give up innocence and self-defense, taking moral responsibility for an evil act."[3]

Confession is never easy, but it is a fairly straightforward act—when we can look the offended individual in the eye. There are, however, other situations in which it's not quite so clear just how we should proceed. If we're haughty now, we were probably haughty in the past. What if the person to whom we should confess is no longer alive or available? What about the haughtiness we harbor, not so much against anyone in particular but against our racial *other* in general? And, importantly, how and to whom do you confess for doing nothing to combat racial injustice?

If we've offended someone with whom we've simply lost contact over the course of time, with the online tools available today it might not take a great deal of effort to find them. Though the chances of creating or restoring a personal relationship may be slim because of physical and/or temporal distance, I believe that integrity requires a good faith effort to clear the air.

Even if that person has passed away, we may still be able to pursue some form of proxy personal closure. In 2 Samuel 9:1 "David asked, "Is there anyone still left of the house of Saul to whom I can show kindness for Jonathan's sake?" His friend, Jonathan, was gone, but taking the lame Mephibosheth into the royal court turned out to be a personally significant way for David to express his affection. Granted, expressing charity and making a confession involve two very different dynamics, but the idea of locating a descendant, other relative, or some person significant to both parties may suggest a practical way forward for the confessor.

When our moral failings have been directed not against an individual but against the African-American collective, it's even trickier to know what confession means. We can't very well buttonhole random black people to hear our confession and grant us absolution on behalf of an entire race. Or walk around with a permanently dour expression, hoping that someone will give us an open door by asking what in the heck is wrong with us.

You can, however, share your personal journey of discovery and your sense of penitence with people of other races as opportunity permits. In this case, it does not take the form of a personal apology but rather a confessional conversation, as in, "You know what I've discovered/been learning recently?" Such sharing should never be forced, but it can nevertheless be intentional.

Of course, most white people have limited social outlets of this sort. But verbalizing the turning points in our moral transformation can be a powerful confirmation that change is happening, as well as an encouragement to continue in the process we've begun. That confessional conversation is even worth sharing with other whites, because putting it "out there" objectifies our experience and brings other people into the process in a constructive way.

The matter of indirect offense continues to exert a powerful influence over interracial relationships. Even if I, as a white person, have never done anything inappropriate to an individual black person, we are likely to begin with an invisible barrier between us. That's because the collective of which I am a part and in which I have participated has quite a shameful track record with regard to their collective. I say "participated," because, though I may not bear moral responsibility simply by virtue of being white, once I admit to any form of racial haughtiness, I am also admitting to a certain solidarity with the larger white legacy. It's not just that I have *been identified* with the sins of whiteness; I have *identified* with the sins of whiteness.

Though white Americans (individualistic as we are) tend to have limited appreciation for shared moral responsibility, this identification with the legacy of haughtiness is very real. It is both a moral as well as a relational reality. In other words, there is some of *me* in that *we*. I have benefitted from its immorally-gained advantage. I have often been conveniently ignorant of its collateral damage. And by both action and inaction I have perpetuated an oppressive racial hierarchy.

The relational reality is this—in the social space that is our racialized society, I represent that white legacy. By default, whether I like it or not. It's not a choice; it's just a fact.

Now, I don't like that fact—because I trust that this haughty legacy does not define the person I am becoming by the grace of God. Nevertheless, as a white person living in the historical vortex of white racial identity, I cannot escape my association with whiteness by pleading individuality. I cannot escape my association with whiteness by trying to prove that I am an exception to the rule. After all that we've seen over the course of this book, I certainly can't escape my association by denying the legacy of haughtiness itself. The only effective way of escaping this association is by confession— by owning up to the validity of the pattern and my own collusion in it. I must recognize and reject that legacy, not as a self-righteous outsider but as a complicit insider.

This would be a good point at which to elaborate a bit on the relationship between confessing and asking for forgiveness. As mentioned, the implicit *telos* of confession, as we've been discussing it, is reconciliation. And when the other party offers forgiveness, it represents a significant step forward in the reconciliation process.

It is precisely here, however, that we must exercise caution, because there are at least three possible permutations in what we might call *asking for forgiveness*. If your relationship with the other individual is close, communication is frank, and the sin you're confessing has not led to major trauma or a breakdown in the relationship; then it may be possible to ask for and to receive forgiveness more or less immediately.

If these conditions do not exist, however, it may be both unfair as well as unwise to ask for forgiveness. Because, rather than *asking* for forgiveness, we may well be *extracting* forgiveness. When one person confesses, it creates a considerable moral counterweight for the other individual, who then feels compelled to respond in a conciliatory manner, lest they be left looking like the bad guy, the obstacle to a restored relationship.

So, what happens? When you ask for forgiveness from someone who isn't yet ready to grant it, you might pressure them to say something inauthentic, introducing a modicum of farce into the relationship. Once people have said, "Oh, that's okay," they feel obligated to act as if everything is all right, even if it isn't. You wanted to feel absolved, and perhaps you do. But better to not be fully reconciled and know that you're not, than to not be fully reconciled and think that you are.

Why might the other party hesitate to grant forgiveness? Maybe they don't think we fully appreciate the seriousness of the offense or the hurt it caused. After all, when we voluntarily confess, it is often the confessor who defines the wrong that was done. Maybe they think we're more interested in finding relief for ourselves than in righting a wrong. Maybe they want to see that the confession is, indeed, linked to real transformation.

It could also be, as one black minister confided to me in the midst of a seminar on the multiracial church, that the hurt feels so great as to seem insurmountable. It could also be that granting forgiveness would leave the absolvers without any justification for their own negative feelings. Black identity, after all, has been forged as a counterpart to white identity. So, if we start to tinker with whiteness, it sends a ripple through blackness as well.

When it comes to racial haughtiness, where whites have a history of moral tone-deafness, these are all good reasons why someone may not be ready to grant forgiveness at a given point in time. Articulating those reasons in the face of a penitent petitioner, however, can be problematic. That's why programmed interracial encounters designed to elicit immediate reconciliation make me nervous. What can a black person say to a tearful white counterpart, who just took the huge step of confessing and is hoping to go home forgiven?

That's why I believe that, generally speaking, confession should be made with a *view* to reconciliation but without the *expectation* of immediate, hand-holding, hunky-doryness. The end product of confession is going to be far more satisfying in the long run if the other party is allowed to process the implications of forgiveness without the pressure of immediate absolution. After all, it may have taken us many years to recognize our haughtiness and to be willing to confess it. It is, therefore, rather unrealistic to expect that someone else will be able to process our penitence and respond in the most ideal fashion in the span of five minutes.

We all like it when confession is transactional—we bare our souls, say our piece, and move on. But not all offenses are created equal. This is a sin that requires not just an act of confession but an ongoing spirit of confession, a more permanent penitence. I say that, not because I have stock in *Sackcloth and Ashes 'R Us*, but because of the nature of this particular sin.

Racial haughtiness is hard to diagnose and even harder to dispel. Disguised, as it is, in plain sight as a "normal" feature of whiteness, this cancer of the soul is likely to be far more extensive and pernicious than we ever imagined. So, even when we do our best to eradicate the haughtiness in our hearts, we must still shy away from triumphant claims that we "got it all."

This confessional spirit must also continue because of the very nature of confession itself. Confession is agreeing with God and with those we have offended about the nature of our offense, taking responsibility for it, and seeking restoration. Though confession and the transformational process should allow us to live without being consumed by shame, if we put our faults so far behind us that we cease to have a sense of shame about the shameful legacy in which we have participated, we can end up minimizing the extent of our failure to the point that we are no longer in agreement with God or others.

To breezily move on from a shameful legacy of historic proportions would be a bit like Germany "getting over" the Holocaust. Indeed, recent polls show that many Germans would like to do just that.[4] Fortunately, their leaders have a more realistic view of the matter. Prime Minister Angela Merkel, in her address to the Israeli Knesset in 2008, stated that Germany continues to be "filled with shame"[5] for atrocities that occurred before her birth.

Some Christians think that forgiveness should vanquish all notions of shame. And it's certainly true that forgiveness helps us to not be dominated by shameful feelings. But once we have confessed our involvement in shameful things, we cannot subsequently diminish their importance or their impact on others without undermining the very agreement that made our confession meaningful and made forgiveness possible.

In Scripture shame remains an active principle even for those who have been forgiven. Paul, in his letter to the Romans, refers to the sins they used to commit as "the things you are now [currently] ashamed of." (Romans 6:21) The apostle himself never seems to have lost a sense of shame about his former persecution of the Church. He has the sense that it makes him unworthy to be an apostle (1 Corinthians 15:9) and thinks of himself as "the worst of sinners" (1 Timothy 1:15-16). While this apostle was a champion of justification, he never claimed to be "just-as-if-I'd" never sinned.

A continuing spirit of confession allows us to retain an appropriate sense of shame, one that keeps us in agreement with what God and others feel about haughtiness. Importantly, that penitent spirit also demonstrates that even if we are transformed and have ceased to exude haughtiness, we still accept responsibility for our sins, and we never cease to be sorry for them.

The ultimate purpose of confession is relational restoration. But even when we manage to reconcile with a certain individual, we are still a long way from racial reconciliation on a broad scale. If we want a truly "beloved community" we need an ongoing *spirit* of confession. If we hope to complete the healing process, the offending party can't just "get over it" and "move on," while the offended are still suffering the consequences of the offense,

Confession, therefore, should not be followed by a period. Confession, even when accompanied by forgiveness, is not the finish line, either personally or relationally. It is a right and restorative step, but it is still just a step in the process of relational healing and personal transformation.[e] As the title of this chapter indicates, confession is a bridge to reconciliation. But just as a bridge is not the same as the destination that lies on the other side, confession is not the same as reconciliation or transformation. In order to complete this process, other crucial steps remain. We continue exploring those steps in the next chapter, addressing the matter of redress.

---

[e] For a powerful example of an honest spirit of confession that incorporates some of the principles set forth in this chapter, see the following exchange between two men in my own congregation.
https://www.youtube.com/watch?v=IK4h7WmrsJI&t=5s

Chapter 26
The Case for Redress

I'll never forget Deacon Vaughn. I can still hear his voice today as if it were last Sunday. In the early eighties I had the privilege of serving as an associate minister in a black Baptist church, where the tradition of call and response was alive and well. And Deacon Vaughn was one of our more prolific participants. Whenever the preacher went on for a while about something that wasn't as it should be, "Deke" would let loose with his favorite line: "Fix it up now, Doc. Fix it up."

We've spent the lion's share of this book focusing on the problem of haughtiness from every angle. So much so that if Deacon Vaughn were still around, about now he'd be urging me to "fix it up." Indeed, in some ways we've already begun that conversation. We've discussed the preliminary steps to transformation, including confession. But there's a big difference between 'fessing up and fixing it up. Confession communicates regret about the past and an implicit desire for a distinct future, but it does not really remedy either the past or the future. "Fixing it up," however, requires substantive change.

But wait a minute. How can you change the past? The future, sure, it's still malleable. But changing the past? That seems counter-intuitive and just plain impossible. Yesterday has come and gone. We can confess it, but we can't change it. Or can we?

Well, yes and no. We cannot change the fact that an event occurred or the way that it impacted people in the past. We may, however, be able to change the construct of the past that exists in our individual and collective memory—and, hence, the way the past continues to project into the future. There is, you see, no neat dichotomy between past and present reality. What *is* right now is largely the continuation of what *has been*.

Though the past occurred some time ago, it is not really over, because we continue to experience it in the present—not as a current event but as a contextualized memory, one that is couched in the meaning that we associate with it and the consequences that have ensued from it. And because the past continues to project itself into the present, when we act to change the contemporary meaning and consequences of the past, we are, in a very real way, changing not only the present but the past as well.

Abraham Lincoln is a good example of someone who changed the past. When we consider how Lincoln changed history, we're usually thinking about how he affected the *future* course of American history. But in the process of changing the nation's future he also changed his own past.

In 1832, after losing his job, Lincoln ran for the state legislature. He lost that race. The next year he started a new business. It failed. Three years later he had a nervous breakdown. Along the way he was elected to the Illinois House of Representatives, but in 1838 he lost his bid to become the Speaker. Over the next ten years he tried twice to be nominated for a seat in Congress, losing both times. In 1856 he failed in his bid to be nominated for Vice President. Two years later, he lost a Senate race to Stephen Douglas.

By 1860, Lincoln's career was characterized by far more failures than successes. He could have allowed that loser status to define his present and, ultimately, his future. Like us, he couldn't change what had happened, but he did find something he could do in his present to alter the meaning and the ongoing consequences of the past. And, so it was, that when Abraham Lincoln became the 16th President of the United States, he changed his past legacy from one of frustrated failure to one of preparation for greatness.

Like Lincoln, we confront a past that needs a lot of changing—in this case a legacy of racial haughtiness and its resulting injustice. Like Lincoln, we can't change the historic acts and facts. White oppression and black disadvantage are what they are. But we can alter their meaning for the present and the future. We can do something about the resulting inequities that continue to undermine black wellbeing and poison black/white relations. And when we do—when we bring justice to bear upon injustice—we so alter its legacy that, in a very real sense, we are changing the past itself.

This is not some kind of mind-over-matter delusion. This is not revisionist history. It is not only *possible* to bring substantive moral change to the past; it is *essential* if we want to change our collective future. And one of the most powerful past-patching tools at our disposal is called redress.

When we hear the term *redress,* we naturally think of *seeking* redress. To seek redress is to demand justice for wrongs committed against you. That's a perfectly legitimate use of the word and, indeed, the most frequent one. My focus here, however, is on the far less common phenomenon of proactively redressing a situation—not *seeking* redress but *providing* redress.

If redress must be sought, that typically means that its provider is unwilling to voluntarily and proactively provide such compensation. Of course, even involuntary redress may offer a measure of justice and a useful benefit to those who have been wronged. But if the unjustly advantaged must be obligated, perhaps by force of law, to relinquish all or part of their advantage, such sacrifice says nothing about their own personal transformation and does little to promote relational healing.

There is, however, another option—voluntary redress. Voluntary redress contributes to all three of these goals: just compensation, personal transformation, and racial reconciliation. The only problem with voluntary redress is the lack of volunteers. That is, many whites balk at the prospect of providing redress to African Americans for the legacy of racial haughtiness and its social consequences. In this chapter we shall see *why* that mindset must change, and in the following chapter we'll examine *how* it can change.

There are two typical objections to the notion of racial redress. The first comes from whites who don't feel any personal responsibility for perpetrating racial injustice. They may genuinely regret the oppression suffered by African Americans; they just don't believe it's their fault. As a result, they would balk not only at the provision of redress but at the prospect of confession as well.

A second objection comes from those who might be willing to take responsibility for their own attitude of racial haughtiness—maybe even confess it. Perhaps they recognize a certain moral solidarity with the broader white legacy of haughtiness. Nevertheless, in their minds that broader connection remains rather fuzzy and indirect. They do not consider themselves substantially and personally responsible for the disadvantages borne by African Americans. Hence, they are not open to the idea of redress.

If, however, we want to experience the personal and interpersonal benefits of true moral transformation, it is precisely this overly individualistic white mindset that must be deconstructed. It is true, of course, that few white people living today took part in the overt and infamous acts of racial discrimination that systematically oppressed African Americans under legal cover. But the matter of our relationship to those bygone people and to the larger phenomenon of racial disadvantage is not so (pardon the pun) black and white.

Let's imagine that forty years ago my father conned your father out of his considerable life savings, allowing our family to become wealthy and plunging yours into poverty.[a] Your family naturally cried foul, and the police investigated, but they were never quite able to pin the crime on dear old dad. Eventually, he died and left that fortune to me.

For my part, I've tried my best to lead an honest life. I don't approve of my father's sometimes less-than-savory business practices. And I really wish you didn't have to struggle like you do. That's why every Thanksgiving I make sure that you're on the list at my church to receive a full turkey dinner. I just wish we could just let bygones be bygones, but you don't seem to be able to get over what happened way back when. What I need you to understand here is that I'm not the bad guy, just an innocent beneficiary.

Now, in your mind—and in the mind of any neutral observer—my efforts to distance myself from this injustice probably ring somewhat hollow. As far as you're concerned, I'm still implicated. Not because I personally took your family's money, but because I continue to benefit from the very injustice that continues to bring you misery. You're not interested in my "turkey" charity; what you want is justice. Unless and until I give the money back—or at the very least share it—you're not interested in being buddies.

Granted, my father was the original culprit and should, therefore, bear the primary moral responsibility. He should have recognized the error of his ways and redressed this situation himself. Of course, he didn't—but, then again, the original oppressors are rarely repentant.

But does his personal failure to redress this situation absolve the beneficiaries of his injustice from responsibility? And does my lack of personal participation in the original wrong give me the right to enjoy the advantages of injustice while you suffer the consequences? My guess is that most of those reading this parable are having a similar gut reaction—that my family owes your family something. That something is called redress, bringing justice to bear on injustice by some compensatory mechanism.

At this stage, I am clearly the only party capable of assuming moral responsibility, not because I created this problem but because of my solidarity with its injustice. Whether I like it or not, in this conflict the parties are defined along family lines. One family got fleeced, while the other family got rich. And I represent the offenders. I didn't ask for that role. Nonetheless, my social solidarity with the offender bequeathed it to me.

---

[a] This hypothetical situation is strictly a literary device and stands in stark contrast to my real father's upstanding character.

My solidarity is not only social but moral as well, because for all the years I have been the responsible party, I have in some sense followed in my father's footsteps by allowing this injustice to stand. In fact, I have deepened the offense, allowing its cruel consequences to endure while enjoying the ongoing benefits of my inaction. By ignoring the injustice with which I am associated, I have become a moral accessory after the fact.

My solidarity with this matter is also circumstantial. As the beneficiary of this ill-gotten gain, not only is it my duty to make redress, I am the *only* one in a position to do so. My father cannot do so—nor can the victims. I am the one holding your family's lost assets, and justice can be served only when I return them. Again, I didn't ask to be put in this position, but the circumstances of this case dictate the nature of my solidarity and, therefore, the nature of my moral responsibility.

So, the ball is in my court. But let's say that I drop that ball. That is, I live my life in comfortable style and never get around to redressing this injustice. As a result, its fruits are passed along to the next generation.

Are my heirs going to be more likely than I was to redress this wrong? Probably not. They have grown up with this money. It feels as if it's their own. And since I didn't want to tarnish the family legacy too much, they got a somewhat redacted version of the original story. Plus, now the wealth is split up among several people—and their spouses, who married into money and have absolutely no compunctions about keeping it.

If that generation fails to make redress, justice will almost certainly become an even less likely outcome as time goes on. It's hard to generate much moral outrage over some dastardly deed committed by one's great-great-great-great grandfather. Once injustice is diffused across an entire clan and across the centuries, the focus of moral responsibility begins to blur.

So, I recognize that, *subjectively* speaking, with the passing of various generations our sense of accountability for past injustices gets watered down. Those who enjoy a relative advantage *feel* more and more entitled to it and *feel* less and less responsible for the original injustice that created that gap.

Naturally, those on the opposite side of that divide are likely to entertain very different sentiments. But, over time, even their flame of initial outrage will likely turn into smoldering resentment or resignation. As demands for redress go unheeded, happy or not, people eventually settle into a new normal.

The question before us, however, is not just about the *feeling* of moral responsibility but about the *fact* of moral responsibility. Returning to my parable, does moral responsibility actually erode over time? If my family continues to ignore the demands of justice for four or five or even ten generations, do those very demands somehow, at some point, become illegitimate? Should we be rewarded for our persistent callousness?

Clearly, there is no magical moment in which past injustice ever turns into anything other than injustice. There is no statute of limitations on sin. Time may heal at least some wounds, but it does not rehabilitate evil actions. As long as injustice endures, redress remains the appropriate response.

Of course, the history of the world is replete with injustices (both individual and corporate), and these have left a convoluted legacy of winners and losers. It's neither possible nor practical to sort them all out, much less figure out what just compensation would look like in every case. Though redress remains theoretically appropriate, it's become hopelessly complicated. Many of the parties involved are no longer even identifiable as such.

But how about racial injustice? Has the passage of time so complicated the identification of oppressors and oppressed as to render redress impossible? Admittedly, it is more complicated—but not that complicated. The constituent aspects of solidarity—starting with social solidarity—can help us define contemporary moral responsibility. Does an identifiable social solidarity exist between the original perpetrators of racial injustice and its current beneficiaries? Between the original victims and the currently disadvantaged?

Social solidarity doesn't mean that all the beneficiaries are formally related to the original perpetrators or to each other, either biologically or otherwise. Social solidarity doesn't mean that every member of the beneficiary group participates equally in their relative advantages. Social solidarity doesn't even mean that everyone in the beneficiary group is better off than everyone in the disadvantaged group. Nor does it mean that everyone in the beneficiary group has consciously opted into it.

In my earlier parable, I didn't want to be the face of my family legacy, but, clearly, I was. In our current social setting the question is whether white people, as a collective, represent the legacy of racial oppression. Given the fact that the injustice in question was defined by race, that its benefits and disadvantages were distributed along racial lines, and that the same color line still largely defines the distribution of social wellbeing in this country, it would be hard to ignore or deny that color-coded identity.

Personally, I don't want to be identified with this oppressive legacy—but I am. That is the nature of being part of a collective. Sure, it's possible for people to distance themselves from that identification—but not by denying its existence or their association with it. Rather, we distinguish ourselves from that legacy by participating in the transformational process we're describing.

One of the reasons we need that transformational process is that our solidarity is, in fact, more than social; it's moral as well. We may not have reprised every form of past oppression, but, as we have seen repeatedly in these pages, we have likely participated in the legacy of haughtiness. To whatever extent we continue to embody this same moral flaw, albeit in a different historical context, we stand in moral solidarity with our forebears.

The survival of the racial hierarchy itself testifies to the endurance of haughtiness. It must somehow seem like a generally acceptable idea to us whites that we should continue to be the beneficiaries of injustice while black people continue to suffer its consequences. If we truly believed that the status quo was unacceptable, then we'd be hard pressed to explain why we have accepted it—unless we want to explain away our haughtiness by admitting to avarice or some other immoral motivation.

Our circumstantial solidarity with the white legacy also speaks to our moral responsibility. The white collective, vis-à-vis the black collective, has emerged from our historical milieu with a significant material advantage. As already noted, the median net worth of white families is ten times that of black families. That advantage is not just due to the luck of the draw. Nor is it due to white exceptionalism, an explanation that circles back to haughtiness. No reasonable, historically viable explanation for the ongoing asymmetry of our racial reality can ignore the role of institutionalized injustice.

We can blame past generations of now dead white people for marginalizing African Americans from economic opportunity. But we cannot deny the fact that we, the living generation, have maintained the structures that define that divide. Moreover, as the most recent beneficiaries of the racial hierarchy, we are the only ones who can redress this injustice. Neither the dead perpetrators nor the living victims can do so. Justice can be brought to bear on injustice only by the beneficiaries of that injustice.

Okay, so let's just say that we whites *do* bear some moral responsibility for the continuing impact of haughtiness, one that warrants redress. Haven't we, in fact, already provided that redress by leveling the racial playing field in our time? Haven't we already provided that redress by the many billions of dollars we've pumped into social welfare programs? Haven't we already provided that redress in the form of affirmative action?

Let's examine those questions one by one. First, is the leveling of the playing field a form of redress? As a society we did, of course, recognize that the racial injustices of yesteryear could not and should not continue, that it was necessary to create an infrastructure of equal opportunity. And we have moved in that direction, at least conceptually and legally.

Note, however, that even if equal opportunity were more of reality than it has yet become, it would *not* constitute a form of redress. Equal opportunity, as understood by most whites, means that everyone must play by the same rules going forward. But it contains no mechanism for compensating past injustice or even for rolling back its ongoing consequences. Such "leveling," even if effective, simply caps historic inequities at a given level.

Consider the case of two baseball teams. For lack of a better name we'll call them the White Sleeves and the Black Sleeves. Their contest is not a typical nine-inning game but a season-long marathon. The White Sleeves have the responsibility of supplying the baseballs for these games and see therein an opportunity. The balls used when they are at the plate are highly compressed and fly off the bat. When the Black Sleeves come to bat, however, the White Sleeves substitute squishier balls that rarely leave the infield.

The Black Sleeves team protests this unequal treatment, but the White Sleeves own the stadium, the baseballs, and, indeed, the league, so the objections fall on deaf ears. Not so surprisingly, two months into the season the White Sleeves hold an impressive lead of 300-30 (coincidentally, a 10:1 ratio). Though the Black Sleeves are totally demoralized, they nonetheless keep on playing, because the players need a paycheck.

Finally, however, the Black Sleeves have had enough and, risking their very livelihoods, they refuse to continue the game unless both teams use the same baseballs. This move takes the White Sleeves by surprise. They had never imagined that their underpaid opponents would risk it all in a game of financial chicken. The White Sleeves soon realize, however, that if the Black Sleeves don't play the game, there's no one to beat up on, and eventually they won't have a paycheck either. So, they agree to the Black Sleeves' demands and start using the same baseballs for everyone. This they do amidst great fanfare, trumpeting their own enlightenment and denouncing the "unequal era" as an anomaly in the illustrious White Sleeves baseball tradition.

It certainly does seem like progress. After all, everyone is now playing by the same rules. But just how long will it take the Black Sleeves to catch up? The obvious answer is that, if the two teams are of roughly equal ability, the

White Sleeves will always be ahead. (In fact, it's possible that such a huge deficit will tempt the Black Sleeves to play in a desperate style that ends up putting them even further behind, but let's not press the metaphor.) This is not a situation in which a couple of big innings will get the Black Sleeves back in the game. The only way they could ever catch up before the end of the season is if they are the far superior team.

The White Sleeves could, of course, create a truly level playing field by resetting the score to a tie. But that would require them to give up their advantage, something they're not about to do. So, there may be more than one way to define "level," but you can't expect to accomplish more than what you aim for. Without redressing past inequities, you can keep the game going with the perennial champs still in the lead, but it will never be a fair contest.

This illustrates the two reasons why our current version of a level playing field is not a form of redress. First, it is not designed to be compensatory, to achieve actual parity. And, second, the model works pretty much as designed.

Another favorite leveling metaphor is that of the rising tide that lifts all boats. But creating equality by means of a rising tide is not only ineffective—it's impossible. A rising tide does, indeed, have the advertised effect on boats, but, hydraulics and economics are governed by different principles. On the water, whether the tide is rising or falling, all boats in a given location are already on the same level. Not so in the world of people.

For the metaphor to have any relevance at all, we would have to imagine that, contrary to the laws of physics, the boats in question could actually rest on the water at very disparate elevations. Then along comes a rising tide that lifts them all. Of course, that doesn't really eliminate the problem either, because the relative differences remain.

Truth be told, even an appeal to science fiction can't rescue this analogy. Because, as it turns out, certain "boats" have a tendency to rise a lot faster than others.[b] Recent studies, including the bestselling *Capital in the Twenty-*

---

[b] According to the U.S. Census Bureau, between 1979 and 2014, income for the top 1% of households rose 221% (in constant dollars). Income for the next 19% rose by 69%. Meanwhile, working downward, income for the middle 60% of households (the middle class) rose only 28%. The bottom 20% rose even less—only 26%. So, even though all boats rose, those that were already highest rose fastest. During that same period, the top 1 percent's share of national income nearly doubled, from 11% to 20%. See: U.S. Census Bureau, "The Distribution of Household Income, 2014." March 2018. See the

First Century by French economist Thomas Picketty,[1] demonstrate that income generated by invested wealth (overwhelmingly controlled by whites) increases far more rapidly than wages, which depend on a growing overall economy. Òscar Jordà is an economist for the Federal Reserve Bank of San Francisco. In his working paper "The Rate of Return on Everything," he concludes: "Globally, and across most countries, the weighted rate of return on capital was twice as high as the growth rate in the past 150 years.[2/c]

If equal opportunity measures do not count as redress, then what can we say about the governmental assistance programs that have directed so many billions of dollars toward the needy in our society? Doesn't this amount to a huge wealth transfer—in effect, a form of redress?

However the cost of public assistance is calculated (and it has been calculated in a wide variety of ways by people trying to make their point), we can stipulate that public assistance amounts to a lot of money. But what is the relationship between that expenditure and the provision of redress for racial injustice? It's important to keep the following facts in mind.

Though the face of poverty in the mind of whites is likely to be a black face, and though African Americans are nearly three times as likely as whites to be living below the poverty line, the fact is that only about one in four Americans living in poverty is actually black.[3/d] So, yes, blacks benefit disproportionately from public assistance programs (because they represent a disproportionate slice of the poor), but the money in question can hardly be considered a race-*based* wealth transfer of any sort, much less redress for racial injustice, when its recipients are 70% more likely to be white than black.

Even if these programs were race-based, they still would not erase the historic wealth gap, simply because they are not designed to do so. Rather, they are designed to ameliorate certain *effects* of the income differential, not to alter its fundamental asymmetry. For proof we need look no further than

---

underlying data figures, "Figure 10: Cumulative Growth in Average Income Before Transfers and Taxes, by Income Groups, 1979 to 2014." Also, Jonathan Rothwell, "Myths of the 1 Percent: What Puts People at the Top." *The New York Times*. Nov. 17, 2017.
www.nytimes.com/2017/11/17/upshot/income-inequality-united-states.html.
[c] 6.25% (capital growth rate) vs. 2.87% (wage growth rate)
[d] I'm using the poverty line as a general demographic indicator of those who are likely to receive public assistance. Of course, many people living above the poverty line receive some form of public assistance, and others (both above and below that line) do not receive all the assistance they could.

the fact that we have been doing various forms of public assistance for decades, and the relative racial inequities haven't changed all that much.

What we're dealing with is not an actual transfer of "wealth." Yes, money is sacrificed on one side, a side that is disproportionately, but not exclusively, white. But the individual amounts received on the other side are insufficient to create genuine "wealth." Despite the oft-repeated anecdotal accounts of people who game the system to get rich, the actual number of such individuals might be compared to the people who amass money by stealing it from the bank as opposed to those who amass money by putting it in the bank.

I don't mean to say that public assistance is ineffectual—if its purpose is understood. It is a safety net that helps keep people from becoming destitute, a platform from which a limited number of exceptional or exceptionally lucky people may even work their way out of poverty. But that is not redress. It is not a tool for righting racial injustice, because it is not race-based and is not even designed to solve the problem of relative disadvantage.

The case of affirmative action is somewhat different. Affirmative action *is* designed to compensate for historic disadvantage along racial lines. And, over the last half century, it has boosted black opportunities in education, employment, contracts, etc. The American Civil Liberties Union (ACLU) calls it: "one of the most effective tools for redressing the injustices caused by our nation's historic discrimination against people of color and women, and for leveling what has long been an uneven playing field."[4]

But there are problems with this "solution." Some of the problems are legal in nature, as the Supreme Court has become increasingly antagonistic to the very premise of affirmative action. The Court now requires that any law based on racial distinctions be justified by a "compelling state interest" and "narrowly framed to accomplish that purpose."[5/e] Some justices, however, consider this filter, known as "strict scrutiny," to be always or nearly always fatal to any race-based distinctions. The late Justice Antonin Scalia made it quite clear: "In my view, government can never have a "compelling interest" in discriminating on the basis of race in order to "make up" for past racial discrimination in the opposite direction."[6] Whatever its constitutional merits, this legal predisposition drastically limits governmental options for redressing historic, multi-generational injustice and its continuing effects.

---

[e] This is still the case at this writing, but the Court is evolving in a direction that would seem even less friendly to affirmative action.

Not only does affirmative action face significant legal obstacles; it has political problems as well. Promoting affirmative action is not a priority for white voters, which means that it doesn't generate much enthusiasm in Congress. A 2016 PRRI/Brookings survey showed that 57% of whites consider discrimination *against whites* to be as big a problem as discrimination against blacks.[7] When asked which racial groups face "a lot of discrimination" today, those who voted for Donald Trump are twice as likely to name whites as to name blacks.[8] Those whites who do support affirmative action are more likely to favor it for women than for racial minorities.[9]

Though some polls have historically found that most whites *favor* affirmative action, on closer inspection this support starts to look a bit too shaky to make much difference in the real world. Indeed, it's hard to find recent polling on this subject, I suspect because it's increasingly hard to ask the question in a meaningful fashion. For instance, in 2013, Gallup asked: "Do you generally favor or oppose affirmative action programs for racial minorities?" 51% of whites said "yes."[10] But an NBC/Wall Street Journal poll from that same year asked respondents to choose between two statements, one supporting affirmative action for minorities and the other suggesting that affirmative action unfairly discriminates against whites. Framed this way, only 34% of whites supported affirmative action, while 56% opposed it.[11]

So, yes, some people will still support something called "affirmative action"—if it doesn't advantage black people at the expense of white people. But doesn't such a view of affirmative action beg the entire question? To mean anything at all, affirmative action must mean more than just anti-discrimination in an infinitely expanding pool of opportunity.

It seems that a lot of people miss the following simple yet critical distinction: how much opportunity exists and how equitably it is distributed are two entirely different questions. Just creating more opportunity will not automatically increase the share of it enjoyed by those who have been categorically denied. But even if those who have been categorically denied were to achieve equal access to all current and future opportunities, that still would not serve as compensation for the deprivations of the past.

Given the current legal and political landscape, affirmative action is simply not a viable mechanism for large-scale redress. Even in its most ambitious moment it was never applied on a scale capable of resolving the problem of racial inequality. And we are way beyond its most ambitious moment. If we can't even keep straight who the victims are, then the whole notion of redress itself is reduced to absurdity.

One aspect of the unfairness complaint may have some merit, though not for the reasons typically adduced. The way in which affirmative action is conceived and applied forces a very limited number of individuals to bear the brunt of white sacrifice—and those few miss out on a contract, a job, or a university admission. The problem, then, is that because we have been unwilling to collectively assume the responsibility of redress, to jointly bear the burden of creating an equitable society, we allow a major burden to fall upon a few rather than placing a minor burden on the many—and then conclude that the concept itself rather than its execution is faulty.

White concerns about the unfairness of affirmative action would logically apply to any form of redress. The bottom line is that we don't want to be stuck providing compensation for somebody else's sins. But, as we have seen, when the benefits and the deprivations of injustice are passed down in a multi-generational fashion, the only people who have the wherewithal to effectively address that inequality are the current beneficiaries. Without redress, injustice is left to stand without any mechanism for bringing justice to bear on it.

Maybe redress is not always "fair." But what constitutes fairness in a benign moral equilibrium must certainly be different than what constitutes fairness in a malignant moral disequilibrium such as the one we have created throughout our history. Once an unfair advantage is created, there is no pool of neutral advantage from which the corresponding disadvantage can be compensated. Are we so naïve or callous as to think that historic injustice must inconvenience only its intended victims? If it seems unfair to be stuck with a moral responsibility based on one's solidarity with past injustice, consider the alternative of being stuck with a material disadvantage because of the legacy of haughtiness. Is that fair? A proprietary focus on fairness that looks forward but not backward is a luxury enjoyed only by those holding the advantage.

The biblical writers spend a great deal of time talking about how to bring justice to bear upon injustice. In Scripture, justice is meted out upon the guilty in the form of judgment. Justice is sacrificially satisfied in the case of the redeemed. And justice compensates the disadvantaged in the case of redress.

Perhaps the most common form of redress to be found in the pages of Scripture is that of restitution. This compensation took a variety of forms, ranging from the simple return of the unjust gain (Ex. 21:33-36); to the addition of 20% (Lev. 6:1-7); to the return of two (Ex. 22:4), four (Ex. 22:1), or even five (Ex. 22:1) times the lost value. Some of these cases may involve a mixing of retributive and compensatory considerations, like in the case of punitive damages granted in our civil justice system. Though compensatory justice may be applied somewhat differently from one era to another, whether we're talking about ancient Israel or contemporary America, the principle of restitution is an essential part of righting a past injustice—and of fulfilling our responsibility to God and others.

Indeed, our willingness to redress past wrongs is a sign of the sincerity of our repentance. The story of Zacchaeus, recorded in Luke chapter 19, is instructive in this regard. More than just a tax collector, Zacchaeus was a *chief* tax collector in the important trade city of Jericho, one of the three principle tax centers the Romans had established in Palestine. He was, therefore, a major player in a thoroughly corrupt system.

Now, tax collectors are never going to win any popularity contests, even when they are honest and represent a government that the taxpayers consider legitimate. But, as a collaborator with the occupying Roman government, Zacchaeus was viewed as a traitor to Jewish interests. Moreover, tax collectors enriched themselves by extorting more money than was due to Rome. So, when the people criticized Jesus for eating at the house of a "sinner" like Zacchaeus, that classification represented both public perception and spiritual reality. This man was undoubtedly guilty of both oppression and injustice.

The result of Jesus' visit, however, was a happy one. Before he left, the Lord announced that salvation had come to the house of Zacchaeus on that very day (Lk. 19:9). Note, however, what prompted Jesus' observation. It was not Zacchaeus's profession of faith as such but his promise of making redress. The previous verse tells us that "Zacchaeus stood up and said, "Look, Lord! Here and now I give half of my possessions to the poor, and if I have cheated anybody out of anything, I will pay back four times the amount."[f]

The law would have required Zacchaeus to refund his ill-gotten gain plus a 20% penalty (or at most double the amount stolen). It's not clear whether Zacchaeus was aware of this legal obligation, but his offer to voluntarily (and perhaps intuitively) go above and beyond speaks to his change of heart.

---

[f] The phrase "if I have cheated…" does not put Zacchaeus's guilt in doubt. The Greek grammar (a first-class condition) makes it clear that the protasis of the conditional statement was, in fact, true. In any case, the matter was not in doubt, as everyone knew that tax collectors made their money by cheating.

In addition to his exaggerated, voluntary restitution, however, he also made another commitment not required by the law in any form—that he would give half of all his possessions to the poor. It is impossible to know the moral logic that led Zacchaeus to this determination, so I don't want to go too far out on a speculative limb here. But, unless this is just a penitent reflex devoid of any practical connection to existing inequities, this money would seem to be yet another form of redress. In this case, Zacchaeus was not offering compensation to individual taxpayers whom he had defrauded, as that offense was addressed by his fourfold restitution. Here it seems that he was concerned about a basic structural issue, the divide between rich and poor. Zacchaeus was under no illusion that he could singlehandedly eliminate poverty across the entire Jewish society. But it does seem as if his repentance motivated him to make a significant personal contribution toward the closing of that gap.

Yes, Zacchaeus's redress was inspired by the implications of personal righteousness, but it clearly had a social/relational element as well. His offenses were committed against people who were, as a result, defrauded and disadvantaged by his actions. We don't know how the relationship between Zacchaeus and the Jewish community proceeded from that point. But his over-the-top actions at the very least paved the way for reconciliation, something he could not have accomplished by offering his victims ten cents on the dollar.

The impressive thing about Zacchaeus was how his desire to make redress followed spontaneously from his repentance. He did not have to be cajoled; he didn't come kicking and screaming or ranting and rationalizing. Relational justice does not respond to the demands of either retribution or strict compensation. Rather, it urgently and passionately goes beyond what is required in order to lovingly restore trust and repair relationships. How different might today's racial landscape look, if the contemporary white followers of Jesus had taken their cue from this enthusiastic example of redress?

There is another biblical passage that speaks powerfully to the notion of redress, not so much on a personal level as on a community/societal level. In Isaiah 58 the nation of Israel was seeking after God (v. 2), trying to gain his favor by an act of religiosity—that is, by fasting. Jehovah, however, insisted that he was looking for a different kind of fast (vv. 6-7), a practical activity that will "loose the chains of injustice and untie the cords of the yoke, to set the oppressed free and break every yoke... to share your food with the hungry and to provide the poor wanderer with shelter—when you see the naked, to clothe them, and not to turn away from your own flesh and blood."

The good news was that the "haves" of Hebrew society did not have to continue in their role of oppressors. They had it in their power to rebuild what was broken, qualifying for the title, "repairer of the breach" (v. 12, KJV). How? In verses 9b-11 the prophet called upon them to "do away with the yoke of oppression...[and] spend yourselves in behalf of the hungry and satisfy the needs of the oppressed." That is, they had to dismantle their institutionalized injustice and sacrificially help those they had disadvantaged.

If we substitute our own unjust racial hierarchy for the social injustices in ancient Israel, what might God be calling us to do? Perhaps we have done *something*. But God doesn't say to do *something*. He says to *fix* the problem. Anything less is less than justice, and anything less than justice is injustice.

We continue to clamor, "God bless America," but there's no indication in Scripture that societal blessings are extended to those who clamor but don't qualify. God does not take orders from the entitled. If we desire to see his benevolent hand, we must pay attention to his conditions.

Whether the American people are ready to embrace justice, even when it hurts, seems somewhat doubtful, given our track record. But what about the people of God, those who are ostensibly committed to obeying his voice? We surely want God's blessing. But if our vision and our practice of social justice is not up to God's expressed standard, how can we expect his approval?

If we are sincerely seeking God's favor, we must begin by doing whatever is within our personal and institutional power to redress racial injustice. Then, in our prophetic role vis-à-vis the secular state, we must speak truth to power, advocating on behalf of justice for those to whom it has been denied. In other words, we must do the very thing we haven't done.

In recent times many white Christians, along with their institutions, have recognized and even decried the legacy of racial injustice. But that should not be confused with moral leadership. Ours has not been a pro-active, prophetic voice. We have far more often been the caboose than the locomotive of social change, dragged in the direction of justice by secular societal enlightenment.

Now is the time, however, to recognize our complicity in this injustice and to "fix it up." We have it in our power to become repairers of the breach, part of the solution rather than part of the problem. It is a challenge only we can meet, and we can meet it only when we enthusiastically embrace redress.

Chapter 27
The Provision of Redress

Having made a case for why redress is both appropriate and necessary, we now move from the principle of redress to its provision. I may have lost some readers in the last chapter—those who are unwilling to contemplate redress in principle, regardless of what it looks like. I may well lose some more readers in this chapter, once they see what redress might actually look like. Nevertheless, for those of us who take this moral responsibility seriously, it would be irresponsible not to talk about the how-to.

I do not pretend that this is an easy question to answer. That's why it's important to be convinced of the rightness of racial redress before fleshing out its practical particulars. Otherwise, we'll be put off by the sheer complexity of the matter, not to mention the sacrifice. Let's begin with the question of who should provide redress, focusing on three possibilities: a national response, an ecclesiastical response, and a personal response.

A broad national and official program of compensation would acknowledge the breadth of this injustice and the complicity of our government in perpetuating it. Because of the resources it can muster, such a response offers the best chance for dealing with racial advantage and disadvantage, to really accomplish redress rather than simply work toward it.

There are, however, a couple of major problems with redress at this level. The first is political; indeed, few initiatives are more unpopular among white Americans than racial redress at the federal level.

A 2014 YouGov poll registered white opinion on the matter.[1] Only 21% believed the federal government should even apologize for slavery.[a] Only 19% favored education or job training programs for slave descendants,[2] and only 6% supported cash payments.[3/b] A 2016 Marist poll posed the question a

---

[a] For a review of "official" apologies already offered and why this question is still being asked, see: www.scottgarber.com/was_notes.pdf, Note 27.1

[b] For the first two questions/answers cited here the black response was almost the exact opposite of its white counterpart. On the question of cash payments, blacks still came down on the opposite side of the question, but their responses were less monolithic than those of whites. 59% of blacks supported cash reparations, 19% opposed them, and 22% were unsure.

bit differently, asking about unspecified reparations for African Americans. 81% of whites opposed reparations for the descendants of slaves, and 85% opposed reparations for black U.S. citizens in general.[4]

At present there are some 2020 Democratic primary hopefuls who are making noise about reparations. It's encouraging to see the notion of redress enter the national conversation, but thus far the amounts being bandied about are rather symbolic. So, we may now face a two-pronged challenge: overcoming the injustice of doing nothing, while avoiding the injustice of doing too little—making a mockery of real redress and then washing our hands of the matter. It's not going to be easy. Congressman John Conyers introduced reparations legislation in every Congress from 1989-2017.[5/c] It never got out of committee.

A second option for providing redress would be to spearhead a racial justice movement within churches. Indeed, many of the church bodies in the U.S. have already voiced some sort of an apology, though few of these have been accompanied by any substantive redress.

Nevertheless, churches have the institutional potential to make a significant contribution. Because of the continuing racial divide in American congregations, such redress would be more demographically fine-tuned than a national response. That is, it would be a mostly white Christian overture toward the black population. By contrast, a national response might very well involve every racial collective, including African Americans, in the provision of redress. An ecclesiastical initiative would also help turn churches into the societal locomotive on a moral issue on which they have long been the caboose. In addition, the Church's spiritual framework would allow redress to function in the context of moral transformation. That would enhance its value as a healing overture.

Despite the promise and the benefits inherent in this sort of church-based cooperation, however, there are difficulties. Many white Christians don't see this kind of action as part of the mission of the Church, so they would just categorically dismiss it. For them, if this is an issue at all it is a "political" issue, and that would preclude the possibility of it also being a spiritual issue.

---

[c] Conyers died in 2019 after his retirement in 2018. Rep. Sheila Jackson Lee took up this mantel in the 116th Congress, re-sponsoring Bill H. R. 40 (named for the infamous 40 acres and a mule). See endnote for text of the bill.

While Christians might differ about whether promoting social harmony is part of the core mission of the Church, at the very least, it should be clear to all that haughtiness is antithetical to the mission of the Church. When the Church and its constituents become notorious for their haughtiness, failing in their fundamental responsibilities of righteousness and unity, rectifying that failure surely goes to the heart of what God has called us to be and to do.

An ecclesiastical approach also has its practical complications. Fewer and fewer "white" churches are *entirely* white. In fact, as of 2012, only 11% of all churchgoers attended an *entirely* white congregation.[6/d] Though the minority presence in white churches is typically quite small, this mixing nevertheless tends to blur the lines between those providing redress and those receiving it.

A bigger practical problem is that church leaders are sensitive to political issues that divide their constituents, as this one most certainly would. Unlike the citizens of a country, church attenders are not a captive audience.[e] Support redress, and a lot of people will vote with their feet. Therefore, even if convinced of the moral relevance of redress, church leaders are unlikely to go to the mat for something that might derail everything else.

A third option would be to foment acts of redress among individual white Christians who are sensitive to the issue. This approach enjoys several advantages. From a demographic perspective, the redress would be accurately targeted. It could create a positive atmosphere for reconciliation among the people involved. It would maximize the potential for personal transformation on the part of the white participants. And it bypasses the sticky wicket of using institutional church/governmental resources to accomplish redress.

It's not clear, however, how many individuals would participate in such redress without some measure of institutional direction. Will white leaders dare to beat that drum? There is also the matter of scale. The anecdotal good that an *ad hoc* group can accomplish might be inspirational, but does it have the critical mass necessary to alter the landscape of black disadvantage? Can it ever be scaled to a tipping point that generates a broader movement toward racial reconciliation? And if the goodwill of these few is juxtaposed with the overwhelming unwillingness of the rest, which message will resonate?

---

[d] 69% of white churches contained one or more blacks, 62% one or more Hispanics, and 48% one or more Asians.

[e] Technically, Americans could emigrate to any number of countries, but that is not a realistic option for very many people.

Given these limitations, it would seem unwise to limit efforts at redress to the individual level. And, yet, I believe that personal initiative is essential. Why? As we have seen, individuals are implicated in haughtiness and its concomitant sins and, therefore, bear a personal responsibility regarding redress. If we care about our personal integrity, we do not have the luxury of waiting for consensus-building to reach critical mass.

I don't mean to suggest that individual initiative is a replacement for broader action. But we must begin by taking responsibility for that which we can control rather than allowing our moral reactions to be dictated by that which we cannot control. How can we expect others to join us in broader action until we first demonstrate our fidelity to godly justice by putting our money where our mouth is?

What might these individual acts of redress look like? If those providing the redress had some historical connection to a specific person or persons to whom they feel indebted, that would certainly shape their response. For most of us, however, the channeling of redress ends up being more symbolic. That does not mean that the benefit it offers is less substantial, only that its targeting is more indirect, with the recipients determined by opportunity rather than by an individual's connection to some specific racial injustice.

Individual redress is a compensatory act by someone on one side of the historic racial hierarchy to a person or persons on the other side of that hierarchy, bringing justice to bear on injustice. This may take the form of a financial investment and/or some personal engagement designed to enhance the well-being of others. For our family, it involves both. We open our home to young people who are pursuing internships, and we help create networking opportunities for those seeking employment. But it also means dedicating a significant portion of our retirement savings to this sort of economic justice.

Individual redress recognizes historic injustice and seeks to balance the scales by providing some of what has so often been denied. That compensation could be for collective and inter-generational sin and/or for our own personal haughtiness and its accompanying injustice. Though individual efforts cannot singlehandedly right all wrongs, attempts at redress must be both intentional and substantive if they are to be meaningful.

Speaking of meaning, that brings us to a rather tricky aspect of individual redress. Naturally, such redress has meaning for the provider, but one must take care in choosing how that redress is directed. Just because black Americans have been collectively disadvantaged relative to white Americans, it does not follow that every black person either wants or is willing to receive compensation. Understandably, some would resent the social stigma inherent in receiving assistance from a white peer, and hardly anyone wants to be cast as the proxy for an entire race.

Of course, there are many fine organizations to which white individuals could channel finances in a way that would benefit both the African-American community as well as particular people who have been disadvantaged because of racial haughtiness. These organizations are not, however, set up to facilitate such giving as an expression of (Christian) racial redress, so it's unlikely that the beneficiaries would know why the money was given. The financial transfer would still be a kind of compensatory justice, but when the meaning behind it gets lost, so too does the opportunity to express remorse and to create a climate for relational healing.

Observing these difficulties, I got to thinking. I saw the importance of providing redress through some entity that provided a layer of anonymity, while communicating the moral rationale behind that redress. I saw that pooling the funds of concerned whites could accomplish more and make a more poignant statement about our desire to penitently do justice and to humbly seek racial healing. But I also saw that, apparently, nobody was facilitating that kind of response. And I was convinced that few white individuals were going to figure it out on their own.

In the end, it just didn't seem responsible to call on readers to respond to this message of this book without pointing them to a practical path forward. So, I started a non-profit to do just that. *Overcoming* identifies opportunities to make a difference within historically disadvantaged communities. It partners with organizations that have the infrastructure to maximize our impact, and it directs financial and personal resources in the name of Christian racial redress. This might take the form of scholarships, reintegration assistance for those who have been incarcerated, micro-loans, etc. It can also mean putting people who have knowledge and skills and opportunity to offer in touch with those who would benefit from such contacts.

I am donating all the net proceeds from this book to benefit the mission of *Overcoming*. I am also inviting others to consider how they can partner with us to fulfill their own personal responsibility and to be part of a Christian movement for racial redress. Visit www.RedemptiveRedress.org to see how *Overcoming* might help you fulfill God's call to racial justice and healing.

In this chapter, we have discussed three different approaches to racial redress (individual, ecclesiastical, governmental). Each has its own strengths and weaknesses. In order to maximize their strengths and minimize their weaknesses, ideally, we need to pursue all three simultaneously. Government action offers the most comprehensive response, but I'm not holding my breath that it's going to happen soon, at least not on any significant scale. That's why individuals, churches, and organizations like *Overcoming* must step up and provide moral leadership that translates into moral leverage.

The faithfulness of individual Christians and the churches to which they belong can function as a moral lever, inviting even broader participation. But consider how a lever works. It's a useful tool for lifting heavy loads, but a lever provides leverage only when you push on it. As Christians, we have an individual and collective responsibility to do what is right (the lever); but we also have a prophetic responsibility to urge our society/government to do what is right (the push).

That brings me to the question of what an official national approach to redress might look like. To some extent I hesitate to go there, because my purpose in this chapter is not to advocate for a particular program of reparations. The point I'm trying to make is that redress is a necessary moral response, if we want to transform the white legacy of haughtiness. That said, it is neither fair nor helpful to advocate a response that is so vague as to be inscrutable. What principles, then, should govern a national response?

In order to accomplish the moral and social purposes outlined above, national redress must be *substantial*, moving the marginalized toward real parity. Redress must mean more than just the right to maintain one's current level of disadvantage or to inch in the direction of equality. It must recognize the value of what has been taken from black Americans in uncompensated or undercompensated labor over the centuries, what Ta-Nehisi Coates has called "the national sin of plunder."[7]

How much would it take to redress this national sin of plunder? Various calculations have been undertaken to quantify the value of uncompensated slave labor. These inevitably involve some speculation, but it's not difficult to arrive somewhere north of a trillion dollars (without even considering the value of underpaid work during the Jim Crow era or compounded interest on the debt, which can balloon the figure considerably).[f]

---

[f] For a sample of such calculations, see: www.newrepublic.com/article/

If redress were based on the phantom "forty acres and a mule" formula, in today's dollars it would come to $2.1 trillion.[g] And that's just the land value, not counting the mules. There is, however, an actual precedent for reparations by the federal government—the compensation paid to Japanese Americans who were incarcerated in internment camps during World War II. Take the $20,000 paid to each eligible Japanese American and factor it by the scale of officially-sanctioned black bondage, and the result is $2 trillion.[h] Professor Thomas Craemer of the University of Connecticut has done excellent and detailed calculations based on relevant reparations theory and practice across the globe and throughout history. He estimates "the present value of U.S. slave labor in 2009 dollars to range from $5.9 to $14.2 trillion."[8]

I use these calculations for illustrative purposes, not to lobby for this or that one as the most appropriate basis for redress. It is important, however, to acknowledge the true scale of the plunder. For once that scale is acknowledged, it becomes obvious that any less-than-substantial attempt at redress could end up being be more offensive than conciliatory.

This kind of historical redress is necessarily symbolic to some degree, because nothing can ever recompense the staggering material and intangible losses suffered by a whole people throughout nearly the entirety of our history. Ta-Nehisi Coates stated it so eloquently:

> Perhaps no number can fully capture the multi-century plunder
> of black people in America. Perhaps the number is so large
> that it can't be imagined, let alone calculated and dispensed.

117856/academic-evidence-reparations-costs-are-limited.

[g] That's approximately 17,000,000 black households x 40 acres at $3,080/acre. Sources: Households – *U.S. Census Bureau, Current Population Survey, 2016, Annual Social and Economic Supplement*, "Table H1: Households by Type and Tenure of Householder for Selected Characteristics," $/Acre – *Land Values 2017 Summary*, USDA, August 2017, p. 4. www.usda.gov/nass/PUBS/TODAYRPT/land0817.pdf.

[h] The average Japanese internment was about 2.5 yrs. The average life of a slave was something more than 25 yrs., or 10x longer. Approximately 10 million blacks were enslaved in what is now the U.S. Multiply the $20,000 paid to each Japanese victim by 10 (years) and then again by 10 million people, and it comes to $2 trillion—about $65,500 per adult African American (per 2016 American Community Survey, U.S. Census = 30,520,180). Even if this calculation were limited to those enslaved after the U.S. became an independent nation, the total figure would still be more well above $1 trillion. For further background, see: www.scottgarber.com/was_notes.pdf, Note 27.2.

> But I believe that wrestling publicly with these questions
> matters as much as—if not more than—the specific answers
> that might be produced. An America that asks what it owes its
> most vulnerable citizens is improved and humane. An America
> that looks away is ignoring not just the sins of the past but the
> sins of the present and the certain sins of the future.[9]

Perhaps the best way to approach redress is not by means of a mathematical calculation but rather a moral one. If whites and blacks are truly equal, and if truly equal opportunity had existed throughout our history, then per capita wealth should now be roughly equal across racial lines. So, if we really want to know the extent to which black people have been defrauded, not only during slavery but even since that time, all we have to do is observe the current racially-defined economic disparity—and redress that disparity.

Now, I imagine that this accounting proposal will prove unacceptable (or at least unappealing) to many whites. But is there, in fact, a flaw in my moral logic or, rather, is the problem simply that I am taking the notion of racial equality to its morally logical conclusion? Does our carefully camouflaged haughtiness inadvertently blow its cover at the suggestion that black people might have achieved actual parity with whites in a truly equal environment?

Not only should redress be *substantial*; to be truly transformational, it must also be *ethically intentional*. That is, at least a significant number of whites must be committed to this course of action because they desire justice for others and desire to do justice themselves. If used merely to mollify black demands or to assuage white guilt, redress becomes little more than a stratagem designed to maximize those results with the least possible sacrifice.

Of course, any level of redress, regardless of its motivation, provides a practical benefit for the disadvantaged. But I am aiming higher than that, because only ethically intentional redress has the power to be restorative. A sincere apology reinforced by substantial compensation can elevate our act of penitence to what law professor Roy Lavon Brooks calls "atonement."[i]

---

[i] Christians, of all people, should be sensitive to the relationship between atonement and reconciliation. Brooks explains it's importance: "Atonement makes reconciliation possible by satisfying the demands of justice. Atonement, however, entails much more than the tender of an apology. It also requires making restitution… reparations commensurate with the atrocity. Reparations are essential to atonement, because they make apologies believable." (Roy Lavon Brooks, *Atonement and Forgiveness: A New Model for Black Reparations.* (Berkeley, University of California Press) 2004, 142).

Atonement satisfies the offended in a way that invites forgiveness and lays the foundation for a beloved community. This sort of redress is, according to Coates: "…more than recompense for past injustices—more than a handout, a payoff, hush money, or a reluctant bribe. What I'm talking about is a national reckoning that would lead to spiritual renewal."[10]

Is this too much to hope for? It seems safe to say that there is presently no groundswell of white moral momentum in the direction of racial redress. But momentum doesn't just happen; it is created by motion. And that motion will be generated by those who recognize the sin of haughtiness, who sorrow over it, who turn away from it, who confess it, and who then engage in and press for redress from whatever platform is theirs. This generation of white Christians has the power to unlock the transforming power of redress, and in so doing to unlock the door to genuine reconciliation.

Chapter 28

Replacement Therapy

"When is a door not a door?" asks the old children's riddle. The answer? "When it's ajar." Okay, it's not hilariously, ha-ha funny, but in some sideways fashion this riddle serves to remind us of an important moral principle—that we cease to be what we used to be only when we become something else.[1]

Think about it. A liar, someone characterized by deceit, does not become a truthful person because today that liar told the truth. You do not cease to be a thief because you haven't stolen anything this week or this month. You don't cease to be unfaithful just because you are between affairs.

Moral transformation occurs only when we regularly begin to do right in the very situations in which we used to do wrong. That is, we cease to be characterized by a given moral failure only when we become characterized by its opposite orientation. The Apostle Paul referred to this dynamic in Ephesians 4:28, saying: "Anyone who has been stealing must steal no longer, but must work, doing something useful with their own hands, that they may have something to share with those in need."

I began this book wondering aloud about the kind of people we white people are—what it is it about white identity that has long prompted us to not only *do* wrong to our black counterparts but, even more fundamentally, to *be* wrong in our relational orientation. The answer I have proposed is that this dysfunction is driven by racial haughtiness, a sinful attitude deeply embedded in white identity. In order to demonstrate the reality of this immoral constant, we have tracked its many manifestations, connecting the dots from yesterday to today and from society in general to each of us individually. Before we can right what is wrong, we must first recognize what is wrong.

Recognition is an important first step, but it is just one step. Recognition must lead to sorrow and to a determination to turn from haughtiness, to confess it, and to redress its consequences. But even when we have done all this, we still have not completed process of transformation. Thoroughgoing transformation does not occur until the door becomes "a-jar," until we become something other than what we used to be. This change is not just the tweaking of our outward behavior, but the very renewing of our minds (Rom. 12:2).

This moral metamorphosis is a kind of replacement therapy in which a sinful orientation is supplanted by its moral opposite. In the case of racial haughtiness, we are not just talking about something bad we sometimes do, or even something bad we habitually do. This is a *state of being* sin. It is about our identity, about who we are (and who *I* am as a subset of that *we*) with respect to another group of people. Until we replace that flawed aspect of our identity with its moral opposite, we have not truly addressed our moral failure.

Before I comment on the opposite of haughtiness, let's review the nature of the problem itself. As we have seen, haughtiness is a condescending form of pride that rests on our own supposed superiority and is bolstered by the supposed unworthiness of others. In past eras, this relative worth was typically viewed as inherent in the respective racial identities themselves and was regarded as a matter of fact. Today that sense of superiority may not be regarded as objectively true but remains subjectively real, an affective attitude that is more likely to be based on culture and/or circumstance. But make no mistake; haughtiness it was and haughtiness it remains.

But this spiritual problem does not exist in a social vacuum. Haughtiness wants to structure society and social relationships in such a way as to reflect its hierarchy of deservedness. Therefore, as we seek to replace haughtiness with its moral opposite, we must also pay careful attention to the social structures and institutions that have grown up around it. We may not have the unilateral power to undo all of this, but in order to replace haughtiness with its opposite we must at least become a hierarchy-attenuating individual rather than a hierarchy-enhancing individual. That is, we must move from active or even passive support of the racial hierarchy to active opposition.

Trying to change our own personal haughtiness without also changing the racial hierarchy that fosters and sustains it, is morally short-sighted. Our social structures have created well-worn relational and attitudinal ruts. If we do not change that hierarchy—or at least distance ourselves from it—we will continue to fall back into the same old historic patterns, perhaps changing our minds but not significantly altering our behavior or relationships.

Speaking of relationships, until we stand actively and intentionally opposed to the racial hierarchy, we cannot bridge the racial divide. It's rather incongruous to try to create personal community with our black brothers and sisters, while continuing to identify with, tolerate, and even protect the racial hierarchy that relegates them to a disadvantaged position.

Inevitably, this relational consideration has political implications. That consideration may or may not dictate a party affiliation, for in recent American history one party has been largely tone-deaf to these considerations, while the other has been more talk than action, and even the actions it has taken have generally lacked both imagination and a heart for the true moral issues. When it comes to voting, we may have to choose between existing options, but the pressure we put on the political process itself should be that of a prophetic moral voice, urging our society toward racial justice and broad reconciliation, rather than an adversarial and entrenched inequality. The best answers to these problems may not be any of the existing ones, so godly creativity is needed to move our society toward racial healing.

In order to carry out that prophetic role with integrity, however, we must begin by changing ourselves. The world within us is where we possess the greatest control over the transformational process and where we gain the leverage to transform the world around us.

So, then, what is the opposite of haughtiness? What would this door look like if it were not a door?

There is certainly a sense in which *equality* is the flip-side of haughtiness. Ontologically we are all equal as fellow bearers of the image of God. Hamartiologically we are all equal as fellow sinners in need of God's grace. Soteriologically we are equal as undeserving recipients of God's grace. As the Apostle Paul made clear, that leaves no room for boasting or any sense of superiority whatsoever (Rom 3:27 ff.).

As we have seen, however, it is possible to intellectually accept the principle of equality without relinquishing our affective attitudes of haughtiness. Moreover, Scripture seems to suggest that the real opposite of haughtiness is not just equality but, rather, humility.

We tend to think of humility as a self-reflexive attitude of mind that involves a relative devaluation of one's worthiness or importance. The biblical notion includes this sense, of course, but it is more robust, as determined by the several Greek/Hebrew words so translated and the broad range of contexts in which they appear. Quite often *humility* is associated with the non-aggressive quality of meekness or gentleness. It is frequently a literal abasement of status or living conditions. Sometimes humility is a recognition of our lowliness vis-à-vis God's glory and/or holiness.

The notion of humility as the attitudinal antithesis of haughtiness, however, also appears in Scripture. David affirmed that God saves the humble, while bringing down the haughty (2 Sam. 22:28, Ps. 18:27). David's son, Solomon, observed that haughtiness leads to a downfall, whereas humility brings honor (Prov. 18:12). In Isaiah 13:11 the Lord promised to impose humility as an antidote to haughtiness (cf. Zeph. 3:11).

Without actually using the term, the Apostle Paul references haughtiness in Rom. 12:3, beginning by framing haughtiness and humility as we often do—thinking or not thinking of ourselves more highly than we ought. But a few verses later he challenges his readers to take humility to the next level, that is, to "honor one another above yourselves." (Rom. 12:10)

The key to replacing haughtiness with its opposite is not just a matter of denying our superiority (affective or ideological or both) by insisting on our literal inferiority. (After all, we can't all actually *be* inferior to everyone else.) Rather, as the Apostle Paul says in Philippians 2:3 (ESV), the trick is to "in humility *count* others as more significant than yourselves." This involves not so much a literal assessment of others' relative significance, as a decision to relate to them *as if they were* more significant. The attitudinal and the practical/social aspects of humility must work together.

The broader context of Philippians 2 makes it clear that this approach to humility is exactly what Paul has in mind, because imitating Christ's attitude involves looking out for the interests of others in addition to our own (2:4). Of course, it would have been irrational for Christ to have deemed us to be worthier than he was. Indeed, Romans 5:8 makes it clear that Christ died for us though fully aware of our unworthiness. What is significant is that he did not try to conserve his well-deserved advantages, but rather humbled himself for our sake (Phil. 2:6-8), acting as a servant.

Humility, then, expresses itself by our willingness to value others above ourselves by prioritizing their wellbeing above our own. If Christ could humble himself while in fact being more worthy, it shouldn't be too much for us to follow his example, given the fact that we are not starting from a status of greater inherent worth than other people but one of actual equality.

If we understand humility as elevating others and their wellbeing above our own, it becomes immediately apparent that humility is, indeed, the moral opposite of racial haughtiness—for it represents the exact opposite of the way whites have treated black people throughout our history. Rather than counting our racial other as more worthy and therefore serving them, we have devalued and disadvantaged them, expecting them to serve us. Spiritual transformation, then, means more than just pledging allegiance to equality. It means giving *preference* to those we have devalued ("in honor *preferring* one another" Rom. 12:10, KJV), working on their behalf, and serving their interests.

If such sacrificial preference sounds something like love, well, that's hardly an accident. For if humility is the particular alter ego of haughtiness, then love, as the ultimate fulfillment of every moral obligation (Mt. 22:40), must also be the ultimate antithesis of every moral failure.

What kind of humility functions as a replacement for haughtiness? The kind that comes bundled with love. It is not enough to become humbler by simply adjusting the valuations we place on ourselves relative to our racial counterparts. That re-valuation must result in acts of love that reflect it.

I can think of no more instructive example of this kind of humble love in a racially-charged context than that of the Good Samaritan. Let's see how this story informs our efforts to replace haughtiness with its moral opposite. Here's the parable, as Jesus told it in Luke 10:30-37:

> A man was going down from Jerusalem to Jericho, when he was attacked by robbers. They stripped him of his clothes, beat him and went away, leaving him half dead. [31] A priest happened to be going down the same road, and when he saw the man, he passed by on the other side. [32] So too, a Levite, when he came to the place and saw him, passed by on the other side. [33] But a Samaritan, as he traveled, came where the man was; and when he saw him, he took pity on him. [34] He went to him and bandaged his wounds, pouring on oil and wine. Then he put the man on his own donkey, brought him to an inn and took care of him. [35] The next day he took out two denarii and gave them to the innkeeper. 'Look after him,' he said, 'and when I return, I will reimburse you for any extra expense you may have.'

The backstory to this parable is highly significant. For centuries, the Jews had demeaned the Samaritans, considering them inferior, on account of their pagan inbreeding and heterodox religious practice. The resulting segregation was quite extreme. John 4:9 informs us that the Jews did not associate with Samaritans. In fact, the Jews would literally go out of their way to avoid their racial other. The Samaritans' homeland was located between Judea and Galilee, and the Jews would circumvent Samaria on their travels between their own northern and southern territories, even though doing so might add considerable distance to the journey.

We don't know how the Samaritan in this story *felt* about that historic condescension or what his personal track record was with his racial other. The text doesn't say. What we do know, however, is what he *did*—an example at once inspirational and at the same time deeply disquieting.

On the surface, the Samaritan's ancient example might seem an odd one to apply to modern American whites. After all, in the racial hierarchy of his day, the Samaritan was not associated with the oppressor class but with the marginalized. But keep in mind the circumstances that prompted the parable. A legal scholar had asked Jesus a question about the nature of spirituality. So, it was to that *Jewish* interlocutor and the accompanying *Jewish* audience that Jesus told this story.

Though Christ's casting choices may at first seem counter-intuitive, in reality they make the story more relevant. For we can rest assured that the Samaritan's actions were not the product of paternalism or some sense of guilt-by-association syndrome. There's no indication that he feels responsible because the roadside assaulters were his ethnic kin. Though the bad guys are not identified, the incident did not take place in Samaritan territory. As far as we can tell, his actions reflect his own personal sense of moral duty, which is, after all, the question the story purports to answer.

What is important about this setting for our purposes is that: 1) a man had been the victim of an injustice for which the Samaritan bore no personal responsibility; 2) this victim was still suffering from the consequences of that injustice; and 3) the Samaritan's response took place against a backdrop of longstanding racial tension fueled by haughtiness.

The story features two negative examples, both religious Jews. They ignore their fellow countryman and walk right on by, leaving him to an ignominious end (or, at best, to be tended to by someone else). Their "not my fault, not my problem" attitude clearly does not pass Jesus' moral muster. They just kept on moving, perhaps wagging their heads and wondering what in the world the world was coming to.

The Samaritan, in contrast, does not take refuge in his personal innocence. He's not focused on the bad things he didn't do. He's not focused on the fact that the Jews should have helped their own. He's focused on what he can do for someone in need.

So, the Samaritan takes pity on a natural enemy and demonstrates his compassion by getting involved. And I don't mean by calling 911. At the risk of becoming the next victim, he spends time by the injured man's side, personally administering first aid.

He also put his resources to work in order to lift up his fallen *other*. He had to use his *own* clothing, or strips of it, to make bandages, as the man's clothing had been taken from him. He put the victim on his *own* donkey, meaning that he probably had to walk so that the injured man could ride. He took him to a hotel and used his *own* money to pay for his room. That began with a down payment of about two day's wages, but it didn't end there. The Good Samaritan essentially wrote a blank check for his continuing care and promised to return to settle the account.

This certainly represents a remarkable effort on behalf of someone who, had they met under other circumstances, would probably not have given the Samaritan the time of day. So, our hero was not obligated by the other person's deservedness. He was not acting with the expectation of reciprocity—or even of recouping his investment in this man's rehabilitation.

But if this remarkable story is one-part inspiration, it is two-parts indictment. Consider the questions that Jesus answers with this parable. The first appears in Luke 10:25: "On one occasion an expert in the law stood up to test Jesus. 'Teacher,' he asked, 'what must I do to inherit eternal life?'"

The question is not, "What can I do to be a spiritual superstar?" or "How can I earn some extra credit?" Rather, he wants to know what he *must* do to inherit eternal life, to be right with God. So, this parable responds to the question: "What are the demands of divine justice?"

Jesus puts this expert on the defensive, however, by returning the rhetorical serve, lobbing the ball back into his questioner's court.

> [26] "What is written in the Law?" he replied. "How do you read it?" [27] He answered, "'Love the Lord your God with all your heart and with all your soul and with all your strength and with all your mind'; and, 'Love your neighbor as yourself.'" [28] "You have answered correctly," Jesus replied. "Do this and you will live."

So, this man who has come to "test" Jesus finds himself being tested. For even if the standard is easy to identify, it is not easy to keep, and now he's afraid that he *can't* do what he *must* do. A pious, hardcore religious type like him might be able to defend the fact that he loved God, who is both eminently lovable as well as invisible. But it's downright hard to love anyone else as thoroughly as he loves himself, let alone *everyone* else. …Unless he could somehow gerrymander his neighborhood, restricting it to his own ingroup and thereby making the lofty standard somewhat less lofty.

So, he adds a second question: "And who is my neighbor?" Of course, Jesus sees this stratagem—a smart guy trying to "justify himself." The scholar first wanted to know the demands of divine justice; now he wants to know how to get around them. Jesus' brilliant response—this parable of the Good Samaritan—answers both questions in a way that doesn't allow either his questioner (or us) to control the parameters of his (or our) 'hood.

In this parable *neighbor* is not defined by geography or by chosen associations or by natural affinities. It is defined by the people God places in our pathway, in our sphere of influence, so that we might *be* a neighbor to them. According to Jesus' example and teaching, that might be the outcast or the enemy or the "least of these"—or the racial *other*. It's not a matter of *distinguishing* those who are our neighbors, as opposed to those who are not, and then loving the neighborly sorts. It's a matter of acting in a sacrificially loving manner toward whomever we can. Which is why Jesus asks:

> [36] "Which of these three do you think was a neighbor to the man who fell into the hands of robbers?" [37] The expert in the law replied, "The one who had mercy on him." Jesus told him, "Go and do likewise."

We don't know if this legal scholar took Jesus' words to heart, but, like him, we are all unnerved by this demanding standard. It is so demanding, in fact, that it inevitably sends us scrambling in the direction of grace. Note, however, that God dispenses his grace not in the form of a lowered standard or even simply in the form of forgiveness for our failings. Ultimately, God's grace has a transformational *telos*; it is the divine enablement to live in the prescribed manner, to love your neighbor as yourself. So that when Jesus says, "Go, and do likewise," what he really means by that is, "Go, and do likewise."

What, then, does this parable teach us about the process of transformation in general and, specifically, about replacing racial haughtiness with its moral antithesis? As amply documented in the preceding pages, the historical pattern of whites relating to blacks has been precisely the opposite of the Good Samaritan's example. Throughout all the various incarnations of haughtiness, whiteness has never focused on loving our black neighbor as ourselves but on loving ourselves at the expense of our black neighbor. From slavery's brutal oppression to our current colorblind maintenance of the racial hierarchy, wherever you find haughtiness, you will also find an unloved neighbor.

And, yet, like this long-ago legal scholar, we persist in finding ways to justify ourselves by gerrymandering our neighborhood. We tell ourselves that we are not to blame for the historic abuses of African Americans. And because this mess is not our *personal* fault and therefore not our *personal* responsibility, we can choose to walk on by, wishing them well in the search for their own bootstraps.

Let's imagine for a moment that we do not, in fact, bear *any* responsibility for the trauma suffered by African Americans or for the inequities that are still their lot. That would put us squarely in the position of the Good Samaritan, wouldn't it? Which means that walking on by is still not an option. And if it's not an option for the innocent, it is certainly not an option for the implicated.

Jesus is not calling us to engage in some extraordinary act of generosity here, though that is how this parable is sometimes understood. Jesus is not trying to illustrate the optional nature of philanthropy. He is illustrating the obligatory nature of love—fulfilling our moral duty by assuming the difficulties of our racial other as if they were our own.

Obviously, we are not able to lift all of the fallen wherever they might be. Neither was the Good Samaritan. He was simply responding faithfully to the need that appeared in his pathway. Many modern-day whites have tried their best to put the African-American experience out of sight and out of mind by isolating themselves from it. But there is no escaping from the fact that white-on-black oppression has taken place in our historical back yard and that the resulting inequities continue to dominate our social landscape.

Regardless of where we think we are headed—as individuals, as a Church, as a nation—racial injustice stands squarely in our pathway. America's original sin remains America's unfinished business. Even worse, racial haughtiness and all its corollaries remain the great unfinished business of American Christianity. We, too, have been told to "go and do likewise," and doing likewise will require us to also do something different than we are doing now. In other words, it will involve replacement therapy.

Doing *likewise* is not just doing something. The Good Samaritan did not simply get involved until it became inconvenient or uncomfortable or expensive. He stayed involved until the problem was solved. Because love does whatever it takes.

It's not possible to precisely define the "whatever" in *whatever it takes*. Otherwise it would be a known quantity rather than a *whatever*. But w*hatever it takes* to fix the problem must surely be the opposite of *whatever it took* to create it. And the moral opposite of haughtiness is this humble love so beautifully illustrated by the example of the Good Samaritan and, ultimately, by the example of Christ himself—a love that puts the good of others, and of our *other*, ahead of our own.

Humble love celebrates the ontological and theological equality of our racial other, leaving us no room to think or even feel that our own racial identity imbues us with any greater worthiness whatsoever. But while humble love recognizes equality in theory, in practice it overshoots equality, prompting us to count, to consider, to treat others as *more* important than ourselves. Which means eschewing the modern white legacy that gives lip service to equality, while in actual practice prioritizing its own worth.

Many of us wish that the black/white relationship could be different going forward. But in order for that *relationship* to change fundamentally, *we* must change fundamentally. And that requires replacement therapy, exchanging racial haughtiness for humble love. Only then will we be willing to redress the wrongs of the past. Only then will we be ready to listen and to learn and to follow—not just to talk and to teach and to lead. Only then can we experience true racial harmony, "the beloved community" of which Dr. King and, more importantly, Jesus dreamed. It is to that dream that we now turn in our final chapter.

Chapter 29

The Beloved Community

Part of the gospel's good news is that even though we are sinners, we can find forgiveness by putting our faith in Christ's sacrificial death for us. Indeed, it is that promise of forgiveness that attracted many of us to the Christian message in the first place. And rightly so. We desperately need the forgiveness that God so graciously provides. As Ephesians 1:7 tells us: "In him we have redemption through his blood, the forgiveness of sins, in accordance with the riches of God's grace."

Forgiveness, however, is not the beginning and end of the gospel; it's only the beginning. God did not save us simply so that we could be forgiven for being the kind of people we are; he saved us so that we could become the kind of people we aren't yet. The really good news is that we are not only saved from the penalty of sin through forgiveness; we are also saved from the power of sin through transformation.

I'm not talking about some sort of extra-credit Christianity here. God's transformative *telos* for our lives was built right into the vicarious death of Christ, and when we associated with his death by faith, we were also initiated into this divine purpose. Romans 6:6 tells us that "our old self was crucified with him." Why? "[So] that we should no longer be slaves to sin." Verse four calls it "living a new life."

Over the last few chapters, we have been taking that transformative purpose seriously, actualizing our emancipation from the sin of racial haughtiness. But even when we overcome the strongholds of sin in our individual lives, we have not yet maximized the power of the gospel. Because Jesus didn't die just for me; he died for *us*. Ephesians 5:25 tells us that "Christ loved the *church* and gave himself up for her." The text goes on to say that he did this with the same sort of transformational purpose he had in mind for individual believers: "to present her to himself as a radiant church, without stain or wrinkle or any other blemish, but holy and blameless."

Now, if Christ doesn't want his Church to be stained or wrinkled, then I think we can agree that he doesn't want it to be torn either. But isn't that exactly what the racially-divided American Church amounts to—a Church torn in two? Just as the legacy of haughtiness constitutes a threat to God's transformational purpose in our individual lives, it also constitutes a threat to his transformational purpose in our corporate life.

The good news, however, is that the gospel can mend not only our personal brokenness but our interpersonal brokenness as well. Indeed, unless and until we take transformation to that level, we have not experienced the fullness of the gospel.

Not wanting to sell that good news short, we're going to spend this final chapter thinking about what collective transformation would look like with regard to race. To guide our thinking about this broader purpose of the gospel, I'm going to borrow Martin Luther King's evocative phrase "the beloved community." I say "borrow," because that which follows is far more than an exegesis of his thinking. I'm taking the liberty to re-cast his vision of *the beloved community* as I think it would be most helpful to understand it today.

And just where do I get the *chutzpah* to tinker with such an iconic phrase? Well, the fact is that, though Dr. King referred to *the beloved community* with some frequency, he never really fleshed out its practical application. Indeed, at the end of his life he seemed to be at something of a loss regarding how to pursue it. Moreover, I feel at liberty to adapt this notion, since Dr. King had already adapted it from the person who (evidently) invented it.

That story begins with a turn-of-the-century philosopher named Josiah Royce (1855-1916). Royce's philosophy revolved around the concept of community, defined as the loyalty of those who subscribed to a common experience. Though he found some forms of community to be mundane, Royce believed that others achieved transcendence, acquiring a very real personhood that involved true loyalty, or "loyalty to loyalty." These he called "genuine communities" or "communities of grace." Above and beyond even these, however, lay the ideal to which they aspired, *the beloved community*.[1]

Royce's vision of this archetypical collective was not specifically or necessarily Christian, though he did regard the Church as an excellent paradigm and the Early Church under the influence of Paul as the finest exemplar of a graced community. Royce's theological "vision," however, was more than a bit quirky, placing greater emphasis on the work of the Spirit as the fomenter of Christian community than on Christ as its founder.

How, then, did this phrase make its way from Royce's original formulation to Martin Luther King's usage? It appears that as a student King was exposed to Royce's work and that he found more to like about *the beloved community* than just its literary catchphrase value. Both men considered community to be bigger than the sum of its parts and made it central to their thinking. Royce became the founder of the Fellowship of Reconciliation, an organization of which Dr. King would eventually become a member.

King, however, couched his communitarian vision in a far more orthodox Christian framework. According to Charles Marsh, Professor of Religious Studies at the University of Virginia: "The logic of King's dream was theologically specific: beloved community as the realization of divine love in lived social relation."[2] That vision "was founded in a specific theological tradition, and no amount of post-modern complexity can remove that intention and claim. 'I am many things to many people,' King said…, 'but in the quiet recesses of my heart, I am fundamentally a clergyman, a Baptist preacher.'"[3]

As far back as the Montgomery bus boycott in 1956, Dr. King already had his visionary eyes on the prize, affirming that "the end is reconciliation; the end is redemption; the end is the creation of the beloved community."[4] A decade later, even after the most heady and historic victories of his civil rights career, he remained committed to that philosophy: "I do not think of political power as an end. Neither do I think of economic power as an end. They are ingredients in the objective that we seek in life. And I think that end [or] that objective is a truly brotherly society, the creation of the beloved community."[5]

Part of what made King's articulation more specifically Christian was that, rather than relying on the relatively bland notion of loyalty, he developed his *beloved* community around the more robust, biblical concept of *agapic* love. In a 1957 address to The Conference on Christian Faith and Human Relations, King referenced this love that

> can transform opposers into friends. The type of love that I stress here is not *eros*, a sort of esthetic or romantic love; not *philia*, a sort of reciprocal love between personal friends; but it is *agape* which is understanding goodwill for all men. It is an overflowing love which seeks nothing in return. It is the love of God working in the lives of men. This is the love that may well be the salvation of our civilization.[6]

The following year he explored how this connection between love and community informed his entire approach to racial reconciliation:

> *Agape…* is love in action. *Agape* is love seeking to preserve and create community. It is insistence on community even

> when [some]one seeks to break it. *Agape* is a willingness to go
> to any length to restore community. It doesn't stop at the first
> mile, but it goes the second mile to restore community....
>
> The cross is the eternal expression of the length to which God
> will go to restore broken community.... The Holy Spirit is the
> continuing community creating reality that moves through
> history. He who works against community is working against
> the whole of creation.
>
> Therefore, if I respond to hate with... hate I do nothing but
> intensify the cleavage in broken community. I can only close
> the gap in broken community by meeting hate with love.[7]

This ideal of community guided the young preacher from Montgomery as
he framed the civil rights struggle. It was not enough to win freedom for black
Americans; he insisted on doing so in a way that would lay the foundation for
a beloved community. He believed that "love is creative and redemptive. Love
builds up and unites; hate tears down and destroys. The aftermath of the 'fight
fire with fire' method... is bitterness and chaos; the aftermath of the love
method is reconciliation and the creation of the beloved community."[8]

Dr. King spoke of this ideal far more often at the outset of his career than
he did toward the end, and with good reason. Over time, he found himself
unable maintain the discipline of non-violence within his own ranks and he
found white haughtiness to be even more recalcitrant than he had imagined.
Marsh observes that in 1964, "despite an impressive slate of civil rights
legislation enacted that same year and the following, the vision of the beloved
community began to fragment."[9]

In March of 1968, Martin Luther King spoke at the National Cathedral in
Washington, D.C. His was a somber reflection on the dream of a beloved
community, the "brotherly society" he had sought to create: "Through our
scientific and technological genius, we have made of this world a
neighborhood and yet we have not had the ethical commitment to make of it
a brotherhood. But somehow... we have got to do this. We must all learn to
live together as brothers or we will all perish together as fools."[10]

A week later, Dr. King's quest for the beloved community came to a
tragic end. But did his dream die with him? Was the beloved community just
a flight of 1960s romantic fancy, a Christianized "Age of Aquarius?"

Keep in mind that the struggle to create a beloved community in the face
of historic divisions does not date from the sixties but from the fifties. And I

don't mean the 1950s but the A.D. 50s, when the Apostle Paul found it necessary to address the ethnic/religious discord present in the Early Church.

Given the seemingly irreconcilable differences between Jews and Gentiles, the path of least resistance would have been to follow the apartheid American model and create two parallel tracks. And, yet, it is noteworthy that Paul refused to even contemplate such a solution, choosing, rather, to "preserve the Union" at any cost. And in his response to that existential threat, he affirmed that the indivisible unity of the Church trumped ethnic identities.

Ethnic inclusiveness is more than just a firewall against division, however; Scripture presents it as a positive good to be pursued. The New Testament begins with the visit of the Magi and ends with the New Jerusalem, composed of people from every tongue and tribe and nation. And at pivotal points in between Jesus sends his Church out into all nations (*ethne*), and the Spirit comes in a powerful Pentecostal affirmation of ethnic inclusivity. The fully equal integration of all peoples into God's salvific purpose is an indispensable template for understanding the New Testament message.

As my pastor, Dr. David Anderson, points out, Paul confirms the essential and necessary role of ethnic diversity within the unity that is the body of Christ in 1 Corinthians 12:12-13: "Just as a body, though one, has many parts, but all its many parts form one body, so it is with Christ. For we were all baptized by one Spirit so as to form one body—whether *Jews or Gentiles*, slave or free—and we were all given the one Spirit to drink." Only after adding this overlay of ethnic diversity to the diversity of gifts does the Apostle go on to insist on the inalienable interdependence of that body's diverse parts.[11]

Note, however, that the unity Paul prescribed was not the kind that could simply be affirmed from afar. It had to be lived out in community. Paul addressed his teaching on this subject to congregations who were dealing with ethnic and religious tensions. And he did not allow congregational community to be defined by history or by ethnicity or by social circumstance—or by any consideration that was secondary to their oneness in Christ.

The theological fact of unity makes this multiethnic community both necessary and appropriate for the people of God. But as history more than amply illustrates, the theological fact of unity does not guarantee that practical community will ensue. What, then, is the secret ingredient that makes it possible for a group of people to create a genuine existential community?

I wish I had some advanced exegetical acumen to offer about the nature of the beloved community, but it strikes me as tautologically simple to parse.

A beloved community is a community characterized by love. But while the beloved community may be simple to define, the implications of its constituent elements are, perhaps, not quite so obvious.

Let's begin with the communal aspect. To be meaningful, community must also be existentially functional. Of course, it's possible to contemplate the universal Church as a "community of believers" bound together by the love of God and by a common "loving" commitment. But this kind of loving commitment smacks a bit too much of Royce's "loyalty," because the "love" required at this level is rather abstract. It doesn't require anyone to put up with the interpersonal obnoxiousness that often characterizes human behavior.

More specific to the current context, love at this level may not require us to face up to, let alone overcome, racial haughtiness. I suppose that many of the perpetrators of racial haughtiness throughout the centuries were convinced in their own minds that they loved the body of Christ. When we bring that macro vision down to street level, however, it becomes clear that they were not involved in the lives of people across the racial divide in any way that added up to meaningful community or love. Kind of like Charlie Brown, who once said, "I love mankind... it's people I can't stand!!"[12]

American Christianity represents two parallel, racially-defined realities, a circumstance that denies us the opportunity to be in true community. Because there can be no actual community without meaningful contact. And without *actual* community, there surely can be no *beloved* community.

A lot of white Christians are convinced that they have positive feelings about the people on the other side of the color barrier, but unless they interact with those people, how do they really know? Long-distance "love" is easy. But real community can't happen from opposite sides of the tracks.

Let's not think that interracial community happens just because a group of white Christians welcomes a certain number of black Christians into their midst. If those black believers are simply being assimilated into a white environment—that is, if they appreciate and adapt to white ways of being and doing—then of course we get along. It's only when we whites opt to accommodate others, rather than insisting they assimilate, that the rubber of real interracial community hits the road. Accommodation requires *us* to adapt. So, how do we feel when we must do things their way, when we have to follow their lead, when our sons and daughters want to date and marry their sons and daughters? We can't even begin to talk about a beloved community until we create communal structures that allow us to experience life together.

This lack of communal infrastructure is one of the reasons why Dr. King's vision of the beloved community was never realized. During the era of forced segregation, it might have seemed reasonable to think that once the dam of segregation was destroyed, the waiting waters of racial harmony would rush to flow freely. But such a view vastly underestimated the recalcitrance of haughtiness and all that it hath wrought.

What replaced forced segregation was not racial harmony but voluntary separation—even, and perhaps especially, in the Church. Some people seem to think that voluntary separation between Christians is a far more benign arrangement than forced segregation. While that may be true from a socio-political point of view, from a spiritual point of view it seems like quite the opposite. If society keeps you from pursuing loving unity within the body of Christ, you have something of an excuse. But if you simply *choose* not to pursue loving unity within the body of Christ, there really is no excuse.

So, in this tautologically simple exposition of the beloved community, the first step is to create an existentially functional community. By definition, however, a *beloved* community must also be a *loving* community. What does that look like?

Dr. King argued that a loving community must begin with *agape*—a godly, overflowing love that asks for nothing in return. Where there is no loving community, somebody must go that extra, sacrificial mile to establish it and to draw others into it. Note, however, that this *agape*, as Dr. King describes it, is an initiatory love. It is the kind of love that God showed us while we were still sinners and even his enemies (Romans 5:8-10). He took that first step to establish a loving relationship with us where there was none.

King, envisioning a beloved community that did not yet exist, realized that such a unidirectional, initiatory love was necessary to bridge the gap from the state of race relations that existed to the beloved community.[a] But note that while unidirectional, initiatory love is necessary to *create* a beloved community, something more is required to *sustain* one. To sustain a beloved community that initiatory love must lead to mutual love. You can't have a beloved community in which only one party is doing all the loving.

---

[a] Dr. King's *agapic* emphasis notwithstanding, it's not clear that he ever tried to exclude *philia* from the beloved community. He was simply focused on the *establishment* of such a community. As he insisted in a 1962 letter to Robert Epstein, King believed that *agape* "[made] possible the "beloved community." (www.thekingcenter.org/archive/document/letter-mlk-robert-epstein).

But doesn't this sort of mutual love push us beyond the bounds of what Dr. King described as *agape* and into the "reciprocal love" of *philia*? Well, yes and no. Yes, because a beloved community clearly requires reciprocal love. But here we must be careful here to avoid overly rigid assumptions about the equivalence between concepts and their linguistic symbols.

It's true that *philia* (along with its verbal form, *phileō*) is often used in the New Testament to designate just the sort of mutual love necessary to a beloved community. Note, however, that *philia* is also used not so infrequently for the love of sinful things that cannot love in return (Mt. 6:5, Lk. 22:46, John 12:25, Rev. 22:15). For its part, *agape* (along with its verbal form, *agapaō*), can also be used for the love of sinful things (John 12:25, 2 Tim. 4:10, 1 Jn. 2:15) and, like *philia*, can also refer to reciprocal love between people (John 13:34-35, 2 Thess. 1:3, 1 Pet. 1:22, 1 Jn. 3:11, 23; 1 Jn. 4:7, 11, 12; 2 Jn. 1:5). In fact, in both the Septuagint as well as the New Testament, *philia* and *agape* are sometimes used synonymously (1 Thess. 4:19 / 2 Thess. 1:3, 1 Pet. 1:22).[b]

Since the semantic ranges of these two terms are rather broad, it seems best not to rely too heavily on such morphological distinctions. What seems inescapably clear is that the entire range of the loving dynamic is necessary to create and sustain the beloved community.

Even *eros* has its place. This Greek term, which is not used in the Bible, refers to the sensual/romantic aspect of love. Of course, this kind of relationship would not be appropriate between any and all members of the community, but for that community to establish the bonds necessary to be truly *beloved*, there must be an aesthetic appreciation that crosses racial lines, making mutual attraction and intermarriage a natural occurrence. As a practical matter, the resulting racially-mixed families serve as powerful hierarchy-attenuating institutions, undermining the we/they otherness of racial differentiation at its most basic level.

It is not just the nature and focus of love that matters to the beloved community, however. It is also the quality of that love. Naturally, the love shared between forever friends is different than the love shared between those who were once estranged. The former is as comfortable as an old shoe, so much so that it might even be taken for granted. There is, however, a certain

---

[b] For more on the usage of these words, see: D. A. Carson, Exegetical Fallacies, 2nd ed. (Grand Rapids: Baker, 1996), 31-32, 51-53.

sweet triumph to a love won over. It cannot be taken for granted, in part because it required an effort to obtain and requires an effort to maintain.

Because white identity has for so long been so thoroughly infused with haughtiness, unless white folks make a conscious effort to think and act and feel differently, they can quite easily fall back into their legacy patterns of relating to black folks. On the other side of the ledger, African Americans, who are used to whites relating to them from a posture of haughtiness, can easily adopt a here-we-go-again mentality. Contemporary Christians can't afford to ignore this history, because, whether we like it or not, we're part of it. We do, thank God, have the power to create a new history, but that takes time and effort and pushing back against the old one.

My car was manufactured in 1995. It's not a classic; it's just old. So, it has a lot of "features" I could do without. But it has one I like; it has a stick shift. I must admit, though, that driving a manual transmission requires more attention than driving an automatic. Especially if I'm going uphill from a standing start. I have to coordinate the release of the clutch and the pressure on the accelerator at just the right moment, or the car will stall.

Interracial relationships are an uphill climb. You can't just ease into them. They require extra attention and at least a little bit of skill. If you ignore that reality, the relationship will stall—or worse, slide backwards.

So, in order to overcome history's uphill grade, white people must bring a very specific kind of love to the beloved community. I'm talking about a transformed and a transformational love, a love that turns history on its head. This transformed love must be respectful, not condescending. This transformed love must be humble, not paternalistic. This transformed love must be willing to listen, not just to talk. This transformed love must follow, not just lead. This transformed love must value the wellbeing of our racial other above our own. This transformed love must be willing to do whatever it takes to right the wrongs of the past. And this transformed love cannot rest until our brothers and sisters are truly our equals, enjoying a just distribution of God's material blessings.

Where, then, might we incubate such a community? It must be a setting suitable for the genuine sharing of life together across racial boundaries. It must be characterized by radically re-oriented values. And it must be populated by people who have, themselves, been transformed.

If you look at his pronouncements on the matter, Dr. King seems to have envisioned the beloved community operating on a societal level. One can hardly blame him for concluding that at least certain sectors of society were more open to racial healing than most sectors of the church, because that's exactly what he observed. Not only that, but those were the sixties, and he was not alone in his aspirations for a Great Society.

Nevertheless, given what we have seen about the ingredients necessary to create a beloved community and the evolution of race relations over the last half century, to begin with such an ambitious application now seems like an overreach. Secular society may be capable of producing some sort of vapid, let's-call-the-whole-thing-off tolerance, but it lacks any socio-spiritual mechanism capable of dealing with haughtiness and its collateral damage. If we are to take the notion of the beloved community seriously, we must see it as a divine institution infused with a morally transcendent, supernatural ethos.

We, of course, have the advantage of seeing something that Dr. King did not, the actual proliferation of multiracial churches. The fact that a church is multiracial does not, of course, make it a beloved community, but this multiracial phenomenon at least points us in the direction of a realized ideal. It allows us to at least envision how congregational life could and should function as the incubator of a beloved multiracial community.

In order for the multiracial church movement to further fulfill the promise of the beloved community, two critical issues remain—quantity and quality. Before we can even begin to refer to the broader Church as a beloved community in this racially-specific sense, there must to be many more multiracial congregations, as right now these still represent a niche minority of the whole. Not only that but (as noted earlier) many of those congregations classified as "multiracial" have not come to terms with the fundamental problem of racial haughtiness. Many have achieved a degree of mechanical integration without a corresponding level of relational reconciliation. And, frankly, too many are still racial hierarchy-enhancing institutions.

I should also say a word about those congregations that, because of their local demographics (as in some rural settings), are not candidates for significant multiracial mixing. How can they participate in this beloved multiracial community in a meaningful way? To really delve into the nuts and bolts of this matter would require a separate treatment, but the short answer, I believe, has three parts.

First, white Christians can work through the process of self-examination and transformation, as outlined above. Close physical proximity to a racial other is helpful in that process, but some spiritual approximation can be accomplished even at a distance. Second, even where significant racial mixing within the congregation is not a viable option, personal and corporate connections with Christians across racial lines (joint initiatives, periodic sharing) can still be meaningful, even if they are somewhat less frequent or intimate. And, third, keeping in mind that racial disadvantage is a national and not just a local issue, white Christians can engage in personal and corporate advocacy on behalf of African-American wellbeing and genuine equality, even when they do not live in areas with a significant black population.

While I believe that the Christian Church is uniquely qualified to create a home for the beloved community, I am not writing off secular American society. Like Dr. King, I am deeply concerned that the message of racial reconciliation be disseminated and digested as broadly as possible. The Church should be the messenger, but the broader audience is also important, because a messenger without an audience is rather superfluous.

If the people of God are, as Jesus said, the light of the world, then the purpose of that light is not primarily to remind others that they are in the dark but to illumine that darkness. Setting a positive moral example shows the beauty of doing things God's way, demonstrates how it is done, and invites others into the process. There could be no more convincing testimony of the power of God than an actual solution to America's original sin and most recalcitrant problem.

The creation of a beloved interracial community also affords Christians a platform from which to speak truth to power and to influence the policies that sustain the racial hierarchy itself. But that moral leverage doesn't come from just talking about the beloved community. It comes from incarnating the beloved community and thereby representing an interracial voice that transcends the typical interest groups.

The problem, as we've seen throughout this book, is that for Christians to become part of the solution, they must first quit being part of the problem. As 1 Peter 4:17 warns, "It is time for judgment to begin with God's household." We cannot change the society without changing the Church. And we cannot change the Church without changing the people who comprise it. Only those who have experienced a transformation from racial haughtiness to racial humility can be builders of a beloved community. And, make no mistake, it will take a beloved community to light the way forward for a society steeped in racial haughtiness and all that it hath wrought.

Am I anticipating a utopian turnaround, a national catharsis? Well, it wouldn't be the first time America has experienced a Great Awakening, but I am not anticipating heaven on earth on this side of the eschaton. The beloved community is not a beatific community. It is a striving, albeit imperfect human collective made up of imperfect individuals who are, at best, growing in grace.

What I am calling for here, what I am hoping and praying for, is what Francis Schaeffer referred to as "substantial healing," a supernatural work of God through which the eternal kingdom infiltrates our contemporary experience. While substantial healing does not make all things new, it foreshadows that coming reality and demonstrates that the God who will bring that kingdom about is already at work.

As Schaeffer makes clear in his classic book, *True Spirituality*, substantial healing includes "a substantially restored relationship among Christians in this life."[13] For the power of God to be maximized and manifested in substantially restored relationships, however, it cannot be applied only to the easy cases that are likely to work themselves out anyway. We can neither demonstrate nor even appreciate the supernatural character of "substantial healing," unless we apply it to the seemingly impossible. And there can be no more thoroughly intractable relational challenge in the history of American society and American Christianity than our racial dysfunction.

What, then, would a "substantially restored relationship among Christians in this life" look like when applied to our racialized reality? It would look like none other than the beloved community, that idyllic human experience for which Jesus prayed and for which Jesus died—and for which Jesus has been waiting quite a long time in this America. The good news is that today more Christians are buying into this dream than at any other time in history. But dreams don't come true just because we dream them; they come true only when we pursue them.

Why, then, have we not pursued this one more fervently than we have? Martin Luther King once observed that the creation of a truly beloved community, "will require *a qualitative change in our souls* as well as *a quantitative change in our lives*."[14] So, there you have it. Dreaming about a beloved community is easy, but realizing that dream is hard—because it requires change, and change is hard.

The very changes Dr. King referred to have been the focus of this book. The qualitative change in our souls is that process of transformation from racial haughtiness to loving humility. The quantitative change in our lives involves embracing racial justice by redressing the consequences of our sin. The divine demands of righteousness make this change necessary, and God's grace makes it possible—but it is still a very hard thing to do.

If personal transformation is challenging, the going doesn't get much easier on the interpersonal level. It takes a lot more than warm, fuzzy feelings to build a beloved community. Building a beloved community requires sacrifice and patience and understanding that you don't yet possess. Building a beloved community reveals vestiges of haughtiness that you thought you had overcome. And building a beloved community will remind you that not every member of the beloved community is quite as lovely as you'd like.

If you've ever built a house or had one built or endured the frustrated rants of someone who has, you know that the cost is considerable at every level, from the financial to the emotional. And, yet, when you're done, you have a place that was built just for you. And you are home.

That is the beauty of the beloved community—it is a home built just for us. Its architect is God himself, who knew exactly what he wanted and what we needed. His design was a mystery hidden from eternity past, to be realized in the fullness of time. In this beloved community we lay aside the color-coded identities that have so long divided and oppressed and stratified us. We take up our true identity, the children of God gathered as the family of God. And when we do, we are home.

Index

Endnotes

Note: Citations of online sources do not contain an "Accessed on" date, because most were accessed multiple times, and all were re-checked for viability prior to publication.

Chapter 1

[1] "Across Racial Lines, More Say Nation Needs to Make Changes to Achieve Racial Equality," Pew Research Center for the People and the Press RSS, August 5, 2015, www.people-press.org/2015/08/05/across-racial-lines-more-say-nation-needs-to-make-changes-to-achieve-racial-equality/.

[2] Ibid.

[3] *"New York Times*/CBS News Poll on Race Relations in the U.S.," *The New York Times*. July 22, 2015, www.nytimes.com/interactive/2015/07/23/us/document-new-york-timescbs-news-poll-on-race-relations-in-the-us.html. This is the detailed polling data related to the article: "A Growing Divide on Race," *The New York Times*, July 22, 2015, www.nytimes.com/interactive/2015/07/23/us/race-relations-in-america-poll.html. See also: Krissa Thompson and Scott Clement, "Poll: Majority of Americans think race relations are getting worse," *The Washington Post*, July 16, 2016, www.washingtonpost.com/national/more-than-6-in-10-adults-say-us-race-relations-are-generally-bad-poll-indicates/2016/07/16/66548936-4aa8-11e6-90a8-fb84201e0645_story.html. In this poll 63% of whites characterized race relations as "generally bad," while 32% answered "generally good.

[4] Pew Research Center, "Across Racial Lines, More Say Nation Needs to Make Changes to Achieve Racial Equality," Aug. 5, 2015, http://www.people-press.org/2015/08/05/across-racial-lines-more-say-nation-needs-to-make-changes-to-achieve-racial-equality/.

[5] Pew Research Center, "Most Americans Say Trump's Election Has Led to Worse Race Relations in the U.S.," December 19, 2017, http://www.people-press.org/2017/12/19/most-americans-say-trumps-election-has-led-to-worse-race-relations-in-the-u-s/.

[6] Ibid.

Chapter 2

[1] Barack Obama, "A More Perfect Union," speech, National Constitution Center, Philadelphia, March 18, 2008, http://constitutioncenter.org/amoreperfectunion/.

Chapter 3

[1] "Romanus Pontifex," Papal Encyclicals Online: Pope Nicholas V, www.papalencyclicals.net/Nichol05/index.htm.

[2] Gomes Eannes De Azurara, and Charles Raymond Beazley, *The Chronicle of the Discovery of Conquest of Guinea* (London: Hakluyt Society, 1896), 81.

[3] Ibid. 79.

[4] Ibid. 80.

[5] Ibid, 83.

[6] Ibid, 81-82.

[7] Ibid, 81.

[8] Ibid, 84-85.

[9] Pedro Lage Reis Correia, "Father Diogo De Mesquita (1551-1614) and the Cultivation of Western Plants in Japan," *Bulletin of Portuguese/Japanese Studies*, December, año/vol. 7, (2003): 76.
[10] Willie James Jennings, *The Christian Imagination* (New Haven: Yale University Press, 2010), 102-104.
[11] Charles Ralph Boxer, The Christian Century in Japan, 1549-1650 (Berkeley: University of California Press, 1951), 94.
[12] Jennings, *The Christian Imagination*, 35.
[13] Charles Ralph Boxer, *The Church Militant and Iberian Expansion, 1440-1770* (Baltimore: Johns Hopkins University Press, 1978), 23.
[14] Charles Ralph Boxer, *Four Centuries of Portuguese Expansion, 1415-1825: A Succinct Survey* (Berkeley: University of California Press, 1961), 43.
[15] Josef Franz Schütte, *Valignano's mission principles for Japan, Vol 1.* (St. Louis, Institute of Jesuit Resources, 1985), 131.
[16] Jennings, *The Christian Imagination*, 79.

Chapter 4

[1] "Modern History Sourcebook: Jules Ferry (1832-1893): On French Colonial Expansion," Fordham University, www.fordham.edu/halsall/mod/ 1884ferry.html. / From: Jules François Camille Ferry, "Speech Before the French Chamber of Deputies, March 28, 1884," Discours et Opinions de Jules Ferry," Paul Robiqueta, ed. (Paris: Armand Colin & Cie., 1897), 199-201, 210-11, 215-18. Translated by Ruth Kleinman in *Brooklyn College Core Four Sourcebook*.
[2] BBC, "Press Office," http://www.bbc.co.uk/pressoffice/proginfo/tv/2010/wk7/sun.shtml.
[3] John Spencer Hill, *John Milton: Poet, Priest and Prophet: A Study of Divine Vocation in Milton's Poetry and Prose* (London: Macmillan, 1979), 88.
[4] Isaac Watts with Calvin College, "The Psalms and Hymns of Isaac Watts with all the Additional Hymns and Complete Indexes," Christian Classics Ethereal Library, www.ccel.org/ccel/watts/psalmshymns.html.
[5] John B. Judis, "The Chosen Nation: The Influence of Religion on U.S. Foreign Policy," Visiting Scholar, Carnegie Endowment for International Peace, Carnegie Endowment for International Peace, no. 37 (March, 2005): 1, http://carnegieendowment.org/2005/03/15/chosen-nation-influence-of-religion-on-u.s.-foreign-policy-pub-16668.
[6] Mary Beth Norton, et. al., eds., *A People and a Nation: A History of the United States, 6th ed.* (Boston: Houghton Mifflin Company, 2001), 40.
[7] Thomas K. McCraw, "It Came in the First Ships: Capitalism in America," Harvard Business School Working Knowledge: A First Look at Faculty Research, October 12, 1999, http://hbswk.hbs.edu/item/0896.html. Excerpted with permission from Thomas K. McGraw, *Creating Modern Capitalism: How Entrepreneurs, Companies, and Countries Triumphed in Three Industrial Revolutions,* (Cambridge: Harvard University Press, 1997).
[8] Ibid.

Chapter 5

[1] James A. Rawley and Stephen D. Behrendt, *The Transatlantic Slave Trade: A History* (Lincoln: University of Nebraska Press, 2005), 2. On this subject David Pott comments, "It is likely that the underlying motive for his passion about enslaving

Native Americans was that he believed it was the quickest way to cancel the debts he had incurred on his voyages." David Pott, "Roots of the Atlantic Slave Trade," www.lifelineexpedition.co.uk/content/view/38/86/.

[2] Ibid, 2-3.

[3] Tzvetan Todorov, *The Conquest of America: The Question of the Other* (Norman, Oklahoma: Univ. of Oklahoma Press, 1999), 146.

[4] See: Allison Keyes, "Thanksgiving Origins: More Than Just 'Turkey Day,'" interview with Jim Adams of the Smithsonian Institution's National Museum of the American Indian. Nov. 25, 2010, www.npr.org/templates/story/story.php?storyId=131565906.

[5] Cotton Mather, *Magnalia Christi Americana; or, The ecclesiastical history of New-England; from its first planting, in the year 1620, unto the year of Our Lord 1698, Vol. 1* (Hartford: S. Andrus and Son, 1855), 558-559. Mather had an important impact on the missiology of his time. His more than 400 published works include *India Christiana*, his discourse to the commissioners for the propagation of the gospel among the American Indians.

[6] Forrest B. Wood, *The Arrogance of Faith* (New York: Alfred A. Knopf, 1990), 18.

[7] Barbara A. Moe, *The Charter of the Massachusetts Bay Colony: A Primary Source Investigation* (New York: Rosen Primary Source, 2003), 94.

[8] Ibid.

[9] John Winthrop, *Winthrop Papers*,(Boston: Massachusetts Historical Society, 1929), 171-172.

[10] Ibid.

[11] Elizabeth Prine Pauls, "Native American," In *Encyclopædia Britannica Online*, https://www.britannica.com/topic/Native-American.

[12] "Immigration: Native American," Library of Congress, www.loc.gov/teachers/classroommaterials/presentationsandactivities/presentations/immigration/alt/native_american8.html. See also: Guenter Lewy, "Were American Indians the Victims of Genocide?" George Mason University's History News Network, 11/22/04, http://hnn.us/articles/7302.html.

[13] Guenter Lewy, "Were American Indians the Victims of Genocide?"

[14] Seymour Drescher, *Abolition: A History of Slavery and Antislavery* (Cambridge: Cambridge University Press, 2009), 44.

[15] Robbie Ethridge, "English Trade in Deerskins and Indian Slaves," in *The New Georgia Encyclopedia*, www.georgiaencyclopedia.org/nge/Article.jsp?id=h-585.

[16] Robert Baker, "Manifest Destiny and the Peculiar Institution," *Prezi* online, Sept. 25, 2017, https://prezi.com/-argza0ekrui/manifest-destiny-and-the-peculiar-institution/.

[17] Ibid.

[18] Seymour Drescher, *Abolition*, 6-7.

[19] John Madden, "Slavery in the Roman Empire," article excerpted by Dr. Miland Brown on *World History Blog*, June 29, 2005, www.worldhistoryblog.com/2005/06/slavery-in-roman-empire.html. The article formerly appeared as John Madden, "Slavery in the Roman Empire - Numbers and Origins," University College, Galway, Classics Ireland, 1996 Volume 3. This article appears to no longer be available online.

[20] Ibid.

[21] The Civil War Home Page, "Results from the 1860 Census," www.civil-war.net/pages/1860_census.html.

[22] "Slavery in the North: Northern Profits from Slavery," www.slavenorth.com/profits.htm.

[23] "Slavery in the North: Northern Emancipation," www.slavenorth.com/emancipation.htm.

[24] Herbert S. Klein, *The Atlantic Slave Trade* (Cambridge: Cambridge University Press, 1999), 46.
[25] Slavery in the North, www.slavenorth.com/slavenorth.htm.

Chapter 6

[1] Jennings, *The Christian Imagination,* 242.
[2] John Dixon Long, *Pictures of Slavery in Church and State* (Philadelphia: Published by the Author, 1857), 198.
[3] Ibid, 198-199.
[4] Eugene D. Genovese, *A Consuming Fire: The Fall of the Confederacy in the Mind of the White Christian South* (Athens, Georgia: University of Georgia Press, 1998), 84.
[5] Abraham Lincoln and Stephen Douglas, John G. Nicolay and John Hay, eds., "First Joint Debate at Ottawa, August 21, 1858," in *The Complete Works of Abraham Lincoln, Vol. 3* (New York: Francis D. Tandy Company, 1894, 1858), 217, http://lincoln.lib.niu.edu/islandora/object/niu-lincoln%3A36541.
[6] Ibid, 229-230.
[7] Joseph Doddridge, Narcissa Doddridge, William Thomas Lindsey, *Notes on the Settlement and Indian Wars in the Western Parts of Virginia and Pennsylvania* (Pittsburgh: John S. Ritenour and Wm. T. Lindsey, 1912), 48. This is the third printing of Doddridge's original 1824 work, to which his daughter adds a memoir.
[8] Eugene D. Genovese, *The World the Slaveholders Made: Two Essays in Interpretation,* (Hanover, NH, University Press of New England, 1988), xv.
[9] Ibid.
[10] Ibid, 196.
[11] George Washington, "Statement to David Humphreys," ca. 1788-1789, quoted in Peter R. Henriques, "'The Only Unavoidable Subject of Regret': George Washington and Slavery," http://chnm.gmu.edu/courses/henriques/hist615/gwslav.htm.
[12] Ibid.
[13] Stuart Hall, *Representation: Cultural Representations and Signifying Practices* (London: Sage, Milton Keynes; Open University, 2007), 243.
[14] Winthrop D. Jordan, *The White Man's Burden: Historical Origins of Racism in the United States* (New York: Oxford University Press, 1974), 105.
[15] Frederick Douglass, *Narrative of the Life of Frederick Douglass: An American Slave,* (New York: Cosimo Classics, 2008), 38. (Original work published in 1845.)
[16] W.E.B. DuBois, *Darkwater: Voices From Within The Veil* (New York, Harcourt, Brace and Howe, 1920), 172.
[17] Henry Louis Gates, Jr. "Michelle's Great-Great-Great-Granddaddy—and Yours." *History News Network* of The George Washington University, https://historynewsnetwork.org/article/118292. Originally published in "The Root," Oct. 8, 2009.
[18] Rose Williams, enslaved in Texas, interviewed ca. 1937 [WPA Slave Narrative Project], http://nationalhumanitiescenter.org/pds/maai/enslavement/text6/masterslavesexualabuse.pdf.
[19] Sylvia Watkins. enslaved in Tennessee, interviewed ca. 1937 [WPA Slave Narrative Project], http://nationalhumanitiescenter.org/pds/maai/enslavement/text6/masterslavesexualabuse.pdf.
[20] Harriet A. Jacobs, *Incidents in the Life of a Slave Girl* (Rockville, MD; Arc Manor, 2008), 32-33. Originally published in 1860, the historical validity of this book was at

one time questioned, but modern scholarship has validated its historicity. For more background information, see: http://docsouth.unc.edu/fpn/jacobs/bio.html.
[21] Ibid, 38.
[22] Thomas Cary Johnson, *The Life and Letters of Robert Lewis Dabney, Volume 3* (Richmond, Virginia: Presbyterian Committee of Publication, 1903), 68.
[23] Frederic Bancroft, *Slave Trading in the Old South* (New York: Ungar, 1959), 68.
[24] Frances Ann Kemble, *Journal of a Residence on a Georgian Plantation 1838-1839* (Teddington, Middlesex: Echo Library, 2008), 122.
[25] Robert Edgar Conrad, *In the Hands of Strangers: Readings on Foreign and Domestic Slave Trading and the Crisis of the Union* (University Park, PA: Penn State University Press; London: Eurospan, 2003), 231-232.
[26] F. Forrester Church, *So Help Me God: The Founding Fathers and the First Great Battle over Church and State* (Orlando, Harcourt, 2008), 280.
[27] Rose Williams, *supra.*
[28] Frederick Douglass, *The Life and Times of Frederick Douglass* (Hartford, Park Publishing Co., 1881) 118-119.

Chapter 7

[1] *The Christian Examiner* [compiled journal], (Boston: O. Everett, New York: C.S. Francis, 1824-1869), 234.
[2] Roland De Vaux, *Ancient Israel: Its Life and Institutions* (Grand Rapids, Michigan: W.B. Eerdmans,1997), 74.
[3] David M. Goldenberg, *The Curse of Ham: Race and Slavery in Early Judaism, Christianity, and Islam* (Princeton: Princeton University Press, 2003), 1. Goldenberg's excellent book covers the early history of the Curse, while two other quality treatments are helpful with later periods. See David M. Whitford, *The Curse of Ham in the Early Modern Era: The Bible and the Justifications for Slavery* (Farnham, England: Burlington, VT; Ashgate Publishing Ltd., 2009) and Stephen R. Haynes, *Noah's Curse: The Biblical Justification of American Slavery* (Oxford: Oxford University Press, 2002).
[4] John Henry Hopkins, *A Scriptural, Ecclesiastical, and Historical View of Slavery, from the Days of the Patriarch Abraham, to the Nineteenth Century* (New York: W.I. Pooley & Co., 1864), 7.
[5] Pope Pius IX, "A Prayer to Implore the Conversion of the Descendants of Cham in Central Africa," Oct. 2, 1873. Collected by the Catholic Church, "Congregatio indulgentiarum et sacrarum reliquiarum" in *The Raccolta; or, Collection of Prayers and Good Works, to Which the Sovereign Pontiffs Have Attached Holy Indulgences* ([Woodstock], Maryland: Woodstock College, 1878), 413.
[6] Cyrus Ingerson Scofield, The Scofield Reference Bible: the Holy Bible, containing the Old and New Testaments (New York: Oxford University Press, American Branch; London : H. Frowde, 1909), 16.
[7] Ibid.
[8] David M. Goldenberg, *The Curse of Ham,* 143.
[9] Ibid, *144.*
[10] Augustin Calmet and C. Taylor, *Calmet's Dictionary of the Holy Bible* (Boston, Crocker and Brewster, 1832), 476.
[11] David M. Goldenberg, *The Curse of Ham,* 143.
[12] See: William F. Albright, "Reviewed Work(s)," *Hebrew Union College Annual Journal of Biblical Literature*, Vol. 64, No. 2 (June, 1945): 294. Also, Joshua Blau,

"On Polyphony in Biblical Hebrew," *Proceedings of the Israel Academy of Sciences and Humanities*, 6 (1982), 144-178. Also, David Noel Freedman, ed., "Ham." In *Eerdmans Dictionary of the Bible*, 543. Edinburgh, Alban Books, 2002.

[13] Lorenzo Johnston Greene, *The Negro in Colonial New England, 1620-1776* (New York: Columbia University Press, 1942), 62.

[14] David Humphries, *An Historical Account of the Incorporated Society for the Propagation of the Gospel in Foreign Parts* (New York: Arno Press, 1969 [1730]), 232-233.

[15] Ibid, 235-236.

[16] Ibid, 139.

[17] Albert J. Raboteau, *Slave Religion: The "Invisible Institution" in the Antebellum South* (Oxford: Oxford University Press, 2004), 149.

[18] Samuel Parsons Scott, translator; Alfonso X (King of Castile and Leon), Robert I. Burns, ed., *Las Siete Partidas* (Philadelphia: University of Pennsylvania Press, 2001), xxiv.

[19] Ibid.

[20] Seymour Drescher, *Abolition: A History of Slavery and Antislavery*, 15.

[21] Samuel Parsons Scott, et. al., *Las Siete Partidas*, xxiv.

[22] Forrest G. Wood, *The Arrogance of Faith*, 116.

[23] Samuel L. Chatman, "'There Are No Slaves in France': A Re-examination of Slave Laws in Eighteenth Century France," *The Journal of Negro History* (2000): www.jstor.org/pss/2649071.

[24] George Fisch. Nine Months in the United States During the Crisis (London: James Nisbet & Co., 1863), 114.

Chapter 8

[1] Historic Germantown: Philadelphia, PA, "Thones Kunders House Site," http://www.ushistory.org/germantown/lower/kunders.htm.

[2] James O. Lehman and Steven M. Nolt, *Mennonites, Amish, and the American Civil War* (Baltimore: Md. Johns Hopkins Univ. Press 2007), 30.

[3] Rodney Stark and Roger Finke, "American Religion in 1776: A Statistical Portrait," *Sociology of Religion*, Volume 49, Issue 1, 1 (March 1988): 39–51, https://doi.org/10.2307/3711102.

[4] "Quakers: From Slave Traders to Early Abolitionists," www.pbs.org/thisfarbyfaith/. (Most easily located in the "Printable Version" link on the lower part of the main page.)

[5] J. William Frost, "George Fox's Ambiguous Anti-slavery Legacy," http://trilogy.brynmawr.edu/speccoll/quakersandslavery/commentary/people/fox.php.

[6] Robert Smith, ed., "The Friend: Religious and Literary Journal," vol. xvii, *The Friend*, (1844): 125.

[7] William H. Phillips, "Cotton Gin," http://eh.net/encyclopedia/cotton-gin/.

[8] Stark, and Finke, "American Religion in 1776," 43.

[9] Frederick Douglass, "Baptists, Congregationalists, the Free Church, and Slavery: An Address Delivered in Belfast, Ireland, on December 23, 1845." Belfast News Letter, December 26, 1845 and Belfast Northern Whig, December 25, 1845. John Blassingame, et. al., eds., *The Frederick Douglass Papers: Series One–Speeches, Debates, and Interviews, Vol. I* (New Haven: Yale University Press, 1979), https://glc.yale.edu/baptists-congregationalists-free-church-and-slavery.

---

[10] Richard Morgan Cameron (Methodist Church (U.S.). Board of Social and Economic Relations), *Methodism and Society in Historical Perspective* (New York: Abingdon, 1961), 97.

[11] Ibid, 99.

[12] Ibid.

[13] William Peter Strickland, History of the Discipline of the Methodist Episcopal Church (New York: Carlton & Porter, 5th ed., 1857), 328. For a fuller discussion of the evolution of this issue in the Methodist church see this same volume, pp. 327 ff.

[14] Forrest G. Wood, *The Arrogance of Faith*, 309.

[15] Ibid.

[16] For a fuller discussion of the slavery issue in the Baptist and Presbyterian churches, see Forrest G. Wood, *The Arrogance of Faith*, 295-307, 318-332. See also: James G. Birney, *The American Churches: The Bulwarks of American Slavery*; "The Schism of 1861: Presbyterian Church History, Chapter 7," www.americanpresbyterianchurch.org/apc-history/presbyterian-history/the-schism-of-1861/.

[17] Cotton Mather, Paul Royster, ed., The Negro Christianized: An Essay to Excite and Assist that Good Work, the Instruction of Negro-Servants in Christianity (Lincoln: DigitalCommons@University of Nebraska – Lincoln, originally published 1706), 28. http://digitalcommons.unl.edu/etas/28.

[18] Ibid, 29.

[19] Charles Colcock Jones. "A Catechism for Colored Persons." Cited in Jeffrey Robert Young, *Proslavery and Sectional Thought in the Early South, 1740 – 1829: an Anthology* (Columbia, SC: Univ. of South Carolina Press 2006), 162.

[20] Ibid,163.

[21] Ibid.

[22] Mia Bay, *The White Image in the Black Mind: African-American Ideas about White People, 1830-1925* (New York [u.a.]: Oxford Univ. Press, 2000), 179-180.

[23] Ibid, 179.

[24] Ibid.

[25] Ibid, 181.

[26] Paul Finkelman, *EPDF*, "Milestone Documents in African American History: Exploring the Essential Primary Sources," Section 24, "Virginia's Act III: Baptism Does Not Exempt Slaves from Bondage," https://epdf.tips/milestone-documents-in-african-american-history-exploring-the-essential-primary-.html.

[27] Eugene D. Genovese, "Black Conversion and White Sensibility," in Cornel West and Eddie S. Glaude, African American Religious Thought: an Anthology (Louisville, Kentucky: Westminster John Knox Press, 2003), 292.

[28] Forrest G. Wood, *The Arrogance of Faith*, 119.

[29] The National Archives, "Black Presence: Slave or Free?," www.nationalarchives.gov.uk/pathways/blackhistory/rights/slave_free.htm.

[30] Francis Le Jau, "The Carolina Chronicle of Francis Le Jau (1706-1717),"; in Kirsten Fischer and Eric Hinderaker, *Colonial American History* (Malden, MA: Blackwell Publishers, 2002), 179.

[31] Federal Writers' Project, Virginia: A Guide to the Old Dominion (New York: 1952), 78.

[32] Rudolph Lewis, "Up From Slavery: A Documentary History of Negro Education," www.nathanielturner.com/educationhistorynegro6.htm.

[33] Eugene D. Genovese, "Black Conversion and White Sensibility," 294.

[34] Janet Duitsman Cornelius, *Slave Missions and the Black Church in the Antebellum South* (Columbia: Univ. of South Carolina Press, 1999), 30. See also: Larry M. James,

"Biracial Fellowship in Antebellum Baptist Churches," in John B. Boles. *Masters & Slaves in the House of the Lord: Race and Religion in the American South, 1740-1870.*

[35] James G. Birney, *The American Churches*, 6.

[36] Junius P. Rodriguez. *The Historical Encyclopedia of World Slavery* (Santa Barbara, California: Oxford, ABC-Clio, 1997), 28.

[37] Ibid.

[38] Ibid.

[39] "The Emigrationist Movement: A New Home or a Forced Exodus?" www.pbs.org/thisfarbyfaith/. (Most easily located in the "Printable Version" link on the lower part of the main page.)

[40] Forrest G. Wood, *The Arrogance of Faith*, 295. Calculations for the number of emigrants varies, but this is the most generous number I have found for this period of time.

[41] See: Phillip W. Magness and Sebastian N. Page, *Colonization After Emancipation: Lincoln and the Movement for Black Resettlement* (Columbia, Missouri: University of Missouri Press, 2010).

[42] Abraham Lincoln, "Address on Colonization to a Deputation of Negroes; August 14, 1862," in *Collected Works of Abraham Lincoln, Vol. 5*, Ann Arbor, Michigan: University of Michigan Digital Library Production Services 2001, https://quod.lib.umich.edu/l/lincoln/lincoln5?page=viewtextnote;rgn=full+text, 371-373.

[43] Janet Duitsman Cornelius, *Slave Missions and the Black Church*, 9.

[44] James Mellon, *Bullwhip Days: The Slaves Remember: An Oral History* (New York, Grove Press, 1988), 195.

[45] "Santa Barbara Ring Shout Project," www.ringshout.org/.

[46] C. Eric Lincoln, *The Black Church in the African American Experience* (Durham, Duke University Press, 1991), 23.

[47] Ibid, 65.

[48] Janet Duitsman Cornelius, *Slave Missions and the Black Church*, 117.

[49] Richard Allen describes the event in his autobiography. Richard Allen, *The Life Experience and Gospel Labors of the Rt. Rev. Richard Allen* (New York: Abingdon Press, 1960), 25.

[50] The Official Website: African American Episcopal Church, "Our History," https://www.ame-church.com/our-church/our-history/.

Chapter 9

[1] William Garrot Brown, "The Tenth Decade of the United States," *Atlantic Monthly*, July, 1905, 362. This quote also appears in the museum at the Lincoln Memorial in Washington, DC.

[2] The National Archives, "The Emancipation Proclamation: Transcript of the Proclamation," https://www.archives.gov/exhibits/featured-documents/emancipation-proclamation/transcript.html.

[3] Mary Beth Norton, Carol Sheriff, David M Katzman, et al., *A People & a Nation Volume One, To 1877* (Boston: Houghton Mifflin, 1990), 418.

[4] John David Smith "The Enduring Myth of 'Forty Acres and a Mule'." The Chronicle of Higher Education (July 14, 2011), http://chronicle.com/article/The-Enduring-Myth-of-Forty/32583.

[5] Ibid.

[6] Ibid.

[7] Ibid.

[8] For the actual text of this provision see: United States Congress. Journal of the House of Representatives of the United States: Second Session of the Thirty-Eighth Congress (Washington, DC; Government Printing Office, 1865), 483.

[9] Ibid.

[10] Ibid.

[11] For the text of these amendments: http://topics.law.cornell.edu/constitution.

[12] Andrew Johnson, "Third Annual Message," State of the Union Address, Washington, DC, December 3, 1867, http://www.presidency.ucsb.edu/ws/?pid=29508.

[13] George Mason University: Roy Rosenzweig Center for History and New Media "The Civil Rights Act of March 1, 1875," http://chnm.gmu.edu/courses/122/recon/civilrightsact.html.

[14] The National Archives, "African American Heritage: African American Records: The Freedmen's Bureau," www.archives.gov/research/african-americans/freedmens-bureau/.

[15] James C. Giesen, "Sharecropping," The New Georgia Encyclopedia, updated 5/1/2009, www.georgiaencyclopedia.org/nge/Article.jsp?id=h-3590.

[16] Ronald E. Butchart, last edited by NGE staff on 4/13/2016, "Freedmen's Education during Reconstruction," in *New Georgia Encyclopedia*, www.georgiaencyclopedia.org/nge/Article.jsp?id=h-634.

[17] David Blight, "Black Reconstruction in the South," (lecture, HIST 119: The Civil War and Reconstruction Era, 1845-1877, Open Yale Courses, Yale University, 2018), https://oyc.yale.edu/history/hist-119/lecture-23.

[18] David Stricklin and Chris Stewart, "Philanthropy," In *The Encyclopedia of Arkansas History and Culture*, updated 12/18/2017, www.encyclopediaofarkansas.net/encyclopedia/entry-detail.aspx?entryID=4853.

[19] Keith S. Hébert, "Ku Klux Klan (KKK) During the Reconstruction Period," In *Encyclopedia of Alabama*, published September 14, 2010, updated Jan. 5, 2015, www.encyclopediaofalabama.org/face/Article.jsp?id=h-2934.

[20] David Blight, "After Appomattox: Book review of *The Bloody Shirt* by Stephen Budiansky" in *The New York Sun*, January 30, 2008, https://www.nysun.com/arts/after-appomattox/70434/.

[21] Richard M. Valelly, *The Two Reconstructions: The Struggle for Black Enfranchisement* (Chicago: University of Chicago Press, 2004), 32.

[22] David Blight, "Retreat from Reconstruction: The Grant Era and Paths to 'Southern Redemption,'" lecture, HIST 119: The Civil War and Reconstruction Era, 1845-1877, Open Yale Courses, Yale University, 2018, https://oyc.yale.edu/history/hist-119/lecture-24.

[23] Lerone Bennett Jr., "Black Power in Dixie," *Ebony*, vol. 7, no. 9, Sept. 1962, 88.

[24] David Blight. "Black Reconstruction in the South," https://oyc.yale.edu/history/hist-119/lecture-23.

[25] Anne H. Pinn and Anthony B. Pinn, *Fortress Introduction to Black Church History* (Minneapolis: Fortress Press, 2002), 37.

[26] William B. Gravely, "Christian Methodist Episcopal Church," in *Encyclopedia of Religion in the South* (Macon, GA: Mercer University Press, 2005), 189.

[27] Daniel W. Stowell, *Rebuilding Zion: The Religious Reconstruction of the South, 1863-1877* (New York: Oxford Univ. Press, 1998), 92.

[28] Lucius Henry Holsey, Autobiography, Sermons, Addresses, and Essays of L. H. Holsey, D.D. (Atlanta: The Franklin Printing and Publishing Co., 1898), 218, https://docsouth.unc.edu/neh/holsey/holsey.html.

[29] Charles Eric Lincoln and Lawrence H. Mamiya, *The Black Church in the African-American Experience* (Durham: Duke University Press, 1990), 27.

[30] Eric Foner, *A Short History of Reconstruction* (New York: Harper Collins, 2010), 42.

[31] Frederick Douglas, "The Color Question," (The Frederick Douglass Papers at the Library of Congress) www.loc.gov/rr/program/bib/douglass/.

[32] David Blight. "Black Reconstruction in the South," https://oyc.yale.edu/history/hist-119/lecture-26.

[33] Eric Foner, "A Massacre and a Travesty," *The Washington Post*, March 23, 2008, www.washingtonpost.com/wp-dyn/content/article/2008/03/20/AR2008032003067.html.

[34] Mark A. Noll, God and Race in American Politics: A Short History (Princeton and Oxford: Princeton University Press, 2008), 72.

[35] Ibid.

[36] Nicholas Lemann, *Redemption: The Last Battle of the Civil War* (New York: Farrar, Straus and Giroux, 2007), 69.

[37] Martin Luther King, Jr., "Letter from a Birmingham Jail," http://mlk-kpp01.stanford.edu/kingweb/popular_requests/frequentdocs/birmingham.pdf.

[38] Ibid.

Chapter 10

[1] David Pilgrim, "Who Was Jim Crow?" Jim Crow Museum of Racist Memorabilia, Ferris State University, 2000, edited 2012, https://ferris.edu/news/jimcrow/who/.

[2] Michael O. Emerson and Christian Smith, *Divided by Faith*, (Oxford: Oxford University Press, 2000), 42.

[3] Henry McNeal Turner, *Civil Rights : The Outrage of the Supreme Court of the United States upon the Black Man* (Philadelphia: Publication Department of the AME Church, 1889), 14, Transcribed text at https://docsouth.unc.edu/church/turnercivil/turner.html.

[4] Henry McNeal Turner, *The Barbarous Decision of the United States Supreme Court Declaring the Civil Rights Act Unconstitutional And Disrobing the Colored Race of All Civil Protection* (Atlanta: Published by the author, 1893), 3. Transcribed text at https://docsouth.unc.edu/church/turnerbd/turner.html.

[5] Richard Wormser, *The Rise and Fall of Jim Crow* (New York: St. Martin's Griffin, 2004), xii.

[6] National Park Service, "Jim Crow Laws," Martin Luther King National Historical Site, www.nps.gov/malu/forteachers/jim_crow_laws.htm.

[7] L. C. Allen, "The Negro Health Problem," American Journal of Public Health; vol. 5, number 3 (March, 1915): 194, 196.

[8] Bruno Bettelheim and Morris Janowitz, Social Change and Prejudice, Including Dynamics of Prejudice, (New York, Free Press of Glencoe, 1964), 142. This study was first published in 1950, re-published in 1964 and 1975 ith additional comments.

[9] Paul Finkelman, *Encyclopedia of American Civil Liberties, Volume 1* (New York, Taylor & Francis Group, 2006), 1022.

[10] Massachusetts General Court, *The Charters and General Laws of the Colony and Province of Massachusetts Bay* (Boston: T.B. Wait and Co., 1814), 747.

[11] New York Historical Society, *Proceedings of the New York Historical Society, Volume 1843* (New York: Press of the Historical Society, 1844-49), 104.

[12] "Anti-miscegenation Laws in the United States," http://en.wikipedia.org /wiki/Anti-miscegenation_laws_in_the_United_States. Note on Wikipedia: Due to the uneven reliability of its entries, I have generally avoided citing this source. In this case, however, it offers a set of tables that display the dates of repeal by state. This same historical information is corroborated by other sources, none of which organizes it in such a useful fashion.

[13] Somini Sengupta, "November 5-11; Marry at Will" *The New York Times*, November 12, 2000, https://www.nytimes.com/2000/11/12/weekinreview/november-5-11-marry-at-will.html.

[14] Somini Sengupta, "Ideas & Trends: The Color of Love; Removing a Relic of the Old South," *The New York Times*, Nov. 5, 2000, https://www.nytimes.com/2000/11/05/ weekinreview/ideas-trends-the-color-of-love-removing-a-relic-of-the-old-south.html.

[15] Joseph Carroll, "Most Americans Approve of Interracial Marriages." Aug. 16, 2007, www.gallup.com/poll/28417/most-americans-approve-interracial-marriages.aspx.

[16] "Table 1. Race of Wife by Race of Husband: 1960, 1970, 1980, 1991, and 1992," www.census.gov/population/socdemo/race/interractab1.txt. While the overall interracial marriage rates of all groups increased significantly from 1960-1970, if white and black marriages to other races are excluded, the percentage of interracial marriages between whites and blacks rose only from 0.12% (.0012) to 0.13% (.0013) during the decade. These percentages (cited here and below) are based on my black/white calculations from the data presented in Census documents but do not appear in this extracted form in the documents themselves.

[17] Eugene D. Genovese, *A Consuming Fire: The Fall of the Confederacy in the Mind of the White Christian South* (University of Georgia Press, Athens and London, 1998), 93.

[18] Albert Bushnell Hart, *The Southern South* (New York, London: D. Appleton, 1910), 154.

[19] United States Bureau of the Census, *Thirteenth census of the United States taken in the year 1910. Abstract of the census, statistics of population, agriculture, manufactures, & mining for the United States, the States, & principal cities, with supplement for Michigan, containing statistics for the state, counties, [etc.]* (Washington: Government printing office, 1913), 79.

[20] Quoted in Horace Mann Bond, Julia W. Bond, Adam Fairclough, *The Star Creek Papers* (Athens, Georgia: University of Georgia Press, 1997), 132.

[21] Janet Browne, *Darwin's Origin of Species: a Biography* (New York: Atlantic Monthly Press, 2006), 128.

[22] Genovese, *A Consuming Fire*, 94.

[23] F. F. Bruce *The New International Commentary on the New Testament: Acts* (Grand Rapids: Michigan; William B. Eerdmans, 1988), 337.

Chapter 11

[1] "Strange Fruit" by Billie Holliday, words and music by Lewis Allan (a pseudonym for Abel Meeropol), 1939, http://www.songfacts.com/detail.php?lyrics=543.

[2] Josh Sanburn, "Strange Fruit," *TIME*, "All-TIME 100 Songs, Populist: Lists about Entertainment," Oct. 21, 2011, http://entertainment.time.com/2011/10/24/the-all-time-100-songs/slide/strange-fruit-billie-holiday/.

[3] "Strange Fruit: Anniversary of a Lynching," NPR: "All Things Considered," Aug. 6, 2010, https://www.npr.org/templates/story/story.php?storyId=129025516.

[4] D. A. Graham, "Some Facts About Southern Lynchings," (1899) in Philip Sheldon Foner, Robert J. Branham. Lift Every Voice: African American Oratory, 1787-1900 (Tuscaloosa, University of Alabama Press, 1998), 882.

[5] William Ferris. *Blues from the Delta* (New York, London: Da Capo, 1984), 19.

[6] Steve Martinot, *The Machinery of Whiteness: Studies in the Structure of Racialization* (Philadelphia: Temple University Press, 2010), 68.

[7] Pete Daniel, *The Shadow of Slavery: Peonage in the South, 1901-1969* (Urbana: University of Illinois Press, 1990), 126. The source of this citation is: Mary F. Berry, "Do Black People Have a Constitutional Right to Life: A Consideration of Federal and State Concern about the Murder of Black People, 1877-1969," paper delivered to the *Southern Historical Association Convention*, Nov. 12, 1970, 22-28.

[8] Christopher Waldrep, *Jury Discrimination: The Supreme Court, Public Opinion, and a Grassroots Fight for Racial Equality in Mississippi* (Athens, Georgia: University of Georgia Press, 2010), 4.

[9] Jeffrey B. Abramson, *We, the Jury: The Jury System and the Ideal of Democracy* (Cambridge: Harvard University Press, 2000), 112.

[10] William Bradford Huie, "The Shocking Story of Approved Killing in Mississippi," *Look*, January 24, 1956, 46-49. Quoted in Philip Dray. *At the Hands of Persons Unknown: The Lynching of Black America* (New York: The Modern Library, 2003), 432.

[11] Robert A. Gibson, "The Negro Holocaust: Lynching and Race Riots in the United States, 1880-1950." www.yale.edu/ynhti/curriculum/units/1979/2/79.02.04.x.html.

[12] William S. Beard, ed., *The American Missionary*, Volume 73, Issue 5 (New series, Vol. 11, No. 2) American Missionary Association, Congregational Home Missionary Society (May, 1919): 102.

[13] Manfred Berg, *Popular Justice: A History of Lynching in America* (Chicago: Ivan R. Dee, 2011), 3.

[14] Jessie Parkhurst Guzman, ed., *1952 Negro Year Book: A Review of Events Affecting Negro Life, 1941-46* (Tuskegee, Alabama: Dept. of Records and Research, Tuskegee Institute; 1947), 303.

[15] Michael Laris, "Emmett Till's trial and other civil rights milestones still vivid for reporter," *The Washington Post*, August 27, 2013, www.washingtonpost.com/local/emmett-tills-trial-and-other-civil-rights-milestones-still-vivid-for-reporter/2013/08/27/e4b565bc-0f31-11e3-bdf6-e4fc677d94a1_story.html.

[16] University of Missouri-Kansas City School of Law, "Lynchings: By State and Race, 1882-1968," http://law2.umkc.edu/faculty/projects/ftrials/shipp/lynchingsstate.html.

[17] The calculations are my own, based on: University of Missouri-Kansas City School of Law, "Lynchings Statistics by Year and Race," http://law2.umkc.edu/faculty/projects/ftrials/shipp/lynchingyear.html.

[18] George Mason University. "History Matters: The U.S. Survey Course on the Web The Body Count: Lynching in Arkansas," http://historymatters.gmu.edu/d/5467/.

[19] Richard Lacayo, "Blood At The Root," *Time*, Sunday, Apr. 02, 2000, www.time.com/time/magazine/article/0,9171,42301,00.html.

[20] For more information see James M. Sorrell, "The 'Waco Horror:' The Lynching of Jesse Washington," in Bruce A. Glasrud, *The African American Experience in Texas: An Anthology* (Lubbock, Texas: Texas Tech University Press; 2007), 183, ff. See also: Amy Louise Wood, *Lynching and Spectacle: Witnessing Racial Violence in America, 1890-1940* (Chapel Hill: University of North Carolina Press, 2009), 179, ff. See also:

Patricia Bernstein, *The First Waco Horror: The Lynching of Jesse Washington and the Rise of the NAACP* (College Station: Texas A&M University Press, 2006).

[21] The postcard and the inscription from the reverse side can be viewed at http://en.wikipedia.org/wiki/Lynching_of_Jesse_Washington.

[22] James Cutler, *Lynch-Law: An Investigation into History of Lynching in the United States* (New York: Longmans, Green, and Company, 1905), 1.

[23] Reinhold Niebuhr, Christian Century, April 19, 1923, 502. quoted in Robert Moats Miller, "The Protestant Churches and Lynching, 1919-1939," The Journal of Negro History," Vol. 42, No. 2, (April, 1957): 118-131.

[24] Henry Ward Beecher, "Reconstruction," *Independent*, July 6, 1865, 8, quoted in Michael A. Bellesiles, *1877: America's Year of Living Violently* (New York: New Press, 2010), 58.

[25] Ibid.

[26] Lyle W. Dorsett, *A Passion for Souls: The Life of D. L. Moody* (Chicago: Moody Press, 1997), 246.

[27] Sam P. Jones, Randall J. Stephens, ed., *Sam Jones' Own Book: A Series of Sermons* (Columbia: University of South Carolina Press in cooperation with the Institute for Southern Studies of the University of South Carolina, 2009), back cover of book.

[28] Kathleen Minnix, *Laughter in the Amen Corner: The Life of Evangelist Sam Jones* (Athens: University of Georgia Press, 2010), 200.

[29] Ibid.

[30] Ibid, 201.

[31] Ibid.

[32] For greater detail on the stands taken by various groups see: Robert Moats Miller, "The Protestant Churches and Lynching, 1919-1939," *The Journal of Negro History*, Vol. 42, No. 2; (April, 1957): 118-131.

[33] For more background on the Southern Baptist response, see: Robert Moats Miller, "The Protestant Churches and Lynching," 119. Miller culled this material from three unpublished doctoral dissertations cited in his work.

[34] Robert A. Gibson, *The Negro Holocaust: Lynching and Race Riots in the United States, 1880-1950* (Yale-New Haven Teachers Institute), www.yale.edu/ynhti/curriculum/units/1979/2/79.02.04.x.html.

[35] Congressional Record, (67th Congress; 2nd Session; Volume 62; part 2; January 18, 1922), 1706.

[36] Ibid,1721.

[37] Thomas Dixon, *The Leopard's Spots* (New York: Doubleday, Page, 1902), 5.

[38] "Biggest Money Pictures," *Variety* (June 21, 1932): 1.

[39] Jessie Parkhurst Guzman, ed., "Table 8: Causes of Lynchings Classified, 1882-1951," in *1952 Negro year Book, Vol. 1: A Review of Events Affecting Negro Life* (New York: WM. H. Wise & Co., Inc., Tuskegee Institute, 1952), 278. www.archive.org/stream/negroyearbook52tuskrich/ negroyearbook52tuskrich_djvu.txt.

[40] Maria DeLongoria, *"Stranger Fruit": The Lynching of Black Women the Cases of Rosa Richardson and Marie Scott*. PhD thesis, University of Missouri–Columbia, 2006, 1, 77, 142, https://mospace.umsystem.edu/xmlui/bitstream/handle/10355/4447/ research.pdf?sequence=3. Per this author a total of 159 black women were lynched.

Chapter 12

[1] Paul Harvey, *Freedom's Coming: Religious Culture and the Shaping of the South from the Civil War through the Civil Rights Era* (Chapel Hill, Univ. of North Carolina Press, 2005), 8.

[2] For more information see: Juan Williams and Quinton Hosford Dixie, *This Far by Faith: Stories from the African American Religious Experience* (New York: Amistad, 2003), 101-123. Also, "This Far by Faith: People of Faith: Henry McNeal Turner," www.pbs.org/thisfarbyfaith/people/henry_mcneal_turner.html.

[3] W. Edward Orser, "Racial Attitudes During Wartime: The Protestant Churches during the Second World War," *Church History*, Vol. 41, No. 3, (Sept., 1972): 337.

[4] Benjamin Elijah Mays, Orville Vernon Burton, *Born to Rebel: An Autobiography* (Athens: University of Georgia Press, 2002), 253.

[5] Ibid. Both white and black church leaders were involved in elaborating this statement.

[6] Peter C. Murray, *Methodists and the crucible of race 1930-1975* (Columbia: University of Missouri Press, 2004), 57.

[7] Barry Hankins, *American Evangelicals: A Contemporary History of a Mainstream Religious Movement* (Lanham: Rowman & Littlefield, 2009, 2008), 124.

[8] Troy A. Murphy and William Jennings Bryan, "Boy Orator, Broken Man, and the 'Evolution' of America's Public Philosophy," *Great Plains Quarterly*, vol. 22, no. 2, (Spring, 2002): 83.

[9] Josiah Strong, *Our Country: Its Possible Future and Its Present Crisis* (New York: Baker & Taylor Co. for the American Home Missionary Society, 1885), 178.

[10] Ibid, 177.

[11] Albert Jeremiah Beveridge, "Our Philippine Policy," Speech delivered on the Senate floor January 9, 1900 in *The Meaning of the Times: And Other Speeches*, (Indianapolis, Bobbs-Merrill Co., 1908), 85.

[12] For more information see: Morris J. MacGregor, *The Emergence of a Black Catholic Community: St. Augustine's in Washington* (Washington, DC: Catholic University of America Press; 1999), 28-30.

[13] David W. Southern, *John LaFarge and the Limits of Catholic Interracialism, 1911-1963* (Baton Rouge: Louisiana State Univ. Press, 1996), 72.

[14] Forrest G. Wood, *The Arrogance of Faith*, 363.

[15] David W. Southern, *Limits of Catholic Interracialism*, 81.

[16] William Edward Burghardt Du Bois, Herbert Aptheker, ed., "Correspondence with Joseph B. Glenn; March 24, 1925"; in *The Correspondence of W. E. B. Du Bois, Vol. 1: Selections, 1877-1934* (Amherst: University of Massachusetts Press, 1997), 311.

[17] Ibid.

[18] Cheryl J. Saunders, Saints in Exile: The Holiness-Pentecostal Experience in African American Religion and Culture (New York: Oxford University Press, 1996), 29.

[19] "Harvey Cox, Fire from Heaven: The Rise of Pentecostal Spirituality and the Reshaping of Religion in the twenty-first Century (Cambridge, Massachusetts: Da Capo Press; 2001), 61.

[20] Ibid.

[21] Harvey Cox, *Fire from Heaven*, 63.

[22] Edward L. Queen, Stephen R. Prothero, Gardiner H. Shattuck, eds., *Encyclopedia of American religious history, Volume 3* (New York: Facts On File, 2009), 162.

Chapter 13

[1] Cynthia L. Clark, *The American Economy: A Historical Encyclopedia, Volume 1* (Santa Barbara, California: ABC-CLIO; 2011), 646.

[2] "Table 1.1 – Summary of Receipts, Outlays, and Surpluses or Deficits (-): 1789–2023," Office of Management and Budget: Historical Tables, https://www.whitehouse.gov/omb/historical-tables/. The figures in this chart are not adjusted for inflation, but the inflation rate for the period in question was negligible.

[3] Randall G. Holcombe, "The Growth of the Federal Government in the 1920s," *The Cato Journal*, Vol. 16, No. 2 (Fall, 1996): Figure 1, 176. https://www.cato.org/cato-journal/fall-1996.

[4] Cpl. Rupert Trimmingham, Correspondence with *Yank* magazine, April, 1944, in *The Best from Yank, the Army Weekly*. (USA, Franklin S. Forsberg, 1945), 212-213.

[5] Cpl. Henry S. Wootton Jr., Correspondence with *Yank* magazine, in *The Best from Yank, the Army Weekly*, (USA: Franklin S. Forsberg, 1945), 213.

[6] Nelson, Jack, "The Civil Rights Movement: A Press Perspective." Human Rights 28, no. 4 (2001): 3-6, http://www.jstor.org/stable/27880281.

[7] Harry S. Truman, as quoted in Raymond H. Geselbracht, The *Civil Rights Legacy of Harry S. Truman* (Kirksville, Missouri: Truman State University Press, 2007), 110.

[8] Harry S. Truman Library and Museum, https://www.trumanlibrary.org/whistlestop/study_collections/desegregation/large/index.php?action=pdf&documentid=2-7.

[9] Martin Luther King Jr, "Letter from a Birmingham Jail," African Studies Center, University of Pennsylvania, www.africa.upenn.edu/Articles_Gen/Letter_Birmingham.html.

[10] U.S. Supreme Court, "Brown V. Board of Education Of Topeka, 347 U. S. 483, 1954," U. S. Supreme Court Center, http://supreme.justia.com/us/347/483/case.html.

[11] See the chapter, "Mixed Blessings: Martin Luther King, Jr., and the Lessons of an Ambiguous Leader," in Michael Eric Dyson, *The Michael Eric Dyson Reader* (New York: Basic Civitas Books, 2004), 287-305. See also: Michael Eric Dyson, *I May Not Get There with You: The True Martin Luther King, Jr.* (New York: Free Press, 2000). See also: Ralph Abernathy, *And the Walls Came Tumbling Down: An Autobiography* (New York: Harper & Row, 1989), 471.

[12] Editorial, *The New York Times*, Nov. 13, 1990, www.nytimes.com/1990/11/13/opinion/what-dr-king-wrote-and-what-he-did.html.

[13] "A Statement to the South and to the Nation," in "Martin Luther King, Jr. Papers Project," Southern Negro Leaders Conference on Transportation and Nonviolent Integration, Atlanta, January 10–11, 1957, http://mlkkpp01.stanford.edu/primarydocuments/Vol4/11-Jan-1957_AStatementToTheSouth.pdf, 105.

[14] David L. Chappell, *A Stone of Hope: Prophetic Religion and the Death of Jim Crow* (Chapel Hill and London: The University of North Carolina Press, 2004), 87.

[15] Fred Shuttlesworth, "President's Address to ACMHR," July 11, 1958, Shuttlesworth Papers, box 1, sw, July 9, 1958, 1. Quoted in: Andrew M. Manis, *A Fire You Can't Put Out: The Civil Rights Life of Birmingham's Reverend Fred Shuttlesworth* (Tuscaloosa, London: University of Alabama Press, 1999), 174.

[16] Martin Luther King, Jr., "Letter from a Birmingham Jail."

[17] Martin Luther King, Jr., *Stride Toward Freedom: The Montgomery Story* (Boston: Beacon Press, 2010); 196.

[18] Joseph Carroll, "Race and Education 50 Years After *Brown v. Board of Education*," Gallup, May 14, 2004, https://news.gallup.com/poll/11686/race-education-years-after-brown-board-education.aspx.

[19] Gallup Poll of June 28, 1961, quoted in Hazel Erskine, "The Polls: Speed of Racial Integration," *The Public Opinion Quarterly*, Vol. 32, No. 3, (Autumn, 1968): 513.
[20] "The Southern Manifesto of 1956: March 12, 1956", Office of the Clerk: U.S. House of Representatives, http://history.house.gov/Historical-Highlights/1951-2000/The-Southern-Manifesto-of-1956/.
[21] Sondra Gordy. "Lost Year," in *The Encyclopedia of Arkansas History & Culture*, updated 6/2/2017, http://www.encyclopediaofarkansas.net/encyclopedia/entry-detail.aspx?search=1&entryID=737.
[22] "Timeline of Events Leading to the Brown v. Board of Education Decision, 1954," National Archives, www.archives.gov/education/lessons/brown-v-board/timeline.html.
[23] Charles C. Diggs, quoted in James W. Vander Zanden, "The Impact of Little Rock," *Journal of Educational Sociology*, Vol. 35, No. 8 (Apr., 1962): 381.
[24] "African American Odyssey: The Civil Rights Era—Sit-ins, Freedom Rides, and Demonstrations," Library of Congress, http://memory.loc.gov/ammem/aaohtml/exhibit/aopart9b.html.
[25] Robert E Dewhirst, *Encyclopedia of the United States Congress* (New York: Facts on File, 2007), 529.
[26] Lyndon B. Johnson, "LBJ's Election Analysis," private conversation with Hubert Humphrey at All the Way with LBJ, https://allthewaywithlbj.com/lbjs-election-analysis/.
[27] Robert E Dewhirst, *Encyclopedia of the United States Congress*, 529.
[28] Library of Congress, "Sit-ins, Freedom Rides, and Demonstrations."
[29] Robert E Dewhirst, *Encyclopedia of the United States Congress*, 529.
[30] Robert D. Loevy, *The Civil Rights Act of 1964: The Passage of the Law that Ended Racial Segregation* (Albany, NY: State University of New York Press, 1997), 69.
[31] David L. Chappell, *A Stone of Hope: Prophetic Religion and the Death of Jim Crow* (Chapel Hill and London: The University of North Carolina Press, 2004), 101.
[32] Martin Luther King, Jr., *The Strength to Love* (Philadelphia: Fortress Press, 1981, 1963), 37-38.
[33] Martin Luther King, Jr., "Where Do We Go from Here?" in Martin Luther King, Jr. and James Melvin Washington, *A Testament of Hope: The Essential Writings of Martin Luther King, Jr.* (San Francisco: Harper & Row, 1986), 560.
[34] Ibid, 559.
[35] "Labor Force Statistics from the Current Population Survey, (White vs. Black)" Bureau of Labor Statistics Data Tool, https://data.bls.gov.
[36] Jessica Firger, "Black and White Infant Mortality Rates Show Wide Racial Disparities Still Exist," *Newsweek*, July 3, 2017, www.newsweek.com/black-women-infant-mortality-rate-cdc-631178.
[37] Snyder, Howard N.; Cooper, Alexia D.; and Mulako-Wangota, Joseph. Bureau of Justice Statistics. "U.S. Arrest Estimates, Arrest Rate of Blacks 2014" and "U.S. Arrest Estimates, Arrest Rate of Whites 2014." Generated using the Arrest Data Analysis Tool at www.bjs.gov.
[38] Zhen Zeng, BJS Statistician, "Jail Inmates in 2016: Table 2: Jail incarceration rates, by sex and race/Hispanic origin, 2000, 2005, and 2010-2016," U.S. Department of Justice, Office of Justice Programs, Bureau of Justice Statistics, NCJ 251210, February, 2018, 3, and "Appendix Table 1: Number of confined inmates in local jails, by characteristic, 2000, 2005, 2010-2016," 9. Also, E. Ann Carson, Ph.D., BJS Statistician, "Prisoners in 2016." (U.S. Department of Justice, Office of Justice Programs, Bureau of Justice Statistics), NCJ 251149, January, 2018, and "Table 6: Imprisonment rate of sentenced prisoners under jurisdiction of state or federal

correctional authorities by jurisdiction and demographic characteristics, December 31, 2006-2016," and "Table 13: Number of sentenced prisoners under jurisdiction of state correctional authority, by most serious offense, sex, race, and Hispanic origin, December 31, 2015."

Since the government publications mentioned above tabulate the figures for jails vs. prisons (both state and federal) separately, in order to come up with an overall figure the two incarceration rates must be weighted by the respective populations of jails vs. prisons, which I did by comparing the various tables mentioned in the endnote. The ratio of blacks to whites in the jail population was 4.14 to 1, with a total of 242,200 blacks vs. 338, 700 whites. The ratio of blacks to whites in the prison population was 5.87 to 1, with a total of 489, 900 blacks vs. 439,800 whites.

[39] Jessica L. Semega, Kayla R. Fontenot, Melissa A. Kollar, "Income and Poverty in the United States: 2016," Report Number: P60-259. U.S. Census Bureau, Sept. 12, 2017. www.census.gov/library/publications/2017/demo/ p60-259.html.

[40] Lisa J. Dettling, Joanne W. Hsu, Lindsay Jacobs, Kevin B. Moore, and Jeffrey P. Thompson, with assistance from Elizabeth Llanes, "Recent Trends in Wealth-Holding by Race and Ethnicity: Evidence from the Survey of Consumer Finances," *The Board of Governors of the Federal Reserve System: Feds Notes*. Sept. 21, 2017. https://www.federalreserve.gov/ econres/notes/feds-notes/recent-trends-in-wealth-holding-by-race-and-ethnicity-evidence-from-the-survey-of-consumer-finances-accessible-20170927.htm.

[41] Jeff Guo, "Black-White Wage Gap Widens Among Educated," *The Washington Post*, Oct. 4, 2016, section A, page 10. This article (also available online under the title, "Why black workers who do everything right still get left behind") is a helpful distillation of the much longer report by the Economic Policy Institute (www.epi.org/publication/black-white-wage-gaps-expand-with-rising-wage-inequality/#epi-toc-7). While EPI is, as noted by *The Post*, a "left-leaning think tank," the research itself seems quite carefully done, with multiple controls for other possible explanations.

[42] Martin Luther King, Jr., "MLK Speech at SCLC Staff Retreat," Nov. 14, 1966, 6, www.thekingcenter.org/archive/document/mlk-speech-sclc-staff-retreat.

Chapter 14

[1] Felicia Pratto, Jim Sidanius, Shana Levin, "Social dominance theory and the dynamics of intergroup relations: Taking stock and looking forward," *European Review of Social Psychology*, 17, (2006): 271.

[2] Iaian Walker and Heather J. Smith, "Fifty Years of Relative Deprivation Research," in Iaian Walker and Heather J. Smith, eds., *Relative Deprivation: Specification, Development, and Integration* (Cambridge: Cambridge University Press, 2002), 16.

[3] Jack Levin, Jim Nolan, *The Violence of Hate: Confronting Racism, Anti-Semitism, and Other Forms of Bigotry* (Boston: Allyn & Bacon, 2011), 12.

[4] Bruno Bettelheim and Morris Janowitz, *Social Change and Prejudice, Including Dynamics of Prejudice* (New York: Free Press of Glencoe, 1964), 142.

[5] Robert D. Putnam, David E. Campbell, Shaylyn Romney Garrett, *American Grace: How Religion Divides and Unites Us* (New York: Simon & Schuster, 2010), 118.

[6] "Behind Closed Doors: Evangelicals Are Having Sex... and Abortions," in *NAE Insight*, National Association of Evangelicals; Spring, 2012, 1-2.

[7] "A Report on Juvenile Homicide in the District of Columbia, 2002-2004," District of Columbia Metropolitan Police Department: Office of Organizational Development/Intergovernmental Relations Division, www.washingtonpost.com/ wpsrv/metro/documents/dcjuvenilehomicide_2005.pdf, 2. Two other young ladies (the intended victims, and not juveniles) survived the same attack that killed Myesha.
[8] U.S. Justice Department, Federal Bureau of Investigation, "Crime in the United States: Murder Victims by Age, Sex, and Race – 2009." 2010, www2.fbi.gov/ucr/cius2009/offenses/expanded_information/data/shrtable_02.html.

Chapter 15

[1] Lydia Saad, "On King Holiday, a Split Review of Civil Rights Progress." Gallup; January 21, 2008. www.gallup.com/poll/103828/civil-rights-progress-seen-more.aspx.
[2] "The Big Man Is Martin Luther King," *Newsweek*, July 29, 1963, quoted in Taylor Branch. *Parting the Waters: America in the King Years, 1954-63* (New York: Simon & Schuster, 1989), 856.
[3] Michael O. Emerson and Christian Smith, *Divided by Faith*, (Oxford: Oxford University Press, 2000), 46.
[4] Stuart A Wright, *Making War: Patriots, Politics, and the Oklahoma City Bombing* (Cambridge: New York: Cambridge University Press, 2007), 57. This figure includes the 48% who answer "a lot" and the 27% who answered "some." Had they not considered the influence significant they had the option of answering "minor," "not at all," or "don't know."
[5] William Martin, *A Prophet with Honor: The Billy Graham Story* (New York: William Morrow and Co., 1991), 168.
[6] David L. Chappell, *A Stone of Hope: Prophetic Religion and the Death of Jim Crow* (Chapel Hill and London: The University of North Carolina Press, 2004), 107.
[7] Ibid, 131.
[8] Ibid.
[9] Andres T. Tapia, "Matters of Opinion: Racial Reconciliation: After the Hugs, What?" *Christianity Today*, February 3, 1997. www.christianitytoday.com/ct/1997/february3/7t2054.html.
[10] "Billy Graham Urges Restraint in Sit-ins," *The New York Times*, April 18, 1963, *21.*
[11] Ibid.
[12] Martin Luther King, Jr. and James Melvin, *A Testament of Hope: The Essential Writings of Martin Luther King, Jr.* (San Francisco: Harper & Row, 1986), 219.
[13] William C. Martin, *A Prophet with Honor*, 295-296..
[14] Martin Luther King, Jr., James Melvin; *A Testament of Hope*, 218.
[15] David L. Chappell, *A Stone of Hope*, 4.
[16] "Lewiston Evening Journal," Lewiston, ME; Dec. 6, 1963, 10.
[17] David L. Chappell, *A Stone of Hope, 4.*
[18] Ibid.
[19] Ibid, 3-4
[20] The Bishops of the United States of America, "Racial Discrimination and the Christian Conscience," *American Catholic History Classroom*, 1. https://cuomeka.wrlc.org/items/show/912.
[21] Ibid, 2.
[22] *The Evening Independent*, St. Petersburg, Florida (Holiday Isles Edition); Sept. 19, 1963, p. A-3.

[23] National Black Catholic Congress, "What We Have Seen and Heard: A Pastoral Letter on Evangelization from the Black Bishops of the United States," https://www.cctwincities.org/wp-content/uploads/2015/11/What-We-Have-Seen-and-Heard.pdf.

[24] Ibid.

[25] *The Evening Independent*, St. Petersburg, Florida (Holiday Isles Edition); Sept. 19, 1963, p. A-3.

[26] Robert Furlow, "Black Bishops Accuse Catholic Church Of Discrimination," *Associated Press: AP News Archive*, Nov. 13, 1985; 7:14 PM ET. www.apnewsarchive.com/1985/Black-Bishops-Accuse-Catholic-Church-Of-Discrimination/id-3ee3a19f288c2fd06a0f059d7747aef7.

[27] Ibid.

[28] U.S. Conference of Catholic Bishops, "Discrimination and the Christian Conscience," 5.

[29] Mark A. Noll, *God and Race in American Politics: A Short History* (Princeton and Oxford: Princeton University Press, 2008), 166.

[30] National Conference of Black Churchmen, "Black Power," statement, in *The New York Times*, July 31, 1967, quoted in Milton C. Cernet. *African American Religious History: A Documentary Witness* (Durham: Duke University Press, 1999), 558.

[31] Ibid.

[32] James Cone, "Martin, Malcolm, and Black Theology," in J. Deotis Roberts and Michael Battle, *The Quest for Liberation and Reconciliation: Essays in Honor of J. Deotis Roberts* (Louisville: Westminster John Knox Press, 2005), 56.

[33] Ibid.

[34] Ibid, 59.

[35] James H. Cone, *Black Theology and Black Power* (New York: Seabury Press, 1969), 16.

[36] James H. Cone, *Black Theology and Black Power*, 40.

[37] Ibid, 74.

[38] A. Roger Williams. "A Black Pastor Looks at Black Theology," *Harvard Theological Review*, No. 64, (1971): 559-567.

Chapter 16

[1] Kenneth J. Neubeck and Noel A. Cazenave, Welfare Racism: Playing the Race Card Against America's Poor (New York, Routledge, 2001), 118.

[2] Hazel Erskine, "The Polls: Speed of Racial Integration," *The Public Opinion Quarterly* Vol. 32; No. 3; (Autumn, 1968): 515. Respondents also had the option of answering "about right" or expressing no opinion.

[3] Ibid, 522.

[4] Timothy J. Minchin, John A. Salmond, *After the Dream: Black and White Southerners since 1965* (Lexington, Kentucky; University Press of Kentucky, 2011), 37 ff.

[5] Ibid, 38.

[6] Ibid, 41.

[7] Bob Woodward and Scott Armstrong, *The Brethren* (New York, Simon & Schuster, 2005), 39.

[8] Burger, C.J., "Opinion of the Court, Supreme Court of the United States, 402 U.S. 1, *Swann v. Charlotte-Mecklenburg Board of Education*" No. 281 Argued: October 12,

1970 / Decided: April 20, 1971,
www.law.cornell.edu/supct/html/historics/USSC_CR_0402_0001_ZO.html
[9] Minchin and Salmond, *After the Dream,* 109.
[10] Ibid, 177.
[11] Ibid, 177-178.
[12] Ibid, 11.
[13] George C. Wallace, "The1963 Inaugural Address of Governor George C. Wallace," speech delivered in Montgomery, Alabama, Jan. 13, 1963, quoted in Alabama Department of Archives and History,
www.archives.alabama.gov/govs_list/inauguralspeech.html.
[14] Daniel Patrick Moynihan, Steven R. Veisman, Daniel Patrick Moynihan: A Portrait in Letters of an American Visionary (New York, Public Affairs, 2010), 214.
[15] Ibid.
[16] George Packer, "The Fall of Conservatism," (The New Yorker, May 26, 2008), 2. Quoted material comes from a memorandum shared with Packer by Buchanan, who warned that it was "a little raw for today."
www.newyorker.com/reporting/2008/05/26/080526fa_fact_packer/.
[17] Ibid.
[18] James Boyd, "Nixon's Southern Strategy: 'It's All in the Charts," in *The New York Times, (1857-Current file); May 17, 1970; ProQuest Historical Newspapers The New York Times (1851-2003)*, 215, www.nytimes.com/packages/html/books/phillips-southern.pdf.
[19] For an excellent discussion of welfare reform as a component of the backlash phenomenon, see: Kenneth J. Neubeck and Noel A. Cazenave, *Welfare Racism: Playing the Race Card Against America's Poor*, (New York, Routledge, 2001). Here I have drawn on his pages 120-121.
[20] Harry R. Haldeman, *The Haldeman Diaries– Inside the Nixon White House*, (New York: Berkley Books, 1994), 53.
[21] "Nixon Raps Johnson on Crime," AP story from New York appearing in Daytona Beach Morning Journal, (May 7, 1968) 8,
http://news.google.com/newspapers?nid=1873&dat=19680507&id=nG4eAAAAIBAJ&sjid=g8kEAAAAIBAJ&pg=1828,1854686.
[22] "Jimmy Carter; Transcript," PBS American Experience,
https://www.pbs.org/wgbh/americanexperience/films/carter/ - "Transcript."
[23] Robert A. Strong, "Jimmy Carter: Life before the Presidency," UVA: Miller Center: U.S. Presidents: Jimmy Carter, https://millercenter.org/president/carter/life-before-the-presidency.
[24] E. Stanly Godbold, *Jimmy and Rosalynn Carter: The Georgia Years, 1924-1974* (Oxford, New York; Oxford University Press, 2010), 170.
[25] John D. Saxon, "Wallace Saw It First,"
https://www.nytimes.com/1981/01/13/opinion/wallace-saw-it-first.html.
[26] Drew S. Days III, "Turning Back the Clock: The Reagan Administration and Civil Rights," Faculty Scholarship Series, Paper 1492, 1984,
http://digitalcommons.law.yale.edu/fss_papers/1492.
[27] "ABC-Post Poll Says Reagan Still Not Popular Among Blacks," Associated Press, AP News Archive, Jan. 17, 1986, www.apnewsarchive.com/1986/ABC-Post-Poll-Says-Reagan-Still-Not-Popular-Among-Blacks/id-18cdbe0fd75eae9d50208d9d7a0b2b34, 2012.

[28] Kyle Longley, Jeremy D. Mayer, Michael Shaller, John W. Sloan, *Deconstructing Reagan: conservative mythology and America's fortieth president* (Armonk, NY, M.E. Sharpe, 2007) p. 76.

[29] Laurence I. Barrett, *Gambling with History, Ronald Reagan in the White House* (New York, Doubleday, 1983), 426.

[30] William Raspberry, "Reagan's Race Legacy," *The Washington Post*, Monday, June 14, 2004, A17.

[31] Ronald Reagan, "Remarks at a Reagan-Bush Rally in Macon," The American Presidency Project: Ronald Reagan, speech, Macon, Georgia, October 15, 1984, http://www.presidency.ucsb.edu/ws/index.php?pid=39242.

[32] Joe P. Dunn and Howard Lawrence Preston, The Future South: A Historical Perspective for the Twenty-First Century (Urbana, University of Illinois Press, 1991), 61.

[33] Alexander P. Lamis, *Southern Politics in the 1990s* (Baton Rouge, Louisiana State Univ. Press, 1999), 8. Lamis, who conducted the original interview, revealed the respondent's true identity years later in this book.

[34] Martin Luther King, Jr. and Jesse Jackson, *Why We Can't Wait* (New York, New American Library, 2000), 124.

[35] Martin Luther King, Jr.; Coretta Scott King; Vincent Harding, *Where Do We Go from Here: Chaos or Community?* (Boston, Beacon Press, 2010), 95.

[36] Robert L. Carter, "Public School Desegregation: A Contemporary Analysis," St. Louis University Law Journal, No. 37, (1993): 885.

[37] "Gravely Ill, Atwater Offers Apology," *The New York Times,* AP story, January 13, 1991, www.nytimes.com/1991/01/13/us/gravely-ill-atwater-offers-apology.html.

[39] Charles P. Henry and Ralph Bunche, Model Negro or American Other? (New York, New York Univ. Press, 1999), 4.

[40] Joe Klein, The Natural: The Misunderstood Presidency of Bill Clinton (New York, Broadway Books, 2002), 150-151.

[41] Robert C. Smith, *Encyclopedia of African American Politics* (New York, NY; Facts On File, 2003), 78.

[42] David Burnham and Susan Long, "The Clinton Era By the Numbers: His Legacy: More Money for Enforcement, Less Money for a Range of Services," *The Nation*, January 29, 2001, www.thenation.com/article/clinton-era-numbers.

[43] James Carney, "Affirmative Action: Mend It, Don't End It," *Time*, July 31, 1995, www.time.com/time/magazine/article/0,9171,983257,00.html.

[44] William Jefferson Clinton, "Mend It, Don't End It," speech delivered at the National Archives on July 19, 1995, 4, web.utk.edu/~mfitzge1/docs/374/MDE1995.pdf.

[45] Barbara Bobejda, "Clinton Signs Welfare Bill Amidst Division," *The Washington Post*; August 23, 1996), A1.

[46] George W. Bush, "The Duty of Hope," speech delivered in Indianapolis, Indiana on July 22, 1999, quoted in its entirety in Marvin N. Olasky, *Compassionate Conservatism: What it is, What it Does, and How it Can Transform America* (New York, The Free Press: A Division of Simon & Schuster, 2000), 216.

[47] George W. Bush, "First Inaugural Address," speech in Washington, DC, Jan. 20, 2001, The American Presidency Project: George W. Bush, http://www.presidency.ucsb.edu/ws/?pid=25853.

[48] "Redefining Rights in America: The Civil Rights Record of the George W. Bush Administration, 2001-2004," U.S. Commission on Civil Rights, Office of Civil Rights

Evaluation, vii,
https://www.law.umaryland.edu/marshall/usccr/documents/cr12r24.pdf.
[49] "United States Department of Justice; Information on Employment Litigation,
Housing and Civil Enforcement, Voting, and Special Litigations Sections'
Enforcement Efforts from Fiscal Years 2001 through 2007," For the full text of the
report, see: Government Accountability Office, United States Department of Justice;
October, 2009, www.gao.gov/assets/300/297337.pdf.
[50] UPI article, Washington dateline, Dec. 3, 2009, www.upi.com/Top_News/US/2009/
12/03/GAO-looks-at-Bush-civil-rights-enforcement/UPI-29611259846651/.
[51] Jerry Markon, "Justice Department's Civil Rights Division steps up enforcement,"
The Washington Post, June 4, 2010, http://www.washingtonpost.com/wp-
dyn/content/article/2010/06/03/AR2010060304938.html. This information originally
appeared in Ryan J Reilly, "Report Delivers Hard Numbers on Bush Civil Rights
Division," United States Department of Justice; December 7, 2009,
www.mainjustice.com/2009/12/07/report-delivers-hard-numbers-on-bush-civil-rights-
division/. This website has vanished since my original research, but numerous news
outlets have commented on the report.
[52] "Redefining Rights in America," 9.
[53] Bootie Cosgrove-Mather, "Poll: Katrina Shakes Confidence," February 11, 2009,
https://www.cbsnews.com/news/poll-katrina-shakes-confidence/.

Chapter 17

[1] David Maraniss, Barack Obama: The Story, (New York, Simon & Schuster, 2012), as
quoted in "Barack Obama: A masterful portrait of a guarded politician," *The
Washington Post*; June 5, 2012, C9.
[2] Rush Limbaugh, "The Rush Limbaugh Show," Premiere Radio Network; June 22,
2009.
[3] Carol Morello and Ted Mellnik, "Census: Minority babies are now majority in
United States," *The Washington Post*, May 17, 2012,
www.washingtonpost.com/local/census-minority-babies-are-now-majority-in-united-
states/2012/05/16/gIQA1WY8UU_story.html.
[4] Leonard Pitts Jr., "Pitts: The black self-loathing of Herman Cain, *The Baltimore Sun*,
October 16, 2011, http://www.baltimoresun.com/news/opinion/oped/bs-ed-pitts-cain-
20111016-story.html.
[5] Frederick Harris, "Still Waiting for Our First Black President," *The Washington
Post*; June 3, 2012, B5.
[6] Cheryl I. Harris, "An Affirmative Act? Barack Obama and the Past, Present, and
Future of Race-Conscious Remedies," in Charles, P. Henry, Robert Allen, Robert
Chrisman, eds., *The Obama Phenomenon: Toward a Multiracial Democracy*, (Urbana,
University of Illinois Press, 2011), 292.
[7] Ibid, 298.
[8] Barack Obama, news conference in the White House Press Office, March 24, 2009,
as quoted in Cheryl I. Harris, "An Affirmative Act," 293.
[9] Barack Obama, Speech to the Congressional Black Caucus, as quoted in Associated
Press, "Obama Tells Congressional Black Caucus to 'Stop Complaining,'" September
25, 2011, http://www.foxnews.com/politics/2011/09/24/obama-set-to-speak-to-
frustrated-congressional-black-caucus.html.
[10] William Yeomans, "Rebuilding Civil Rights Enforcement," Human Rights
Magazine, American Bar Association, Vo. 37. Nov. 4,

https://www.americanbar.org/publications/human_rights_magazine_home/human_righ
ts_vol37_2010/fall2010/rebuilding_civil_rights_enforcement.html.
[11] Jennifer Agiesta, "Misperceptions persist about Obama's faith, but aren't so
widespread." CNN Politics, September 14, 2015, https://www.cnn.com/2015/
09/13/politics/barack-obama-religion-christian-misperceptions/.
[12] Ibid. The more exact figure was 29%, as reported in the full polling results at
http://i2.cdn.turner.com/cnn/2015/images/09/12/iranpoll.pdf.
[13] "Racial Attitudes in America: Post-Racial in the Age of Obama Fails to Exist:
Findings from the Blair-Rockefeller poll," Blair Center-Clinton School Poll, Diane D.
Blair Center of Southern Politics & Society, University of Arkansas,
https://blaircenter.uark.edu/polling-data-reports/2010-poll/racial-attitudes/. Also, "New
York Times/CBS News Poll: National Survey of Tea Party Supporters," *The New York
Times*, http://documents.nytimes.com/new-york-timescbs-news-poll-national-survey-
of-tea-party-supporters?ref=politics.
  I have taken the liberty of recalibrating some of the statistics from *The New York
Times/CBS News Poll*, because of the way in which they were presented. These poll
results compare the answers of Tea Party supporters with those of the general
American public. But 18% of that general public identified as Tea Party supporters, so
lumping them together conflates the two groups. Therefore, I disaggregated Tea Party
opinion from that of the general population in order to compare the two more directly.
[14] Michael Grunwald, "The Party of No: New Details on the GOP Plot to Obstruct
Obama," Time Magazine, Aug. 23, 2012, http://swampland.time
.com/2012/08/23/the-party-of-no-new-details-on-the-gop-plot-to-obstruct-obama/.
This blog includes information from Grunwald's book, The New New Deal: The
Hidden Story of Change in the Obama Era, which details the exchanges cited here,
among others.
[15] See: Patrick Caldwell, "Senate Republicans Are Blocking Obama's Judges at a
Nearly Unprecedented Rate," *Mother Jones*, Nov. 4, 2015, www.motherjones.com/
politics/2015/11/senate-republicans-block-obama-judge-nominations.
[16] Mugambi Jouet, "Trump Didn't Invent 'Make America Great Again': How
conservatives hijacked the idea of American exceptionalism." *Mother Jones*,
January/February, 2017. www.motherjones.com/politics/2017/01/american-
exceptionalism-maga-trump-obama/.
[17] Andrew McGill, "Just When Was America Great?" *The Atlantic*, May 4, 2016.
www.theatlantic.com/politics/archive/2016/05/make-the-sixties-great-again/481167/.
[18] Michael D'Antonio, "Is Donald Trump Racist? Here's What the Record Shows,"
Fortune, June 7, 2016, http://fortune.com/2016/06/07/donald-trump-racism-quotes/.
[19] Ben Jacobs, "Republicans denounce bigotry after Trump's latest Charlotte remarks,"
www.theguardian.com/us-news/2017/aug/15/donald-trump-charlottesville-republicans-
react-bigotry.
[20] "Trump Holds Steady After Charlottesville; Supporters Think Whites, Christians
Face Discrimination," Public Policy Polling,
https://www.publicpolicypolling.com/polls/trump-holds-steady-after-charlottesville-
supporters-think-whites-christians-face-discrimination/.
[21] Rebecca Savransky, "Trump's Approval Rating Holds Steady after Charlottesville,"
The Hill, Aug. 23, 1017, http://thehill.com/homenews/administration/347633-poll-
trumps-approval-steady-following-charlottesville-response.
[22] George Will, "A Ruinous Triumph for the GOP," *The Washington Post,* Nov. 9,
2016, www.washingtonpost.com/opinions/a-ruinous-triumph-for-the-
gop/2016/11/09/18b9e804-a6a3-11e6-ba59-a7d93165c6d4_story.

[23] Frank Newport, "Obama Approval Rating Jumps to Four-Year High," Nov. 15, 2016, www.gallup.com/poll/197495/obama-job-approval-jumps-four-year-high.aspx. This Gallup tracking poll was taken during the week of the 2016 election, Nov. 7-13. Trump voters clearly did not share this enthusiasm, as only 5% indicated approval, with 90% disapproving of Obama, according to a Public Policy Polling poll released on Dec. 9. In that poll, Obama enjoyed an overall 50% approval rating. See: www.publicpolicypolling.com/pdf/2015/PPP_Release_National_120916.pdf.

Chapter 18

[1] Jim Sidanius and Felicia Pratto, Social Dominance: An Intergroup Theory of Social Hierarchy and Oppression (Cambridge, New York; Cambridge University Press, 1999), 16.
[2] David O. Sears and P. J. Henry, "Interpersonal Relations and Group Processes: The Origins of Symbolic Racism," Journal of Personality and Social Psychology, American Psychological Association, Inc., Vol. 85, No. 2, (2003): 259 –275.

Chapter 19

[1] "Trends in U.S. Corrections," The Sentencing Project, May 2012, 2, https://www.sentencingproject.org/wp-content/uploads/2016/01/Trends-in-US-Corrections.pdf.
[2] E. Ann Carson, "Prisoners in 2016, Table 14: Percent of sentenced prisoners under federal correctional authority, by most serious offense, sex, race, and Hispanic origin, September 30, 2016." U.S. Department of Justice: Bureau of Justice Statistics, NCJ 251149, January, 2018, 20, www.bjs.gov/content/
pub/pdf/p16.pdf, 17. The exact percentage is 47.5%.
[3] Snyder, Howard N.; Cooper, Alexia D.; and Mulako-Wangota, Joseph. Bureau of Justice Statistics. "Arrests by Race and Age in the U.S., 2014," Generated using the Arrest Data Analysis Tool at www.bjs.gov., April 27, 2018. Compared with: E. Ann Carson, "Prisoners in 2016: Table 12: Percent of prisoners under state correctional authority, by most serious offense, sex, race, and Hispanic origin, December 31, 2015. Also: "Table 14: Percent of prisoners under federal correctional authority, by most serious offense, sex, race, and Hispanic origin, September 30, 2016," U.S. Department of Justice: Bureau of Justice Statistics, NCJ 251149, January 2018, pages 18 and 20, https://www.bjs.gov/index.cfm?ty=pbdetail&iid=6187.
[4] E. Ann Carson, "Prisoners in 2016: Table 12…Table 14." Compared with: "Annual Estimates of the Resident Population by Sex, Age, Race, and Hispanic Origin for the United States and States: April 1, 2010 to July 1, 2016." Source: U.S. Census Bureau, Population Division, released, June 2017.
[5] Center for Behavioral Health Statistics and Quality, "Table 1.31B: Illicit Drug Use in Lifetime, Past Year, and Past Month among Persons Aged 12 or Older, by Age Group and Demographic Characteristics: Percentages, 2015 and 2016,"in "2016 National Survey on Drug Use and Health: Detailed Tables." Substance Abuse and Mental Health Services Administration, Rockville, MD, 228.
www.samhsa.gov/data/sites/default/
files/NSDUH-DetTabs-2016/NSDUH-DetTabs-2016.pdf.
[6] Laura E. Gomez, Misconceiving Mothers: Legislators, Prosecutors, and the Politics of Prenatal Drug Exposure (Philadelphia, Temple University Press, 1997), 14.
[7] Charles Krauthammer, *The Washington Post*, July 30, 1989; C7.

---

[8] Kyle Graham, "Sorry Seems to Be the Hardest Word: The Fair Sentencing Act of 2010, Crack and Methamphetamine," University of Richmond Law Review; Vol. 45, (March, 2011):765. http://lawreview.richmond.edu/wp/wp-content/uploads/2011/04/Graham-453.pdf), 774.

[9] Ibid.

[10] "Congressional Record," Vol. 156, No. 112. July 28, 2010. H6202.

[11] Kyle Graham, "Sorry Seems to Be the Hardest Word," 766.

[12] Ames Grawert, Tim Lau, "How the FIRST STEP Act Became Law—and What Happens Next," Jan. 4, 2019, https://www.brennancenter.org/blog/how-first-step-act-became-law-and-what-happens-next.

[13] David Anderson, *Gracism: The Art of Inclusion* (Downers Grove, Illinois; Intervarsity Press) 2010, 9 ff.

[14] See the Bureau of Justice Statistics website for the list of publications on this topic, especially those in the (ostensibly) triennial series "Contacts Between the Police and the Public." The 2011 contribution to this series bears the title "Police Behavior during Traffic and Street Stops." It is more narrowly focused but goes into greater depth, and I relied heavily on this document in an earlier draft of this book. However, after comparing it with an earlier and now the most current edition (from 2015, finally published in October, 2018), the reporting inconsistencies from one iteration to the next left me no longer willing to rely on its results at any level of detail. The BJS study suffers from its relatively small sample size, especially when examining smaller subsets, like the percentage of black vs. white drivers who are arrested in a traffic stop situation. See: https://www.bjs.gov/index.cfm?ty=tp&tid=70#data.

[15] Emma Pierson, et. al., "A large-scale analysis of racial disparities in police stops across the United States," Stanford Open Policing Project, 2017, https://5harad.com/papers/traffic-stops.pdf.

[16] Ibid, 6.

[17] Ibid, 7.

[18] Ibid, 9.

[19] Ibid, 11.

[20] John Sides, What data on 20 million traffic stops can tell us about 'driving while black', *The Washington Post*, July 17, 2018, https://www.washingtonpost.com/news/monkey-cage/wp/2018/07/17/what-data-on-20-million-traffic-stops-can-tell-us-about-driving-while-black/?utm_term=.3fac05405345.

[21] Ibid.

[22] Missouri Attorney General Josh Hawley, "2017 Vehicle Stops Executive Summary," https://www.ago.mo.gov/home/vehicle-stops-report/2017-executive-summary#summary.

[23] "Illinois Traffic Stops Statistic Study: 2007 Annual Report," (Evanston, IL; Northwestern University Center for Public Safety, http://www.idot.illinois.gov/assets/uploads/files/transportation-system/reports/safety/traffic-stop-studies/2007/2007%20illinois%20traffic%20stop%20summary.pdf, 10-11. This report combines citations and arrests in a single category, making arrest comparisons with other jurisdictions impossible.

[24] "Minnesota Statewide Racial Profiling Report: All Participating Jurisdictions, Report to the Minnesota Legislature," September, 2003, www.law.umn.edu/metro/index/inst.-metro.-opp/school-studies/27-racial-profiling-aggregate-report.pdf), 1.

[25] United States Department of Justice: Civil Rights Division, "Investigation of the Ferguson Police," www.justice.gov/sites/default/files/opa/press-releases/attachments/2015/03/04/ferguson_police_department_report.pdf, 1.

[26] Ibid, 18.

[27] United States Department of Justice: Office of Public Affairs, "Justice Department Announces Findings of Investigation into Baltimore Police Department." Aug. 10, www.justice.gov/opa/pr/justice-department-announces-findings-investigation-baltimore-police-department.

[28] Mark Berman and Mark Guarino, "After a blistering report, what's next for the embattled Chicago police?" *The Washington Post*, April 16, 2016, www.washingtonpost.com/news/post-nation/wp/2016/04/16/after-a-blistering-report-whats-next-for-the-embattled-chicago-police/?utm_term=.ef1f8f396a4c.

[29] John Sullivan, Julie Tate, Jennifer Jenkins, "Fatal police shootings of unarmed people have significantly declined, experts say," *The Washington Post*, May 7, 2018, www.washingtonpost.com/investigations/fatal-police-shootings-of-unarmed-people-have-significantly-declined-experts-say/2018/05/03/d5eab374-4349-11e8-8569-26fda6b404c7_story.html?utm_term=.e3a9561d7da9.

[30] "Fatal Force," *The Washington Post*, Feb. 6, 2019, https://www.washingtonpost.com/graphics/2018/national/police-shootings-2018/?utm_term=.c0a1dbf5fa40.

[31] U.S. Census, "Quick Facts: Population Estimates July 1, 2016: White Alone, Not Hispanic or Latino vs. Black or African American Alone." www.census.gov/quickfacts/fact/table/US/PST045216.

[32] Samuel R. Gross and Michael Shaffer, "Exonerations in the United States, 1989-2012: Report by the National Registry of Exonerations," University of Michigan, June, 2012, www.law.umich.edu/special/exoneration/Documents/exonerations_us_1989_2012_full_report.pdf, 42.

[33] National Registry of Exonerations, www.law.umich.edu/special/exoneration/Pages/about.aspx.

[34] Exonerations in the U.S., 1989-2012 Key Findings," National Registry of Exonerations, May 20, 2012, www.law.umich.edu/special/exoneration/Documents/exonerations_us_1989_2012_summary.pdf, 5.

[35] Samuel R. Gross and Michael Shaffer, "Exonerations in the United States, 1989-2012," 49.

[36] BJS' Federal Justice Statistics Program website, http://bjs.ojp.usdoj.gov/fjsrc/. The source data used by BJS comes from the U.S. Sentencing Commission—USSC Offender Data Set (Standard Research data file) FY 2014 (as standardized by the FJSRC).

[37] Glenn R. Schmitt, Louis Reedt, Kevin Blackwell, "Demographic Differences in Sentencing: An Update to the 2012 *Booker* Report," United States Sentencing Commission. November, 2017, www.ussc.gov/research/research-reports/demographic-differences-sentencing, 2.

[38] Ibid.

[39] Ibid, 4.

[40] BJS' Federal Justice Statistics, http://bjs.ojp.usdoj.gov/fjsrc/.

[41] "Overview of Mandatory Minimum Penalties in the Federal Criminal Justice System," United States Sentencing Commission, July, 2017, www.ussc.gov/sites/default/files/pdf/research-and-publications/research-publications/2017/20170711_Mand-Min.pdf, 11.

[42] BJS' Federal Justice Statistics, http://bjs.ojp.usdoj.gov/fjsrc/.

[43] "Overview of Mandatory Minimum Penalties in the Federal Criminal Justice System," 53.

[44] "Mandatory Minimum Sentences for Firearms Offenses in the Federal Criminal Justice System," United States Sentencing Commission, March, 2018, www.ussc.gov/sites/default/files/pdf/research-and-publications/research-publications/2018/20180315_Firearms-Mand-Min.pdf, 6.

[45] Ibid, 24.

[46] "Report to Congress: Mandatory Minimum Penalties in the Federal Criminal Justice System, Chapter 12," United States Sentencing Commission, October 2011, www.ussc.gov/Legislative_and_Public_Affairs/Congressional_Testimony_and_Reports/Mandatory_Minimum_Penalties/20111031_R tC_PDF/Chapter_12.pdf, 353-354.

[47] Ibid, /Chapter_05.pdf., 102.

[48] Ibid, 101.

Chapter 20

[1] Doris Layton Mackenzie, et. al., "Sentencing and Corrections in the 21st Century: Setting the Stage for the Future," University of Maryland, July, 2001, https://www.ncjrs.gov/pdffiles1/nij/189106-2.pdf, 2.

[2] Pamela E. Oliver and Marino A. Bruce, "Tracking the Causes and Consequences of Racial Disparities in Imprisonment," A proposal to the National Science Foundation, Aug. 2001, www.ssc.wisc.edu/~oliver/RACIAL/Reports/nsfAug01narrative.pdf, 2-3.

[3] Lauren E. Glaze, "Correctional Population in the United States, 2010: Appendix Table 3: Estimated number of inmates held in custody in state or federal prisons or in local jails per 100,000 U.S. residents, by sex, race and Hispanic/Latino origin, and age, June 30, 2010," U.S. Department of Justice, Office of Justice Programs, Bureau of Justice Statistics, Bulletin, December 2011, NCJ236319, 8. www.bjs.gov/content/pub/pdf/cpus10.pdf.

[4] Danielle Kaeble and Mary Cowhig, "Correctional Populations in the United States," U.S. Department of Justice, Office of Justice Programs, Bureau of Justice Statistics, NCJ 251211, April, 2018, 1, https://www.bjs.gov/content/pub/pdf/cpus16.pdf.

[5] E. Ann Carson. "Prisoners in 2016: Table 9: Percent of sentenced prisoners under jurisdiction of state or federal correctional authorities, by sex, race, Hispanic origin, and age, December 31, 2016," 15. Also, Zhen Zeng, "Jail Inmates in 2016: Appendix Table 1: Number of confined inmates in local jails, by characteristic, 2000, 2005, and 2010-2016," 9. Also, Danielle Kaeble, "Probation and Parole in the United States 2016: Appendix Table 5: Adults on parole, 2016," 18. Also, "Appendix Table 8: Characteristics of Adults on parole, 2000, 2015, 2016," 24. Also, "Appendix Table 2: Characteristics of Adults on probation, 2016," 13. Also, "Appendix Table 4: Characteristics of Adults on probation, 2000, 2015, 2016," 17, U.S. Department of Justice, Office of Justice Programs, Bureau of Justice Statistics, April, 2018, NCJ251148.Also, U.S. Census Bureau, 2016 American Community Survey, 1-year estimates, Table CO1001: Sex by Age (Black or African American Alone). https://factfinder.census.gov/.

[6] E. Ann Carson, "Prisoners in 2016: Table 9: Percent of sentenced prisoners under jurisdiction of state or federal correctional authorities, by sex, race, Hispanic origin, and age, December 31, 2016." 15. Also: U.S. Census Bureau, 2016 American Community Survey, 1-year estimates, Table CO1001: Sex by Age (Black or African American Alone). https://factfinder.census.gov/.

[7] E. Ann Carson, "Prisoners in 2016: Table 10: Imprisonment rate of sentenced state and federal prisoners per 100,000 U.S. residents, by sex, race, Hispanic origin, and age, December 31, 2016," 15.

[8] FBI, Uniform Crime Reports as prepared by the National Archive of Criminal Justice Data, www.ucrdatatool.gov/Search/Crime/State/RunCrimeStatebyState.cfm.

[9] Laruen E. Glaze, "Bulletin: Correctional Populations in the United States, 2009, U.S. Department of Justice, Office of Justice Programs, Bureau of Justice Statistics, NCJ 231681, December, 2010, https://www.bjs.gov/content/pub/pdf/cpus09.pdf.

[10] Roy Walmsley, "World Prison Population List, 11th ed."; (London, International Centre for Prison Studies), May 9, 2018. www.prisonstudies.org/news/international-prison-news-digest-issue-44.

[11] Danielle Kaeble and Mary Cowhig, "Correctional Populations in the United States." U.S. Department of Justice, Office of Justice Programs, Bureau of Justice Statistics, April, 2018. Also: U.S. Census Bureau, Population Division, "Annual Estimates of the Resident Population for Selected Age Groups by Sex for the United States, States, Counties and Puerto Rico Commonwealth and Municipios: April 1, 2010 to July 1, 2016," https://factfinder.census.gov/.

[12] "Digest of Education Statistics: Table 306.10: Total fall enrollment in degree-granting postsecondary institutions, by level of enrollment, sex, attendance status, and race/ethnicity of student: Selected years, 1976 through 2015." U.S. Department of Education, National Center for Education Statistics, https://nces.ed.gov/programs/digest/d16/tables/dt16_306.10.asp. Cross-referenced with E. Ann Carson, "Prisoners in 2015" and Zhen Zeng, "Jail Inmates in 2016."

[13] Roy Walmsley, "World Prison Population List, 11th ed.," International Centre for Prison Studies, May 9, 2018, www.prisonstudies.org/news/international-prison-news-digest-issue-44. Compared with E. Ann Carson, "Prisoners in 2015" and Zhen Zeng, "Jail Inmates in 2016."

[14] Bruce Western, and Becky Pettit, "Incarceration and Social Inequality," *Daedalus*, The American Academy of Arts and Sciences, (Summer, 2010): 8, www.amacad.org/publications/daedalus/10_summer_western.pdf. I am indebted to Professors Western (Harvard) and Pettit (U. of Washington) for their helpful article on which I have relied heavily to illustrate this point.

[15] Mariel Alper, Matthew R. Durose, Joshua Markman, "2018 Update on Prisoner Recidivism: A 9-Year Follow-up Period (2005-2014)," U.S. Department of Justice, Office of Justice Programs, Bureau of Justice Statistics, May, 2018. NCJ250975, www.bjs.gov/content/pub/pdf/18upr9yfup0514.pdf, 6.

[16] Devah Pager, "The Mark of a Criminal Record," *American Journal of Sociology*, Volume 108, Number 5, (March 2003): 937–975, https://www.journals.uchicago.edu/doi/abs/10.1086/374403. See also: Devah Pager, *Marked: Race, Crime, and Finding Work in an Era of Mass Incarceration* (Chicago, University of Chicago Press, 2008).

[17] Christopher Wildeman and Bruce Western, "Incarceration in Fragile Families: "Table 2. Cumulative Risk of Paternal and Maternal Imprisonment by Age Fourteen for Children Born in 1978 and 1990, by Race and Parental Education.," *The Future of Children*, vol. 20, no. 2, (Fall, 2010): 162, https://files.eric.ed.gov/fulltext/EJ901827.pdf.

[18] Bruce Western and Becky Pettit, "Collateral Costs: Incarceration's Effect on Economic Mobility," The Pew Charitable Trusts, 2010, www.pewtrusts.org/~/media/legacy/uploadedfiles/pcs_assets/2010/collateralcosts1pdf.pdf, 21.

[19] Danielle Kaeble and Mary Cowhig, "Correctional Populations in the United States," 1.

[20] Lauren E. Glaze, "Correctional Population in the United States, 2009," 1.

[21] Howard N. Snyder, Alexia D Cooper, Joseph Mulako-Wangota, Bureau of Justice Statistics. (U.S. Arrest Estimates: Arrests of Black, 1980-2014). Generated using the Arrest Data Analysis Tool at www.bjs.gov. (June 6, 2018).

[22] Todd D. Minton "Jail Inmates at Midyear 2010 – Statistical Tables:Table 6: Number of inmates in local jails, by characteristics, midyear 2000 and 2005–2010," U.S. Department of Justice, Office of Justice Programs, Bureau of Justice Statistics; April, 2011, NCJ 233431, 3. Also, Zhen Zeng, "Jail Inmates in 2016: Appendix Table 1: Number of confined inmates in local jails, by characteristics, 2000, 2005, and 2010-2016," U.S. Department of Justice, Office of Justice Programs, Bureau of Justice Statistics, NCJ 251210 February, 2018, 9. Also, E. Ann Carson, "Prisoners in 2016: Table 3: Sentenced prisoners under jurisdiction of federal or state correction authorities, by jurisdiction, sex, race, and Hispanic origin, December 31, 2006-2016," U.S. Department of Justice, Office of Justice Programs, Bureau of Justice Statistics, Bulletin, September, 2015, 5.

[23] FBI, "Uniform Crime Reports as prepared by the National Archive of Criminal Justice Data," June 6, 2018, www.bjs.gov/ucrdata.

[24] Marc Fisher, "Guns in America: As streets get safer, who gets the credit?" *The Washington Post*, March 4, 2013, A5.

[25] Paul Guerino, Paige M. Harrison, William J. Sabol, "Prisoners in 2010," U.S. Department of Justice, Office of Justice Programs, Bureau of Justice Statistics; December, 2011 (Revised 2/9/12), bjs.ojp.usdoj.gov/content/pub/pdf/p10.pdf. Note: only 47 states participated in this survey.

[26] Adam Liptak, "Justices, 5-4, Tell California to Cut Prisoner Population," *The New York Times*, May 23, 2011, www.nytimes.com/2011/05/24/us/24scotus.html?pagewanted=all&_r=0.

[27] Christian Henrichson and Ruth Delaney, "The Price of Prisons: What Incarceration Costs Taxpayers," Vera Institute of Justice; January, 2012 (updated 7/20/2012), 9, https://www.vera.org/publications/price-of-prisons-what-incarceration-costs-taxpayers. See: second Key Fact: $31,286, average inmate cost, 2010 or download PDF file.

[28] "Attorney General Holder Urges Changes in Federal Sentencing Guidelines to Reserve Harshest Penalties for Most Serious Drug Traffickers," press release, U.S. Department of Justice, Office of Public Affairs, March 13, 2014, www.justice.gov/opa/pr/2014/March/14-ag-263.html.

[29] Ibid.

[30] "Announcing New Clemency Initiative, Deputy Attorney General James M. Cole Details Broad New Criteria for Applicants," press release, U.S. Department of Justice, Office of Public Affairs, April 23, 2014, www.justice.gov/opa/pr/2014/April/14-dag-419.html.

[31] @realDonaldTrump, Thanks to Leader McConnell for agreeing to bring a Senate vote on Criminal Justice this week! These historic changes will make communities SAFER and SAVE tremendous taxpayers dollars. It brings much needed hope to many families during the Holiday Season." 2:09 PM ET, Dec. 11, 2018.

[32] Attorney General Jeff Sessions, "Memorandum for All Federal Prosecutors: Department Charging and Sentencing Policy," May 10, 2017, www.justice.gov/opa/press-release/file/965896/download. Also, Attorney General Eric Holder, "Memorandum to the United States Attorneys and Assistant Attorney General for the Criminal Division: Department Policy on Charging Mandatory Minimum

Sentences and Recidivist Enhancements in Certain Drug Cases," Aug. 13, 2013, www.justice.gov/sites/default/files/oip/legacy/2014/07/23/ag-memo-department-policypon-charging-mandatory-minimum-sentences-recidivist-enhancements-in-certain-drugcases.pdf.

[33] Jess Sessions, "Jeff Sessions: Being soft on sentencing means more violent crime. It's time to get tough again." *The Washington Post*, June 16, 2017, https://www.washingtonpost.com/opinions/jeff-sessions-being-soft-on-sentencing-means-more-violent-crime-its-time-to-get-tough-again/2017/06/16/618ef1fe-4a19-11e7-9669-250d0b15f83b_story.html?utm_term=.18eca691df30.

[34] "Remarks by President Trump in Roundtable with County Sheriffs," The White House, Feb. 7, 2017, www.whitehouse.gov/briefings-statements/remarks-president-trump-roundtable-county-sheriffs/.

[35] John Gramlich, "5 facts about crime in the U.S.," Pew Research Center, Jan. 9. 2019, http://www.pewresearch.org/fact-tank/2019/01/03/5-facts-about-crime-in-the-u-s/.

[36] "Crime," Gallup, Feb. 12, 2019, https://news.gallup.com/poll/1603/crime.aspx.

[37] Raymond V. Liedka, Anne M. Piehl, Bert Useem, "The Crime-Control Effect of Incarceration: Does Scale Matter?" *Criminology and Public Policy*, 5 (2), (2006). Quoted in "One in 31: The Long Reach of American Corrections," The Pew Center on the States, March, 2009, www.pewtrusts.org/~/media/assets/2009/03/02/pspp_1in31_report_final_web_32609.pdf, 19.

[38] "One in 31: The Long Reach of American Corrections," 20.

[39] The statistics in this paragraph are taken from Jenni Gainsborough and Marc Mauer, "Diminishing Returns: Crime and Incarceration in the 1990s," The Sentencing Project; September, 2000, https://www.prisonpolicy.org/scans/sp/DimRet.pdf, 7-10.

[40] E. Ann Carson, "Prisoners in 2016," Table 9: Percent of sentenced prisoners under jurisdiction of state or federal correctional authorities, by sex, race, Hispanic origin, and age, December 31, 2016," 15. Also, Zhen Zeng, "Jail Inmates in 2016: Appendix Table 1: Number of confined inmates in local jails, by characteristic, 2000, 2005, and 2010-2016," 9. Also, Danielle Kaeble, (U.S. Department of Justice, Office of Justice Programs, Bureau of Justice Statistics), "Probation and Parole in the United States, 2016 April, 2018, NCJ251148." "Appendix Table 5: Adults on parole, 2016," 18.,"Appendix Table 8: Characteristics of Adults on parole, 2000, 2015, 2016," 24..."Appendix Table 82 Characteristics of Adults on probation, 2016," 13, "Appendix Table 4: Characteristics of Adults on probation, 2000, 2015, 2016," 17. Also, U.S. Census Bureau, 2016 American Community Survey, 1-year estimates, Table CO1001: Sex by Age (Black or African American Alone). https://factfinder.census.gov/.

Chapter 21

[1] John Perkins, With Justice for All (Ventura, California: Regal Books, 1982), 40.

[2] Ibid, 84.

[3] George Yancey, *Reconciliation Theology: Results of a Multiracial Evangelical Community*. Paper presented at the "Color Lines in the Twenty-First Century" conference, Chicago, IL, 1998. As reported in Michael O. Emerson and Christian Smith, *Divided by Faith*, (Oxford: Oxford University Press, 2000), 54.

[4] Michael O. Emerson, "A New Day for Multiracial Congregations," *Yale University Reflections*, April 11, 2013, https://reflections.yale.edu/article/

future-race/new-day-multiracial-congregations.

[5] Scott Thumma, "Racial Diversity Increasing in U.S. Congregations," The Huffington Post, May 21, 2013, www.huffingtonpost.com/scott-thumma-phd/racial-diversity-increasing-in-us-congregations_b_2944470.html.

[6] Vincent Synan, "Memphis 1994: Miracle and Mandate," http://www.pccna.org/about_history.aspx.

[7] "Resolution on Racial Reconciliation on the 150th Anniversary of the Southern Baptist Convention," June 1995, http://www.sbc.net/resolutions/899.

[8] Kevin Eckstrom, "Methodists Offer Sweeping Apology for Church's Racism," *Religious News Service*, May 5, 2000, http://www.beliefnet.com/news/2000/05/methodists-issue-sweeping-apology-for-churchs-racism.aspx.

[9] *Journal of the General Convention of...The Episcopal Church, Columbus, 2006,"* General Convention, (2007): 664-665.

[10] E. J. Dionne, "Pope Apologizes to Africans for Slavery," *The New York Times*, Aug. 14, 1985, A3. www.nytimes.com/1985/08/14/world/pope-apologizes-to-africans-for-slavery.html.

[11] Robert J. McClory, "Family Gathering," *National Catholic Reporter*, September 13, 2002, www.natcath.org/NCR_Online/archives/091302/091302a.htm.

[12] United States Conference of Catholic Bishops, "Brothers and Sisters to Us: U.S. Catholic Bishops' Pastoral Letter on Racism," www.usccb.org/issues-and-action/cultural-diversity/african-american/brothers-and-sisters-to-us.cfm.

[13] Ibid.

[14] Ibid.

[15] Mike Allen, "Male Bonding for the Evangelical Set," *The New York Times*, August 23, 1999, www.nytimes.com/1999/08/23/nyregion/male-bonding-for-the-evangelical-set.html?pagewanted=all&src=pm.

[16] Charles Honey, "United Against Evil: Promise Keepers says its Ministry is Needed now More Than Ever," *The Grand Rapids Press*, March 11, 2005, http://menscenter.org/spirituality/promise-keepers/.

[17] Ibid.

Chapter 22

[1] Mark DeYmaz and Harry Li; *Ethnic Blends: Mixing Diversity into Your Local Church*, (Grand Rapids: Zondervan, 2010), 23.

[2] Michael O. Emerson, "A New Day for multiracial Congregations," *Yale University Reflections* April 11, 2013, https://reflections.yale.edu/article/future-race/new-day-multiracial-congregations.

[3] Mark Chaves and Alison Eagle, "National Congregations Study: Religious Congregations in 21st Century America," 2015, 20, www.soc.duke.edu/natcong/Docs/NCSIII_report_final.pdf.

[4] Ibid, 21.

[5] Scott Thumma, "Racial Diversity Increasing in U.S. Congregations," The Huffington Post, May 21, 2013, www.huffingtonpost.com/scott-thumma-phd/racial-diversity-increasing-in-us-congregations_b_2944470.html.

[6] Campbell Robertson, "A Quiet Exodus: Why Black Worshipers Are Leaving White Evangelical Churches," *The New York Times*, March 9, 2018, https://www.nytimes.com/2018/03/09/us/blacks-evangelical-churches.html.

[7] Ibid.

[8] Curtis Paul DeYoung, Michael O. Emerson, George Yancey, Karen Chai Kim. *United by Faith*, (Oxford: Oxford University Press, 2003), 166. The broader discussion of this issue from which these three categories are derived appears on pages 163-169.
[9] Ibid, 168.
[10] Michael O. Emerson, "A New Day for multiracial Congregations.
[11] Ryon J. Cobb, Samuel L. Perry, Kevin D. Dougherty; "United by Faith? Race/Ethnicity, Congregational Diversity, and Explanations of Racial Inequality," Sociology of Religion, 76:2, (2015): 17, www.researchgate.net/profile/Ryon_Cobb/publication/276257767_United_by_Faith_RaceEthnicity_Congregational_Diversity_and_Explanations_of_Racial_Inequality/links/55f28a0108ae199d47c4814e.pdf.
[12] Desmond Tutu, "Foreword by the Chairperson," in *Truth and Reconciliation Commission of South Africa Report, Vol. 1*; The Commission, 1998, 4.
[13] John Lewis, "John Lewis spent 15 years fighting for the museum — now the dream is realized, www.washingtonpost
.com/lifestyle/magazine/john-lewis-spent-15-years-fighting-for-the-museum--now-the-dream-is-realized/2016/09/14/eeb0ca10-64bb-11e6-96c0-37533479f3f5_story.html.

Chapter 23

[1] Richard W. Scholl, "Dispositions: Attitudes, Values, & Personality," University of Rhode Island, http://web.archive.org/web/20150315232151/www.uri.edu/research/lrc/scholl/webnotes/Dispositions.htm. Can also be accessed at https://www.scottgarber.com/was_notes.html.
[2] Ibid.
[3] Ibid.
[4] Ibid.

Chapter 24

[1] Michael Eric Dyson, "Giving Whiteness a Black Eye," in *The Michael Eric Dyson Reader*, (New York: Basic Civitas Books, 2004), 113 ff. Dr. Dyson has recently published a more readable though no less confrontational address concerning whiteness, *Tears We Cannot Stop: A Sermon to White America*, (New York: St. Martin's Press, 2017).
[2] Louis Farrakhan, "Self Improvement: The Basis for Community Development" in Back Where We Belong: Selected Speeches, (Philadelphia, International Press, 1989), 188-189.
[3] John Dryden and Walter Scott; *The Works of John Dryden: Now First Collected in Eighteen Volumes* (Edinburgh, A. Constable & Co., 1821), 474.
[4] See: J. Goetzmann, "Repentance," in Colin Brown, ed., *New International Dictionary of New Testament Theology, Vol. 1*, (Grand Rapids, Zondervan, 1975), 358.

Chapter 25

[1] Allen Aubrey Boesak and Curtiss Paul DeYoung, *Radical Reconciliation: Beyond Political Pietism and Christian Quietism*, (Maryknoll, NY: Orbis Books, 2012), 1.
[2] Susan Wise Bauer, The Art of Public Grovel: Sexual Sin and Public Confession in America, (Princeton, Princeton University Press, 2008), 2.
[3] Ibid, 3.

---

[4] "Study: 80 Percent of Germans Want to Put the Holocaust Behind Them," *The Algemeiner,* Jan. 26, 2015, www.algemeiner.com/2015/01/26/study-80-percent-of-germans-want-to-put-holocaust-behind-them/.
[5] Tom Chivers, et. al, "Germany is 'filled with shame' over Nazi holocaust, Angela Merkel tells Israel," *The Telegraph,* March 18, 2008, www.telegraph.co.uk/news/worldnews/1582102/Germany-is-filled-with-shame-over-Nazi-holocaust-Angela-Merkel-tells-Israel.html.

Chapter 26

[1] Thomas Picketty, *Capital in the Twenty-First Century.* Translated by Arthur Goldhammer (Cambridge, Massachusetts; The Belknap Press of Harvard University Press, 2017).
[2] Òscar Jordá, Katharina Knoll, Dmitry Kuvshinov, Moritz Schularick, Alan M. Taylor, "The Rate of Return on Everything, 1870–2015" Federal Reserve Bank of San Francisco Working Paper, 2017, 25 and 49, https://www.frbsf.org/economic-research/publications/working-papers/2017/25/.
[3] Carmen DeNavas-Walt and Bernadette D. Proctor, "Income and Poverty in the United States: 2013: Table 3: People in Poverty in the United States," U.S. Department of Commerce / U.S. Census Bureau, September, 2014, 13.
[4] ACLU, "Affirmative Action," www.aclu.org/racial-justice/affirmative-action. It's not clear to what other tools they might be comparing affirmative action as a method of redress.
[5] "Grutter v. Bollinger," 539 U.S. 30 (2003), https://supreme.justia.com/cases/federal/us/539/306/case.pdf.
[6] "Adarand Constructors v. Pena (93-1841)," 515 U.S. 200 (1995), https://supreme.justia.com/cases/federal/us/515/200/case.pdf.
[7] Betsy Cooper, Daniel Cox, PhD, E.J. Dionne Jr., Rachel Lienesch, Robert P. Jones, PhD, William A. Galston: "How Immigration and Concerns about Cultural Change are Shaping the 2016 Election | PRRI/Brookings Survey." June 23, 2016. www.prri.org/research/prri-brookings-poll-immigration-economy-trade-terrorism-presidential-race/.
[8] Ariel Edwards-Levy, "Nearly Half of Trump Voters Think Whites Face a Lot of Discrimination," Nov. 21, 2016, www.huffingtonpost.com/entry/discrimination-race-religion_us_5833761ee4b099512f845bba.
[9] Rebecca Riffkin, "Higher Support for Gender Affirmative Action Than Race," Aug. 26, 2015, http://news.gallup.com/poll/184772/higher-support-gender-affirmative-action-race.aspx, accessed: April 16, 2018.
[10] Jeff Jones and Lydia Saad, "Gallup Poll Social Series: Minority Rights & Relations," Gallup News Service; 6/13–7/55, 2013, www.gallup .com/file/poll/163679/Affirmative_Action_130724.pdf, 3.
[11] Hart/McInturff, "NBC News/Wall Street Journal Survey, Study #13200"; May 30-June 2, 2013, http://online.wsj.com/public/resources/documents/WSJpoll060513.pdf.

Chapter 27

[1] *YouGov* poll conducted May 23-27, 2014, http://cdn.yougov.com /cumulus_uploads/document/ckcdgrxspy/tabs_OPI_1_discrimination_20140527.pdf, 7.
[2] Ibid, 9.

[3] Ibid, 8.

[4] Marist Poll, "Reparations for Slavery in the United States?" Poll conducted in late April and early May, 2016. http://www.pbs.org/wgbh/point-taken/blog/marist-reparations-slavery-united-states/.

[5] House Bill H. R. 40: "To acknowledge the fundamental injustice, cruelty, brutality, and inhumanity of slavery in the United States and the 13 American colonies between 1619 and 1865 and to establish a commission to examine the institution of slavery, subsequently de jure and de facto racial and economic discrimination against African-Americans, and the impact of these forces on living African-Americans, to make recommendations to the Congress on appropriate remedies, and for other purposes." https://www.congress.gov/bill/116th-congress/house-bill/40/text

[6] Ibid.

[7] Ta-Nehisi Coates, "The Case for Reparations," *The Atlantic*; June, 2014, 68. Coates re-ignited the debate about reparations with this important article, which also documents a great deal of ongoing discrimination, especially in the field of housing.

[8] Thomas Craemer, "Estimating Reparations: Present Value Comparisons of Historical Multigenerational Reparations Policies," *Social Science Quarterly*, Volume 96, No. 2, June 2015, 639. See also: Thomas Craemer, "International Reparations for Slavery and the Slave Trade," *Journal of Black Studies*, Vol. 49, No. 7, 2018, 694-713. Douglas Main, "Slavery Reparations Could Cost up to $14 Trillion, According to New Calculation," *Newsweek*, August, 9, 2015, https://www.newsweek.com/slavery-reparations-could-cost-14-trillion-according-new-calculation-364141.

[9] Ibid, 70.

[10] Ibid.

Chapter 28

[1] Jay Adams, A Theology of Christian Counseling: More Than Redemption, (Grand Rapids, Ministry Resources Library) 1986, 236 ff. Though I don't subscribe to Adams' approach to psychology, he makes a good point about the nature of spiritual change.

Chapter 29

[1] "Josiah Royce," *Stanford Encyclopedia of Philosphy*, https://plato.stanford.edu/entries/royce/.

[2] Charles Marsh, The Beloved Community: How Faith Shapes Social Justice from the Civil Rights Movement to Today (New York: Basic Books, 2008), 2.

[3] Ibid, 6.

[4] Martin Luther King, Jr., "Facing the Challenge of a New Age," speech delivered at the First Annual Institute on Nonviolence and Social Change, Montgomery, Alabama, December 3,1956, quoted in "The Martin Luther King, Jr. Papers Project," http://okra.stanford.edu/transcription/document _images/Vol03Scans/451_3-Dec-1956_Facing%20the%20Challenge%20of %20a%20New%20Age.pdf, 458.

[5] "The King Philosophy," The King Center, quoted *in Christian Century Magazine*, July 13, 1966, http://thekingcenter.org/king-philosophy/.

[6] Martin Luther King, Jr., "The Role of the Church in Facing the Nation's Chief Moral Dilemma," speech delivered at the Conference on Christian Faith and Human Relations, Nashville, TN, April 25, 1957, in "Proceedings of the Conference on

Christian Faith and Human Relations, "Black Mountain, N.C., 1957, 190. See: "Martin Luther King Papers Project," http://okra.stanford.edu/transcription/document_images/Vol04Scans/184_1957_The%20Role%20of%20the%20Church.pdf.

[7] Dr. Martin Luther King, Jr., "An Experiment in Love," in *A Time to Break Silence: The Essential Works of Martin Luther King, Jr. for Students* (Boston, Beacon Press, 2013) np. (Originally published in *Stride Toward Freedom: The Montgomery Story*, New York, Harper & Brothers, 1958).

[8] Martin Luther King, Jr., "Advice for Living," in *Ebony*, November, 1957, 106, https://kinginstitute.stanford.edu/king-papers/documents/advice-living-1.

[9] Marsh, *The Beloved Community*, 4.

[10] Martin Luther King, Jr., "Remaining Awake Through a Great Revolution," sermon delivered at the National Cathedral, Washington, D.C., March 31, 1968, https://kinginstitute.stanford.edu/king-papers/publications/knock-midnight-inspiration-great-sermons-reverend-martin-luther-king-jr-10.

[11] David Anderson, *Gracism: The Art of Inclusion* (Downers Grove, Illinois; Intervarsity Press) 2010, 33 ff.

[12] Charles M. Schulz, The Complete Peanuts, 1959-1960 (Vol. 5), 2016.

[13] Francis A. Schaeffer, *True Spirituality* (London: Hodder and Stoughton, 1972), 147.

[14] Martin Luther King, Jr.; "Nonviolence: The Only Road to Freedom," *Ebony*; October, 1966, Vol. XXII, No. 12, 30.

CPSIA information can be obtained
at www.ICGtesting.com
Printed in the USA
FSHW020647071219